MONROE COUNTY
TENNESSEE

TOMBSTONE
INSCRIPTIONS

W.P.A. Records

Heritage Books
2023

HERITAGE BOOKS

AN IMPRINT OF HERITAGE BOOKS, INC.

Books, CDs, and more—Worldwide

For our listing of thousands of titles see our website
at
www.HeritageBooks.com

A Facsimile Reprint
Published 2023 by
HERITAGE BOOKS, INC.
Publishing Division
5810 Ruatan Street
Berwyn Heights, MD 20740

International Standard Book Number
Paperbound: 978-0-7884-8840-5

W.P.A. RECORDS

The WPA Records are, for the most part, carbon copies of the original that was typed on onion skin paper during the Depression. Since these records were typed on poor machines by people who did not type in some cases and at the same time, they were read by persons not always sure of the older handwritten materials, the results are often less than perfect.

We have made every attempt to make as clear a copy as can be made from these older papers. Sometimes there are water stains and burned edges around the paper. This is the results of a fire at the home of one of the workers, Mrs. Penelope Allen, who was over most of the project. Sometimes, the index will be misleading in that they index by the middle name when a list of names are given in one family, i.e. "... the children of John Smith are, John, Jr., Mary Warren, and Oscar Sims. The indexer would list a Warren and a Sims in the index, when they should be Smith. Mountain Press has acquired a rather large number of finished and un-finished manuscripts. Many of these latter manuscripts are being typed and index now.

The WPA Records are now very scattered between the Tennessee State Library, various Public and Private Libraries and other collections. Some day, there is a hope that all of these can be collected and stored in one place. In spite of their many mistakes and problems, these are still the most complete collection of Tennessee records found anywhere.

MONROE COUNTY

TOMBSTONE INSCRIPTIONS

Table of Contents

Copied by:: Lawrence McConkey, Englewood, Tennessee
Date:

The Allison Family Cemetery was established on the Allison
farm. It is thought that the Allisons migrated from North
Carolina, and settled at this place when first settlers came
to this part of the Country. J. F. Allison, born Aug. 13, 1863,
died Oct. 9, 1914, is buried in the City Cemetery at Madisonville.
He was a son of William D. Allison and a grandson of Jessee
Allison. J. F. Allison was Registrar of Deeds for Monroe County
for several years. His widow, Saleatha, is still living.

The Jessee Allison Family Cemetery is located 19 miles South
of Madisonville and can best be located by going to Mt. Vernon
then to Jalapa then on to road leading toward Ivy, to the farm
of Wm. R. Cain. The Allison family owned slaves and one of them
is buried in this cemetery.

There are 18 inscriptions and 10 unmarked graves, some of them
being of people not related to the Allison family.

PEEL

Eliza Peel
Died 1903
Aged about 65 years.

John Peel
Died 1898
Aged about 22 years.

Robert Peel
Died 1936
Aged about 40 years.

Henry Peel
Aged 3 months

George Peel
Infant

Mary Peel
Died 1891
Aged 23 years.

ALLISON

William D. Allison
Born Oct. 5, 1824
Died June 25, 1902
He was a good man
and full of faith.

Elizabeth P. Stephenson
Wife of
W. D. Allison
Feb. 3, 1829
July 15, 1915
Asleep in Jesus.

Rev. W. P. Allison
Son of
W. D. & E. P. Allison
Feb. 6, 1866
July 21, 1896
A name engraved in our
hearts is -------
--- not here the sainted
Spirit -------

Part of the inscriptions is
not readable.

ALLISON FAMILY CEMETERY

Lowery Allison
Apr. 30, 1855
May 20, 1855
Gone but not forgotten.

Polenia Allison
Oct. 3, 1869
May 20, 1871
Gone but not forgotten.

Susan Jane Allison
Jan. 26, 1855
Mar. 8, 1901
She believed in
Holy living.

(Note: Susan Jane Allison
was buried beside the
Rev. W. P. Allison,
might be his wife. LMcC.)

Jessee Allison

-------- Allison
Wife of
Jessee Allison

Mose (Col.)

(Note: Salve of Allison family.)

CAIN

Susan A. Allison Cain
Daughter of
W. D. & Elizabeth Allison
July 7, 1856
April 3, 1932
Gone but not forgotten.

Eveline Peel
Wife of
Wm. R. Cain
Died 1928
Aged about 70 years.

WISE

Ellie B. Wise
Sept. 3, 1890
Oct. 19, 1890
At Rest.

MONROE COUNTY

TOMBSTONE INSCRIPTIONS

BIG CREEK BAPTIST CHURCH CEMETERY

Copied by: Lawrence McConkey, Englewood, Tennessee
Date:

The Big Creek Baptist Church and Church Cemetery are located
about 6 miles Southeast of Madisonville. They may be reached
by taking the Madisonville to Belltown road for about 5 miles
then turning right on to the Big Creek road. The church was
constituted in 1834 on land given by Thomas Divine. He also
furnished the land for the cemetery wh'ch is up on the hill
from the church. The cemetery was established about the same
time as the church, but the earliest inscriptions readable
are dated in 1839. Later Elijah Cagle gave additional land
for the cemetery and a few years ago more land for the graveyard was secured from John Saffles. There cemetery land
comprises about 10 acres and approximately 6 acres is in graves.
Several soldiers are buried in Big Creek Baptist Church Cemetery.
There are 231 inscriptions; several fragments of inscriptions;
114 Field Stones; 174 or more unmarked graves and 12 graves
whose inscriptions have been destroyed.

HICKS OR HIX

Mary
Wife of
Abraham Hicks
Died June 22, 1910
Age 78 years
Though thou art gone
fond memory clings to thee.

Abraham Hicks
Oct. 10, 1834
Sept. 23, 1906
He was a member of
Big Creek Church.
(Note: He was a Confederate
Soldier so says Robt. N.
Cagle.) LMcC.)

Hicks
Rittie Hicks
1871-1937

B. H. Hicks
1868-(Living)

(Note: One unmarked grave at South
of the above Husband & wife. LMcC.)

N. T. H. H.

(Note: The above inscription
is in the Hicks section. LMcC.)

Loise Hicks

Alford
Son of
Mr. & Mrs. L. V. Hicks
Oct. 30, 1928
Mar. 8, 1929
Our darling.

John A. Hicks
June 5, 1875
June 3, 1906

William Osbin Hicks
Mar. 25, 1916
Aug. 13, 1917
At Rest.

BIG CREEK BAPTIST CHURCH CEMETERY

Vestie Hicks
daughter of
M. A. & Loucinda Hicks
Aug. 20, 1900
Oct. 18, 1901
At Rest.

1 Stone North of above.

Mrs. R. K. Hicks
Died Apr. 24, 1936
Aged 58 yrs. 4 mos. & 24 days.

T. P. Hix

(Note: The above inscription,
for a member of the Hicks
family, is on a field rock.
There are also 2 field stones
South and 1 field stone North
of above. These graves are in
the old section of cemetery.
LMcC.)

M. E. Hicks

J. D. Hicks

TOWNSEND

Nannie Townsend
Sept. 11, 1918
Dec. 27, 1924
Safe in the arms of Jesus.

Eugene Townsend
June 2, 1922
May 13, 1923
Safe in the arms of Jesus.

SUTTON

Jesse H. Sutton
June 1880
Dec. 1900

John Sutton
Died June 14, 1871

3 field stones South & 1
field stone North of above.

W. H. Sutton
Sept. 9, 1879
Feb. 18, 1907

2 stones South of above.

G. H. Sutton
Apr. 23, 1849
July 20, 1892

----- James ------

(Note: Remainder of inscription
unreadable. It is in Sutton
rows. LMcC.)

J. O. Sutton
Died Sept. 28, 1856

(Note: 2 field stones South of
above. Many unmarked graves in
area that seem to be graves of
the Sutton family. LMcC.)

EVANS

Jasper
Son of
J. H. & M. A. Evans
Sept. 21, 1888
May   3, 1890
Asleep in Jesus.

Jennis Ugene
Son of
Mr. & Mrs. Marion Evans
July 16, 1924
Feb. 22, 1926
Darling we miss thee.

AVANS

Infant
Son of
I. A. & S. E. Avans
Mar. 27, 1911
Feb. 7, 1912
Asleep in Jesus.

J. P. Avans
Decd July 17, 1841

BIG CREEK BAPTIST CHURCH CEMETERY

(note: The two top inscriptions
are of graves side by side. May
be Evans and Avans same name.
J. P. Avans was at another
location. LMcC.)

CARROLL

J. H. Carroll
June 24, 1880
Dec. 6, 1902

Sarrah Jane Carroll
Sept. 17, 1849
July 1, 1910

George R. Carroll
Sept. 17, 1850
Sept. 15, 1925
Gone but not forgotten.

TOOMEY

Thomas L. Twomey
Mar. 15, 1841
Mar. 20, 1899
At Rest but not
forgotten. Belong to
Big Creek Church 22 years.

(Note: The name is spelled Twomey
on the marker but it is incorrect.
The name is Toomey. LMcC.)

Mrs. Winnie Toomey
Died May 24, 1931
Aged 82 yrs. 6 mos. & 24 days.

Forest
Son of
J. W. & C. F. Toomey
June 28, 1904
Budded on earth to bloom
in Heaven.

Infant
of
T. J. & D. A. Toomey

Henry L. Toomey
Mar. 17, 1892
Dec. 20, 1934
Asleep to wake again.

HENSLEY

Thomas Hensley
July 7, 1892
Dec. 6, 1918
Gone but not forgotten.

SAFFLES OR SAFFLE

Infant
Son of
Earnest & Cordie Saffles
Dec. 28, 1906
Dec. 30, 1906
Asleep in Jesus.

Infant
of
Luther & ------- Saffles

Thomas Saffles
Co. D.
3rd Tenn.
Mt'd Inf.

Nancy Saffles
Aug. 27, 1828
Mar. 2, 1914

G. W. Saffles
Oct. 1, 1863
Nov. 21, 1910

1 Stone North of above.

DOYLE

(Mason Emblem)
Jacob Doyle
Jan. 2, 1819
Nov. 4, 1864
He has gone on the last
march to the land where
never more shall the bugle
sound revellle or the dread-
ful cannon roar. He who for
the country dies, dies not.
Erected by his wife & son.

Jakie Doyle
Born March 27, 1864
and took flight to Heaven
Feb. 17, 1865
Thou art gone little Jakie
(continued on next page)

BIG CREEK BAPTIST CHURCH CEMETERY

Sweet child of our love,
from earth's fairy strand
to bright mansions above.
Erected by her brother
and mother.

(Note: Jacob Doyle was a
Civil War Soldier and a
Representative of Monroe
Co. in State Legislature.   LMcC.)

Sallie J. Doyle
Born May 17, 1859
and Went to Heaven
July 10, 1879
at 4 o'clock and
30 minutes.
With prospects bright
and budding fair just
rising into bloom,
death came in an untimely
hour and snatched her to
the tomb.
Erected by her mother & brother.

3 field stones to South of
Jacob Doyle's graven and 1
field stone to North of
Sallie J. Doyle's grave.

SHARP

Father
Robert P. Sharp
Oct. 10, 1861
Mar. 25, 1932

Pearl
Jan. 14, 1912
Jan. 20, 1912

Infant son
Born & died
Dec. 31, 1910
Children of
R. P. & M. J. Sharp

Infant
daughter
Born & died
July 4, 1902

Infant
Son
Born & died
Nov. 1, 1905
Children of
R. P. & M. J. Sharp.

1 unmarked grave North of above.

BRUNER

Billy L. Bruner
June 27, 1934
Sept. 28, 1938

Margaret Joan Bruner
Jan. 23, 1936
July 4, 1936

CROWDER

William E.
Son of
W. J. & M. D. Crowder
June 7, 1893
Sept. 11, 1893
Asleep in Jesus.

2 stones North of above.

Susan A.
dau. of
W. J. & M. D. Crowder
June 7, 1891
Aug. 3, 1891
Asleep in Jesus.

Robert A.
Son of
W. J. & M. D. Crowder
Oct. 23, 1889
--- 20, 1889

Arrie
Son of
J. R. & A. D. Crowder
May 28, 1898
Dec. 10, 1898

Freddie
Son of
J. R. & A. D. Crowder
Jan. 15, 1897
Feb. 19, 1897

BIG CREEK BAPTIST CHURCH CEMETERY

1 Field stone North of above.

J. R. Crowder
Died Apr. 9, 1931
Aged 62 yrs. 10 mos. & 15 days.

(Note: 1 grave, possibly wife,
South and 1 stone, possibly
for a child, on North of
above. LMcC.)

Bertha
Daughter of
J. R. & A. D. Crowder
Oct. 16, 1895 - Jan. 3, 1902

Earl
Son of
J. A. & Ellie Crowder
Nov. 5, 1899
Feb. 24, 1900
Asleep in Jesus.

Etta
Daughter of
C. A. & M. C. Crowder
June 22, 1903
June 27, 1903

(Note: The following are in
a different section of
cemetery. LMcC.)

Crowder
Amanda
Nov. 15, 1863
Oct. 22, 1937

Neal C.
May 3, 1858
Dec. 26, 1924

(Note: Thomas Crowder, a
Federal Soldier, buried here
but has no marker says Robt.
N. Cagle. LMcC.)

C. W. C.

(The above inscription is at head
of grave of Neal C. Crowder. LMcC.)

W. C. Crowder

(Note: Above is at north side of
grave of C. W. C. Both are
infants graves, it seems. LMcC.)

YOUNG

Georgia Young
Sept. 20, 1910
Oct. 20, 1910

MORGAN

Henry Morgan
Died Aug. 9, 1928
Aged 63 yrs. 10 mos.

Carl Morgan
Died Feb. 8, 1933
Aged 22 years.

Francies Morgan
1864 (child's grave)

3 field stones South of
Frances Morgan's graves.

Sacred to the memory of
William Morgan
Who ceased this life on
the second day of June
1840 in the fifty-sixth year
of his age. He profest relegion
in 1812 or 13.
Remember friends as you pass by,
as you are now so wonst was I.
As I am now so you must be.
Prepare for death and follow me.

3 field stones South and 1 field
stone North of above grave.

Polly Morgan
Feb. 25, 1831
Apr. 9, 1905

(Note: James Morgan, Polly Morgan's
husband, is buried on North side of
her grave. LMcC.)

BIG CREEK BAPTIST CHURCH CEMETERY

Deny Morgan

Mary Jane Morgan
Was born Feb. 8th 1840
Dec. Nov. 17th 1862

Lillian Morgan
Died Dec. 3, 1935
Aged 13 yrs. 6 mos & 12
                    days.

ALLEN

Alice Allen
Died June 1, 1938
Aged 67 yrs. 9 months
and 8 days.

Charlie
Son of
Mr. & Mrs. J. R. Allen
Oct. 1, 1911
Dec. 1, 1918
A fairer bud of promise
never bloomed.

1 field stone South of
                    above.

BELCHER

Caroline Raper
Wife of
A. S. Belcher
Oct. 7, 1847
May 7, 1879

1 field stone marks grave of
a child on North of above.

Clarasa E. Belcher
Dyed Feb. the 17, 1872

3 field stones North & 1
field stone South of above.

Danul Lafayett Belcher
Oct. 18, 1883
Apr. 23, 1915

Molie Angeline Belcher
April 4, 1898
April 19, 1913

LONDON

Sarrah E. London
March 9, 1820
July 26, 1911

MULLINS

Ines Eona Mullins
Sept. 16, 1915
Jan. 13, 1917
Our darling.

Joseph Wesley Mullins
Apr. 29, 1847
Aug. 8, 1913

GIVENS

Rev. James Givens
Oct. 17, 1837
Sept. 15, 1910

1 field stone South of above.

Eliza Avans
Wife of
Rev. James Givens
Jan. 13, 1842
Nov. 12, 1916

Eliza J. Givens
Died Aug. 30, 1933
Aged 68 years.

(Note: Harris Givens is
buried on South side of wife,
of Eliza J. Givens.   LMoC.)

RICHARDS OR RICHARD

Mother
L. L. Richards
Mar. 16, 1856
Feb. 12, 1907
Gone but not forgotten.

A. B. Richard
Feb. 12, 1854
June 23, 1920
Beloved father farewell.

MOSES

BIG CREEK BAPTIST CHURCH CEMETERY

Tommie Moses
Died July 7, 1938
Aged 25 years.

Infant
of
Jack & Aney Moses

Clester
Son of
Mr. & Mrs. O. G. Moses
Mar. 3, 1917
Nov. 4, 1917
Darling we miss thee.

Gemilia
Wife of
S. C. Moses
Oct. 17, 1901
Aug. 1, 1925

Francis Moses
Jan. 4, 1913
Apr. 7, 1913
At Rest.

Birdie D.
Daughter of
A. & R. E. Moses
Aug. 24, 1903
May 22, 1904
Asleep in Jesus

John Moses

Charlie L.
Son of
Andy & Ren Moses
Aug. 29, 1901
Feb. 12, 1928
A precious one from us
is gone. A voice we
loved is stilled. A
place is vacant in our
home that never can be
filled.

J. M. Moses
Feb. 1, 1857
Dec. 4, 1889

Johnie Moses
1815 - 1890

Mollie Moses
1823- 1894
Father & mother.

Sara Moses
Jan. 4, 1890
Mar. 8, 1899

Robert Moses
Sept. 12, 1894
Feb. 10, 1895

Connie Moses
Mar. 30, 1895
July 2, 1909

J. B. Moses
Feb. 17, 1879
June 5, 1906

3 field stones South of Above.

Jessee Moses
Jan. 16, 1837
Apr. 2, 1893

Juley An Moses
Deced May the 7th 1858
(at another location in cemetery)

BREEDEN

John Breeden

(Nore: Confederate Soldier,
according to information from
Robt. N. Cagle. LMcC.).

Nancy C. Breeden
Gone but not forgotten.

(Note: Nancy C. Breeden was the
wife of John Breeden. LMcC.)

SLOAN

J. E. Sloan
July 15, 1881
Dec. 7, 1889

BIG CREEK BAPTIST CHURCH CEMETERY

S. L. Sloan
April 30, 1841

Reba Sloan
Daughter of
Paul & Lovie Moses

DIAL

--------- Dial

(Note: A plot about 10X30
feet has a concrete wall
around it & in the enclosure
is one grave. On the
concrete is the name Dial.
LMcC.)

CAGLE

Blanche
Daughter of
Robert & Ida Cagle
Born & died
April 30, 1896
At Rest.

Alvin Walter Cagle
Feb. 14, 1889
July 19, 1890

Blanche Elisabeth Cagle
Apr. 16, 1904
Oct. 30, 1907

Amy Janette Cagle
March 27, 1901
April 11, 1908

In memory of
Elijah Cagle
Nov. 2, 1841
Aug. 29, 1911

(Note: Between the above 2
graves is the grave of Susie
Cagle, the second wife of
Elijah Cagle. Elijah Cagle
was a Confederate Soldier, so
says Robert N. Cagle. LMcC.)

Jenettie Webb
Born April 2, 1846
Died May 30, 1889
Married E. Cagle
Aug. 20, 1863
Joined the Baptist Church
at Big Creek Nov. 15, 1860

W. H. Cagle
Dec. Aug. 7, 1870

------ Cagle
The dau of
M. H. & M. E. Raper
Born June 14, 1847
Died ------------

Jane Cagle
Died April 26, 1937
Aged 70 years and
9 months.

Mother
Martha A. Cagle
Jan. 13, 1835
Sept. 13, 1915

Father
Martin Cagle
Mar. 15, 1828
Sept. 18, 1893

HITSON

Cagle
Argin Cagle
Feb. 4, 1855
Dec. 21, 1926
Thy trials ended thy
rest is won.
Wife of
Joe Hitson.

GANN

Henry Gann
Died March the 12 184-

ISBILL

Col. P. Isbill
Born Sept. 18, 1807
Died July 2, 1887
In God I trust.

BIG CREEK BAPTIST CHURCH CEMETERY

Our mother
Mary M.
Wife of
C. P. Isbill
Born Feb. 4, 1815
Died Feb. 6, 1895
At Rest.

(Note: Following were at
another location in cemetery
but are of same family as
above. LMcC.)

Elizabeth Ann Isbill
Aug. 4, 1909
Nov. 30, 1918

Rufus R. Isbill
July 11, 1917
June 26, 1938
Gone but not forgotten.

Emerson W. Isbill
Jan. 12, 1932
Feb. 25, 1932
Asleep in Jesus.

I. A. Isbill
Sept. 18, 1868
Feb. 22, 1935
Gone but not forgotten.

Annie Collake
Wife of
I. A. Isbill
Nov. 22, 1879
Dec. 5, 1918
Mother
At Rest.

Emerson O.
Son of
I. A. & Annie Isbill
June 3, 1912
Dec. 10, 1918
At Rest.

Mary Jane
Daughter of
I. A. & Annie Isbill
June 19, 1904
Dec. 15, 1918
Gone but not forgotten.

DAVIS

Davis
W. A. Davis
May 17, 1861
Feb. 27, 1930
The Lord giveth and
the Lord taketh away.

GRAVES

Abraham Graves
July 1, 1816
Aug. 20, 1891

(Note: On South side of above
with a field stone as marker is
the grave of Peggie, the wife of
Abraham Graves. LMcC.)

Winnie Graves
Aug. 28, 1894
Sept. 21, 1894

Webster
Son of
Alph & Vertie Graves
Nov. 3, 1918
Oct. 15, 1919

1 grave South of above.

Mary
Wife of
S. H. Graves
Apr. 14, 1899
Nov. 20, 1918

Little Mary
Daughter of
Mr. & Mrs. S. H. Graves
Nov. 5, 1918
Jan. 2, 1919

Bettie Graves
Died Feb. 24, 1937
Aged 47 years, 2 mos. 19 days.

1 grave South of grave of
Bettie Graves.

BURK

BIG CREEK BAPTIST CHURCH CEMETERY

Baby Burk
Budded on earth to
bloom in Heaven.

(Note: This child was an
infant son of James Burk. LMcC)

V. B. Burk
May 29, 1850
April 4, 1897
Gone but not forgotten.

(Note: Jane, the wife of
V. B. Burk, is buried on
North side of his grave
with field stone as a
marker. LMcC.)

COOK

Cook
Wade Cook
Feb. 16, 1907
Oct. 6, 1911

WEBB

Rhoda Webb
July 10, 1812
Sept. 7, 1900
Gone but not forgotten.

Larkin Webb
Died Jan. 18, 1859

(Note: This grave is at head
of grave of another Larkin
Webb. LMcC.)

S. Webb

Jasper Webb
March 20, 1860
July 15, 1881

2 unmarked graves.

Larkin Webb
April 29, 1833
Mar. 2, 1862

Note: Larkin Webb was a
Confederate Soldier so says
Robert N. Cagle. LMcC.)

3 graves with field stones
South of above.

Father
James Roche Webb
Apr. 8, 1815
June 5, 1884

Mother
Lucinda Divine Webb
Oct. 9, 1823
Jan. 7, 1917

1 field stone North of above.

James M. Webb
May 7, 1864
Nov. 18, 1924

Rebecca Webb
1864 - 1897
At Rest.

(Note: Grave of Rebecca Webb's is
not same location as others
above it. LMcC.)

ROY

1840
Aug. 13
Harrison Roy

STEPHENS

James
Son of
H. L. Stephens
June 28, 1914

Virgie Lee
Dau. of
H. L. Stephens
July 19, 1913
Aug. 14, 1913

RAPER

I. C. Raper
Dec. Sept. 18, 1872

L. W. Raper
Dec. July 22, 18--

J. S. Raper

M. L. Raper

R. C. Raper

BEALS

Mary Beals
Aug. 11, 1918
July 2, 1938
At Rest.

LAUGHTER

William H. Laughter
Died --- -- ----

(Note: Above is on a
worn, very old field rock.
LMcC.)

Louisa Laughter
Jan. 1, 1853
Aug. 16, 1893
Gone but not forgotten.

(Note: Louisa Laughter's
husband, George Laughter,
married again. Had his
name changed to George
Denton by going before the
Court at Madisonville and
swearing that Denton was his
real name. He is believed to
be buried by side of above wife.
This information secured from
Robert N. Cagle. LMcC.)

GRAY

Nancie C.
Wife of
S. B. Gray
Dec. 7, 1867
July 23, 1898
Safe in the arms of Jesus.

1 field stone North of above.

TAYLOR

J. P. Taylor
Oct. 19, 1872
Mar. 10, 1914
Our father.

1 field stone South of above.

Mary Jane Taylor
Died Nov. 17, 1931
Aged 79 yrs. 10 mos & 22 days.

2 field stones and one unmarked
grave at South of above.

DIVINE

Elisabeth Avans
Born Feb. 24, 1797
Died Jan. 12, 1877
Married to
Thomas Divine
Sept. 12, 1824
Joined the Baptist Church
Oct. 19, 1866
lived a member until death.

Thomas Divine
Born Feb. 24, 1795
Died June 16, 1856

Matilda Divine
Oct. 14, 1856
Sept. 11, 1857

W. H. Divine
Aug. 28, 1840
Oct. 17, 1859

Joseph M. Divine
Feb. 16, 1842
Feb. 15, 1860

Joseph Divine
Mar. 6, 1812
Jan. 22, 1865

BIG CREEK BAPTIST CHURCH CEMETERY

(note: Joseph Divine, was
a Captian in the Fedsral
Army in Civil War, possibly
in home guards. He had been
rough on Confederates. It
is said that he was trapped in
basement of Dr. Upton's home &
was asked to surrender but would
not. One man went in after
him and was killed by Divine.
They promised him not to kill
him if he would come out but
he wouldn't until they decided
to burn the house. They shot
him several times in legs and
arms and he was alive next
morning and he was shot in the
head. Data secured from
Robt. N. Cagle. LMcC.)

1 field stone N. of above.

(Note: At another location 1
North of Col. P. Isbill's grave
is an area of many graves
believed to be all Divine
family burials. Most of the
field rock markers are not
readable but some are as
follows. LMcC.)

M. Divine
Decd August 12, 1848

E. V. Divine

R. R. D.
May 24, 1833

A. Di-----
Was B. the 20th 1820
Decd Ap 16 18--

W. Divine

J. L. Divine.

CAMPBELL

M. Campbell
Dec. June 4th 1843

M. R. C-----
D. June 5th 1839

(Note: Above two graves are close
and presumably the persons buried
here were of same family. Inscriptions on field rocks. LMcC.)

J. S. Campbell.

HUFF

In loving memory of
Alezan
Wife of
G. W. Huff
Aug. 3, 1860
July 7, 1894
Gone but not forgotten.

Lucile Huff
Died Nov. 11, 1918
Aged 19 yrs.

Mrs. W. H. Huff
Died Oct. 24, 1918
Aged --------------

Infant
of
W. H. & Emma Huff

HAWKINS

Goldia Norma
Daughter of
A. & R. E. Moses
Wife of
R. P. Hawkins
June 27, 1905
Mar. 19, 1925

IVENS

Lillian
Our darling
daughter of
R. A. & V. G. Ivens
June 4, 1910
June 11, 1910
Asleep in Jesus.

Father
W. S. Ivens
Dec. 25, 1834
(Date of death not given.)

BIG CREEK BAPTIST CHURCH CEMETERY

Mother
M. L. Ivens
July 26, 1838
Jan. 1, 1911
Here are they that kept
the commandments of
God and the faith of Jesus.

Athalonia L. Ivens
Feb. 4, 1868
Aug. 10, 1890
With prospects bright
and budded fair just
rising into bloom,
death came in at an
untimely hour and
snatched her to the tomb.

James M. Ivens
Died July 18, 1933
Aged 72 yrs. 0 mos. &
24 days.

Louvenia Ivens
April 3, 1898
April 13, 1898
Asleep in Jesus.

Carelee Ivens
Sept. 24, 1905
Budded on earth to
bloom in Heaven.

Elmer Leon Ivens
Feb. 23, 1908
Oct. 28, 1918
Asleep in Jesus.

Kenneth Keith Ivens
Oct. 3, 1917
Feb. 11, 1918
From Mothers arms
to the arms of Jesus.

1 grave North of above.

Mamie Lois Ivens
June 6, 1914
Sept. 26, 1915
Gone but not forgotten.

Robert L. Ivens
June 23, 1896
June 2, 1904
Gone but not forgotten.

H. Clay Ivens
June 19, 1894
July 25, 1896
Gone but not forgotten.

MCCONKEY

Wallis McConkey
Sept. 23, 1909
Nov. 23, 1913
The morning after the
resurrection we shall
see Wallis then.

WHITE

Infant
Twin Son of
J. W. & M. M. White
Born & died
Jan. 30, 1895
Asleep in Jesus.

Mrs. Kitty White
Died May 13, 1936
Aged 36 years.

Roxey Mae White
July 3, 1916
Sept. 8, 1916

Dewey White
Died Nov. 8, 1935
Aged 35 years.

David White
Died Aug. 22, 1929
Aged 23 yrs. 9 mos. & 19 days.

Mrs. James White
Dec. ---- --- 189-

Cecil White
Jan. 30, 1921
Apr. 2, 1924
At Rest.

BIG CREEK BAPTIST CHURCH CEMETERY

James B. White
Aug. 6, 1894
Feb. 29, 1932
Gone but not forgotten.

HARRIS

Father
James Harris
1822 - 1917

Mother
Elizabeth Harris
1824 - 1911

1 grave North of above.

MOSER

Iva Lee Moser
Nov. 17, 1901
May 26, 1902

Mary
Wife of
Joseph Moser
Aged 53
Died Jan. 5, 1910
At Rest in Jesus.

Lucinda Moser
Feb. 8, 1879
May 31, 1902
At Rest.

Infant
of
J. P. & Mary Moser
March 17, 1913

3 field stones North of above.

P. F. Moser
Feb. 26, 1881
Jan. 30, 1917

(Note: 2 field stones South of
above without inscriptions mark
the graves of Doke Moser & -----.
Moser, brothers of P. F. (Pete)
Moser. LMcC.).

KINSLOW

Texie Kinslow

THRASHER

Roxie Thrasher

(Note: The above two graves
were close. Persons buried here
are possibly related. LMcC.)

PAYNE

Hettie Ann
daughter of
J. W. & Annie Payne
Oct. 20, 1873
Nov. 9, 1873
Asleep in Jesus.

Jennie Payne
Born 1801
Died April 11, 1864

(Note: Verse by M. S. C. Doyle
but unreadable. LMcC.)

CURTIS

G. W. Curtis
Mar. 14, 1879
Mar. 1, 1882
Our darling baby.

Minnie Curtis
Aug. 13, 1893
July 4, 1894
Our darling baby.

Mamie Curtis
Aug. 13, 1893
July 7, 1894
Our darling baby.

Nannie Curtis
Apr. 23, 1883
July 10, 1894
Our darling.

BIG CREEK BAPTIST CHURCH CEMETERY

In memory of
Our Father & Mother
J. H. Curtis
Feb. 6, 1848
Aug. 24, 1894

E. J. Curtis
Jan. 6, 1856
May 28, 1905
At Rest.

Joseph Curtis
Apr. 21, 1873
Aug. 27, 1894
At Rest.

FREDLE

Sacred to the memory of
David Fredle
Who Dec. this life
June the 19 1850
He was born the
27 Sept. 1833

3 field stones South of
the above.

The body of
James Fredle
lies her food for worms
while his soul is with
Christ above.
He deceased this life the
second day of June 1850.
He was born Nov. 28, 1828.

(Note: The 2 above inscriptions
are on hewn lime stone rocks.
LMcC.)

DAILEY

John R. Dailey
Died Apr. 12, 1927
Aged 72 years, 7 months
& 3 days.

Senia
Wife of
John R. Dailey

WATSON

Kenneth Watson

Lois Watson

TALLENT

W. Morris Tallent
Nov. 1, 1899
Dec. 31, 1899

1854
Thos Tallent
Dos. Sept. 24

(Note: Jepp Tallent and his
wife, Betsy, are buried in this
cemetery. Their graves formerly
had markers with inscriptions.
It is thought by some of his
descendants that Jepp Tallent
was a Revolutionary Soldier.
Joseph Moses, an old man, 90
years old, says that, Jepp
Tallent told him that he was
in the Revolutionary War.
Tallent died at a real old
age when Moses was young. 'Tis
said that the older set of
Tallents lived to be real old.
LMcC.)

H. B. H.
M. Mc
Oct.

S. S. H.
M
M. V.
Decd M
12 1841

S. B.   March the
----- 1831

B. & D May 26, 1839

(Note: This grave is at foot of
grave of Jacob Doyle. LMcC.)

BIG CREEK BAPTIST CHURCH CEMETERY

Hairl Hi-s---
Died Aug. 27, 1839

(Note: The six inscriptions
above are in the oldest
part of the cemetery. LMcC.)

Henson F. ----------
Sept. 12, 1922

(Note: The above is on
East side of cemetery. LMcC.)

Ransey
died Sept. 25
aged 1 yr.

LUTHER M. BLACKMAN FAMILY CEMETERY

Copied by Lawrence McConkey, Englewood, Tennessee
Date:

The Luther M. Blackman Family Cemetery is on the farm of William
D. Blackman, J. P., 10 miles North of Madisonville. It may be
reached by taking the road that leads to Loudon, via Oak Grove
Baptist Church and Oak Grove County School, Fowlers Cemetery and
Fowlers County School. The farm is at the right.

Luther M. Blackman, born in Connecticut, was a major in the U. S.
Army in the War between the States. He married Margaret Cook of
Monroe County. To this union were born the following children:
Mollie, who married M. H. Rausin; Callie, who married Lee Leslie;
Lou Emma, who married J. S. Tipton; William D., who married Ruth
McLendon; Newland, never married and Electa, never married.

After the war between the States Luther M. Blackman was, a member
of the State Legislature 1865-1867; Government Pension Claim Agent;
U. S. Commissioner of Pensions and Justice of the Peace. He is
buried in the National Soldiers Cemetery at Knoxville.

There are no unmarked graves.

BLACKMAN

Margaret Blackman   Electa Blackman
Born March 3, 1840   Born Mar. 11, 1872
Died March 12, 1908   Died June 22, 1911

Newland Blackman
Born Dec. 7, 1869
Died Nov. 27, 1897

MONROE COUNTY

BLAIR CEMETERY

Copyied by Lawrence McConkey, Englewood, Tennessee
Date: September 20, 1939

The Blair Cemetery, at one time known as Morrow Cemetery,
is on a farm now owned by John Blair. It is part of a 210
acre tract on the Tellico River bought circa 1840 by
Armstrong Morrow from John McGhee. The cemetery is about
1½ miles East of Vonore on the Ball Play Road. Vonore is
approximately 9 miles N. E. of Madisonville.

When the farm was purchased in 1840 there was one unknown
grave on it, this covered with a rock wall. Armstrong
Morrow later allowed a community cemetery to be established
on this property.

Martha W., daughter of Armstrong and Margaret Morrow,
married J. T. Blair. The farm fell in possession of the
Blairs and has benn owned by them or their children ever
since.

J. T. Blair and Judge John J. Blair, deceased were related.
The latter served as Criminal Judge of his District.

There are possibly 15 or more unmarked graves in Blair
Cemetery.

MONROE COUNTY

TOMBSTONE INSCRIPTIONS
BLAIR CEMETERY

MORROW

Armstrong Morrow
Feb. 1, 1801
Mar. 23, 1880
"His Memory is blessed."

Margaret Morrow
June 14, 1808
Aug. 19, 1875
"She was the sunshine of
our home."

BLAIR

Father
J. T. Blair
Jan. 30, 1826
July 10, 1897
Aged 71 yrs, 5 mos &
10 days.
"Gone but not forgotten."

Mother
Martha W. Blair
Wife of
J. T. Blair
Dec. 27, 1833
April 17, 1880
Aged 55 yrs. 3 mos. &
20 days.
"Her many virtues makes
Noblest monument to her
Memory."

Laura Blair
June 7, 1851
Oct. 3, 1917
"Faithful to her trust."

William Blair
May 4, 1868
Feb. 13, 1924
"Christ loved him
and took him home."

Joe Blair
Oct. 6, 1862
July 4, 1931
"We will meet again."

DENTON

In memory of
Elizabeth
Daughter of
Wm. & A. Denton
Feb. 12, 1843
Nov. 8, 1843
Aged 8 mos. & 26 days.

In memory of
Patton L.
Son of
Wm. & A. Denton
Aug. 2, 1847
Nov. 6, 1848
Aged 1 year, 3 months & 4 days.

In Memory of
Amanda C. L.
Daughter of
Wm. & A. Denton
Mar. 23, 1845
Nov. 15, 1848
Aged 3 years, 7 months & 22 days.

In Memory of
Mary
Daughter of
Wm. & Amanda Denton
July 20, 1834
Jan. 15, 1852
Aged 17 years, 5 months & 25 days.

In Memory of
William Denton
March 22, 1800
July 31, 1856
Aged 56 years, 4 months & 9 days.

In Memory of
Francis A
Son of
Calvin Denton
July 3, 1833
Oct. 25, 1856
Aged 23 years, 3 months & 22 days.

SMITH

MONROE COUNTY

TOMBSTONE INSCRIPTIONS
BLAIR QEMETERY

SMITH

Leona
Daughter of
Wm. M. & A. Smith
Died July 21, 1858
Aged 1 yr. & 23 days.

HAGLER

B. B. Hagler
Aug. 20, 1811
Jan. 8, 1890
"Gone but not forgotten."

Mary Jane Hagler
Mar. 11, 1838
June 30, 1925
"Gone but not forgotten."

WAYMAN

Jula Ann Wayman
Feb. 23, 1842
Oct. 7, 1916

KEYES or KEYEES

John Keyes
Sept. 14, 1817
Mar. 6, 1904

M. E. Keyees
June 13, 1853
July 15, 1918
"Though lost to sight
to memory dear."

TOMBSTONE INSCRIPTIONS

BLAIR FARM CEMETERY

Copied by: Lawrence McConkey, Englewood, Tennessee.
Date:

The Blair Farm Cemetery is about 4½ miles East of Tellico Plains on
the road leading to Belltown and Ball Play. Tellico Plains is 16
miles South of Madisonville. The cemetery was established before
the Civil War and it is not known by whom. The Blair family has
owned the farm for over 50 years. It is now owned by Mrs. Mary
Sneed Blair. The cemetery covers a patch in the woods of about
30X50 feet. The last burial, that of Nancy Lynn, was in 19001
There will not likely be any more burials in this cemetery. There
are 8 graves marked with field stones and 22 unmarked graves.

LYNN

Nancy Lynn
Born   1850
Died June 27, 1900

GILES

Infant
of
Delia Giles

Infant
of
Sallie Giles

HUMPHREYS

Alfred Humphreys.

(Note: He died about 1883
at an old age, 75 possibly
LMcC.)

Mrs. Alfred Humphreys.

(Note: She also died about
1883 at an old age. LMcC.)

MONROE COUNTY

BEULAH SOUTHERN M. E. CHURCH CEMETERY

Copied by Lawrence McConkey, Englewood, Tennessee
Date:

The Beulah Southern M. E. Church Cemetery is located 5
miles N. E. of Tellico Plains. To reach the cemetery from
Tellico Plains follow Big Creek Road to Sink Creek Bridge
then turn left. The church and cemetery were established
on three-fourths acres of land bought from John Henderson
Payne and E. W. Harrison. The church was constituted 55
years ago. The first burial, that of John Henderson (Jack)
Payne, was on December 19, 1903. J. W. Payne, a Civil War
soldier is buried in Beulah Southern M. E. Church Cemetery
according to Frazier Styles.

The cemetery contains 24 field stones and 8 unmarked graves.

MONROE COUNTY

TOMBSTONE INSCRIPTIONS
BEULAH METHODIST CHURCH SOUTH CEMETERY

CANTRELL

Simon Cantrell
Feb. 14, 1830
Jan. 1, 1907

PATTERSON

Virgel Patterson
June 12, 1910
Sept. 17, 1912

Note: There are 3 graves
with stones on north
side and 7 stones east
very likely same family.

PAYNE

Father
J. W. Payne
Born Feb. 25, 1845
Co. D. 3 Tenn.
Mt. Inf.

Mother
Annie Parks
Wife of
J. W. Payne
Mar. 11, 1851
Jan. 16, 1924
"A link that binds us
to Heaven."

(Note: Both inscriptions
are on the same marker.)

Wesley
Son of
F. M. & M. E. Payne
Jan. 19, 1894
June 20, 1912

John Henderson Payne
Feb. 15, 1842
Dec. 19, 1903

Sarah Shadden Payne
Oct. 13, 1845
June 17, 1907

(Note: George Payne is buried
at the head of the grave of
John Henderson Payne.)

HARBIN

William Edgar Harbin
Died Aug. 27, 1937
Aged 18 years, 4 months &
28 days.

Sadie Harris
Wife of
S. A. Harbin
Sept. 28, 1884
Dec. 8, 1920

S. A. Harbin

HARRIS

Jimmie H.
Son of
Wm. & S. P. Harris
June 28, 1894
Mar. 4, 1910
"Gone but not forgotten."

Leona Harris
Died Jan. 28, 1937
Aged 9 years, 4 months &
15 days.

CANUP

Mary E. Canup
Mar. 29, 1849
Dec. 15, 1936

J. T. Canup
Mar. 7, 1847
Sept. 2, 1916

STEWART

Milton Stewart
Mar. 11, 1877
July 3, 1926

(Note: He married Ollie Canup
daughter of J. T. & Mary E. Canup

BEULAH METHODIST CHURCH SOUTH CEMETERY

STEWART

Infant
daughter of
Milton & Ollie Stewart
Born & died
Jan. 16, 1911

HELEMS OR HELMS

Margaret Shadden
Wife of
John Helems
Nov. 8, 1830
Nov. 23, 1907

(Note: 1 stone south)

S. J.
Wife of
W. W. Helms
June 10, 1858
Oct. 15, 1914
"At Rest."

W. W. Helems

STEPHENS

Elsie Mae Helms
Wife of
T. J. Stephens
Born July 20, 1885
Married
Aug. 31, 1908
"God in his wisdom
has recalled the boom
his love had given and
though the body moulders
here, the Soul is safe in
Heaven."

BROWN

Joe Brown

DARNES

Mary Ann
Wife of
J. G. Darnes
Feb. 23, 1861
Nov. 1, 1928
"Gone but not forgotten."

EAKIN

Lellie
daughter of
J. A. & Dora Eakin
May 31, 1904
Oct. 4, 1904
"Our darling."

(Note: 1 stone north.)

PEARSON

Infant
Son of
Art & Lovie Pearson
June 8, 1911
June 18, 1911

COPPINGER

Lucile Coppinger
Dec. 20, 1912
Oct. 8, 1913
"Asleep in Jesus."

TOMBSTONE INSCRIPTIONS

BOYD FAMILY CEMETERY

Copied by: Lawrence McConkey, Englewood, Tennessee
Date: October 28, 1938

This is a very old cemetery. The Boyd family owned the farm where
the cemetery is located, when it was established but sold it in
1838 to Solomon Wilson. None of the Boyds in this section of the
County seem to be descendants of the family who established the
graveyard nor can information be secured regarding them.

Located 8 miles South of Madisonville, the cemetery may be reached
by taking the McCroskey highway to Chestua Southern Methodist Church
and there taking the road by the church that leads to the old Federal
road. The cemetery is on the farm of Jess Rogers near Colthorp
School.

There are two unmarked graves.

BOYD   Infant

Sacred to the memory of
Our mother   Infant
Jinsey
Wife of
Erby Boyd
Born Nov. 17, 1794
Died May 1, 1836

MONROE COUNTY

TOMBSTONE INSCRIPTIONS

BULLET CREEK BAPTIST CHURCH CEMETERY

Copied by: Lawrence McConkey, Englewood, Tennessee.
Date:

The Bullet Creek Baptist Church Cemetery was started by the Cain family in 1897 but was soon transferred to the church for a public burial ground. The church had been established for some time.

This cemetery is about 22 miles South of Madisonville. The best route is via Mt. Vernon, to Jalapa or Brown Hill, to Ivy then West toward Starr Mountain.

There are approximately 90 unmarked graves.

CAIN

Elvira K. Cain
Jan. 23, 1850
Jan. 28, 1897
In God I trust.

Elizabeth Cain
Born 1822
Died June 3, 1905

Jacob Cain
born 1812
Died Dec. 22, 1897
Farewell dear parents
sweet is thy rest.

Andrew H. Cain
Mar. 14, 1889
Mar. 31, 1918
Gone but not forgotten.

C. A. Cain
Sept. 20, 1871
(Still living)

S. P. Cain
Oct. 11, 1850
Apr. 29, 1936
At Rest.

Infant
of
S. P. & E. K. Cain

John Cain
Died Aug. 8, 1934
Aged 60 years

Mrs. John Cain

Infant
of
Mr. & Mrs. John Cain

Henry Cain

George Cain

Martha Cain

EATON

G. W. Eaton

Betty Eaton

Samuel Eaton
Josie Eaton

HAMPTON

Susie
Daughter of
R. J. & Ida Hampton
Oct. 13, 1888
Nov. 24, 1910

BULLET CREEK BAPTIST CHURCH CEMETERY

Fred
Son of
Mr. & Mrs. D. C. Hampton
Sept. 23, 1930
Sept. 23, 1930
Our darling.

Robert Hampton

Ida Hampton

ARRANTS

Jacob Arrants

Polly Arrants

BURRELL

John Burrell

GARDNER

Nancy E. Gardner
Dec. 15, 1850
Jan. 4, 1937
Having finished lifes
duty she now sweetly rests.

EVANS

Mrs. Lula Evans
July 2, 1906
Feb. 2, 1933

BURCH

Augusta Lou Ida
Daughter of
J. B. & Etta Burch
Dec. 11, 1909
Oct. 30, 1911
Our beloved baby.

FREEMAN

Howard C. Freeman

Sussie Freeman

G. H. Freeman

Charlie Freeman

R. S. Freeman

CHASTAIN

Nell Chastain

(Note: He was killed. LMcC.)

LEDFORD

John Ledford

Sarah Ledford

Baby
Ledford

WILLIAMS

Allen Williams
Dec. 8, 1896
May 3, 1901
Gone but not forgotten.
Our darling.

F. P. Williams
Mar. 8, 1829
Jan. 31, 1907
Gone but not forgotten.

L. D. Williams
July 4, 1825
Nov. 20, 1914
Gone but not forgotten.

L. D. Williams
July 20, 1863
Aug. 18, 1912
Gone but not forgotten.

(Note: Above two inscriptions
are not for the same person. LMcC)

M. J. Williams
Dec. 25, 1867
Apr. 30, 1906
Gone but not forgotten.

Oscar Williams
Oct. 15, 1882
May 8, 1911
Gone but not forgotten.

GREEHR

Arlie Greehr

DUCKETT

L. A. Duckett
Dec. 5, 1885
Sept. 4, 1921
Father gone but not
forgotten.

Ida Duckett

GREEN

Thomas E. Green
Oct. 1, 1901
July 17, 1931
A little time on earth he
spent till God for him his
Angels sent.

Pearley E. Green
Sept. 22, 1905
July 16, 1929
We'll join thee in
that Heavenley Land
no more to take the
parting hand.

Elisha H. Green
Aug. 23, 1859
Apr. 21, 1938
His toils are past, his
work is done. He fought
the fight - the victory
won.

Elizabeth A. Green
Aug. 13, 1861
Feb. 11, 1931
Having finished lifes
duty she now
sweetly sleeps.

Arlis Green

TOMBSTONE INSCRIPTIONS

ROBERT BURTON FAMILY CEMETERY

Copied by: Lawrence McConkey, Englewood, Tennessee
Date:

J. M. Burton deeded ¼ acre for a family cemetery. The graveyard
is on the Burton farm which has been owned by the Burton family
for over 100 years. It is located 8 miles North of Madisonville.
To reach the farm go via Hiwassee College and keep the main straight
road at Rockville. The cemetery is at the Burton Hill County
School off the main road to the left about ¼ mile.

Robert Burton married Mildred Carpenter. Both were Virginians. To
this Union were born the following children: Nancy, who married
Wm. P. Kittrell; Lucy, who married Wm. Griffitt; Jane, who married
Gillespie Montgomery; James Madison, who married Sarah Matthews;
Henry N., who died when young; and William P., married Mallissa
Rausin.

There are 19 inscriptions, and a few unmarked graves - possibly 10,
most of which are of people unrelated to the Burtons.

BURTON

Mother
Sarah Burton
Wife of
J. M. Burton
Born Nov. 8, 1823
Died Sept. 13, 1892
Aged 68 yrs. 10 mos. 5 days.
Her children shall rise up
and call her blessed.

Our Father
James Madison Burton
Born Mar. 11, 1827
Died Oct. 18, 1912
Aged 85 yrs. 7 mos. 7 dys.
His end was peace.

Mary Jane Burton
Born Jan. 5, 1859
Died Feb. 24, 1925

S. E.
Infant Dau. of
J. M. & M. J. Burton
Nov. 5, 1898
June 5, 1900
Budded on earth to
bloom in Heaven.

Mildred
Wife of
R. Burton
Born Mar. 20, 1793
Died Aug. 25, 1839

Robert Burton
Born Aug. 15, 1790
Died Aug. 29, 1839

Henry P. Burton
Born May 1835
Died Apr. 1839

William P. Burton
Born July 24, 1831
Died Oct. 12, 1873

Maggie M.
Daughter of
W. P. & M. M. Burton
Born May 22, 1866
Died Oct. 18, 1895

Our Sister
Nancy J.
Daughter of
J. M. & S. Burton
(continued on next page)

ROBERT BURTON FAMILY CEMETERY

Born Sept. 13, 1856
Died Oct. 9, 1884
I am the Resurrection
and the life.

Our Brother
Joseph Burton
Son of
J. M. & S. Burton
Born June 20, 1854
Died Sept. 2, 1884
I am the Resurrection
and the life.

Nancy J. Burton
Daughter of
J. M. & S. Burton
Born Sept. 13, 1856
Died Oct. 9, 1884

Joseph Burton
Son of
J. M. & S. Burton
Born June 20, 1854
Died Sept. 2, 1884

(Note: Nancy and Joseph each
have a marker and there is an
extra double marker as above.
LMcC.)

Jack Burton
Died Jan. 1929
Aged about 71 years

Elbert W. Burton
Dec. 22, 1883
Nov. 1, 1917

Dave M. Burton
Nov. 1, 1854
Apr. 13, 1893
A sunbeam has vanished.

KITTRELL

Our Father
Wm. P. Kettrell
Born Oct. 4, 1815
Died Dec. 6, 1884

Our Mother
Nancy Kittrell
Born Jan. 18, 1824
Died Nov. 27, 1905

Columbus
Son of
Wm. P & Nancy Kittrell

HAMILTON

Mary Jane
Wife of
John B. Hamilton &
Daughter of
W. P. & N. J. Kittrell
Born Feb. 1, 1848
Died Oct. 20, 1877

Mary J.
Wife of
J. B. Hamilton
Born Feb. 1, 1848
Died Oct. 20, 1877

Robert H.
Son of
J. B. & Mary J. Hamilton
Born Oct. 19, 1876
Died July 21, 1903

TOMBSTONE INSCRIPTIONS

CATHCART FAMILY CEMETERY

Copied by: Lawrence McConkey, Englewood, Tennessee.
Date: Jan. 25, 1939

The Cathcart Family Cemetery was established on the farm of
Joseph and Annie Cathcart at their request. They willed their
farm to the Denton family. It is on the J. F. McCracken farm
which is located about 4½ miles East of Madisonville on the
road leading to Hopewell Springs.

There are no unmarked graves.

CATHCART

Joseph Cathcart   Annie Cathcart
Died July 4, 1895   Died Feb. 1, 1896
At Rest.   At Rest.

FAMILY SKETCH

Joseph Cathcart, came from near Loudon, and married Annie Denton.
He had one brother, named Allen who lived in the same section,
near Loudon. Allan had one daughter who married David Brooks
and one son named George. Some relatives of Joseph Cathcart,
lived in Georgia.

Joseph and Annie Cathcart were not the parents of any children.
There is not any record of their ages but it is thought that
they were between 85 and 90 years old when they died.

MONROE COUNTY

TOMBSTONE INSCRIPTIONS

CENTER PRESBYTERIAN CHURCH CEMETERY

Copied by: Lawrence McConkey, Englewood, Tennessee
Date:

The Center Presbyterian Church and the church cemetery are located
about 3 miles East of Tellico Plains on the road leading to Belltown.
The land for both church and cemetery, comprising about an acre and
a half, was given by Charles A. Scott in 1924. The church is in
one corner of the property. The remainder is to be used for cemetery
purposes as needed. The graves are scattered about.

The first sermon in the Center Presbyterian Church was preached by
the Rev. Sam Wolf on Feb. 17, 1924. His text was from the 10th
Chapter of Hebrews, the 25th verse.

The first burial in the cemetery, that of Robert Harrison Stephens,
took place on July 14, 1933. There are 2 graves marked by field
stones and 7 unmarked graves.

STEPHENS

Stephens
Robert Harrison Stephens
March 15, 1874
July 14, 1933
His memory is blessed.

Etta Frances Stphens
Dec. 28, 1886
(Still Living)
Christ is my hope.

Ben H. Stephens Jr.
July 28, 1933
Jan. 10, 1935
Baby

SHAW

Maggie Shaw
Nov. 19, 1878
Feb. 18, 1939
Gone but not forgotten.

(Note: The grave of Maggie
Shaw is in a separate lot from
the following. LMcC.)

Shaw
Jasper R.
Feb. 8, 1869
Feb. 22, 1935

Nealie
June 13, 1869
Feb. 22, 1935
Gone but not forgotten.

ELLIS

Augustus Weissert Ellis
July 9, 1878
Oct. 7, 1937

MONROE COUNTY

CHESTUA BAPTIST CHURCH CEMETERY

Copied by Lawrence McConkey, Englewood, Tennessee
Date: August 23, 25, 1939

Land for Chestua Baptist Church and Cemetery is said to
have been given by the Rev. John Scruggs who moved to
Monroe County in 1833. Chestua Baptist Church was
constituted in 1825. As the opinion is strong that this
land was donated by the Rev. Mr. Scruggs, it would seem
that church services were held in some one's home.or in
a school house for several years prior to the erection
of the church.

The earliest inscription in Chestua Baptist Church
Cemetery is that of John J., son of John & Theresa N.
Scruggs, who was born February 5, 1839 and died September
10, 1839.

Probably the most prominent person buried in Chestua is
the Rev. John Scruggs, second son of Richard and Eliza
McMahan Scruggs. He was born in Grayson County, Virginia,
and with his parents moved to Greene County, Tennessee,
near Warrensburg.

On September 7, 1824 John Scruggs married Miss Theresa
Newell Carter, daughter of Francis J. and Esther Crocket
Carter of Cocke County, Tennessee. The latter was a
cousin of the celebrated David Crocket. Scruggs moved to
Monroe County in 1833 and purchased 1700 acres of land
on Chestua Creek. He was a reader of Greek. A brick church
at Chestua was built before the Civil War and he furnished
over one third of the entire cost of the building. Two
other prominent men buried in Chestua Cemetery are John
Coltharp, and John B. Wilson. Mr. Coltharp was the son of
a Revolutionary Soldier and a first Deacon of the church.
Mr. Wilson was a son of Charles and Elizabeth (Broyles)
Wilson. His parents migrated from Washington County,
Tennessee. He was a direct descendant of Benjamin Wilson
who was at Watauga Settlement, and a first Esquire of the
first free Government of the world. John B. Wilson married
Louvenia, a daughter of Adam and Elizabeth Lowry Barr, who
lived in Jefferson County, Tennessee, before settling in
Monroe. The early Wilsons, Lowrys, & Broyles emigrated
from Scotland, coming through Virginia to Tennessee.

There are 188 inscriptions and 300 or more unmarked graves
in Chestua Baptist Cemetery. The cemetery is well fenced
and has rocked drive ways. It is about 5½ miles South of
Madisonville, and about ½ mile to the left of McCroskey.

MONROE COUNTY

TOMBSTONE INSCRIPTIONS
CHESTUA BAPTIST CHURCH CEMETERY

SCRUGGS

Rev. John Scruggs
Mar. 4, 1797
Mar. 11, 1867

Rev. John Scruggs &
Theresa Carter married
Sep. 24, 1824

Theresa N. Scruggs
Oct. 8, 1806
Nov. 9, 1888
"Blessed are the dead
which die in the Lord,
from henceforth yea
Saith the Spirit that
they may rest from their
labors and their works do
follows them."

William F. C.
Son of
John & Theresa N. Scruggs
Aug. 28, 1850
Oct. 21, 1856
"Asleep in Jesus."

George W.
Son of
John & Theresa N. Scruggs
Feb. 11, 1841
Nov. 29, 1849

Rufus
Son of
John & Theresa N. Scruggs
Aug. 28, 1850
Oct. 21, 1856

Zachary T.
Son of
John & Theresa N. Scruggs
Jun 11, 1848
Apr. 30, 1849

John J.
Son of
John & Theresa N. Scruggs
Feb. 5, 1839
Sep. 10, 1839

(Note: The above seems to be
the earliest inscription in
this graveyard.)

John Scruggs
Son of
James & Mary E. Scruggs
May 30, 1872
Mar. 23, 1880
"Gone but not forgotten and
though, the body moulders
here the Soul is safe in Heaven."

Anderson

Iola

(Note: The two above inscriptions
were at left of the grave of the
above John Scruggs, son of James &
Mary E., and at the right of the
grave of James Scruggs. They were
infants of James & Mary E. Scruggs.)

James Scruggs
Born May 30, 1840
Married M. E. Carson, Nov. 30, 1869
Died April 1, 1906
"Saved by Grace."

Mother
Mary E. Scruggs
Wife of
James Scruggs
Mar. 7, 1848
May 20, 1916
"Tho lost to sight to Memory dear."

GREEN
In memoriam
Sister
Sarah Green
Sept. 15, 1880
Aug. 21, 1920

(Note: The above inscription was
at foot of a Scruggs marker. From
information; she was the daughter
of James & Mary E. Scruggs and
married a Mr. Green."

CHESTUA BAPTIST CHURCH CEMETERY

WRIGHT

Elsie S. Coltharp
Wife of
Ernest Wright
Mar. 16, 1884
Apr. 18, 1915
"Dying words I am
ready to go."

BALL

Dollie Ball
1886-1938

J. H. Ball

OWNBY

Ethel Ownby
Dec. 21, 1911
Mch. 23, 1935
"Awaiting the resurrection."

CARTER

Esther Carter
Jan.   1773
July 9, 1870

YEARWOOD

Charley
Infant son of
M. B. & E. E. Yearwood
died Jan. 1, 1868

PITTMAN

S. B. Pittman
Oct. 11, 1859
Oct. 19, 1909
Killed by train.

M. A. Pittman
Oct. 4, 1860
(Buried no date given)

In Memory of
Father & Mother.
Asleep in Jesus

Margaret Amy Pittman
Died Aug. 15, 1936
Aged 75 years, 10 months &
11 days.

E. M. Pittman

Narcissa
Wife of
S. A. Pittman
Born 1833
Died Dec. 18, 1908

S. A. Pittman
Born 1824
Died June 10, 1905
"At Rest."

(Note: E. M. Pittman was buried
by and on North side of Narcissa.
Very likely a child of Narcissa
& S. A. Pittman.)

Elizabeth Pittman
June 13, 1855
June 9, 1913
"At Rest."

James F.
Son of
S. A. & N. Pittman
July 25, 1867
Apr. 26, 1890

John N. Pitman
Oct. 10, 1873
Dec. 15, 1929
"He loved his Church."

(Note: Name is spelled Pitman
on Marker, but he was a son of
S. A. & Narcissa Pittman.)

Smith Pittman

Tip Pittman

Sarah, Wife of
Tip Pittman

CHESTUA BAPTIST CHURCH CEMETERY

BENINE

J. L.
Son of
Joseph & Eliza Benine
Mar. 9, 1883
Apr. 15, 1884
"Asleep in Jesus."

McPEEK

Ephraim McPeek
Ephraim McPeek
Dec. 13, 1840
Mar. 21, 1914

Frances Stockdale
Wife of
E. McPeek
Feb. 1, 1841
Sep. 10, 1910
"In my fathers house are
Many mansions.
Farewell dear parents
sweet is they rest."

Edwin S. McPeek
Jan. 1, 1872
Jul. 16, 1908
"In God we trust."

Fannie May
Daughter of
C. H. & L. L. McPeek
Feb. 10, 1906
Sep. 16, 1906
"Absent not dead."

L. L.
Wife of
C. H. McPeek
Jan. 13, 1880
Jul. 21, 1906
"Meet me in Heaven."

Alfred McPeek
Mar. 20, 1874
May 21, 1904
"Remember friends as you
pass by so you are now so
once was I. As I am now
so you must be, prepare for
death and follow me."

LACEWELL

A. E. Lacewell
June 17, 1904
Sep. 29, 1905

JOINES

My Husband
D. H. Joines
Dec. 3, 1820
Aug. 3, 1892
"Blessed are the dead which
die in the Lord."

John H. Joines
Son of
Moses Joines
and husband of
Maggie Joines
Feb. 17, 1837
Apr. 2, 1886

Mary Joines
Mar. 15, 1824
Mar. 22, 1864
Aged 40 yrs. 7 days

In Memory of
Susan Joines
Oct. 18, 1800
Jun 27, 1875
Aged 74 years, 8 months &
9 days.

Moses Joines
Feb. 15, 1798
Jul. 14, 1884
"Blessed are the dead that
die in the Lord."

MURR

Ruby Rhea
Dau of
Mr. & Mrs. Roy A. Murr
Dec. 29, 1927
Apr. 13, 1932
"Of such is the Kingdom of Heaven."

THOMPSON

Pery A. Thompson
Nov. 15, 1885
Aug. 99, 1932
"He was faithful to
every duty."

Ella B. Thompson
Aug. 20, 1887
Jul. 29, 1935
"In loving memory".

Sister
Della Vinna Thompson
Jun. 17, 1889
Mar. 21, 1924
"Gone but not forgotten."

Gleson R. Thompson
May 23, 1938
May 27, 1938
"Budded on earth to
bloom in Heaven."

Thomas Thompson
(No date given)
June 1, 1928

Barbara Haun Thompson
Aug. 15, 1860
Nov. 28, 1918
"At Rest."

ALLEN

Infant
son of
Mr. & Mrs. J. C. Allen
Mar. 29, 1918
Mar. 29, 1918
"Safe in the arms of Jesus."

PHILIPS

Lizia Brady
Wife of
Boyd Philips
Mar. 21, 1896
May 3, 1921
"At Rest."

E. L. Philips

HAUN

Cordelia Elizabeth Gudger Haun
Dec. 13, 1869
Feb. 26, 1900
Mother

Thomas E. Haun
Apr. 9, 1866
Aug. 17, 1931
"All things to the glory of God."

Rankin
Son of
W. S. & Nettie Haun
Nov. 1, 1897
Nov. 9, 1897

Father
Rev. A. Haun
Feb. 4, 1834
Mar. 13, 1897

Mother
A. Haun
May 16, 1832
Dec. 28, 1921
"Having finished lifes duty
they now sweetly rest."

Mother
Sallie Miller Haun
July 31, 1864
July 9, 1916

Father
James O. Haun
May 26, 1862
Jun 21, 1901

WELLS

Mrs. Sis Wells

James Wells

George Wells

LEE

James E. Lee
Aug. 5, 1861
Mar. 27, 1924
His wife
Callie S. Lee
Oct. 11, 1863
(Living)

CHESTUA BAPTIST CHURCH CEMETERY

LEE

Ida Sue Lee
Sept. 30, 1885
Jan. 26, 1909

Oscar J. Lee
Sept. 30, 1893
Sept. 28, 1903

Ralph H.
Son of
J. E. & C . N. Lee
Sept. 18, 1904
July 23, 1917
"At Rest."

P. N. Lee
Nov. 23, 1820
April 30, 1887
"Gone to rest."

Susan Lee
Wife of
P. N. Lee
July 9, 1822
June 12, 1885
"Gone to rest."

Daughter
of
T. B. & S. J. Lee
Mar. 22, 1909

William R. Lee
Apr. 10, 1853
Mar. 13, 1930

His wife
Tezzie Joines
Sept. 13, 1866
Jan.   5, 1936

Vassie Lee
May 17, 1889
Jan. 1, 1906
Aged 16 years, 7 months &
15 days
"The Lord is my Shepherd,
I shall not want."

Della M. Lee
Apr. 28, 1902
Nov. 22, 1903
"Asleep in Jesus."

Martha Lee
Mar. 5, 1851
Aug. 25, 1933

Eliza Lee
Jan. 12, 1849
Feb. 27, 1926
"At Rest."

Zilpha Lee
Dec. 4, 1817
Jun. 16, 1912
"Gone but not forgotten."

Kattie Lee
Dec. 24, 1918
Jan. 26, 1919
"Our darling."

MITCHELL

J. F. Mitchell
July 18, 1848
May 12, 1914
"Having finished lifes duty.
He now sweetly rests."

WILSON

Infant
of
Thomas & Lucinda Wilson
1889

Infant
of
Thomas & Lucinda Wilson
1892

Father
John B. Wilson
Jan. 15, 1827
Sept. 23, 1898

CHESTUA BAPTIST CHURCH CEMETERY

WILSON

Mother
Louvenia Barr Wilson
Mar. 5, 1840
Nov. 23, 1920
"Their Spirits smiles from
that bright shore and softly
whispers weep no more."

Infant
of
Lee & Ella Wilson
1902

William L. Wilson
June 14, 1867
Oct. 17, 1897

His Wife
Sallie A. Manis Wilson Tallent
Jan. 28, 1870
May 11, 1932

(Note: The above named lady
married Wm. L. Wilson and
after his death she married
Mr. Tallent. The Marker
was erected by the Wilson
children.)

COLTHARP

John Colthorp
Apr. 28, 1781
May 28, 1867
(Eng. Decent.)
Son of a Revolutionary
Soldier.)

Susanna
Wife of
John Coltharp
Nov. 3rd 1786
June 17th 1855

Esther A. Lee Colthorp
Jan. 30, 1856
Aug. 10, 1929
"Gone but not forgotten."

J. H. Colthorp
Sept. 5, 1820
Mar. 20, 1896
"But thanks be to God which giveth
us the Victory through our Lord
Jesus Christ 1 Cor. 15-57."

Jane C. Colthorp
Nov. 7, 1820
Jan. 18, 1906

Maggie J.
Wife of
S. J. Colthorp
Dec. 6, 1853
Oct. 30, 1887
"Sweet Home."

Cornelia
Wife of
J. H. Colthorp
June 24, 1819
Sept. 8, 1853

Alva M. Colthorp
Died June 3, 1863
Age 4 Months & 8 days

Hughie H.
Son of
A. J. & M. J. Colthorp
Dec. 11, 1874
Feb. 13, 1881

Ada E.
Daughter of
G. H. & A. L. Colthorp
June 18, 1869
Aug. 10, 1870

Henry H.
Son of
G. H. & A. L. Colthorp
Oct. 11, 1872
Mar. 3, 1873

Caroline E. Colthorp
Dec. 30, 1843
June 16, 1880
"Asleep in Jesus."

CHESTUA BAPTIST CHURCH CEMETERY

COLTHORP

M. A. Colthorp
Son of
G. H. & M. A. Colthorp
May 11, 1864
May 25, 1864

Joanah B. Colthorp
Sept. 5, 1861
July 16, 1862

Martha A.
Wife of
G. H. Colthorp
Born Oct. 15, 1838
Died May 11, 1864

W. D. Colthorp
Son of
G. H. & M. A. Colthorp
Born Jan. 12, 1862

(Note: Marker is broken and
date of death missing. An
infant's grave.)

Our Father
George Hammer Colthorp
Oct. 12, 1833
June 18, 1907
"Gone home."

Mother
Addie L. Colthorp
Feb. 20, 1841
Jan. 24, 1929
"Gods will be done."

BIVANS

Father
E. C. Bivans
Sept. 17, 1835
Mar. 31, 1920

Mother
S. E. Bivans
May 28, 1840
Feb. 27, 1920

STAKELY

Elisabeth L.
Daughter of
F. L. & N. C. Stakely
1915-1936

Moston H. Stakely
Dec. 2, 1852
Apr. 26, 1921

Lucy Lee Stakely
Jan. 3, 1858
Jan. 17, 1928
"Christ loved them and
took them home."

Joe M. Stakely
Oct. 26, 1869
May 28, 1936

John O. Stakely
Aug. 23, 1848
Dec. 19, 1928
"Asleep in Jesus."

(Member of Masonic order)
Abram Stakely
Jan. 29, 1818
May 26, 1905

Mary E. Horner
Wife of
Dr. A. Stakely
Nov. 22, 1833
May 10, 1909
"Gone but not forgotten."

Father & Mother
F. L. Stakely
Sept. 28, 1879
Dec. 30, 1929
"Come quickly Lord Jesus."

Nellie L. Colthorp
Wife of
F. L. Stakely
Feb. 27, 1880
(living)

CHESTUA BAPTIST CHURCH CEMETERY

MORGAN

Tinie Pittman
Wife of
Andrew Morgan

Andrew Morgan
"At Rest."

J. B.
Son of
Mr. & Mrs. O. A. Morgan
Nov. 2, 1919
Sept 22, 1920

WATSON

Martha A.
Wife of
A. J. Watson
Jan. 15, 1844
Jan. 27, 1881

Sarah Watson
Wife of
John Watson

John Watson

Daniel Watson
Died Oct. 29, 1935
Aged 68 years 4 months &
23 days.

J. H. Watson

Mrs. Daniel Watson

HARDIN

John B.
Son of
M. A. & M. F. Hardin
Sept. 13, 1861
May 3, 1862

JARVIS

A. J. Jarvis
Dec. 1, 1827
Feb. 23, 1896

Rebecca B. Jarvis
Sept. 1, 1832
(Date of death missing.)

Joanna
Daughter of
A. J. & R. B. Jarvis
Oct. 10, 1857
Dec. 20, 1861

MCCASLIN

Father
J. H. McCaslin
July 16, 1832
Sept. 6, 1902
"Peace be thy slumbers."

John McCaslin

REYNOLDS

Susan Ellen
Wife of
T. E. Reynolds
Dec. 17, 1858
Aug. 14, 1891

"Savior lead me."
E. A.
Wife of
T. E. Reynolds
May. 22, 1871
Mar. 27, 1909

Thomas E. Reynolds
Oct. 7, 1856
Mar. 4, 1936

Alice McPeek Reynolds
April 28, 1883
(not buried)
"Resting till the resurrection
Morn."

SMITH

Clyde D.
Son of
E. A. & E. L. Smith
Jan. 21, 1926
Dec. 8, 1928
"Earth has no sorrow that Heaven
Cannot cure."

CHESTUA BAPTIST CHURCH CEMETERY

ROBERTS

Infant
of
W. J. & M. E. Roberts
Born & died
July -- 1886

Mary E. Lee
Wife of
W. J. Roberts
Jan. 30, 1847
Feb. 12, 1913
"At Rest."

W. J. Roberts

Lisa Roberts
Sept. 17, 1834
March 8, 1915
"Her Spirit smiles from
that bright shore and
softly whispers weep
no more."

COVINGTON

Mrs. Lucile Covington
Nov. 9, 1891
Feb. 12, 1924
"She is not dead
but sleepeth."

STEPHEN

Vise E. Stephen

Absolum Stephen

(Note: The above man and
wife were pioneers. Nothing
else given on rock markers
but the names. They have
been dead 50 years or more.)

Ja-- Stephen

Rufus Stephen

Amanda Stephen
Wife of
Rufus Stephen

HICKS

Mary L. H.
Daughter of
John S. & Elizabeth V. Hicks
April 21, 1868
July 30, 1886
"Blessed are the pure in Heart
for they shall see God."

John S. Hicks
Apr. 4, 1842
June 14, 1868

Herbert R. Hicks
son of
Mr. & Mrs. Paul Hicks
Nov. 12, 1935
Nov. 18, 1935
"He Will make Heaven more real."

Ara M. Colthorp
Wife of
O. H. Hicks
Sept. 14, 1875
Oct. 15, 1896
"Death is swollowed up in Victory."

DENTON

Amanda Denton
Mar. 29, 1809
Jan. 6, 1887

Joseph Denton

HYATT

Infant
son of
C. W. & M. B. Hyatt

PENNINGTON

Hubert A.
Son of
John D. & Cordie M Pennington
July 1, 1886
Aug. 29, 1888
"Asleep in Jesus."

CHESTUA BAPTIST CHURCH CEMETERY

MANIS

Father
G. S. Manis
Oct. 21, 1833
(No date given)

Mother
N. C. Manis
Oct. 8, 1839
Feb. 18, 1917
"At Rest."

Mother

Josephine J. Falconer Manis
Sept. 18, 1867
Aug. 11, 1925

Father
Joseph A. Manis
May 4, 1859
May 1, 1908
"At Rest."

MCDANIEL

Cora E.
Daughter of
Rev. J. H. & M. V. McDaniel
June 1, 1893
Mar. 4, 1910
"Another link is broken
in our household band but a
chain is forming in a
better land."

Tennie McDaniel
Jan.   18--
Apr.   1918

Bertha L
Daughter of
Rev. J. H. & M. V. McDaniel
Dec. 15, 1895
Apr. 5, 1903
"Asleep in Jesus."

Rhoden C. McDaniel
Oct. 11, 1835
Dec. 18, 1901
"He followed Virtue as his
truest guide. Lived as a
Christian died."

Martha A. McDaniel
Mar. 25, 1850
Mar. 15, 1938
"Gone but not forgotten."

SCOTT

Mrs. --- Scott
Died Sept. 15, 1937
Aged 68 years

GREGORY

Mrs. T. J. Gregory

Wilson Gregory
Son of
T. J. Gregory

PASSMORE

Laura C. Thomas
Wife of
J. C. Passmore
May 2, 1872
Apr. 5, 1911

H. J. Passmore
Aug. 1, 1876
Oct. 22, 1912
"At Rest."

HARRILL

Joe V. Harrill
Died April 2, 19--
Aged 50 years 1 month & 8 days

CHESTUA BAPTIST CHURCH CEMETERY

HARRILL

James R.
Son of
James & Ella E. Harrill
July 3, 1883
June 6, 1890

Cornellia Harrill
Dec. 15, 1865
Feb. 17, 1917
"Gone but not forgotten."

Eliza Stephen
Wife of
James Harrill

James Harrill
Died June 29, 1937
Aged 78 years 2 days.

Richard Harrill
Died Mar. 20, 1937
Aged 39 years 10 months &
14 days.

Earl Harrill

MCCARY

Bess Gudger McCary
Jan. 17, 1897
Mar. 7, 1928
"Having finished lifes duty,
She now sweetly rests."

RABURN

Mary L. Raburn
Feb. 9, 1844
July 27, 1909

Henry Raburn

PRESSWOOD

Lucy J.
Wife of
E. W. Presswood
June 25, 1885
Feb. 22, 1907
"Gone in her young years,
ere sorrow coved stain;
Afar from lifes cares,
its griefs and its pains."

ABERNATHY

Mother
Pollie Barnet
Wife of
Rev. R. P. Abernathy
Apr. 22, 1836
Feb. 26, 1926
"Mother is gone but not forgotten."

Floyd
Son of
Mr. & Mrs. B. M. Abernathy
May 31, 1902
Mar. 4, 1927
"At Rest."

Myra J.
Daughter of
Mr. & Mrs. C. H. Abernathy
Sept. 23, 1924
Nov. 17, 1924
"Asleep in Jesus."

STILES

L. A. Stiles
Died April 192-
Aged 40 years

Mary Stiles

HARRIS

Willie Harris
Wife of
J. S. Harris

John Harris

Mary Harris

CASS

Grace B. Roberts
Wife of
W. M. Cass
Aug. 29, 1887
June 30, 1910
"At Rest."

MONROE COUNTY

TOMBSTONE INSCRIPTIONS

CITICO BAPTIST CHURCH CEMETERY

Copied by: Lawrence McConkey, Englewood, Tennessee
Date: Nov. 1928

The Citico Baptist Church Cemetery was established at the death
of Eas Millsaps in 1860. It became a community cemetery. Later
his son Jesse Millsaps bought the land and then the Citico Baptist
Church was removed from across the Creek to near the cemetery.
The majority of people buried here are either members of the
Millsaps family or related to them. The graveyard is located in
the steep hills, 29 miles East of Madisonville and can be reached
best by going to Vonore then taking the road known as the Citico road.

There are approximately 152 marked graves and possibly more unmarked
ones.

SELF

Myrtle
Daughter of
Luther & Lula Self
May 7, 1916
Sept. 1, 1919
Safe in the arms of Jesus.

Mosurie
Wife of
C. C. Self
June 5, 1859
Aug. 20, 1928
Gone but not forgotten.

Rev. C. C. Self
May 7, 1854
Sept. 7, 1926
Asleep in Jesus.

Mrs. Wash Self

Wash Self

Baby
Self

GOODWIN

Miss Reba Goodwin
Died Sept. 23, 1937
Aged 16 years & 29 days.

DOTSON

Arenie
Daughter of
J. F. & M. D. Dotson
Jan. 10, 1916
Nov. 1, 1916
Safe in the arms of Jesus.

Floyd
Son of
J. F. & M. Dotson
Aug. 24, 1909
Oct. 10, 1915
Safe in the arms of Jesus.

Laura Dotson

Andrew Dotson

Talar
Son of
B. D. & A. N. Dotson
May 11, 1911
May 13, 1918
He was a kind loving son
and affectionate brother.

Laura
Daughter of
Boyd & Anna Dotson
July 15, 1890
June 8, 1893

GITICO BAPTIST CHURCH CEMETERY

A. J. Dotson
Feb. 10, 1886
Dec. 11, 1919

N. A.
Wife of
A. J. Dotson
May 2, 1892
(Still Living.)
Gone to a brighter
home where grief
cannot come.

Clifford R.
Son of
Loney & Laura Dotson
Oct. 13, 1911
July 2, 1915
Gone but not forgotten.

Luther
Son of
A. J. & N. A. Dotson
Jan. 8, 1911
Oct. 9, 1914
Gone but not forgotten.

James A. Dotson
Apr. 15, 1865
Aug. 12, 1896
Another link is
broken in our house
hold band but a chain
is forming in a better land.

John Dotson
May 6, 1833
Apr. 4, 1912
Not lost blest thought
but gone before, where
we shall meet to
part no more.

Martha
Wife of
John Dotson
June 22, 1843
May 1, 1915
She has gone before
where we shall meet
to part no more.

VANCE

Martellus Vance
Co. G.
13 W. Va. Inf.

Mary
Wife of
Martellus Vance

Mother
Annie
Wife of
Martellis Vance
July 31, 1878
Jan. 22, 1922
Gone but not forgotten.

ARDEN

Fred H.
Son of
Sam & Margaret Arden
July 6, 1900
Sept. 15, 1902
We shall meet again.

CATHCART

Neoma Cathcart
Dec. 17, 1909
July 23, 1911
The Angels called him

Hugh Cathcart

Sissie
Wife of
J. H. Cathcart
Feb. 13, 1885
Nov. 2, 1920

BROOKS

Dora Brooks
June 24, 1898
May 24, 1899

CITICO BAPTIST CHURCH CEMETERY

Floyd
Son of
D. C. Brooks
April 21, 1910
May 17, 1911
The Angels called him.

S. L. Brooks

GUNTER

C. W.
Son of
Mr. & Mrs. M. C. Gunter
Mar. 2, 1928
Mar 24, 1928

WILLIAX

Johney Jackson
Son of
J. D. & Janey Williax
Aug. 28, 1906
Feb. 5, 1915
Gone but not forgotten.

Williax

MORRIS

Bertha
Wife of
C. M. Morris
July 16, 1893
Dec. 12, 1921
She believed and
sleeps in God.

ARP

Father
Square G. Arp
Feb. 3, 1871
July 11, 1925
At Rest.

Loney
Son of
Esq. & D. L. Arp
Mar. 15, 1913
Asleep in Jesus.

Austria
Daughter of
Esq & D. L. Arp
Apr. 30, 1903
Nov. 9, 1913

JOHNSON

Addie Mae
Daughter of
J. A. & C. Johnson
Dec. 18, 1899
July 13, 1901

J. A. Johnson
Mar. 6, 1855
Mar. 11, 1910
Father

DUNKIN

J. L. Dunkin
Died Dec. 13, 1937
Aged 8 Mos. 26 days.

J. W. Dunkin
Jan. 26, 1852
Aug. 17, 1869

A. C. Dunkin
Aug. 1, 1886
June 18, 1887

Modena Dunkin
Aug. 23, 1859
Mar. 2, 1890

John L. Dunkin
Died June 4, 1937
Aged 81 years.

Infant
of
J. I. & J. B. Dunkin
Born & Died
Feb. 7, 1893

Tinie Dunkin
Wife of
Noah Dunkin

CITICO BAPTIST CHURCH CEMETERY

Noah Dunkin

Ollie Dunkin

COSTNER

Sarah An Costner
Mar. 8, 1855
Dec. 16, 1916
The souls who die of
Christ passeth Enter
into immediate rest.

BARNARD

Asleep in Jesus
(Member Jr. O.U.A.M.)
J. H. Barnard
Sept. 9, 1873
Sept. 4, 1918
He is not dead but se
sleepeth.

KIRKLAND

Della
Wife of
John Kirkland
Mar. 15, 1895
May 16, 1932
She was a loving wife,
A constant christian.
She died in the triumph
of faith.

Mother
Delilah
Wife of
James L. Kirkland
Mar. 27, 1862
Feb. 4, 1929
In love she lived
in peace she died.

Infant
of
Mr. & Mrs. John Kirkland
July 5, 1929
Gone Home.

Susie
Wife of
J. C. Kirkland
July 16, 1888
Sept. 2, 1916
We trust our loss
Will be her gain and
that with Christ
she's gone to reign.

Anderson C. Kirkland
Died July 21, 1936
Aged 71 years
A loved one gone.

Otis
Son of
J. C. & Susie Kirkland
Feb. 26, 1916
Oct. 12, 1916
The Angels called him.

Infants
of
A. C. & N. Kirkland
Dec. 9, 1893

Infant
of
A. C. & N. Kirkland
Aug. 8, 1887

Nancy A.
Wife of
A. C. Kirkland
Aug. 24, 1869
Dec. 12, 1893
Therefore be ye also
ready for in such an
hour as ye thinketh not
the Son of Man Cometh.

Nancy
Daughter of
A. C. Kirkland
Sept. 28, 1891
Aug. 13, 1908
The will of the
Lord be done.

CITICO BAPTIST CHURCH CEMETERY

James Kirkland Jr.
Died June 30, 1937
Aged 27 years 7 months 17 days.

WILLIAMS

Williams
Laura
Daughter of
Alf. Millsaps
Wife of
W. B. Williams
Oct. 30, 1877
Sept. 18, 1929

W. B. Williams
June 24, 1875
(Still Living)

Benn F.
Son of
M. F. & C. J. Williams
Mar. 29, 1895
Jan. 16, 1916
My trust is in God.

C. J. Williams
Wife of
Melton F. Williams

Artty
Daughter of
W. O. & Thene Williams
Jan. 18, 1896
Jan. 18, 1897
Safe in the arms of Jesus.

Thene
Wife of
W. O. Williams
Apr. 9, 1860
Sept. 15, 1896
Thy life was beauty,
truth, Goodness and love.

Daughter of
O. H. & Lora Williams
Born & Died
Dec. 26, 1915
From mothers arms to
the arms of Jesus.

M. H. Williams
July 15, 1902
May 20, 1903

W. O. Williams

Melton Williams
Died June 20, 1936
Aged 85 years.

WEST

Joe West
Oct. 10, 1878
June 30, 1911
We will meet again.

LAKEY

C. A. Lakey
Oct. 29, 1909
June 15, 1931
He lived as he died
a christian.

DAVIS

Jennie
Wife of
J. C. Davis
June 17, 1899
Mar. 9, 1931

Bula Elizabeth Tallent
Feb. 26, 1909
Dec. 15, 1909
Gone to a better land.

CRISP

William P. Crisp
June 7, 1842
Nov. 27, 1918
At Rest.

WHITESIDE

Rev. J. H. Whiteside
Mar. 19, 1863
July 3, 1902
Gone to a brither home where
grief cannot come.

CITICO BAPTIST CHURCH CEMETERY

TIPTON

Rev. B. C. Tipton
Feb. 6, 1858
Jan. 29, 1919
Our brothers blest, who
is at rest with
Christ forever more.

Butler Tipton

C. C. Payne
Feb. 18, 1905
Murdered July 3, 1920
Gone but not forgotten.

SHIRK

Mary
Wife of
James W. Shirk
Died Feb. 2, 1917
Aged 76 years
In after time
we'll meet her.

MARKIN AND MARKINS

Asleep in Jesus
Tina Markin
July 26, 1873
Sept. 5, 1914
Here is one who is sleeping
in faith and love. With
hope that is treasured in
Heaven above.

Martha L. M.
Daughter of
G. W. & Tina Markin
April 4, 1903
Sept. 29, 1908
Gone but not forgotten.

Infant
Son of
G. W. & Tina Markin
Born & died Dec. 17, 1901
At Rest.

Chester Markins
Grandson of
James W. Shirk
Gone but not forgotten.

POWELL

Amanda McGaha
Wife of
Clay Powell
Oct. 29, 1873
Sept. 12, 1920

HERRON

William Herron
Jan. 23, 1911
Mar. 1, 1927
A precious one is
gone from us.

Infant
Son of
John & Mary Herron
Born & died
July 14, 1907
Asleep in Jesus.

Mary J. Herron
Sept. 8, 1873
July 5, 1937
A dear one has gone
before but we hope to
meet again.

MARTIN

Infant
of
Mr. & Mrs. W. R. Martin

Infant
of M
Mr. & Mrs. W. R. Martin

M. B.
Wife of
W. D. Martin

CITICO BAPTIST CHURCH CEMETERY

W. D. Martin
Dec. 11, 1838
Mar. 7, 1924

NICHOLS

Hazel
Daughter of
Wess & Illie Nichols
Oct. 15, 1923
Apr. 11, 1924
Gone but not forgotten.

MCKELVY

John McKelvy
Apr. 22, 1882
Aug. 18, 1883

Huston McKelvy
Feb. 15, 1834
Mar. 13, 1916
Happy is he whose
hope is in the Lord.

Sally
Wife of
Huston McKelvy
Nov. 27, 1834
Died (No date given)
Sweetly resting
resting in Heaven.

William J. McKelvy
Aug. 12, 1874
June 7, 1897
May the Resurrection
find thee on the bosom
of thy God.

CATHEY

J. A. Cathey
July 17, 1841
Jan. 19, 1899

Ollie Andrew
Son of
Mr. & Mrs. J. M. Cathey
Nov. 12, 1903
Dec. 15, 1903
Gone but not forgotten.

BRUSTER

Alice
Wife of
W. J. Bruster
Aug. 14, 1889
Apr. 7, 1909

GILES

Malicy J. Giles
May 29, 1872
Feb. 28, 1924
In Heaven we trust
God be with you till
we meet again.

SMITH

Alice Haseline Smith
Died April 3, 1936
Aged 22 yrs. 5 mos. 14 days.

ORR

W. A.
Son of
G. A. & C. O. Orr
Born & died
Sept. 30, 1916
Safe in the arms of Jesus.

SHULER

Asleep in Jesus
Roy
Son of
G. E. & M. P. Shuler
Sept. 16, 1911
Oct. 26, 1918

Georgia
Daughter of
G. E. & M. P. Shuler
Nov. 2, 1913
Oct. 25, 1918

AMMONS

Jane Ammons

George Ammons

CITICO BAPTIST CHURCH CEMETERY

LEGUIRE

Mrs. Wm. Leguire

MYERS

Bertha Myers

GOFORTH

Our mother
Louisa Goforth
Oct. 20, 1851
June 19, 1917
At Rest.

James Goforth

MASON

Lillie
Wife of
John Mason
Feb. 7, 1867
Aug. 5, 1905
A tender mother
and a faithful friend.

BRITTON

Charlies C.
Son of
G. W. & Belle Britton
Aug. 23, 1889
Feb. 24, 1890
Gone but not forgotten.

CUNNINGHAM

Rev. D. B. Cunningham
Sept. 1, 1826
Sept. 23, 1898

Mary Cunningham
Apr. 1, 1831
Apr. 23, 1901
This monument
erected by
Kagley's Chapel
Four mile
Citico and
Mt. Zion Churches

MILLSAPS

Infant
of
J. B. & M. Millsaps
Sept. 17, 1908

Father
Alfred Millsaps
June 9, 1835
Dec. 28, 1917
May he find Joy in
life everlasting.

J.B. Millsaps
Oct. 19, 1885
Nov. 28, 1917
Gone but not forgotten.
In Heaven we trust.
God be with you till
we meet again.

Millsaps
Riley Millsaps
1847-1929

His Wife
M. A. Millsaps
1847 -- ----
The rose may fade, the lily
die but the flowers
immortal bloom on high

Andrew
Son of
Olliver & Martha E. Millsaps
Feb. 14, 1890
Oct. 26, 1916
From dust thou art and
into dust shall thou
return. Gen. 111. 19

Mary A.
Wife of
J. B. Millsaps
and daughter of
A. D. Kirkland
Apr. 8, 1884
Sept. 18, 1908

CITICO BAPTIST CHURCH CEMETERY

Sarah
Wife of
Jessee Millsaps
Born April 30, 1866
Died   19(Living)
At Rest.

Carter Millsaps

Sarah C. F.
Second Wife of
Jessee Millsaps
Born Apr. 30, 1866
Died   19(Living)
J
Jessee Millsaps
Born May 8, 1835
Died Sept. 20, 1912

Loucinda
First Wife of
Jessee Millsaps
Born May 9, 1833
Died Sept. 21, 1899
At Rest.

(Note: Sarah Millsaps has
married again. LMcC.)

Loucinda Millsaps
Wife of
Jesse Millsaps
May 9, 1833
Sept. 21, 1889
Mother has gone to
Glory.

Sally Millsaps

Carl Henry
Son of
C. L. & C. Millsaps
Nov. 18, 1912
Jan. 8, 1913

Rose Dorothy
Dau. of
C. L. & Callie Millsaps
Feb. 9, 1911
Dec. 6, 1911

Anna Hazel
Daughter of
C. L. & Calla Millsaps
Jan. 28, 1916
Apr. 9, 1916
Darling we miss Thee.

Jose Millsaps
Oct. 28, 1844
Oct. 29, 1884
Not lost blest thought
but gone before where
we shall meet to
part no more.

Mary
Wife of
Jason Millsaps
Feb. 25, 1841
Apr. 3, 1909
Not lost blest thought
but gone before where
we shall meet to part no more.

Tennie
Daughter of
Andy Millsaps
Feb. 14, 1897
Oct. 28, 1912
Thy memory shall ever
be a guiding star to Heaven.

Sarah L. Millsaps
Jan. 13, 1860
Mar. 1, 1911
Thy memory shall ever
be a guiding star to Heaven.

Andy Millsaps
May 24, 1841
Feb. 9, 1925
Asleep in Jesus
blessed sleep.

I Millsaps
Son of
Andy Millsaps
Jan. 28, 1882
Jan. 16, 1893
A precious one is gone
A voice we loved is stilled.
A place is vacant in our
home that can never be filled.

James Millsaps
Dec. 19, 1837
Feb. 29, 1884
Thy memory shall ever
be a guiding star to
Heaven.

Joe Millsaps.

M. I. Millsaps
Daughter of
Andy Millsaps
May 13, 1873
Dec. 14, 1873

Eliz. E. Millsaps
Wife of
Andy Millsaps
Mar. 1, 1850
Oct. 22, 1873
Oh how we miss Thee.

Gone Home
Bertha E.
Daughter of
C. L. & C. M. Millsaps
May 25, 1901
Apr. 26, 1914
Prepare to meet me
in Heaven.

Mary F. Millsaps
Nov. 10, 1879
Oct. 4, 1889
Our Darling.

Florida J.
Daughter of
J. M. & Mollie Millsaps
Apr. 1, 1899
July 16, 1909
We will meet again.

Our darlings
Ray and
Fay
Son and daughter of
Avery & Ovie Millsaps
July 17, 1927
July 17, 1927
Sleep on sweet babes
and take thy rest. God
called thee home He
thought it best.

Baby
Millsaps
Died Oct. 2, 1937

Polly Millsaps

Clint Millsaps

Julia Millsaps

HUSTON

Mary Huston

(Note: There are two markers
at graves one with letters L. M.
and other S. C. F. M. They are
next to the grave of Loucinda
Millsaps. They may be children
of Jessee Millsaps and footstones
of his two wives graves may have
been as markers. LMcC.)

MONROE COUNTY

TOMBSTONE INSCRIPTIONS

CLEMMER CEMETERY

Copied by: Lawrence McConkey, Englewood, Tennessee
Date:

The Clemmer Cemetery was established on the farm of John Clemmer as
a cemetery for relatives. It was later changed to a neighborhood
cemetery. There are 50 or more unmarked graves. Lorenzo Davis, who
died Nov. 20, 1827, was the first one buried here. The location
is 10 miles North of Madisonville. The nearest route from Madisonville is via Oak Grove Baptist Church, then to Lakeside, there
cross the Vonore - Sweetwater road and go to the farm of Hugh Clemmer.

DAVIS

Lorenzo Davis
Born May 20, 1827
Died Nov. 20, 1827

Wm. E. Davis
Died Oct. 12, 1834

Jacob N. Davis
Died Aug. 24, 1838
Aged 8 Mos. & 1 dy.

Davis
N. J. Davis
Born May 13, 1843
Died May 3, 1907
Blessed are the dead
which died in the Lord.

W. E. Davis
May 16, 1885
May 11, 1903

Susan Davis
Born Oct. 28, 1805
Died Mar. 28, 1889

William Davis
Born Dec. 3, 1802
Died May 18, 1889

Laura Elsie Davis
July 29, 1872
Sept. 11, 1880

Luther Ernest Davis
Dec. 3, 1875
Apr. 9, 1887

Mary Josephine Davis
July 1, 1877
July 20, 1897

Mary M. Davis
Died Mar. 25, 1848
Aged 1 Mo. & 3 dys.

Joseph C. Davis
Born Sept. 12, 1839
Died July 8, 1858

In memory of
My son
O. R. Davis
Died Oct. 22, 1861

Ethel Davis
Apr. 12, 1883
June 4, 1888

CLEMMER

Finis H.
Son of
H. H. & M. M. Clemmer
Feb. 6, 1894
Nov. 28, 1911

Clinton M. Clemmer
Son of
H. H. & M. M. Clemmer
Aug. 20, 1891
Nov. 6, 1910
Gone but not forgotten.

CLEMMER CEMETERY

Floid M. Clemmer
Son of
H. H. & M. M. Clemmer
Dec. 25, 1886
Dec. 27, 1887

John F. Clemmer
Apr. 28, 1852
Nov. 22, 1918
Gone but not forgotten.

John Clemmer
Born Dec. 27, 1778
Died June 24, 1837

In memory of
Our mother
Hannah Clemmer
Who died Dec. 10, 1866
Aged about 79 years.

Julia A.
Daughter of
Wm. & M. A. Clemmer
Born Nov. 6, 1858
Died May 27, 1859

James E.
Son of
G. S. & S. J. Clemmer
Died June 28, 1855
Aged 1 yr. & 14 d's.

SORTON

Sam Sorton
May 24, 1894
Aug. 26, 1918

BLANKENSHIP

Margaret
Dau. of
I. E. & M. E. Blankenship
Sept. 22, 1871
Aug. 20, 1889

Bertha A.
Daughter of
I. E. & M. E. Blankenship
Feb. 11, 1886
Sept. 6, 1886

Nancy E.
Daughter of
I. E. & M. E. Blankenship
Mar. 8, 1884
Mar. 1, 1885

I. E. Blankenship
Dec. 11, 1847
Feb. 6, 1887

Mary E. Clemmer
Wife of
I. E. Blankenship
July 17, 1844-Dec. 25, 1887

FLETCHER

Allie Vincent
Wife of
J. C. Fletcher
Nov. 19, 1875
Sept. 28, 1922

CANSLER

Mrs. Mary Cansler
Died Jan. 24, 1936
Aged 66 years.

CLOWERS

James Clowers
Aug. 10, 1828
Apr. 6, 1919

Martha Clowers
May 10, 1823
Dec. 5, 1920

FRANK

Estie Frank
Wife of
William Frank
Born June 7, 1885
Died June 26, 1917

PEARCE

Mother
Mary J. Pearce
Sept. 3, 1839
Jan. 27, 1897
Gone to rest.

MONROE COUNTY

TOMBSTONE INSCRIPTIONS

CLICK CEMETERY

Copied by: Lawrence McConkey, Englewood, Tennessee
Date:

Archibald McLemore entered and acquired 640 acres of land where
the Click Cemetery is located. It is believed that the cemetery
was established when he owned the farm and that he and his wife
are buried here. The cemetery is called the Click Cemetery for
the Click family, who later owned the farm, deeded the plot for
a burial ground.

The farm, now owned by L. B. Williams, is 10 miles East of
Madisonville, on the Povo Road.

There are 29 inscriptions and approximately 40 unmarked graves.

BARNETT

J. M. Barnett
May 16, 1846
May 31, 1889

CLICK

W. M. Click
Jan. 7, 1806
Oct. 20, 1881
After all his suffering
he's gone to rest.

Catherine Click
Oct. 17, 1818
Oct. 28, 1886
In love she lived
in peace she died.
Her life was craved
but God denied.

Martha E. Click
Jan. 8, 1879
Aug. 16, 1893
She is waiting at the gate.

Nancy C. Click
Dec. 14, 1874
Oct. 19, 1883

BRYSON

William J. Bryson
Jan. 27, 1874
Aug. 10, 1878
Age 4 yrs. 6 mos. 13 days.

Our baby
A. L. & M. L. Bryson

Our Baby
A. L. & M. L. Bryson

WARD

Sam Ward
Dec. Nov. 10, 1873
Age 4 years.
A precious one from us is
gone, from care and pain free.
O God thou gave him unto us.
We give him back to Thee.

WILLIAMS

Bryson Williams
Died Oct. 11, 1932
Age 77 years.

CLICK CEMETERY

HARTSELL

Amanda Hartsell
Died Mar. 19, 1893
Aged about 83 years,
Dear is the spot
where christians sleep,
and sweet the stranes
that angels pour.

C. R. Hartsell
I will lift up mine
eyes to the hills from
whence cometh my help.

STRICKLAN

James E. Stricklan
Born Sept. 28, 1827
Killed Aug. 1, 1864

Amanda Stricklan
Mar. 17, 1837
June 24, 1903

N. A. Stricklan
Jan. 14, 1862
Nov. 15, 1902
This life here was
insane and numb
but Heaven gave a
new life and tongue.

G. W. Stricklan
Nov. 13, 1858
Sept. 27, 1916
Faithful until death
he now wears a
Crown of life.

HAWKINS

John H. Hawkins
Feb. 7, 1832
Sept. 12, 1879

---------- Hawkins

(Note: Must be the wife of
John Hawkins. LMcC.)

MURR

Margaret E.
Daughter of
Andy H. & Martha Murr
Mar. 10, 1884
June 18, 1900
Not lost blest thought
but gone before where
we shall meet to part no more.

Alfred
Son of
Andy & Martha Murr
Aug. 10, 1873
Nov. 15, 1873
God carries the little
lambs in h's bosom.

Martha Murr
Born -- ----
Died -- ----

A. H. Murr
Co. H.
3 Tenn.
Mt'd. Inf.

MULLINS

Charlie Mullins
Nov. 25, 1874
July 2, 1876

MOSER

Carleton Moser
Dec. 24, 1878
Oct. 6, 1884
We will meet thee,
never to part again.

Siles Moser
Nov. 11, 1880
May 12, 1888
We will meet thee
never to part again.

CLICK CEMETERY

DENTON

Dapcus Denton
May 17, 1817
Mar. 13, 1882
Resting in the hope of
a glorious Resurrection.

Alpherd Denton
Oct. 15, 1810
Sept. 13, 1865

CROWDER

Mrs. John Crowder

John Crowder

MOSES

Joseph Moses

MONROE COUNTY

TOMBSTONE INSCRIPTIONS

COCHRAN CEMETERY

Copied by: Lawrence McConkey, Englewood, Tennessee
Date: Feb. 19, 1940

The Cochran Cemetery is located about 1 mile West of the L. &
N. Railroad Station of Kincaid and 6 miles North of Madisonville. To reach it go via Lakeside road to Oak Grove Baptist
Church & Oak Grove School then turn right on to road leading
to Kincaid to the farm of Will Mincey, where the cemetery is
located. It is said that John B. Lillard owned the farm when
the cemetery was established and that his son, William L., who
died Oct. 27, 1861, was the first one buried here. Later the
Cochran family owned the cemetery and farm and it is known as
Cochran (locally pronounced "Cohorn") Cemetery. Other people
are buried here besides the Lillard and Cochran families.
John B. Lillard was related to the Lillards of Meigs County,
many of whom are buried at Upper Goodfield Baptist Cemetery, and
to the Lillards of Polk County who are buried in Benton and
Four Mile Cemeteries. This is a pioneer family. John & Jane
Cochran of Big Springs in Blount County moved to Monroe County
in 1837. Their son, R. L., married Ann Lowry or Lowery,
daughter of William M. and Elizabeth Lowery or Lowry, who also
came from Blount County in 1845. One of this family of
Lowery's was president of Hiwassee College for many years.
There are 27 inscriptions in the cemetery which is fenced
and covers approximately 1 acre. The cemetery is still used
occassionally.

Graves without inscriptions are as follows: 25 field stones,
approximately 3 with inscriptions destroyed, 72 unmarked graves.

PORTER

Elizabeth A.
Wife of
W. W. Porter
Born Jan. 3, 1831
Departed this life
July 12, 1884

W. W. Porter
Born Sept. 23, 1826
Died May 21, 1885
Be thou faithful until
death and I will give
thee a home in Paradise.

HOLLOWAY

Paul Holloway

M. E. Holloway
Jan. 13, 1900
Sept. 20, 1906

J. W. Holloway
Feb. 5, 1902
April 31, 1902

L. U. Holloway
July 14, 1895
Nov. 28, 1895

COCHRAN CEMETERY

Samuel A.
Son of
J. H. & M. Holloway
Feb. 21, 1875
Mar. 14, 1877
Aged 2 yrs. 23 days.

Susan Farmer
Wife of
Jerry Holloway
Aug. 30, 1804
May 30, 1889
The Lord is my Shepherd
I shall not want.

J. H. Holloway
Jan. 13, 1834
Aug. 24, 1911

M. J. Holloway
Apr. 4, 1845
Apr. 25, 1920
Father and Mother
Gone but not forgotten.

Holloway
R. E. L. Holloway
July 16, 1864
July 8, 1918
Gone to rest.

Glenn
Son of
Mr. & Mrs. J. W. Holloway
July 12, 1918
Feb. 4, 1919

(Note: There are several unmarked graves and at least
some of them are believed to
be graves of members of
Holloway family. LMcC.)

LILLARD

Martha E.
Daughter of
J. B. & N. A. Lillard
April 6, 1881
April 25, 1881

Penelope S.
Daughter of
J. B. & N. A. Lillard
April 6, 1881
July 21, 1881

Nancy A.
Wife of
John B. Lillard
Sept. 15, 1843
April 16, 1881

William L.
Son of
J. B. & N. A. Lillard
April 21, 1860
Oct. 27, 1861

Douglass
Son of
J. B. & N. A. Lillard
Born Mar. 14, 1867
3 days old.

(Note: There are 3 or 4
graves without inscriptions
that seem to be graves of
above family, but they could
be of some other family. LMcC.)

LOGAN

Elizabeth Logan
Born July 4, 1776
Died Dec. 4, 1863

(Note: Verse on above marker
is unreadable. There are
graves without inscriptions on
both sides of above marker.
LMcC.)

COCHRAN, LOWERY OR LOWRY & SHEETS

Jane Cochran
July 19, 1804
May 15, 1890

In memory of
John Cochran
June 25, 1795
July 7, 1876
Aged 81 yrs. & 12 days.

COCHRAN CEMETERY

Ann Lowry
Wife of
R. L. Cochran
Feb. 12, 1825
Feb. 20, 1907

Mary J. Sheets
Oct. 18, 1846
July 21, 1918
Gone but not forgotten.

Henry Sheets
Nov. 24, 1831
Mar. 15, 1918
Gone but not forgotten.

Martha E. Cochran
Dec. 28, 1847
Oct. 22, 1886
Asleep in Jesus.

R. L. Cochran
April 26, 1824
Dec. 21, 1909
Aged 85 years, 7 months
& 25 days.

William M. Lowery
Oct. 16, 1798
Nov. 1, 1880
Aged 82 yrs. & 15 days.

Elizabeth
Wife of
William M. Lowery

(Note: Above marker is very
old and is in a house. The
dates are all gone but is is
known that she died before
her husband.

Note: There are also some
graves without inscriptions
that seem to belong to the
Cochran-Lowery and Sheets
families but may not . LMcC.

MONROE COUNTY

TOMBSTONE INSCRIPTIONS

COOKE-KEFAUVER FAMILY CEMETERY

Copied by: Lawrence McConkey, Englewood, Tennessee
Date: Jan. 25, 1939

The Cooke-Kefavuer Family Cemetery is on the Kefauver Dairy
Farm on the edge of Madisonville. There are 9 inscriptions
and no numarked graves.

COOKE

In memory of
Susan Eliza
6th Daughter of
Dr. R. F. & C. Cooke
Died June 8, 1853
Aged 3 years 10 months & 1 day.

In memory of
William Kimbrough
1st Son of
Dr. R. F. & C. Cooke
Died June 11, 1853
Aged 9 years 3 months & 17 days.

In memory of
Marthy Cantrell
4th Daughter of
Dr. R. F. & Charlotte Cooke
Died April 8, 1854
Aged 11 years 11 months & 27 days.

CANNON

Sallie Cannon
Born Mar. 24, 1866
Died Oct. 2, 1902

GAINES

Robert Cooke
Son of
R. J. & Sarah Gaines
Born May 31, 1857
Died Nov. 5, 1857

KEFAUVER

Rev. J. P. Kefauver
Dec. 19, 1819
June 6, 1893
Saved by Grace.

Nancy Reeves Cooke
Daughter of
Dr. Robert Fielding and
Charlote K. Cooke
Wife of
Rev. J. P. Kefauver
Dec. 30, 1839
Feb. 16, 1926

Robert Fielding
Son of
R. C. & P. E. Kefauver
Apr. 19, 1901
Aug. 9, 1914
A fairer bud of
promise never bloomed.

Elizabeth
Daughter of
R. C. & D. F. Kefauver
Dec. 1, 1897
Oct. 8, 1901

COOKE-KEFAUVER FAMILY SKETCH

The Rev. J. P. Kefauver was born December 19, 1819, near Roanoke, Va. He was an only son of Jacob and Nancy (Vineyard) Kefauver. His father was from Maryland and was of German extraction. His mother was from Washington, D. C. and her ancestors were French. The Rev. Mr. Kefauver was a classical scholar, having had good educational advantages from his youth, first in the nearby district schools, and later at what is now Hollins Institute, where he had a five year course. In early manhood he was married to Sarah Sively, of Virginia, who brightened his life for one year and died.

Attthe age of 20 he was converted and received what he felt to be a divine call to the ministry. He was ordained to this work December 11, 1857 by the Authority of the Blue Ridge Church (Baptist) near Roanoke, Va., of which he was a member — the credentials given him by the ordaining council bearing the signatures of "Thomas C. Goggin, David Staley, Geo. W. Leftwich, Pleasant Brown. The Rev. Mr. Kefavuer came to East Tennessee in the Fall of 1861.

On December 12, 1861 he was married to Nannie R. Cooke, daughter of Dr. Robert F. & Charlotte Cooke, of Madisonville. To this union were born two sons, Robert Cooke and Paul, and two daughters Charlotte & Venia.

The Rev. Mr. Kefauver had the pastoral oversight of the First church of Chattanooga for seven years. During and following the Civil War, protecting the sheep as best he could from the dogs of war. At the close of the war, in company with Dr. J. R. Graves, he attended the General Convention of Baptists meeting in Chicago, Ill, and was invited to make a statement before that body of the condition of Baptist affairs in Tennessee and particularly in Chattanooga. Then the convention volted with one accord to furnish money with which to reseat and repair the Chattanooga Church. He served as its pastor until the death of his father-in-law, Dr. Cooke. Then it was necessary for him to take charge of a large farm and business which had been willed to his wife by Dr. Cooke.

The Rev. Mr. Kefauver was later pastor at different times, of Sweetwater, Old Sweetwater, Prospect Madisonville and other Baptist Churches. When he took charge of the Madisonville church it was considerably in debt. Instead of preaching to the church for nothing till it could pay off the debt, he instructed the church to pay on the debt what they owed him as pastor.

Dr. Robert F. Cooke was a Baptist minister, of note. He was a direct descendant of Robert Cooke, a Scotchman, a Saddle and shoemaker by trade, whose wife was Sarah Fielding from Devonshire County, England. This couple came across the waters

2

COOKE-KEFAUVER FAMILY SKETCH

and settled in Maryland, St. Mary's County in the year 1720.
Another Robert Cooke, grandfather of Robert F., was married to
Susannah Watson, in Culpepper Co., Va., on Jan. 6, 1778 and
died at his home in White Co., Tenn., Nov. 12, 1841, in the
90th year of his age.

Estes Kefauver, grandson of the Rev. J. F. Kefauver, is a
prominent attorney of Chattanooga. He served as State Finance
and Taxation Commissioner under Governor Cooper. (Editor's note:
Estes Kefauver was elected a member of Congress in the 3rd
District of Tennessee November 8, 1939, filing out the un-
expired term of the late Sam D. McReynolds.

It is understood that the farm willed to Mrs. Kefauver by her
father, Dr. Cooke, is always to be held by the Kefauver name
as long as there are any male descendants, or unmarried
female members of the family.

MONROE COUNTY

TOMBSTONE INSCRIPTIONS

COPPENGER CEMETERY

Copied by: Lawrence McConkey, Englewood, Tennessee
Date:

The Coppenger Cemetery is about 1 mile East of Tellico Plains,
just across the Tellico River and on the hill near the bridge.
Tellico Plains is 16 miles South of Madisonville. The cemetery
is the oldest one in this section and dates back to the time
when an English Company owned the land known as the Slate and
Iron Company, or even before then when church Johnson owned
the land. There was an Indian Village at the foot of the hill
and the Indians might have established the cemetery. There was
an epedemic of Cholera in the 1830's that killed nearly all the
settlers in this community and they are buried here. When Wm.
Weiss sold the farm to Charles Swainson about 38 years ago, he
reserved in his deed the cemetery which was about 1½ acres.
More has been added and there are now about 2½ acres in the
Graveyard. It is a community cemetery but the majority buried
there are members of the Coppenger family or their relatives.
This is a White people's cemetery. No Negroes ever have lived
in this community. There are graves of two or three Negroes
below the cemetery. They were killed.

The cemetery is still in use. There are 110 inscriptions; 107
graves marked with field stones; 4 tombstones with inscriptions
destroyed and approximately 125 graves without inscriptions,
making a total of some 236 graves having no readable inscription.

BYERS

C. L. Byers
1889 - 1933
At Rest.

--------- Byers
Died --- 8, 1938
Aged

William David Byers
Died March 19, 1939
Aged 7 months.

Haynes
Son of
Lee & Ruthey Byers
July 17, 1898
June 4, 1911
Gone but not forgotten.

(Note: The following graves and
the one before this note (the one
of Haynes Byers) are at another
location in cemetery. LMcC.)

(Note: On South side of above
are graves of Ike Taylor and
his wife Maggie Taylor. LMcC.)

FREEMON

Bell Freemon
May 20, 1897
Apr. 25, 1935
At Rest.

THOMAS

Nancy D.
Daughter of
James & Sarah Thomas
Dec. 9, 1900
Aug. 9, 1901
Gone but not forgotten.

COFFENGER CEMETERY

MURR

Lillie Murr
Died July 10, 1924
Aged 51 years

Joe Murr
Sept. 20, 1860
July   4, 1919
Gods finger touched
him and he slept.

1 Infant's grave at
North of above.

CAUGHRON

A. C. Caughron
Dec. 16, 1850
Dec. 8, 1924
Gone to rest.

(Note: 1 grave North of
above said to be that of
Effie Frye, housekeeper
of A. C. Caughron. LMcC.)

CATHEY

Western Woodrow
Son of
W. L. & Ida Cathey
Feb. 20, 1914
Mar. 9, 1914
A link that binds
us to heaven.

Infant
Daughter of
W. L. & Ida Cathey
Jan. 26, 1904
Jan. 26, 1904
This fair sweet flower in
Paradise shall bloom.

WEISS

Ena
Daughter of
Wm. & Mollie Weiss
Jan. 15, 1908
Dec. 4, 1909
Asleep in Jesus.

(Note: Above child is buried
beside Western Woodrow Cathey.
Their mothers are sisters. LMCC.)

Pitty Mamma Pitty
Walter Weiss
Mar. 9, 1899
Aug. 27, 1901

BUTLER

Alice Butler
July 12, 1891
June 14, 1918

Willie
Son of
Wm. & B. T. Butler
June 13, 1909
Dec. 24, 1913
This fair sweet
flower in paradise
shall bloom again.

2 field stones at South of above.

Nelie
Son of
A. D. & N. J. Butler
Born & died
June 21, 1911

1 field stone North of above.

FRYE

Infant
of
G. C. & E. L. Frye
1918- 1919

Infant of
G. C. & E. L. Frye
1923

Infant
of
G. C. & E. L. Frye
1922

Infant
of
G. C. & E. L. Frye
1923

COPPENGER CEMETERY

(Note: Two infants died in
1923. LMcC.)

3 field stones North of
above and 1 field stone
South of Above.

FRY

(Note: The graves with FRYE
markers are in North end of
cemetery. Those with FRY markers are in the South end of
the cemetery. LMcC.)

Ben
Son of
A. P. & M. A. Fry
Oct. 23, 1892
May 13, 1911

A. P. Fry
Aug. 29, 1854
Apr. 30, 1911

(Note: Above marker
broken in two. LMcC.)

JONES

Neppie Bradley Jones
Jan. 18, 1875
May 6, 1933
Asleep in Jesus.

BRADLEY

John A. Bradley
July 16, 1866
June 26, 1913
A truer, nobler
heart never beat within
a human breast.

(Note: The Jones & Bradley
markers are side by side.
LMcC.)

PRESSWOOD

Velma L.
Daughter of
E. F. & G. Presswood
Jan. 31, 1911
Apr. 20, 1911

Jack Bradley Presswood
Aged 12 days.

Joseph Presswood
Died Nov. 10, 1911
aged 75 years.
Gone but not forgotten.

Margaret
Wife of
Joseph Presswood
Born Aug. 20, 1848
Died Jan. 31, 1912
We will meet again.

EVANS

Billy
Son of
Mr. & Mrs. Rollie Evans
Mar. 2, 1924
Dec. 30, 1924
Asleep in Jesus.

(Mason Emblem)
G. W. Evans
Mar. 17, 1872
Nov. 24, 1928
Weep not dear ones for
me for I am waiting in
glory for thee.

RIDEN

Mamie Riden
Mar. 16, 1903
Jan. 9, 1904

George Riden
Dec. 29, 1898
Dec. 13, 1900

4

COPPENGER CEMETERY

SMITH

Lyllian
Daughter of
Mr. & Mrs. T. H. Smith
Sept. 4, 1918
June 23, 1919
From mothers arms
to the arms of Jesus.

SATTERFIELD

Melvina Clifford Satterfield
Feb. 25, 1922
May 4, 1923
Darling we miss you.
We will meet again.

Clarence Odean Satterfield
Oct. 12, 1923
Mar. 12, 1924
No pains, no griefs, no
anxious fear can reach
our loved one sleeping
here.

Harrison Satterfield
Mar. 20, 1861
May 15, 1924
No pains, no griefs, no
anxious fears can
reach our loved on
sleeping here.

Glen
Son of
Mr. & Mrs. McKinley Satterfield
Feb. 20, 1920
Apr. 22, 1922

BLAIR

Charles L.
Son of
Charlie & Lillie Blair
July 9, 1917
Nov. 26, 1917

SYLVESTER

Bertha Sylvester
Was born Oct. 27, 1906
Died Dec. 16, 1906

Roye Sylvester
Oct. 21, 1907
April 13, 1910

2 field stones South of above.

Mrs. Effie Sylvester
June 10, 1886
July 6, 1934

Mrs. Bitha Ann Sylvester
Died Feb. 28, 1937
Aged 86 years.

1 field stone South of Above.

John R.
Son of
E. C. & T. A. Sylvester
June 26, 1892
Nov. 30, 1903
A little time on earth
he spent till God for
him his angel sent.

Vergie Sylvester

Girtie Sylvester

Eloie Sue Sylvester

Myrtle Sylvester

Lucie Sylvester

Hattie Sylvester

Annie Sylvester

(Note: The above 8 names are on
marble markers. They were children of W. T. & --- Sylvester.LMcC.)

COPPENGER CEMETERY

Father
W. T. Sylvester
Feb. 14, 1864
(still living)

Mother
———————— Coppenger
Aug. 23, 1870
Aug. 7, 1923

Allen Sylvester
Died March 13, 1937
Aged 36 years, 3 months
& 28 days.

Infant
Dau. of
 Mr. & Mrs. R. T. Sylvester
Nov. 11, 1918

Infant
of
Effie & Robert Sylvester
—————————————————————
(Note: Broken can't read
LMcC.)
A little time on earth
he spent till God for
him his angel sent.

John Sylvester

Infant
Son of
D. W. & E. Sylvester.

In memory of
Elizabeth Sylvester
Feb. 9, 1829
Jan. 19, 1877
Age 49 years.

JACK

J. E. Jack
Aug. 2, 1910
Aug. 17, 1910
At Rest.

WILSON-WILLSON

Milly Wilson
Wife of

J. M. Wilson
Sept. 25, 1855
July 26, 1934
Gone but not forgotten
At Rest

Jim Willson
Nov. 6, 1862
April 11, 1936
Father
Gone but not forgotten.

(Note: Above two are husband
and wife. I think their name
is spelled Wilson. LMcC.)

HENSLEY

H. M. C.
Son of
R. M. & Jessie Hensley
May 18, 1898
June 22, 1922
At Rest.

(Note: South of above are the
graves of his mother Jessie
Hensley and his father R. M.
(Matt) Hensley, with tombstones.
LMcC.)

GARREN

Margaret Garren
Born   1832
Died April 8, 1906

Eliza
Wife of
J. W. Garren
May 4, 1873
Jan. 8, 1916
At Rest.

EMORY

Bettie Garren
Wife of
T. A. Emory
June 13, 1858
Aug. 4, 1923
Asleep in Jesus.

(

6

COPPENGER CEMETERY

(Note: Above grave is
near grave of Margaret
Garren. LMcC.)

FLOYD

John Floyd
June 4, 1855
June 4, 1917

Sue Floyd
Died March 29, 1939
Aged 75 years, 4 months
& 5 days.

Homer J.
Son of
John & Sue Floyd
Apr. 7, 1892
Apr. 18, 1912
At Rest.

KIRKLAND

Cecil Kirkland
Aug. 22, 1922
July 7, 1923

1 field stone on each
side of above.

Mattie Kirkland
Aug. 9, 1872
July 24, 1913
Her spirit smiles from
that bright shore and
softly whispers weep
no more. A treasure in
Heaven to beckon us all
to a higher life.

(Note: 9 field stones North
& 1 field stone South & other
graves in this section said to
be graves of members of the
Kirkland family. LMcC.)

MORGAN

Louise
Daughter of
Ross & Marthie Morgan
Aug. 16, 1913
July 25, 1914

MOORE

Infant
of
E. D. & M. E. Moore
April 28, 1915

E. D. Moore
June 7, 1875
Nov. 26, 1925

BERRY

Oplina Berry
Feb. 5, 1904
May 5, 1904
Of such is the kingdom
of Heaven.

2 field stones South of
above.

(Note: At head of John R.
Slylvester's grave is the
grave of Melton Berry
Died About 1909
Aged about 75 years. LMcC.)

GARRETT

Mrs. Bessie Garrett
Died Oct. 12, 1921
Aged 24 years, 2 months &
1 day.

1 field stone at infants
grave North of above.

AKINS

Mary Neal
Daughter of

COPPENGER CEMETERY

Mr. & Mrs. Floyd Akins
June 6, 1929
Sept. 29, 1929
Asleep in Jesus.

FRITTS

Addie Belle
Wife of
H. J. Fritts
Nov. 5, 1873
May 28, 1931
Mother
At Rest.

QUEEN

John Queen
Oct. 15, 1879
(dead no date)

His wife
Freda
Oct. 17, 1894
Aug. 4, 1925
At Rest.

MILLER

Ollie
Wife of
C. H. Miller
Feb. 5, 1871
Sept. 6, 1914
Gone but not forgotten.

COPPENGER-COPPINGER OR CAPPENGER

(Note: The name is generally
spelled Coppenger. - only one
marker Cappenger and it possibly
was engraved wrong. LMcC.)

Frank W. Coppenger
Feb. 20, 1925
Sept. 6, 1925

(Note: a large head stone to
above grave with name Coppenger
also with a Masonic emblem.LMcC.)

Edith Lucica
Daughter of
Geo & Mary Cappinger
Aug. 20, 1906
Dec. 13, 1906
From mothers arms to
the arms of Jesus.

(Note: Two graves South that
are graves of children of
John & Pearl Hines. LMcC.)

Father
Higens C. Coppinger
Oct. 4, 1826
July 12, 1904

(Note: At head of above grave
is the grave of Higens C.
Coppinger's brother, William
Coppenger, who was born before
Higens and died about 50 years
ago. LMcC.)

Mother
Mary E. Coppenger
Jan. 7, 1848
Dec. 21, 1932

(Note: Mary E. Coppenger was
the wife of Higens Coppinger.
At the head of her grave and
beside William Coppenger's
grave is the grave of William's
wife, Lizzie, without a
marker. LMcC.)

John Coppenger
Aug. 15, 1835
Aug. 10, 1911

Martha
Wife of
John Coppenger
Jan. 20, 1844
Mar. 30, 1925
Father & Mother

COPPENGER CEMETERY

Sadie
Daughter of
J. H. & Hattie Coppenger
Born & died
Nov. 15, 1906
Gone but not forgotten.

Gladis
Daughter of
J. H. & Hattie Coppenger
July 15, 1908
Aug. 10, 1909
Gone but not forgotten.

Hattie
Wife of
J. H. Coppenger
June 26, 1891
Sept. 21, 1910
In love she lived, In
peace she died; Her life
was craved but God denied.

John Henry Coppinger
Sleep in Jesus loved one
Died Dec. 22, 1932

Claud Lee
Son of
H. S. & F. L. Coppenger
Mar. 2, 1913
Mar. 23, 1913
Budded on earth to
bloom in Heaven.

S. H. Coppenger
Birth
Mar. 29, 1886
Death
Apr. 23, 1914

(Note: The initials are S. H.
on the above inscription but
on the marker of his son
Claude Lee, his initials are
H. S. One has possibly been
interchanged by the tombstone
Company. LMcC.)

Elbert Coppenger
Nov. 14, 1841
Dec. 3, 1914
Gone but not forgotten.

Alice Coppenger
1847 - 1925
Sleeping in the arms of Jesus.

(W.O.W. Memorial)
John Coppenger
Apr. 15, 1857
Feb. 19, 1910

(Note: On the North are the
unmarked graves of John
Coppenger's brothers as follows:
Worth Coppenger, died about 1901
Aged about 20 years and
Elbert Coppenger died about 1901
aged about 45 years. LMcC.)

Thelma Lea Coppenger
Jan. 29, 1899
Nov. 13, 1899

HAWKINS

Infant
Son of
J. M. & Bettie Hawkins
Born & died
April 27, 1903

PRESLEY

Josie
Wife of
Manuel Presley
(Broke)
Died Oct. 13, 1911
Not lost blest thought
but gone before where we
shall meet to part no more.

1 field stone at North and 1
grave covered with concrete
nearby.

Manuel Presley

William
Son of
Manuel & Josie Presley
Born & died
Aug. 28, 1911

LEROY

9

COPPENGER CEMETERY

Infant
of
Mr. & Mrs. Ben Leroy
At Rest.

Father & Mother
Ben Leroy
1890 - 1928
Gone but not forgotten

Ethel Leroy
1889 - (Still Living)

(Note: Ben Leroy was a
world war soldier accord-
ing to statement of Mrs.
Wm. Weiss. LMcC.)

HAWKE

Ralph Hawke
Died Mar. 31, 1931
Aged 9 years

Ida Hawke
Died 1929
Aged about 55 years.

Gean Hawke
Died 1927
Aged about 60 years.

PRESSWOOD

Wm. Presswood

(Note: He died about 1919,
age about 60 years. LMcC.)

Emma
Wife of
Wm. Presswood

(Note: She died about 1924,
age, about 50 yrs. LMcC.)

Herbert Presswood
Died --- -- 1935
Aged 19 years.

MONROE COUNTY

CROFTS FAMILY SKETCH

George Washington Crofts was born in South Carolina. He
married Elizabeth Boswell also of South Carolina. They
later moved to Monroe County, Tennessee and bought a farm
where this cemetery was established. They were the parents
of twelve children to wit: George, who married Susie Stephens;
Ellen, who married Neal Crofts; James, who married Nancy Jane
Watson; Andrew, who married Nancy Jane Atkins; Mary, who
married Burt Mitchell; Betty, who married John Watson; Rufus,
who married Maranda Grigsby; Eddie, who married Margaret Watson;
Bell, who married Low Ervin; Infant that died; Arthur, who
married Rhoda Watson and Margarette, who married Andrew Rogers.

The name formerly was spelled Crofts but now some members of
the family spell it Croft.

MONROE COUNTY

TOMBSTONE INSCRIPTIONS

G. W. CROFTS FAMILY CEMETERY

Copied by: Lawrence McConkey, Englewood, Tennessee
Date: Oct. 28, 1938

The G. W. Crofts Family Cemetery was established on the farm of
George Washington Crofts about 7 miles South of Madisonville.
The first burial was that of Eddie, son of George Washington
and Elizabeth Crofts. To reach the graveyard take the Tellico
Plains route to Hoe there turn to the right on to the "Old
Federal" road. The cemetery is on the farm of Mrs. Ethel Croft
Harris. There are 14 inscriptions and 8 unmarked graves.

CROFTS OR CROFT

G. W. Crofts
Mar. 20, 1832
Oct. 6, 1915

Elizabeth Crofts
Sept. 11, 1835
Apr. 26, 1917

Susan Stpehens
Wife of
George Crofts
Died Mar. 12, 1936
Aged 72 years.

Rhoda Crofts

Eddie Crofts

Infant
of
Amos & Lizzie Croft

Infant
of
Amos & Lizzie Croft

Oscar L. Croft
Jan. 23, 1896
Dec. 21, 1929
Hdqrs. Co. 76 F. A.

Aaron Croft
May 28, 1905
May 6, 1926

TORBETT

Infant
of
Frank & Dorthy Torbett
1934

ERVIN

O. R. Ervin
Dec. 12, 1912
Dec. 22, 1912

HUSKEY

Infant
of
Sam & Mary Huskey

Infant
of
Sam & Mary Huskey

Huff

Infant
Huff
1918

(Note: The last three listed
were not related to the Crofts
family. LMcC.)

MONROE COUNTY

TOMBSTONE INSCRIPTIONS

CURTIS CEMETERY

Copied by: Lawrence McConkey, Englewood, Tennessee
Date: Nov. --, 1938

This cemetery was established in 1865 when two brothers, Burt and Riley Curtis, were killed. The land was owned by the Curtis family and has been used as a neighborhood burial ground. Later the farm was owned by Peter Moser who was a very prominent Monroe Countian. The plot was deeded for a cemetery by the Moser family and some know it was the Moser Cemetery.

There are 15 inscriptions and possibly 40 unmarked graves. The cemetery is on the farm of Stokley Brothers 15 miles Northeast of Madisonville. To reach it from Madisonville to to Vonore, there take the Ballplay Road.

CURTIS

Burt Curtis
Killed 1865

Riley Curtis
Killed 1865

HAWKINS

Rachel Hawkins
Wife of
Gregg Hawkins
Died 1888
Aged about 70 years.

Gregg Hawkins
Died 1867
Aged about 49 years.

Bettie Jane
Daughter of
Gregg & Rachel Hawkins
Died 1903
Aged about 45 years.

FIELDS

Prudie
Wife of
Cyrus Fields
June 20, 1883
May 5, 1911
Gone but not forgotten.

MOSER

Katie
Daughter of
P. & V. M. Moser
Born Dec. 21, 1874
Died Oct. -- 1884
Our loved one.

Infant
Daughter of
P. & V. M. Moser
Born & died
 1886
Budded on earth to bloom in
Heaven.

Peter Moser
Born Oct. 13, 1839
Died Feb. 14, 1909
We will meet again

Venie M. Hawkins
Wife of
Peter Moser
Born June 17, 1854
Died Nov. 2, 1892
A tender mother and a
faithful frined.

GRAY

John Gray   Elizabeth Gray
  Mary Gray   Sarah Gray   Henry Gray

MONROE COUNTY

TOMBSTONE INSCRIPTIONS
DALE CEMETERY

CROWDER

Daniel B.
Son of
A. O. & N. C. Crowder
Sept. 10, 1868
Nov. 15, 1868
"Gone but not forgotten."

(Note: Another child of above
parents is buried on north
side of above but only the
initial F. of the second name
can be read on the broken marker.

Temsy
Daughter of
A. O. & N. C. Crowder
Aug. 1, 1881
Aug. 9, 1881
"Gone but not forgotten."

Atles O. Crowder
March 13, 1820
Sept. 5, 1895
"He followed virtue as his
truest guide, Lived as a
Christian, as a Christain
he died."

(Note: It is said that his
wife, N. C. Crowder is also
buried here--but it is
doubtful if at his side.)

NICHOLS

J. D. Nichols
Jan. 29, 1858
Jan. 9, 1905
"Death is the crown of life."

MORTON

Nancy Morton
deceased Dec. the 20, 1863.

(Note: No age given--but is a
long grave.)

MONROE COUNTY

DRUID HILL BAPTIST CHURCH CEMETERY

Copied by Lawrence McConkey, Englewood, Tennessee.
Date:

The Druid Hill Baptist Church and Cemetery are located
three miles East of Tellico Plains along the road leading
to the Big Creek Community.

The Druid Hill Baptist Church was constituted in 1934 with
the Rev. Horace Atkins as first pastor. In order to secure
the plot wanted, land for the church and cemetery was
bought from two different people. Most of the church
grounds was purchased from Fred C. Payne and the greater
part of the cemetery was bought from Ben Johnson.

The property comprised approximately $1\frac{1}{2}$ acres. There are
only three graves in the cemetery as yet. The first person
buried in Druid Hill Baptist Church Cemetery was January
7, 1934.

MONROE COUNTY

TOMBSTONE INSCRIPTIONS
DRUID HILL BAPTIST CHURCH CEMETERY

MASSINGALE

John Oscar Masingale
Apr. 9, 1896
May 14, 1937
"It is the sepulchre of
the man of God."

AKINS

Urma Akins
Nov. 26, 1907
Jan. 7, 1934
"At Rest."

BURCHFIELD

Cecil M. Akins
Wife of
V. W. Burchfield
Apr. 23, 1911
Jan. 22 1937
"Darling we miss thee."

TOMBSTONE INSCRIPTIONS

DUGGAN-HAMBY CEMETERY

Copied by: Lawrence McConkey, Englewood, Tennessee
Date: Jan. 6, 1939

This is the burial ground of two families. The Wm. Duggan
family and J. C. Hamby family. Wm. Duggan was a descendant
of Hugh and Matilda Duggan who migrated from Sevier Co., when
this part of the State was being settled. The Hamby family
migrated from North Carolina soon after settlement began in
Monroe County.

This cemetery is about 20 miles South of Madisonville, and
can best be reached from Madisonville by going to Mt. Vernon
then to Jalapa (or Brown Hill School), then to Ivy. The
cemetery is on the farm of Wm. Hamby.

There are 16 inscriptions and 11 unmarked graves.

HAMBY   S. L. Duggan
                                  Wife of
J. C. Hamby   Sherman Frye
Born 1823
Died Aug. 4, 1901   Infant
Gone but not forgotten.   of
                                  Sherman & S. L. Frye
Lilly L. Hamby
Sept. 21, 1896   DUGGAN
Dec. 7, 1898
Gone but not forgotten.   Wm. Duggan

Davie J. Hamby   Sarah Duggan
June 12, 1889
Sept. 20, 1904   J. C. Duggan
Gone but not forgotten.
                                  Infant
M. A. Hamby   of
Feb. 4, 1862   Mr. & Mrs. J. C. Duggan
June 13, 1929
Gone but not forgotten.   Infant
                                  of
Lizzie Hamby   Mr. & Mrs. J. C. Duggan
Oct. -- 1863
Sept. 28, 1929   Infant
                                  of
FRYE   Mr. & Mrs. J. C. Duggan.

Sherman Frye   Infant of
                                  Mr. & Mrs. Wm. Duggan

                                  Margaret --------

                                  (Note: Believe the above is also
                                  a member of the Duggan family. LMcC.)

TOMBSTONE INSCRIPTIONS

EDINGTON OR SAMUEL EDINGTON FAMILY CEMETERY

Copied by: Lawrence McConkey, Englewood, Tennessee
Date: Feb. 7, 1940

This cemetery was established on the farm of Samuel Edington.
It was a neighborhood cemetery as no one buried there, with the
exception of two Axley children and members of the Edington
family, has a tombstone. It was known as Edington family
cemetery, but the Henleys owned the farm later, the cemetery is
mostly known now as Henly Family Cemetery. It is located 5
miled North of Madisonville on the Morganton to Acorn Gap road
on farm of A. C. Irvin. It is about 1 mile West from road and
the Irvin brick home and on a hill. It comprises ½ acre in
the woods. There are 10 inscriptions; 15 graves marked with
field stones and 35 unmarked graves. The cemetery has been
discontinued. It is not known just when it was established but
the oldest date is that of Abijah Fowler who was a Confederate
Soldier and was killed or shot from ambush May 27, 1864. He was
a son-in-law of Samuel Edington. Fowler soldier information
and much of the family history was secured from Abijah Fowler's
daughter, Sarah Frances Fowler Lowry, who is over 80 years of
age.

EDINGTON, FOWLER & HENLEY

My Father
Samuel Edington
Sept. 6, 1793
June 13, 1871

My Mother
Fanny Edington
Feb. 1804
Jan. 13, 1879

Our brother
Samuel A. Fowler
Died Oct. 19, 1878
Aged 19 years, 7 months
& 9 days.
Blessed is he who dies
in the arms of Jesus.

Our Father
Abijah Fowler
Died May 27, 1864
Aged 27 years, 1 month
and 1 day.
Blessed is he who
dies in the arms of Jesus.

(Note: Abijah Fowler was killed
in the Mountains of Monroe near
the North Carolina line. He
and some other Confederate soldiers were shot at by a posse
from the hills. He was killed.
He was on his way home for a
visit. Believed one who killed
him was mistaken as to Fowler's
idenity. LMcC.)

Allen M. Henley
Apr. 22, 1841
Oct. 19, 1877

Bettie
Daughter of
A. M. & M. A. Hensley
Feb. 18, 1875
July 9, 1875

Mary A. Fowler
Wife of
A. M. Henley
Dec. 3, 1840
Jan. 10, 1884

EDINGTON & EDINGTON FAMILY CEMETERY

Georgie
Daughter of
J. R. & E. J. Henley
April 17, 1864
June 25, 1865

(Note: The above
parents later named
another daughter
the same name --
Georgia -- Rather un-
usual. LMcC.)

AXLEY

Infant
Daughter of
S. D. & E. J. Axley
Died Oct. 14, 1864

Henry Mayer
Son of
S. D. & E. J. Axley
Died Aug. 14, 1867
Aged 8 months and
8 days.

EDINGTON FAMILY SKETCH

Samuel Edington married Fannie Browder. He was from Greene Co.,
Tennessee and his wife from Lenore City, Tennessee or that
section. He either entered or purchased early a tract of land
at or by where cemetery is - he later purchased land until he
owned possibly twelve hundred acres in this section. He was
very likely a brother of Jessee Edington of McMinn County.

Samuel and Fannie Edington were the parents of two daughters;
Mary Ann and Eliza Jane.

Mary Ann married Abijah Fowler. They were the parents of:
Mary Jane, Sarah Frances and Samuel A. After Abijah was killed
Mary Ann, his widow, married Allen M. Henley. They were the
parents of: Thomas Owen, Arthur R., Inez, Josie, Maggie and
Bettie. Last three, triplets, were born Feb. 18, 1875.

Eliza Jane Edington married James R. Henley. He was a brother
of Allen M. He was born April 30, 1836, died March 30, 1892.
She was born Nov. 21, 1843 and died May 13, 1899. Both are
buried at New Hope Cumberland Presbyterian Church Cemetery.
They were the parents of: Mary, Samuel, Charles, Nell, Georgia,
Frank, Maude, Joseph, John and also another daughter named
Georgia, the 1st Georgia having died while an infant.

EDINGTON OR SAMUEL EDINGTON FAMILY CEMETERY

The children of Mary Ann Edington and Abijah Fowler married as
follows: Samuel A. never married; Mary Jane married Chas. Price.
Lived at Decatur, Ala.; Sarah Francis married Joseph H. Lowry
of Monroe County.

The children of Mary Ann Edington Fowler and Allen M. Henley,
married as follows: Thomas Owen, born June 6, 1869, died
April 7, 1938, never married; Authur R. born Jan. 14, 1871
married Virginia Smith, died Oct. 15, 1915. No children were
born to above couple. Inez, born Jan. 21, 1873 married J. D.
Clark. They now live at Portersville, Californ'a. Josie
married Oscar M. Clark. They now live at Summerton, Arizonia.
Maggie married Nick B. Hall. She is dead, buried in Southern
M. E. Cemetery at Vonore, Tennessee. Bettie, died July 9, 1875
and the last three were born Feb. 18, 1875.

Children of Mary Jane Fowler and Charles Price were as follows:
Mary Who married Pinkington, he died then she married a Mr.
Moody. Danella, no record; Emma, no record, Annie, no record,
Wesley, no record. Children of Sarah Frances Fowler and
Joseph H. Lowry were as follows: Mary Elizabeth, born May 25,
1882, married C. W. Lancaster, lived at Richmond, Cal.; Martha
Jane, born Oct. 1, 1883, married Ben Hall. Ruth born, Sept. 21,
1885 died. Samuel Anderson, born Feb. 3, 1887, married Bessie
Lomax. Minnie, born July 10, 1888, married T. W. Brunner.
David A., born April 21, 1890 married Maggie Nunn, and live in
New Mexico. Bertha, born Oct. 17, 1891 married S. F. Betifish.
Inez born Sept. 1, 1893, not married. Lives in Chicago, Ill.
Margaret F., born Oct. 3, 1895 not married. Authur Henley born
June 27, 1899, died July 13, 1899. Virginia Lee, born Aug. 20,
1900, married Henry McConkey of Monroe County.   Live at Lenore
City, Tennessee. Children of Inez Henley and husband J. D.
Clark are as follows: Ethel, died; Helen married Harry Gunning,
Eugene, died at age of 2 yrs; Walter married --------; Aleen
married --------; Richard married --------. Children of Josie
Henley and husband Oscar M. Clark are as follows: Ernest never
married; Clifford, married; Owen, married;Sadie, married; Morris,
married; Arthur never married. Children of Maggie Henley and
Nick B. Hall are as follows: Lottie married Pat Horner; James
died, never married; Thomas married Elberta Steele; Barksdale,
married Annie Giles; Artie Lou, died at age 2 yrs; Frances
married Nick Isbell. She is dead. Allen Married Myrtus Giles;
Bettie not married; Maggie, not married; Dortha, not married;
Children of Eliza Jane Fowler and husband James R. Henley married
as follows: Mary, married Ashley Johnson; Samuel, married Emma
Anderson; Charles, married Ressa Johnson; Nell, not married; Georgia
married Frank Johnston; Frank, married Nandy Johnston, Maude,
married Mack Lowery; Joseph married Cora Rogers; John, married
Louella Huston and Georgia, oldest child died in infancy.

MONROE COUNTY

TOMBSTONE INSCRIPTIONS

ELEAZER CAMP GROUND M.E. CHURCH CEMETERY

Copied by: Lawrence McConkey, Englewood, Tennessee
Date:

The Eleazer Camp Ground M. E. Church South and Cemetery are
located about 1½ miles Southeast of Mt. Vernon. Mt. Vernon
is approximately 9 miles South of Madisonville on the road
leading to Tellico Plains. The site for both church and
cemetery was on the land of Col. Joseph Boyd and is said to
have been selected by the Rev. Wm. G. Brownlow, "The Fighting
Parson," who later became governor of Tennessee. The earliest
inscription is that of Thomas M. Boyd, son of Joseph & Margaret
Boyd, who died Oct. 3, 1833. His was not, however, the first
interment in the cemetery. The name of the first person buried
there is not known but it is known that the first burial was
not much earlied than 1833. The cemetery now covers about 3
acres of land. Where the log school house once stood, is now
a part of the cemetery. Soldiers buried there are Pvt. Peter
Davis, Mexican War; Capt. Joseph Marr, Confederate; Lt. Robert
R. Winn, Confederate; Major Benj. P. Reagon, Confederate; Pvt.
Houston Wilburn, Federal; Pvt. Robert London, Federal; Pvt.
Thurber McConkey, World War, Killed in France. Information
regarding the above soldiers was securied from John Lee, of Mt.
Vernon. Preachers buried at Eleazer include the Rev. C. M.
James, M. E. South; the Rev. Melvin Smith, M. E. South; the
Rev. Louis Miller, M. E. South; the Rev. John Burger, Sr.,
M. E. South. Postmasters of Mt. Vernon buried here are:
Grimes A. Spillman, Postmaster at time of Civil War; Wm. M. Lee;
Newton S. Stizlar; Wm. M. Stizlar and James M. McConkey.

There are 345 inscriptions, 127 field stones and approximately
170 unmarked graves in Eleazar Cemetery. Three inscriptions
have been destroyed.

SHADDEN

Alex. Shadden
Mar. 4, 1829
July 6, 1912

Margaret Shadden
Mar. 11, 1842
Nov. 1, 1896

At Rest
G. C. Shadden
Oct. 2, 1874
June 20, 1893

(Note: South of above are
seven graves with a marker at
the four corners with letter
S. These seven graves are
graves of children of Thomas
L. and Lou Shadden. LMcC.)

Ida
Daughter of
J. H. & E. J. Shadden
Mar. 4, 1865
Mar. 5, 1899
We loved her, yes we loved
her but Angels loved her more.

ELEAZER CAMP GROUND M. E. CHURCH CEMETERY

Shadden
In memory of
George Brown Shadden
Dec. 3, 1898
Oct. 6, 1926
Gone but not forgotten.

Urma J.
Child of
A. A. & Florence Shadden
Aug. 8, 1900
Oct. 5, 1901

Joseph Shadden
Feb. 1, 1822
July 3, 1908

Jane Shadden
Nov. 1, 1833
Feb. 11, 1913

Maggie
Wife of
W. M. Shadden
Oct. 27, 1852
Jan. 7, 1900
Meet me in Heaven.

LONDON

Rob't London
Co. B.
1 U. S. V. I.

(Note: Rob't London was a
U. S. Civil War Soldier as
above marker indicates and
also according to John Lee
was the Postmaster of Mt.
Vernon, Tenn. LMcC.)

ERVIN

(Note: Many different branches
of this family are buried here
in several different locations.
LMcC.)

Beatrice Jane Ervin
Died Feb. 2, 1937
Age 3 yrs. & 4 months.

Rebecca
Wife of
James Ervin
Oct. 23, 1812
July 2, 1885
Aged 72 years, 8 months
& 9 days.
Gone on before.

James Ervin
Mar. 18, 1805
Mar. 31, 1887
Aged 82 years & 13 days.

George Ervin
Apr. 15, 1854
Aug. 25, 1887
A father beloved,
A husband most dear,
in death's cold arms
lies buried here.

Infant of
Calvin & Nannie Ervin
Aug. 7, 1888

Alex Ervin
July 13, 1835
April 8, 1913

Martha Austin
Wife of
Alex Ervin
Apr. 8, 1840
Oct. 4, 1912
Father & Mother

M. A. Ervin
At Rest.

1 field stone South of above
grave.

Robert W.
Son of
J. M. & Margaret Ervin
Oct. 11, 1893
Dec. 9, 1901
Gone but not forgotten.

ELEAZER CAMP GROUND M. E. CHURCH CEMETERY

J. M. Ervin
Husband of
Margaret Ervin
June 15, 1871
Sept. 12, 1904
A loved one from us has gone.

Rispa
Wife of
Patrick Ervin
Apr. 18, 1830
Aug. 26, 1897

Ruby Lee Ervin
June 2, 1915
June 18, 1915
Gone but not forgotten.

A. S. Ervin
July 21, 1888
Aug. 14, 1917
At Rest.

Alice Ervin
Nov. 15, 1910
Mar. 16, 1916
Budded on earth to bloom
in Heaven.

Husband
B. E. Ervin
Jan. 30, 1896
(Still living)

Wife
Minnie Ervin
Oct. 17, 1890
May 15, 1934
"Amazing grace how
sweet the sounds,
that saved a wretch
like me" I one was
lost, but not I am
found, was blind but
not I see. Is gone but not
forgotten.

Savior lead me
Earl
Son of
Calvin & N. A. Ervin

April 20, 1889
Aug. 12, 1908
We shall meet but we
shall miss him.
There will be a vacant
chair but though we
no more possess him
still our hearts his
memory bear.

W. L. Ervin
Sept. 16, 1863
Apr. 22, 1933
Gone but not forgotten.

2 graves South of above.

Martha
Wife of
W. L. Ervin Jr.
Apr. 21, 1857
June 22, 1908
O how sweet will be
in that beautiful land,
so free from all sorrow
and pain, with songs on
our lips and with harps
in our hands to meet one
another again.

Patrick Ervin
April 30, 1827
Sept. 27, 1880

(Above marker broken)

Henry M.
Son of
Patrick & Rispa Ervin
Nov. 8, 1859
Aug. 2, 1863

Catherine
Wife of
Joseph Ervin
Died March 5, 1898
Age about 70 years.

Joseph Ervin
May 5, 1828
April 17, 1895

ELEAZER CAMP GROUND M. E. CHURCH CEMETERY

Sarah Jane
Daughter of
Joseph & Catherine Ervin
Dec. 10, 1849
July 14, 1869

Bertha
Daughter of
J. M. & M. J. Ervin
Jan. 14, 1892
Oct. 7, 1896

Mattie Rider
Wife of
J. M. Ervin
Jan. 26, 1870
Sept. 12, 1913
In God we trust.

R. H. Ervin
Nov. 10, 1865
Mar. 12, 1908
Only sleeping

Dorcas
Wife of
R. H. Ervin
June 10, 1861
Oct. 24, 1907
We will meet again.

Dora Ellen
Daughter of
W. L. & Martha Ervin
Mar. 8, 1881
Apr. 21, 1881

Mary Ervin
Oct. 19, 1839
Dec. 9, 1900

(Note: There are 2 field
stones North of above.
One probably marks the
grave of Mary Ervin's
husband. LMcC.)

(Note: The six following
graves are enclosed in a
fence. There are four Ervin
graves, one Burger grave and
one Stiles grave. These
families all are related. LMcC.)

Alice Chester Ervin
Feb. 19, 1890
July 29, 1904
We weep for our darling
who is gone for a sun-
beam that has flown
a missing step of
nameless grace. A tender
voice and a loving face,
but not for the soul,
whose goal is won,
whose perfect joy has just
begun, not for the spirit
robed in white and crowned
where angels are.

Carroll Ervin
May 5, 1852
Oct. 4, 1925

His wife
Susan A. Ervin
Sept. 27, 1852
Dec. 8, 1924

Ervin
S. M. Ervin
Jan. 24, 1878
July 25, 1930
He has gone, to his
rest after a useful life.

BURGER

J. H. L. Burger
July 26, 1886
Sept. 29, 1908

STILES

Infant
of
W. P. & Ella Stiles
June 26, 1911

(Note: The above two graves
are enclosed in a fence with
the graves of Alice, Carroll
and Susan Ervin. LMcC.)

ELEAZER CAMP GROUND M. E. CHURCH CEMETERY

LEE

Mrs. Martha Ann Lee
Died June 21, 1939
Aged 57 years, 9 months
& 29 days.

William Hobart Lee
Nov. 15, 1896
June 27, 1898

Ralph Davis Lee
Sept. 13, 1898
Aug. 13, 1899

Robert Lee
Aug. 23, 1894
Dec. 15, 1912

Father
Arthur A. Lee
April 9, 1872
Feb. 15, 1912
His spirit smiles from
that bright shore and
softly whispers weep no
more.

Maud
Beloved little daughter of
Ras & Randa Lee
Mar. 11, 1899
Aug. 30, 1908
Meet me darling at the gate.

Father
(Masonic Emblem)
Wm. M. Lee
July 12, 1839
Oct. 23, 1900
To live in hearts we
leave behind is not to die.

E. B. Lee
Aug. 25, 1898
Nov. 13, 1931
Asleep in Jesus.

Robert Lee
Aug. 23, 1894
Dec. 15, 1912

(Note: Without inscription
are: the graves of Peter
Davis, Jr., and Attie Reagon
Peter Davis, Jr., is buried
on South side of the above.
The Lee and Davis families
are related. Beside Arthur
A. Lee's grave is that of his
mother.) LMcC.

Attie Reagon
Wife of
Wm. M. Lee
Died about 1917,
aged about 60 years.

DAVIS

Peter Davis
Feb. 29, 1824
June 29, 1899

(Note: 2 graves South of
above - possibly one is
wife of Peter Davis. LMcC.)

ELLIS

Hattie Lou Ellis
Died July 11, 1936
Aged 4 months & 22 days.

Mrs. Salina Ellis
Died March -- 1936
Aged 37 years

Hattie Ellis
July 6, 1872
May 2, 1904

John Ellis
May 11, 1861
Feb. 24, 1907

B. D. Ellis
Bornd   1816
Died Aug. 6, 1911

Starlon Ellis
Feb. 13, 1932
Nov. 21, 1932

6

ELEAZER CAMP GROUND M. E. CHURCH CEMETERY

(Note: 2 graves without
inscriptions South of R. L
Peeler marker.)

Bessie Bryson
Wife of
James Ellis
Died About 1930
Aged about 25 yrs.

Infant
of
James & Bessie Ellis
  Born & died 1930

GRAHAM

L. A. Graham
Born 1861
Died May 21, 1930

CARDIN OR CARDEN

James J. Cardin
Dec. 15, 1807
Oct. 14, 1888

(Note: The wife & daughter
of James J. Cardin are
buried North of this grave
without inscriptions. LMcC.)

Leonard Cardin
Aug. 9, 1814
May 22, 1900
Gone home to be blest
with peace, happiness and
rest.

N. C. Cardin
Dec. 25, 1815
Mar. 1, 1897

Polly
Wife of
John Cardin
Sept. 16, 1821
Sept. 12, 1862

(Note: unmarked grave North
possibly husband of above. LMcC.)

Lilie Mae
Wife of
W. T. Cardin
May 17, 1882
May 13, 1913
At Rest.

Cornelious
Son of
J. T. & H. Cardin
Nov. 6, 1877
Aug. 5, 1904
Gone but not forgotten.

J. T. Cardin
May 6, 1850
Dec. 28, 1925
Kind father of love thou
art gone to thy rest for-
ever to bask in the joys
of the blest.

Hassie
Wife of
J. T. Cardin
Born May 3, 1848
Died May 20, 1917
Gone to rest.

William Harrison
Son of
J. T. & L. H. Cardin
Dec. 18, 1890
Aug. 31, 1891

Alexander
Son of
J. M. & J. E. Cardin
July 18, 1874
Aug. 24, 1874

In memory of
W. J. Carden
Oct. 1, 1832
May 23, 1894
Erected by his wife.

Polly Carden
Sept. 14, 1833
Nov. 27, 1914
Erected by her daughter
Betsy Ann Land.

ELEAZER CAMP GROUND M. E. CHURCH CEMETERY

Mother
Martha Cardin
Dec. 17, 1845
May 31, 1921

Father
W. J. Cardin
Apr. 8, 1839
Mar. 16, 1919

(Masonic Emblem)
Carden
Jordan Carden
Dec. 22, 1877
Jan. 23, 1924
He was beloved by God
and man.

America Cardin
Oct. 1, 1849
Jan. 9, 1921
Blessed are the dead which
die in the Lord.

J. B. Carden
June 26, 1884
May 27, 1904

Elbert Carden
Born Nov. 20, 1895
Age 10 months
In Heaven we hope to
meet him.

Gracie Carden
Born June 23, 1896
Age 4 months
In Heaven we hope to
meet her.

Brother
W. H. Cardin
1886 - 1928
Gone but not forgotten.

(Note: W. H. Cardin was a
son of J. T. & Hassie Cardin.
LMcC.)

Infant
Son of
J. R. & Maggie Carden
Feb. 7, 1909
Feb. 11, 1909

Amos R. Carden
May 25, 1904
Dec. 22, 1908

Buster D. Cardon
Nov. 26, 1912
Dec. 7, 1934
Son of
J. T. Cardon

(Note: The above was son
of Joe Carden. Name spelled
incorrectly on marker. LMcC.)

J. M. Carden
Dec. 19, 1859
Aug. 27, 1891
Blessed are the pure in
heart for they shall see
God.

4 field stones South of above.

LUNSFORD

Husband
J. T. Lunsford
(Jr. O. U. A. M. Emblem)
April 20, 1868
April 28, 1026

STANDRIDGE

Mrs. Nancy Standridge
Died Nov. 5, 1937
Aged 20 years, 5 months
& 19 days.

BATES

Clif
Son of
Mr. & Mrs. O. S. Bates
Oct. 17, 1911
Nov. 25, 1918
Darling we miss thee.

ELEAZER CAMP GROUND M. E. CHURCH CEMETERY

Cyntha Bates
Born   1824
Died Jan. 18, 1907

(Masonic Emblem)
E. M. Bates
Feb. 15, 1822
Oct. 16, 1905

MORGAN

Little Taylor Morgan
At Rest
Erected Apr. 1912

2 unmarked graves South of
above. LMcC.)

Matilda Morgan
At Rest
Erected Apr. 8, 1912

Z. T. Morgan
Born   1850
Died   1904
Age 62 yrs.
In Heaven we hope
to meet him.

(Note: Above dates and age
do not agree. LMcC.)

Cora May Morgan
At Rest
Erected Apr. 8, 1912

DANIEL

Lilly Gertrude Daniel
Dec. 29, 1892
Nov. 7, 1904
Suffer little children
to come unto me.

Mrs. Mary Daniel
Died July 28, 1931
Aged 69 years, 5 months
& 14 days.

Unmarked grave.

James Newton Daniel
Feb. 19, 1866
July 5, 1917
Gone but not forgotten.

Unmarked grave.

STUART

Jane Stuart
Oct. 7, 1853
(Date of death not given)
May
May Stuart
Dec. 1, 1883

ROGERS

M. L. Rogers
April 22, 1845
(date of death not given)

J. W. Rogers
Dec. 25, 1841
Dec. 23, 1909

CROFTS

Caroline Crofts
Jan. 26, 1834
Dec. 6, 1912

(Note: Asbury Crofts, husband
of above, is buried at the
South side of this grave. LMcC.)

M. C.

(Note: Above inscription is
by Asbury Croft's grave. LMcC.)

WHITE

James Harbert White
Dec. 8, 1913
May 21, 1914
Budded on earth to bloom
in Heaven.

Howard White
Aug. 28, 1915
Oct. 20, 1916

ELEAZER CAMP GROUND M. E. CHURCH CEMETERY

SMITH

Martha Smith
Mar.   1859
Aug. 19, 1902
At Rest.

BAKER

Father
G. W. Baker
June 3, 1853
(Date of death not given)

Mother
Julia Baker
June 2, 1864
May 27, 1914
Gone but not forgotten.

Mr. Louise Baker
Died May 16, 1936
Aged 35 years, 1 month
& 17 days.

James Harvey Baker
Died Feb. 6, 1937
Aged 56 years.

BOYD

Joseph Boyd
Jan. 1, 1798
Aug. 18, 1874
Aged 76 years, 7 months
& 17 days.

Margaret
Wife of
Joseph Boyd
July 4, 1893
Aug. 7, 1887

In memory of
Major Joseph C. Boyd
Born Nov. 24, 1835
Died at Vicksburg, Miss
June 11, 1863

Thomas M.
Son of
Joseph & Margaret Boyd
Feb. 14, 1831
Oct. 3, 1833

(Note: Above is earliest
inscription is this cemetery
LMcC.)

VAUGHN

In memory of
Mrs. J. C. Vaughn
Born April 2, 1831
Died in New York
Nov. 12, 1868
Blessed are the pure in
heart for they shall see God.

(Note! Mrs. J. C. Vaughn
was buried near Major Joseph
C. Boyd. The Boyds & Vaughns
were related. LMcC.)

Infant
of
Mr. & Mrs. J. C. Vaughn

Willie H.
Son of
J. C. & N. S. Vaughn
Apr. 10, 1856
Sept. 27, 1856

Infant
of
J. C. & N. S. Vaughn

WILSON

George Lee Wilson
Died Nov. 10, 1937
Aged 4 mos. & 2 days.

Son of
F. M. & Ida Wilson
Sept. 5, 1908
Sept. 8, 1909

Mary Alice
Dau. of
T. & E. Wilson
June 15, 1883
Jan. 16, 1885

ELEAZER CAMP GROUND M. E. CHURCH CEMETERY

Infant
of
J. T. & S. J. Wilson
Born & died
Sept. 7, 18--

Mary A. Wilson
Sept. 12, 1883
Sept. 1, 1887

Francis M. Wilson
Dec. 15, 1844
Feb. 7, 1871

Dianah Wilson
May 30, 1819
March 19, 1897

Mother
Sarah Robison
Wife of
J. T. Wilson
Jan. 30, 1843
Nov. 26, 1925

Father
J. T. Wilson
May 30, 1847
June 21, 1924

BOWERS

A. M. Bowers
Mar. 5, 1822
Aug. 14, 1909
At Rest.

E. M. Bowers
Apr. 6, 1831
June 16, 1916
Gone to rest.

RIDER

Rider
Alex R.
March 15, 1856
(Still Living)

Mary L.
July 15, 1858
July 15, 1935
Gone but not forgotten.

Ida
Daughter of
A. R. & Mary Rider
Sept. 8, 1886
Sept. 27, 1904
At Rest.

Infant
of
A. R. & Mary Rider
Born & died 1899

Infant
of A
A. R. & Mary Rider
Born & died 1897

Infant
of
A. R. & Mary Rider
Born & died 1895

1 Stone unmarked.

Louella
Daughter of
A. R. & Mary Rider
Jan. 17, 1882
Jan. 9, 1896
At Rest.

Infant
of
A. R. & Mary Rider
Born & died 1891

Infant
of
A. R. & Mary Rider
Born & died 1886

J. S.
Son of
A. R. & Mary Rider
April 11, 1879
Aug. 4, 1879

ELEAZER CAMP GROUND M. E. CHURCH CEMETERY

Martha
Wife of
Wm. Rider
Jan. 18, 1855
April 12, 1898
Gone but not forgotten.

4 field stones South of
above.

Infant
of
W. B. & Martha Rider

1 field stone

Robert S.
Son of
W. B. & Martha Rider
Feb. 15, 1888
July 9, 1889

Lida J. Rider
Wife of
J. L. Rider
Mar. 26, 1861
Sept. 19, 1886

Malt Rider
Aug. 13, 1865
Aug. 3, 1871

E. J. Rider
Nov. 22, 1837
Dec. 3, 1889

M. C. Rider
May 5, 1826
Apr. 15, 1868

S. R. Rider
Feb. 3, 1823
June 20, 1910
He was faithful to
every duty.

HAMPTON

E. J.
Son of
T. M. & Louisa Hampton
Aug. 6, 1886
Oct. 27, 1890
Our loved one.

CROFTS

Minnie
Wife of
N. D. Crofts
June 19, 1876
Jan. 14, 1919
Her end was peace.

1 field stone North of above.

HAWKINS

Father
Anderson Hawkins
May 5, 1828
Apr. 24, 1900

Mother
Betsey A.
Wife of
Anderson Hawkins
May 25, 1832
Nov. 1, 1895

CARVER

Nancy A. Carver
Died June 23, 1904
Age about 66 years.

GAMBLE

D. A. Gamble
Aug. 14, 1861
June 21, 1888

HAMPTON

Infant
of
J. H. Hampton & wife

NORRIS

In My fathers house are
many mansions
Lola M.
Wife of
W. T. Norris
Sept. 12, 1886
Aug. 23, 1908
(continued on next page.)

ELEAZER CAMP GROUND SOUTHERN M. E. CHURCH

Oh how sweet it will be
in that land so free from
all sorrow and pain with
songs on our lips and
with harps in our hands to meet
meet another again.

Mrs. Lytton Norris
Died August 27, 1936
Aged 27 years & 17 days.

ROBERTS

Jr. O. U. A. M.
Carter R. Roberts
Oct. 7, 1881
Sept. 3, 1935

Roberts
Mother
Roda An Roberts
Dec. 18, 1855
Jan. 31, 1929

Father
P. M. Roberts
May 17, 1858
Oct. 12, 1929
Loves Remembrance
lasts forever.

J. J. Roberts
March 13, 1886
Jan. 5, 1915

Catherine Roberts
Nov. 4, 1827
June 10, 1906

5 field stones North
of above.

VISAGE

P. J. Visage
May 19, 1895
Oct. 6, 1918

TATE

Father
George W. Tate
Nov. 13, 1858
Jan. 19, 1929
Gone home.

Infant
Son of
G. W. & Jennie Tate
Born Sept. 25, 1898

Sallie Tate
Wife of
M. W. Tate
July 19, 1867
Oct. 27, 1897
Age 30 years 3 months
& 9 days.
Not last but gone before.

GAY

Infant
of
Wiley J. & Mary E. Gay
Born & died June 30, 1903

(Note: This grave is between grave of
Geo. W. Tate and Infant son
of G. W. & Jennie Tate listed
above. LMcC.)

MARR

Grover C. Marr
Mar. 11, 1887
Nov. 26, 1911

John F. Marr
June 9, 1875
Sept. 19, 1889
Farewell brother till we
meet again.

Capt. Joseph Marr
May 29, 1813
March 26, 1884
He was a member of the
M. E. Church South.

ELEAZER CAMP GROUND M. E. CHURCH CEMETERY

(Note: Joseph Marr was a
Captain in the Confederate
Army according to statement
of John Lee. LMcC.)

MERCER

Foster Mercer
Jan. 12, 1879
May 13, 1905
In Jesus he is sweetly
sleeping.

William James Mercer
Sept. 1, 1872
May 13, 1905
Gone but not forgotten.

(Note: There is 1 field
stone between the two
above graves. These 3
graves are between graves
of Grover C. Marr and
John F. Marr; also the
following grave is between
graves of John F. and Capt.
Joseph Marr, apparently
same family. LMcC.)

Minnie A. Mercer
Aug. 10, 1875
Sept. --, 1887
At Rest.

SNIDER

Lizzie
Infant dau. of
W. R. & Jennie Snider
Dec. 13, 1885
Jan. 1, 1886

1 field stone South of
above.

NAILER

Mary L.
Wife of
B. F. Nailer
May 26, 1860
Apr. 15, 1887

Infant
Born & died
Sept. 23, 1882

J. N. Agnes Nailer
Alias Shadden
Wife of
B. F. Nailer
Oct. 13, 1864
Jan. 8, 1893

2 graves North of above.

REAGON OR REAGAN

M. A. Reagon
Died May 7, 1904
Age 55 years.
Gone but not forgotten.

1 field stone North and 4
field stones South of above.

B. P. Reagan
Feb. 12, 1830
Jan. 14, 1909

(Note: The above, Benj. P.
Reagan, Esq., was a Sargeant
in the Confederate Army and
later a J. P. of Monroe Co.)

Eliza Reagon
Sept. 11, 1855
Sept. 19, 1920

HARRISON

Milard Harrison
June 5, 1920
May 10, 1922
Gone but not forgotten.

MIZE

Jimmie
Son of
J. S. & Jane Mize
June 24, 1862
Jan. 11, 1868

WINN

ELEAZER CAMP GROUND M. E. CHURCH CEMETERY

R. R. Winn
Oct. 12, 1836
July 28, 1908

(Note: The above, Robert
R. Winn, was a lieutenant
in the Confederate Army
according to statement of
John Lee of Mt. Vernon.
LMcC.)

MITCHELL

Elmer G.
Son of
J. G. & Catherine Mitchell
Sept. 15, 1891
Sept. 29, 1897
Christ said suffer little
children to come unto me
and forbid them not for
of such is the Kimgdom
of Heaven.

RAPER

Viola Raper
Mar. 18, 1904
Apr. 29, 1904

Lislie
Infant of
R. A. & Cora Raper
Nov. 9, 1917
July 19, 1919
Darling we miss Thee

Ella V. Raper
Feb. 14, 1890
July 8, 1891

COOK

Laura Cook
Sept. 12, 1887
Sept. 10, 1911

(Note: Beside the above
grave are the unmarked
graves of Ernest, Cook,
Died about 1935 aged about
24 yrs, and Benton Cook,
Died about 1936 aged about
52 years. LMcC.)

Sarah J.
Wife of
L. W. Cook
Sept. 6, 1862
Sept. 3, 1907

Martha Cook
Jan. 23, 1882
Mar. 22, 1896
Darling we miss thee at
home but a little time on

Martha Cook
Aug. 25, 1837
Apr. 11, 1901
At Rest.

1 field stone North and 2
South of above.

PEELER

W. D. Peeler
May 3, 1841
Jan. 23, 1907

3 field stones South of
following.

R. L. Peeler

W. H. Peeler

W. W. Peeler
Sept. 13, 1900
Sept. 20, 1900

S. E. Peeler
Apr. 20, 1895
Aug. 30, 1900

Nannie Peeler
Died June 13, 1937
Aged 88 years, 8 months
and 11 days.

(Note: The above age maybe
38 years. LMcC.)

Infant Grave South of Above.

ELEAZER CAMP GROUND M. E. CHURCH CEMETERY

WOODS

Frances Viola Woods
April 1, 1905
May 25, 1906

Dixie May Woods
Mar. 14, 1891
Apr. 16, 1892

Lizzie Clementine Woods
Mar. 11, 1902
Mar. 13, 1902

Robert Clide Woods
Apr. 22, 1910
June 19, 1910

Hugh King Woods
Aug. 16, 1908
Nov. 26, 1909

GAY

Mary J. Gay
Sept. 1, 1825
Jan. 5, 1903

Infant's grave at South and
several graves North of
above.

Note: The grave & inscription below are at another
location. LMcC.)

Elizabeth Gay
Jan. 29, 1827
Jan. 10, 1912

11 stones North of above.

RICHESON

Archie
Son of
E. S. & C. L. Richeson
Apr. 15, 1918
Jan. 29, 1919
Gone but not forgotten.

Mary Ann Richeson
Wife of
I. R. Richeson
Feb. 9, 1859
Aug. 26, 1887

Martha A. Richeson
Born   1809
Died Oct. 9, 1893
Age 84 years.

William Richeson
Died June 4, 1873
Aged 71 years, 3 months
and 20 days.

Mrs. Margaret Richeson
Died April 4, 1935
Aged 82 years, 2 months
and 9 days.

MANIS

Jeanett Manis
Died Jan. 8, 1936
Aged 2 months

1 grave South of above.

BURGER

Martha Emaline Burger
April 1, 1849
July 28, 1922
Asleep in Jesus.

Rev. John Burger Sr.
Dec. 5, 1831
Apr. 6, 1911
He followed virtue as his
truest guide, lived as a
christian and as a christian died.

Mary A.
Wife of
Rev. John Burger
Aug. 30, 1824
Sept. 12, 1897

ELEAZER CAMP GROUND M. E. CHURCH CEMETERY

Kathleen
Daughter of
John & Elsie Burger
Oct. 27, 1918
May 6, 1919

J. L. Burger
May 27, 1860
Nov. 5, 1917
Farewell Father thou
hast loved us long and
well. How we miss thee
none can tell.
Jesus called thee all
is well.

Tabitha Burger
July 18, 1861
Sept. 28, 1916
Blessed are the dead
which die in the Lord.

Infant
of
J. L. & Tabitha Burger
Born 1899
At Rest.

J. H. L. Burger
July 26, 1886
Sept. 29, 1908

GAINES

Cora
Wife of
J. R. Gaines
Nov. 5, 1892
Oct. 1, 1906

(Note: Cora Gaines is
buried by side of infant
of J. L. & Tabitha
Burger. She is very likely
their daughter. LMcC.)

MCCOLLUM

Mary E. McCollum
Apr. 8, 1878
Apr. 15, 1885
Age 7 yrs. & 7 days.

Sumner E.
Son of
R. W. & Addie McCollum
Apr. 1, 1901
Apr. 11, 1901

Dr. S. E. McCollum
Sept. 4, 1835
Dec. 12, 1902
Gone but not forgotten.

Selina
Wife of
S. E. McCollum
Feb. 11, 1838
Sept. 6, 1899
Gone but not forgotten.

WILBURN

Houston Wilburn
Co. D.
2 Tenn. Cav.

Note: Houston Wilburn was
a private in the Federal
Army, so says John Lee. LMcC.)

LAND

Jessie Land
Dec. 18, 1866
Mar. 16, 1902
Gone to rest.

Steller Land
May 9, 1895
Darling we miss thee

Jessie Land
May 1, 1902
May 2, 1902
Darling we miss thee

At Rest.
Mandy Jane Land
June 8, 1862
July 4, 1895

1 grave South of above.

Effie Lee Land
Aug. 25, 1899
July 30, 1920
Gone but not forgotten.

ELEAZER CAMP GROUND M. E. CHURCH CEMETERY

DITMORE

Vivie Ditmore
Died Jan. 12, 1936
Aged 9 years 3 months
and 24 days.

2 field stones South of
above.

BRADLEY

Kenneth Bradley
May 11, 1938
May 13, 1938

BLACK

G. W. Black
Nov. 12, 1888
Aug. 3, 1924
Gone but not forgotten.

W. E. Black
Oct. 20, 1901
Oct. 20, 1908

(Note: The following are
at another location. LMcC.)

Laura Ethel
Infant of
S. N. & Essie Black
Sept. 18, 1907
Sept. 21, 1907

Charles
Infant of
S. N. & Essie Black
April 25, 1908

PICKELSIMER

Margarett Pickelsimer
Aug. 19, 1833
Feb. 8, 1908

1 field stone North
of above.

RUSSELL

Ab Taylor
Son of
W. A. & P. A. Russell
April 15, 1890
Nov. 14, 1891

11 graves South of above.

(Note: The following grave
is at another location. LMcC)

Mary Frances
Wife of
J. B. Russell
Nov. 15, 1900
Feb. 1, 1922
One precious to my heart
has gone. The voice I
loved is still, the place
made vacant in my home
can never be filled.

DISHROON

Hannah Dishroon
April 20, 1862
Jan. 29, 1938

MARSHALL

William Marshall
Sept. 26, 1789
Apr. 21, 1857

Isaac Marshall
Jan. 1, 1833
July 16, 1856
He obtained relegion in
early life and united him-
self with the M. E. Church
South and died a trumphant
death.
Erected in memory of
my father.
By Emma Richardson

(Note: The Marshall and the
Richeson graves are close together. It is very likely the
Emma Richardson above should
have been Richeson. LMcC.)

ELEAZER CAMP GROUND M. E. CHURCH CEMETERY

YOUNG

In memory of
Alafair Young
May 5, 1871
Feb. 10, 1905

KELSO

John C.
Son of
J. H. & Keziah A. Kelso
March 7, 1853
July 6, 1867

3 graves at South of above.

Harriet J.
Daughter of
J. H. & Keziah A. Kelso
Feb. 3, 1860
June 10, 1860

Infant
Daughter of
J. H. & Keziah A. Kelso
Feb. 11, 1864
Feb. 25, 1864

Infant
of
J. H. & Keziah A. Kelso
Jan. 6, 1863
Jan. 9, 1863

(Note: Nearby above graves
and at head of D. A. Gamble
marker South are 4 graves
marked Kelso and there seem
to be other Kelso graves
also. LMcC.)

HAYNES

M. M.
Wife of
A. J. Haynes
Nov. 14, 1852
Oct. 20, 1888

TURK

Here lies the body of
Caroline Turk
deaprted this life
7 December 1850
age 37 years
Happy soul thy days are
ended. All thy mourning
days below.
The wife of
C. L. Turk

V. W. Turk
Departed this life
25 January 1851

(Note: There may be burials beside the
above graves but this is not
certain. LMcC.)

HALE

William Hale
Jan. 11, 1802
Feb. 21, 1845

CHARLES

Oliver A. Charles
Feb. 6, 1830
Sept. 30, 1860
Aged 30 years, 7 months
& 24 days.

Note: There is 1 grave on
South side of above grave
which has a marker with
letters C. C. This was possibly the grave of Oliver A.
Charles' wife. LMcC.)

COLLAQUE OR COLLAKE

Collake
Infant
of
J. C. & M. M. Collake
Jan. 15, 1903
Sweetly sleeping.

Collake
Infant of
J. C. & M. M. Collake
Nov. 20, 1908
Sweetly sleeping.

ELEAZER CAMP GROUND M. E. CHURCH CEMETERY

C. V. Collake
Dec. 25, 1858
Nov. 15, 1912

Sarah Jane Collaque
June   1848
May 28, 1892

Sallie Collaque
Born 1812
Died March 23, 1892

Joseph S. Collaque
Born 1874
Died 1886

John W. Collaque
Born 1877
Died 1878

Harvey Collaque
Oct. 8, 1887

Charles Collaque
Sept. 25, 1889

ABERNATHY

Bonnie
Daughter of
J. L. & M. A. Abernathy
Mar. 31, 1903
Sept. 5, 1907
Thy will be done.

SPILLMAN

Joseph B.
Son of
N. J. & M. A. Spillman
Sept. 1, 1854
June 8, 1855

In memory of
N. J. Spillman
Died April 4, 1859
Age 54 years & 3 days
Blessed are the merciful
for they shall obtain
Mercy. N. J. Spillman
who was always kind
and benevolent to the poor.

G. A. Spillman
June 5, 1826
July 19, 1912

M. C. Spillman
Oct. 6, 1830
Dec. 3, 1911
At Rest.

Gone Home
In memory of
John C. Spillman
Son of
G. A. & M. C. Spillman
June 22, 1860
Sept. 7, 1882
Aged 27 years, 2 months
& 16 days.
Precious in the sight of
the Lord is the death of
his Saints.

JAMES

James
(Mason Emblem)
Rev. C. M. James
Aug. 16, 1845
Aug. 13, 1926

JONES

Mary E.
Wife of
A. B. Jones
May 8, 1814
June 29, 1862

A. B. Jones
Nov. 18, 1799
Aug. 1, 1881

STILES

(Note: The Stiles family graves,
as well as graves of the other
families are divieded because the
cemetery is an old one & other old
burials are nearby. All members
of the Stiles family buried at
Eleazer Cemetery are descendants of
Wm. M. & Eliza Stiles, the first two
listed below. LMcC.)

ELEAZER CAMP GROUND M. E. CHURCH CEMETERY

William M. Stiles
Jan. 2, 1824
Apr. 12, 1880
At Rest.

Eliza Stiles
Dec. 23, 1825
Apr. 6, 1880

Easter A. Stiles
Dec. 29, 1852
Feb. 9, 1929

A. S. Stiles
June 8, 1848
Apr. 7, 1935

Jack L. Stiles
June 29, 1890
Dec. 31, 1908
At Rest.

R. A. Stiles
Wife of
W. H. Stiles
Born Mar. 28, 1860
Died Sept. 27, 1887
Age 27 years, 6 mos
Not lost but gone before.

Sarah J.
Wife of
J. P. Stiles
July 25, 1850
Dec. 24, 1903
Gone but not forgotten.

J. Paschal Stiles
Born   1850
Died Sept. -- 1934

Stiles
Cora Lee
Wife of
Chanler K. Stiles
Feb. 8, 1887
Dec. 27, 1909
One precious to my heart
has gone. The voice I
loved is still. The place
made vacant in my home can
never be filled.

Infant
of
John & Kittie Stiles
Born & died
Dec. 14, 1914
Budded on earth to bloom
in Heaven.

W.O.W. Memorial
Stiles
H. E. Stiles
Sept. 11, 1880
Sept. 24, 1915
At Rest.

Infant
of
J. L. & Lillie Stiles
Born May 13, 1888

Chippy Stiles
Died March 22, 1930
Aged 40 years.

Nellie Dorris Stiles
Apr. 24, 1918
Mar. 21, 1920
Budded on earth to
bloom in Heaven.

HELMS

Virgil Munsey Helms
Died 2-11-1939
Aged (Not given)

SMITH

(Jr. O. U. A. M. Emblem)
J. M. Smith
Age 47 years
Erected by Mt. Vernon
Council No. 214 Jr. O.U.A.M.

1 grave North of above.

MCCONKEY

ELEAZER CAMP GROUND M. E. CHURCH CEMETERY

Emet Athel
Son of
J. F. & T. E. McConkey
Nov. 20, 1891
Jan. 8, 1905

McConkey
James M. McConkey
Born Aug. 13, 1836
Died (date not given.)

Emaline McConkey
Apr. 6, 1838
Mar. 29, 1915
She now sweetly rests.

Lewis M. McConkey
Born Jan. 28, 1858
Met death Feb. 4, 1908
Gone but not forgotten.

Newton Alexander McConkey
Sept. 16, 1867
Apr. 26, 1912
God in his wisdom has
recalled the boon his love
had given and though the
body slumbers here the
soul is safe in Heaven.
A loved one from us has
gone. A voice we loved is
stilled. A place is vacant
in our home which never
can be filled.

Alice
Wife of
Newton Alexander McConkey
Died 1915
Aged 50 years.

Rosa
Wife of
Claude McConkey
Died 1923
Aged 30 years.

Infant
of
Claude & Rosa McConkey
Born & died 1928

Thurber McConkey
A World War soldier
Killed in France in 1917
(Grave unmarked)

SITZLAR

(Note: These graves are in
the same plot as those above
and are graves of same family.
LMcC.)

Sitzlar
Jr. O.U.A.M.
William R. Sitzlar
Sept. 12, 1859
Jan. 10, 1929
Our loved one.

Sarah E. McConkey
Wife of
William R. Sitzlar
Feb. 6, 1860
Oct. 26, 1918
She was a kind and
affectionate wife: a fond
mother and a friend to all.

N. S. Sitzlar
Died Aug. 1930
Aged 68 years.

Fannie McConkey
Wife of
Newton S. Sitzlar
Died 1932
Aged 58 years.

Clyde
Son of
N. S. & Fannie Sitzlar
Born 1902
Died 1934

Mescal
Daughter of
N. S. & Fannie Sitzlar
Born 1918
Died 1932

HOLCOMB

ELEAZER CAMP GROUND M. E. CHURCH CEMETERY

Carrie
May 2, 1881
Jan. 27, 1922
She was the sunshine
of our home.

Brin
Son of
Mr. & Mrs. D. M. Holcomb
July 7, 1915
Mar. 17, 1919

(Note: An infant of Mr. &
Mrs. D. M. Holcomb is
buried on the South side of
above child's grave. LMcC.)

(Note: At another location are th
the following inscriptions on
graves of 2 infants, the children
of Sampson & Ara Holcomb. LMcC.)

Infant
of
S. & A. Holcomb
Died Dec. 2, 1877

Infant
of
S. & A. Holcomb

(Note: Dates, if any
are gone. LMcC.)

Poney Holcomb.

(Note: Field stones mark
3 more grave of above
family. LMcC.)

HOOPER

Hooper
A. C. Hooper
May 27, 1886
Sept. 26, 1909

Juanita Hooper
Died June 15, 1939
Aged 4 yrs. 10 mos. & 17 days.

Narvel Hooper
May 30, 1909
March 16, 1926
Gone to rest.

3 field stones South of above.

BRANNON

James Brannon
Mar. 17, 1839
May 8, 1907
Death is eternal life
why should we weep.

Tiney
Daughter of
James & Bettie Brannon
Born 1879
Died 1879

Bettie McConkey
Wife of
James Brannon
Born 1844
Died June 24, 1879

Elihu
Son of
James & Bettie Brannon
Born 1870
Died 1874

In memory of
Frances Brannon
Dau of
James & Bettie Brannon
Died July 20, 1871
Age 2 years.

Opal Brannon
Nov. 25, 1915
July 21, 1917
Darling we miss thee.

Note: Nancy Sluder was an
Aunt of Opal Brannon & a
sister of Mrs. Lee Brannon.
Her grave has no inscription.
Nancy Sluder
Born 1840
Died 1935. LMcC.)

ELEAZER OAMP GROUND M. E. CHURCH CEMETERY

HOLLOFORD

Mary Elizabeth Holloford
Died Feb. 19, 1936
Aged 86 years.

(Note: The two above ladies
were sisters. LMcC.)

EVERHART

R. M. Everhart
Br. May 15, 1918

Florence
Daughter of
Isaac & America Everhart
Feb. 12, 1875
June 13, 1877

STEWART

Sintha Stewart
Died May 12, 1939
Aged 33 years & 17 days.

GIBSON

Tane Gibson
Nov. 1841
May 1918

PEARSON

W. G. Pearson
Jan. 17, 1855
Mar. 7, 1919
Prepare to meet me
in Heaven.

GIIES

Mae
Daughter of
John & M. Giles
Sept. 21, 1904
Dec. 21, 1915

Mary
Wife of
John Giles
May 3, 1862
Oct. 18, 1915

ROBERTS

William Roberts
Oct. 21, 1838
Apr. 19, 1907

DUGGAN

Mother
At Rest
Grace E. Duggan
Feb. 11, 1903
Mar. 25, 1936
Asleep in Jesus.

CASEEY

John Caseey
Died May 17, 1936
Aged 57 years.

(Note: The above possibly
should be spelled CASSEY, but
have listed name as it appeared
on tombstone. John Caseey's
wife, Collie, died about 1927,
age about 43 years, and is
buried on the South side of
her husband. LMcC.)

WALKER

Sarah E. Walker
June 22, 1850
Mar. 16, 1928
At Rest.

G. W. Walker
June 15, 1836
Oct. 4, 1900
In Heaven we hope to
meet him.

(Note: At side of above is
grave of Jack Ellis, aged 80,
died 1927. LMcC.)

ROBERSON

Mrs. Martha Ann Roberson
Died May 7, 1939
Aged 29 years, 9 months & 2 days.

ELEAZER CAMP GROUND M. E. CHURCH CEMETERY

ROBERTS

Nellie Roberts
Died June 4, 1939
Aged 42 years 4 months
& 5 days.

(Note: At the South side
of Nellie Robert's grave
Teddia, the wife of James
Roberts, is buried. LMcC)

HAMILTON

Lizzie Collake
Wife of
H. T. Hamilton
May 31, 1886
Nov. 19, 1928
Gone but not forgotten.

RICHESON

Mrs. J. B. Richeson
Died April 23, 1926
Aged 22 years, 10 months
& 20 days.

GRAVES

Nannie Graves
Sept. 14, 1925
Feb. 1, 1926
Our darling.

MUELLER OR MILLER

(Note: As the following two
inscriptions indicate this
name was spelled Mueller. It
is, however, spelled Miller by all
descendants of Theodore Charles &
Easter Mueller. Two of the above
sons, Charles Williams and Lewis
E., were doctors and Enos C. was
Representative of Monroe County
LMcC.)

Dr. Theodore Charles Mueller
Born Jan. 9, 1810
At Darmstadt Grand
Duchey of Hessid in Rhine
Germany Europe.
Died Jan. 5, 1885

Easter
Wife of
T. C. Mueller
Mar. 26, 1825
Dec. 23, 1906

To the Memory of
Charles Williams Miller
July 23, 1856
May 27, 1899
One precious to our
heart has gone. The voice
we loved is stilled. The
place made vacant in our
home can never more be filled.
Our father in his wisdom
Called the boon his love had
given and though on earth
the body lies, the soul
is safe in Heaven.

(Note: The above 3 graves are
enclosed in an iron fence.
The following are at different
locations in the cemetery but
are graves of same family. LMcC.)

Arlie Miller
Feb. 7, 1880
Nov. 16, 1908

F. A. Miller
June 2, 1851
Jan. 3, 1911
In Heaven we hope to meet him.

Bob Miller
May 5, 1883
May 11, 1912
Gone to rest.

(W.O.W. Memorial)
Grover C. Miller
Feb. 7, 1890
Aug. 17, 1912
Farewell father & mother
Meet me in Heaven.

Mary J.
Wife of
J. E. Miller
Sept. 10, 1855
Jan. 18, 1897

ELEAZER CAMP GROUND M. E. CHURCH CEMETERY

W. C. Miller
Died Nov. 10, 1935
Aged 78 years.

1 Field stone.

Dr. L. E. Miller
Jan. 25, 1827
Aug. 19, 1902
Gone but not forgotten.

1 Grave North of above.

Vira
Daughter of
W. L. & Lula Miller
Jan. 6, 1909
Apr. 9, 1910
From mothers arms to the
arms of Jesus.

(Note: The following are
Negro graves in the Negro
section of the cemetery.
LMcC.)

CARDEN

Esau Carden
May 2, 1860
Nov. 27, 1893
Gone but not forgotten.

MCDERMOTT

George P. McDermott
Oct. 17, 1875
Nov. 12, 1908
Gone but not forgotten.

MCDURMOTT

W. R. McDurmott
Feb. 13, 1906
Nov. 29, 1920

(Note: The Negro Section
is badly grown up with
briars. There are many more
members of above families
and also members of the Boyd
and other families buried
here. The Rev. Jessee Boyd
and the Rev. Johnnie McDermott, Negro preachers, are
buried here without markers.
The Negro section covers
the low ground in the cemetery and possibly there are
50 or more unmarked Negro
graves. LMcC.)

ELEAZER CAMP GROUND M. E. CHURCH CEMETERY

ELEAZER CAMP GROUND M. E. CHURCH SKETCH

The Rev. Wm. G. Brownlow was pastor of the Tellico Plains
Circuit, of the Methodist Church one year 1830-1831. The
Circuit included the newly established Eleazer Camp Ground
M. E. Church South. The only story told of disturbance of
worship in those early days was once when Brother Brownlow
was preaching. He stopped long enough to find the offender
and deal with him according to the name he gained for himself
and then returned to his sermon. The Rev. W. H. H. Duggan,
another pioneer Methodist Circuit rider, was a member of
Eleazer Camp Ground Methodist Church. When the break in
Methodism came in 1842, he being a union sympathizer, withdrew
in to M. E. membership, the Eleazer Church chaning into the
Southern Methodist body. Two log buildings were originally
erected on the above site, church and school. The Rev. W. W.
Byott, the Rev. Thomas, the Rev. Joseph Wiggins, and the Rev.
Hasten Caste were some of the pastors of the log church. The
arbor was built on the log church prior to 1861. About 1865-
1870 the log building was replaced by the frame building that
burned Sunday March 26, 1933. The church and arbor were
replaced as much like the old ones as possible. The Rev.
Coleman Campbell was probably the pastor at that time.
Sampson Holcomb was the head carpenter, assisted by Crawford
Collaque, Joseph Marr, and others. The Trustees were: Dr.
Louis Miller, James A. Dyer (both local preachers), G. A.
Spillman, Joseph Boyd, and Richard Marshall. About five and
one half acres were deeded to them by Col. Joseph Boyd, Sept.
4, 1871 but the deed has been lost. The trustees disagreed
on the length of the building, and so when the sills had been
laid, some men came one night and sawed off ten feet, making
the ten feet shorter than originally planned. Once when the
Rev. J. C. Harris was preaching to a crowded congregation he
said that the foundation was laid ten feet long, but the devil
cut off the sills. Eleazer became an important gathering
place for camp meetings. Camp cabins were built around the
church on three sides and people gathered annually for many
years. It is estimated that four thousand people have been
there on one camp meeting Sunday. In the early days they came
in wagons drawn by oxen, cooked on one common fire and slept
in the camps. The preachers camped in the church. The Rev.
Uriah Payne from McMinn always came and camped in the school.
Camps were owned by Col. Joseph Boyd, Joseph Marr, G. A.
Spillman, Landerman Cardin, John Burger, Benj. Ellis, Wm.
Richeson, James McConkey, Larkin Cardin and others. The camp
meetings were both international and interracial. The colored
people not only attended camp meetings, but many were members
of the church. As above stated the church was established in
1830-1831 with Wm. G. Brownlow as 1st pastor and for both church
and school as well as the cemetery given by Col. Joseph Boyd.

TOMBSTONE INSCRIPTIONS

FORKNERS CHAPEL SOUTHERN M. E. CHURCH CEMETERY

Copied by: Lawrence McConkey, Englewood, Tennessee
Date: Feb. 23 & 29, 1940

The Forkners Chapel Southern Methodist Church and Cemetery are
located, 7 miles North of Madisonville and 3½ miles Southeast of
Sweetwater in the Fork Creek Community. To reach the cemetery
take the highway from Madisonville to Sweetwater and turn right
at Howards Springs onto road leading to Vonore, go to the
Forkner farm now owned by Joseph Frank Forkner and take the road
to the left and follow for about one mile then turn right.
Cemetery is along this road about ⅛ mile distance. There are 6
graves with inscriptions; 18 marked by field stones and 20 without
markers. The church was established about close of Civil War on
¼ acre of land given by Thomas Forkner. At first a large shed
was built but about 1870 a church building was placed on the property. Lawrence and Thomas Forkner were main contributors. Before
this church was established, there was a school house on the
Lawrence Forkner Sr., farm, that was used as a community church.
The following preachers are buried here: The Rev. Samuel Edward
Hope, the Rev. John Bradshaw. Two Confederate Soldiers are buried
here: Thomas Robinson and ----- Bradshaw.

HARPER

Fred M. Harper
Died Oct. 18, 1931
Aged 1 year, 3 months
& 17 days.

Infant's grave with stone
at North of above.

BRADSHAW

J. R. Bradshaw
Oct. 25, 1876
Sept. 8, 1935

SELVIDGE

John William
Son of
H. G. Selvidge & wife
Apr. 17, 1908
Aug. 6, 1910
Budded on earth to
bloom in Heaven.

Anna Lee Selvidge
Died Dec. 17, 1926
Aged 17 years 11 months
& 7 days.

(Note: Next grave North has
an Odd Fellow Lodge marker
but no inscription. Also
another grave North of this
one. LMcC.)

Alice Marie
Daughter of
T. J. Selvidge & wife
Apr. 7, 1908
Oct. 7, 1909

Infant
Daughter of
T. J. Selvidge & wife
May 21, 1894

J. W. Selvidge
Died July 10, 1895
Aged 68 years.

FORKNERS CHAPEL SOUTHERN M. E. CHURCH CEMETERY

M. J. Selvidge
Wife of
J. W. Selvidge
Died Sept. 7, 1900
Aged 71 years
Gone but not forgotten.

MCGHA OR MCGAHA

R. M. McGha
1877 - 1929
At Rest.

Marren
Son of
Mr. & Mrs. W. R. McGaha
June 18, 1924
Jan. 3, 1926

(Note: There was one field
stone South of R. M. McGha
also above mane Marren is
as on stone. LMcC.)

BLACK

James M. Black
Died Nov. 7, 1900
Aged 84 years

Mary P. Black
Died March 26, 1898
Aged 80 years.

Two field stones North
of above.

STONE

Clark W. Stone
Jan. 30, 1830
Mar. 27, 1901
At Rest.

Sarah D.
Wife of
Clark W. Stone
Born March 13, 1834
Married
March 4, 1855
Died March 23, 1908
At Rest.

(Note: 1 grave between above
and following. ------ also
Stone and Stephens may be
related. LMcC.)

STEPHENS

Samp A. Stephens
Died Nov. 29, 1923
Aged 68 years & 10 months

IRONS

Infant
Son of
F. M. & A. J. Irons
(No date)
Budded on earth to
bloom in Heaven.

Julia Ann Irons
Died Sept. 22, 1908
Aged 16 years.
Resting in the hope
of a glorious resurrection.

(Note: Three graves at head
of above three. They maybe
of same family.)

CLARK

Cornelia Thomas
Wife of
J. F. Clark
Born Dec. 25, 1880
Died May 5, 1908
Gone but not forgotten.

Two field stones North
of above.

James F. Clark
Died May 11, 1911
Aged 32 years
Gone but not forgotten.

BLAIR

Joseph Blair
Died May 28, 1933
Aged 80 years.

FORKNERS CHAPEL SOUTHERN M. E. CHURCH CEMETERY

Sarrah Blair
1829 - 1910

Gilford Blair
1828 - 1913

MCCROSKEY

Marry E. McCroskey
Sept. 11, 1898
June 30, 1926

THOMAS

(W.O.W. Memorial)
William Clarence Thomas
Apr. 25, 1884
Oct. 28, 1915

Earl Thomas
Oct. 7, 1906
Dec. 25, 1923

ROLEN

Dora Bell Rolen
Died March 21, 1933
Aged 16 yrs. & 9 months

(Note: 1 grave between above
and following. Rolen &
Wilford families maybe related
LMcC.)

WILFORD

J. Hugh Wilford
Died Aug. 27, 1923
Aged 64 years, 9 months
& 11 days.

SMITH

Husband
At rest.
Olie Smith
May 23, 1886
Sept. 5, 1918
There is no parting
in Heaven.

2 graves North and 1 South
of above.

LEMONS

Blanche Delena Lemons
April 19, 1913
Nov. 29, 1916
In Heaven there is
one Angel more.

1 field stone

Elijah Lemons
Sept. 25, 1858
April 12, 1916
Gone but not forgotten.

Dewey Lemons
Jan. 3, 1904
Feb. 27, 1905
Asleep in Jesus.

Two unmarked graves.

STEPHENS & STONE

Callie Stone Stephens
Died Dec. 21, 1931
Aged 64 years.

James H. Stone
Died Aug. 25, 1935
Aged 75 yrs. 11 mos.
& 9 days.

HARLESS

Thomas Harless
Died Dec. 13, 1939
Aged 11 months & 19 days.

(Note: At South of Thomas
Harless is a marker at grave
of an infant with only "H"
on it. LMcC.)

VINCENT

FORKNERS CHAPEL SOUTHERN M. E. CHURCH CEMETERY

Josie Vincent
Died Sept. 15, 1937
Aged 61 years, 2 months
& 18 days.

WEBSTER & ERVIN

Our darling
Alice Louise
Daughter of
H. L. & Ada Webster
Jan. 12, 1916
Mar. 29, 1917
In Heaven.

(Note: The above and
following may not be
related but it seems
they are as the are
side by side and none
other close by. LMcC.)

Mrs. J. W. Ervin
Died Dec. 9, 1938
Aged 72 years.

HOPE

Rev. Samuel Edward Hope
Jan. 17, 1870
Nov. 5, 1918
The Lord is my shepherd
I shall not want.

Lydia F. Hope
Died ------------
Aged 59 years.

(Note: Above has an undertaker's paper marker - faded.
LMcC.)

HITSON

Rosie Lee Hitson
Aug. 3, 1918
Age 8 yrs.

Zelter
(No dates)

Nelter
(No dates)

1 unmarked grave North
of above.

BLAIR

Infant
Son of
O. P. Blair
Died May 23, 1929
13 days old.

ROBINSON

Frank Robinson
Died Dec. 21, 1928
Aged 81 years 2 months
& 19 days.

BLAIR

Mattie J. Blair
Died Dec. 16, 1935
Aged 80 years, 10 months
& 7 days.

Father
John R. Blair
March 28, 1856
Nov. 3, 1921

HOPE

(Note: The following Hopes
are descendants of the Rev.
Samuel Hope buried in another
location in this cemetery. LMcC.)

Samuel Hope
Died April 3, 1931
Aged 31 years.

Luther Cecil Hope
Died Oct. 28, 1939
Aged 19 years, 6 months
& 3 days.

Jack M. Hope
Died March 4, 1939
Aged 1 year, 9 month & 29 days.

FORKNERS CHAPEL SOUTHERN M. E. CHURCH CEMETERY

Samuel E. Hope
Died July 10, 1937
Aged 1 year, 5 months
& no days.

CLEMMER

Dorothy E.
Daughter of
Mr. & Mrs. Ben Clemmer
Nov. 9, 1922
Nov. 3, 1924

HICKS

Kate
Wife of
Mark Hicks
1884 - 1926
The rose may fade, the
lily die but flowers
immortal bloom on high.

FRIDLEY

Roseanna Fridley
Died Dec. 16, 1923
Aged 71 years, 1 month
and 0 days.

Benjamin L. Fridley
Jan. 14, 1931
Sept. 18, 1931

SMITH

Betty Jo Smith
1930 - 1930

THOMAS

David Thomas Jr.
Died Sept. 24, 1939
Aged 0 days.

STEPHENS

Florence
Daughter of
S. H. & J. L. Stephens
March 16, 1913
March 19, 1913

LANCE

Mr. ------ Lance
Died June 23, 1933
Aged ----------.

(Note: Above inscription on
a paper marker did not have
given name or age, but very
likely he was husband of
lady buried by his side as
follows.   LMcC.)

Sarah Lance
Died April 4, 1932
Aged 71 years.

(Note: 4 infants graves South
possibly grandchildren of above.
LMcC.)

THOMAS

William G. Thomas
   Oct. 4, 1906
   Aug. 9, 1925

Infant
Son of
Mr. & Mrs. G. W. Thomas
Nov. 8, 1919

Mattie
Daughter of
Mr. & Mrs. G. W. Thomas
Feb. 28, 1915
Mar. 9, 1915

Blanche Lee
Daughter of
Willie & Mattie Thomas
March 22, 1921
Dec. 20, 1922

HICKS

Stephen F. Hicks
March 11, 1900
May 11, 1920

N. J. Hicks
Dec. 25, 1856
(Death date not given)

FORKNERS CHAPEL SOUTHERN M. E. CHURCH CEMETERY

M. A. Hicks
June 5, 1856
March 28, 1913

MASSENGILL

Lena Massengill
Died June 13, 1930
Aged 33 years, 1 month
& 23 days.

JENKINS

Anna Mae
Daughter of
Mr. & Mrs. P. C. Jenkins
Jan. 11, 1915
Apr. 18, 1916
Asleep in Jesus.

TOMBSTONE INSCRIPTIONS

LAWRENCE FORKNER FAMILY CEMETERY

Copied by: Lawrence McConkey, Englewood, Tennessee
Date: Feb. 29, 1940

The Lawrence Forkner Family Cemetery is 6 miles North of
Madisonville or about 5 miles Southeast of Sweetwater. To be
reached from either Sweetwater of Madisonville go on the highway
between them to Howards Springs, then on to the Rookville road
to the farm now owned by Joseph Frank Forkner where the cemetery
consisting of about ¾ acre is located. The cemetery was established on the farm of Lawrence Forkner, Sr., in 1856 as a family
cemetery. There are others who are buried there but none of
them has a tombstone, except Nancy A. Lowry and Wm. H. Fridley.
Probably none other of the non-relatives will have tombstones.
No one has been buried here for about 30 years and not likely
will be. There are 15 inscriptions; 20 graves marked with field
stones and about 20 unmarked graves. The unmarked graves are not
all graves of the Forkner family. These graves, however, will
probably never be marked and the cemetery has been listed as the
Forkner Family Cemetery.

FORKNER & NICHOLDS

E. I.
Daughter of
D. P. & R. Forkner
Jan. 8, 1853
Nov. 22, 1857

3 field stones South
of above.

J. Forkner
Sept. 4, 1854
Sept. 18, 1857

M. F. Forkner
Aug. 2, 1856
Aug. 11, 1856

M. A. W. Forkner
June 24, 1857
July 14, 1859

T. A. Forkner
Mar. 5, 1859
July 18, 1860

1 field stone North
of above.

Jestuana
Wife of
Lawrence Forkner
Died May 20, 1879
Aged 75 years.

(Note: Her husband Lawrnece
Forkner who was born in 1804
died at the age of 84 years
is buried by her side without
inscribed marker. Also there
are one other grave South and
one North with inscriptions.
LMcC.)

Father
Lawrence Forkner
Feb. 7, 1839
Aug. 30, 1881

Mother
Clara N. Forkner
Sept. 8, 1845
Mar. 8, 1889

2 field stones.

LAWRENCE FORKNER FAMILY CEMETERY

Infant
of
J. & M. Forkner
May 10, 1856

4 field stones South
of above.

Josiah Forkner
June 14, 1856
Feb. 6, 1858

Julia A.
Wife of
Thomas Forkner
Born May 1829
married
Nov. 6, 1851
Died May 2, 1898
She is at Rest.

Thomas Forkner
July 2, 1830
Mar. 2, 1906
Asleep in Jesus.

Thomas J. Nicholds
Nov. 3, 1838
Nov. 28, 1858

LOWRY

Nancy A. F.
Daughter of
M. & Tho. Lowry
July 8, 1859
Aug. 6, 1860

(Note: The above no
relation to Forkners.
LMcC.)

2 field stones North
of above.

FRIDLEY

William H. Fridley
Son of
B. L. & Roas A. Fridley
July 25, 1896
Nov. 22, 1887

(Note: Above was not related
to the Forkner's. LMcC.)

(Note: Several members of
the Carroll family, also
buried here, are not re-
lated to Forkners. They
were neighbors. As others
buried who were not related.

LAWRENCE FORKNER FAMILY CEMETERY

LAWRENCE FORKNER FAMILY SKETCH

The Forkner family history is as follows: Lawrence Forkner
was born in North Carolina in 1804. His wife, Jestina (Jestuana)
Golden, was born in North Carolina in 1805. Eight children were
born to this union; one in North Carolina, the others in Tennessee. The family moved to Tennessee about 1830 or 1829 and
settled on Fork Creek in Monroe County. Lawrence Forkner was
probably the first to make the cradle with fingers used in cut-
ting wheat in this part of the country. He also operated a
factory and engaged in the manufacture of chewing tobacco. One
of the oldest churches in this part of the county was founded
on his property, adjoining the homestead, about the year 1840,
where until about the year 1862. Then his sons, Thomas and
Lawrence, led in erecting of a new building on the present site
of the Forkners Chapel Southern Methodist Church.

Lawrence Forkner lived to be 84 years old and his wife, Jestina
(Jestuana), died at the aged of 75 years. A list of their
children and grand-children follows: Their first child, Sarah
was born in N. C. in 1828. She married Pleas Davis. Two
children were born to Sarah and Pleas Davis, William and Hugh.
Sarah and Pleas moved to Texas soon after marriage. There
may have been more than the two mentioned children. Sometimes
between the birth of the first (Sarah) and the second (Thomas)
Lawrence and Jestuana moved from North Carolina to Monroe
County, Tennessee. Thomas their second child was born in 1831
according to the family but the tombstone inscription gives
July 3, 1830 as the date of his birth. He married Julia Ann
McGuire. Six children were born to this union, John, Lawrence,
Steve, James, Thomas, Nannie. Three are still living as follows,
Lawrence in Monroe County, Tennessee, Thomas, Colorado Springs,
Colo., Nannie, Chattanooga, Tennessee. John was residing in
Loudon County, Tennessee at time of his death. Steve before his
death lived in Monroe County. James, lived in State of Washing-
ton at his death. Thomas the father of the above children gave
the land for the Forkners Chapel Southern Methodist Church and
he and his brother Lawrence were the leaders in the erection of
the church. Thomas was Superintendent of the Sunday School
at the above church for forty years. Joseph the third child of
Lawrence & Jestuana was born in 1833. He married Minervia Haley.
Four children were born to this union as follows: Susie,
Lawrence, Thomas and John. Joseph was killed during the Civil
War while a soldier in the Federal Army. His children were
raised by his brother Thomas. Upon reaching maturity they moved
to West to the Indian Territory. Notherin is known of them now
but all are supposed to be dead. John the fourth child of
Lawrence & Jestuana was born in 1835. He married Bettie Nichols.
They had one child named Bettie. John was killed while serving
in the Federal Army during the Civil War. His widow and daughter
moved to Illinois. Bettie, the daughter married a man by the
name of Luracen. She is now dead. Lawrence the fifth child was

LAWRENCE FORKNER FAMILY CEMETERY

LAWRENCE FORKNER FAMILY SKETCH

born Feb. 7, 1839. He married Clara Johnston in 1865 of Monroe County. They were the parents of the following five children; Joseph, Franklin, Fred, Lela, William and Grace. He, the father of above children, was a soldier in the Federal army and a Methodist Minister. He died Aug. 30, 1881 at the old home place on Fork Creek in Monroe County, Tennessee. Three of his children are still living as follows: Franklin lives at the old old home place on Fork Creek, William lives at Sweetwater, Tenn., and Lela, who married Samuel Scott, lives at Tarrytown, New York. Fred or (Ferd) died in 1933 leaving a widow, Mrs. Eva Wilkerson Forkner. Grace, who married Oscar Bolton, died in 1920. Elizabeth, the sixth child was born in 1841. She married Jeff (Thomas J.) Nicholds. They were the parents of one child, a son, Joseph, when they moved to the Indian Territory about 1880. Not much is known about them since. Nancy the seventh child was born in 1844. She married Cap Parsley. They were the parents of four children as follows: Joseph or Joe, Lawrence, Lester, and Richard. Nancy and her husband moved West to the Indian Territory about 1880. All of their children are believed to be living with the exception of Joseph. (Note: Cap Parsley referred to, who married Nancy Forkner, was known to the Forkner family only as "Capp", so Cap does not seem to be a nick name.LMcC. James the eight child was born in 1848. He married Sally Orr. They were the parents of five children as follows: Joe or Joseph, John Jessie, Lizzie, Scruggs. He was a Baptist Minister. He and his family moved west to the Indian Territory about the year 1880. All his children are believed to be living at present, with the exception of Joe. The above list of eight are all the children of Lawrence and Jestuana Forkner were parents of. They owned a good farm on Fork Creek consisting of around five or six hundred acres. The old homestead is still owned by the Forkner Family. It is now owned by Joseph Frank Forkner. It has been owned by the Forkners for over one hundred years.

MONROE COUNTY

TOMBSTONE INSCRIPTIONS

GRAVES FAMILY CEMETERY

Copied by: Lawrence McConkey, Englewood, Tennessee.
Date: Jan. 1939.

The Graves Family Cemetery is located 19 miles South of
Madisonville on the farm of Mrs. Myrtle Q. Gowan. To reach
the cemetery from Madisonville take the Mt. Vernon road to
Jalapa, there take road leading toward Ivy.

There are 5 inscriptions and no unmarked graves.

GRAVES

J. L. Graves   B. C. Graves
1845 - 1934   1816- 1902
(Masonic member)
                                   STEPHENS

S. S. Graves
1854 - 1925   C. B. Stephens
                                   1820 - 1902

G. W. Graves
1825 - 1919
Masonic Member

FAMILY SKETCH

Benjamin Graves married Rachel Asher. They lived at New
River, Yancy Co., N. C. Their son, Solomon, married Nancy
Kinnick,; Polly married --- Braden; Betty married Mike Perkins;
William married --- McGinty; Millie never married but was the
mother of James, Alfred, Samuel, Harrison and a girl who
married ------- Thompson. Solomon and Nancy Graves were the
parents of: Granville, Eliza, Rachel, Sarah and John L.
Granville W., married Bethia C. Stephens; Eliza, married
Solomon Helton; Rachel married John Wickinson; Sarah married
James H. Bailey; John L. married Sarenne Tate. Granville W.
and Bethia C. Graves were the parents of Catherine who married
Dr. Grimshaw; Eliza & Solomon Helton were the parents of Mary,
Thomas and Nancy Jenny. Mary married --------; Thomas married
-------; Nancy Jenny never married. Rachel and John Wilkinson
were the parents of Sallie, Houston, Homer, Benjamin and Neoma.
Sallie married Hugh Smith; Souston married Perky Hampton; Homer
married Kattie Eubanks; Benjamin married Hannah Eubanks; Neoma
married Wm. Anderson. Sarah & James H. Bailey were the parents

GRAVES FAMILY CEMETERY

of Charles M., Walter R., Nancy O., George W., James M.,
Myrtle Q., and Minnie E. Charles M., married Martha Seaton;
Walter R., married Nellie Bell; Nancy O., never married;
George W., married Rachel Maloney; James M., never married;
Myrtle Q., married Robert Gowan; Minnie E., married Tilden
Joiner. John L. and Sarenne S. Graves never had any children.

MONROE COUNTY

TOMBSTONE INSCRIPTIONS

GRIFFITH CEMETERY

Copied by: Lawrence McConkey, Englewood, Tennessee
Date: Jan. 25, 1939

It is not known just when the Griffith Cemetery was
established. Years ago there was a Methodist Church not
far away called Center Methodist Church. The church also
owned a plot of land for a cemetery but it was never used.
Burials were made in the Griffith Cemetery.

This cemetery possibly was established before the Griffith
family owned the land or soon thereafter, although they came
to Monroe County early and either entered or bought a large
boundry of land where this cemetery is located. The Griffith
family were prominent in early days of the county. The
graveyard is 5 miles East of Madisonville on the road leading to Hopewell.

There are 31 inscriptions and possibly 75 or more unmarked
graves. Several Negroes are buried in this cemetery. Some
of them were slaves of the Griffith family.

GRIFFITH

William Griffith
Born Jan. 13, 1791
Died May 11, 1862

Sarah S. Griffith
Born Dec. 11, 1794
Died May 20, 1872

(Masonic member)
Elisha E. Griffith
Born Oct. 16, 1816
Died July 21, 1890
And though the body
moulders here, the Soul
is safe in Heaven.

Rebecca J.
Wife of
Elisha E. Griffith
Born Mar. 25, 1821
Died May 16, 1871
We trust our loss
and will be her gain and
that with Christ
she's gone to Reign.

Callie Griffith
Jan. 12, 1854
July 12, 1898

Sallie J. Griffith
Wife of
Smith Bayless
Oct. 1, 1861
June 11, 1912

Paulina Louise
Wife of
E. E. Griffith
Nov. 23, 1836
Oct. 5, 1914

Charles F.
Son of
J. L. & Cordie Griffith
June 30, 1908
Dec. 23, 1915

Brantly C.
Son of
R. L. & Detie Griffith
Dec. 15, 1898
Sept. 27, 1918

GRIFFITH CEMETERY

Infant
Son of
R. L. & Detie Griffith
Born & died
Oct. 27, 1909
Gone but not forgotten.

Ed Duncan
Son of
R. L. & Detie Griffith
May 28, 1894
Jan. 27, 1908
Not lost blest thought
But gone before where
we shall meet to part
no more.

Charles
Son of
Richard L. & Detie Griffith

Richard L. Griffith
1857 - 1923
At Rest.

Detie Griffith
Wife of
Richard L. Griffith
Died --------
Aged 55 years 4 months

Oliver Y. Griffith
Oct. 7, 1857
Nov. 1, 1897

Charles E. Griffith
Apr. 13, 1865
July 24, 1925

ROBINSON

Elisha Robinson
Ds. Oct. 1837
5

(Note: Suppose the 5 means
age. LMcC.)

ARK

Infant
of
John Ark

BURCHFIELD

J. M. Burchfield
Ds. May 16, 1869

Levind Burchfield
Feb. 18, 1816
Nov. 14, 1884

J. R. Burchfield
Mar. 17, 1819
Mar. 16, 1890

Evalener Burchfield
May   8, 1886
Aug. 12, 1887

WRIGHT

Elisha R. Wright
Oct. 5, 1831
June 18, 1832

MASON

Our Father
Rufus M. Mason
Feb. 10, 1823
Sept. 11, 1891
Age 68 years 7 months
& 1 day
At Rest.

A. W. Mason
July 20, 1851
Jan. 28, 1884

REED

Suson Adalin Reed
Bornd 1844

W. R.

(Note: Remainder chipped off.
LMcC.)

GRIFFITH CEMETERY

E. N. R.

(Note: The 2 inscript-
ions above and those
which follow may mark
Negro graves as it is
said the colored section
is on the lower end of
the cemetery. LMcC.)

M. U.
Nov. 22, 1908

J. H.
------ 1833

E. R. M.
------ 1841
------ 1867

MONROE COUNTY

TOMBSTONE INSCRIPTIONS

HALL CEMETERY

Copied by: Lawrence McConkey, Englewood, Tennessee
Date:

The Hall Cemetery is 2¼ miles North of Vonore on the farm of
J. D. Ramsey on the Little Tennessee river. The farm was formerly
owned by Judge John Blair and before that by the Hall family.
Wm. Hall entered 260 acres of land. It is not known when the
cemetery was established but there was a church at this place,
it seems, very soon after land in this section was entered. The
church, however, has been discontinued for about 75 years. There
have been several markers with inscriptions but they are weather
worn or gone now. There is one acre or more of this cemetery
which contains 3 readable inscriptions, 30 field stones, 6
inscriptions that have been destroyed and 60 or more unmarked
graves.

HALL

Wm. Hall

Ruth Sparks
Wife of
Wm. Hall

Bess Hall

(Note: The above was a
son of Wm. & Ruth Hall. LMcC.)

MONROE COUNTY

TOMBSTONE INSCRIPTIONS

WM. HAMBY FARM CEMETERY

Copied by: Lawrence McConkey, Englewood, Tennessee.
Date:

This cemetery was established on the Secrecy farm, but is now
owned by Wm. Hamby. It is located about 20 miles South of
Madisonville, at Ivy. Only field rocks mark the graves and
there are three or more graves without any markers at all.

SMITH

George Smith

Sarah Smith
Wife of
George Smith

WILLIAMS

Mrs. Betty Williams

(Note: Her son, Alexander,
also his son, Nelse R.,
have served as Esquire in
McMinn County. LMcC.)

SECRECY

Senia Secrecy

Elisha Secrecy

Mary
Wife of
Elisha Secrecy

Baby
Secrecy

MONROE COUNTY

TOMBSTONE INSCRIPTIONS

HAWKINS CEMETERY

Copied by: Lawrence McConkey, Englewood, Tennessee.
Date:

The Hawkins Cemetery was established in 1850, maybe earlier,
on the Hawkins farm or possibly on land of Allen D. Gentry.
Allen D. Gentry, who is buried here, entered and acquired
several hundred acres of land along the Tellico River. He
was a Justice of the Peace for several terms, being a Justice
at the time of his death. The cemetery is on the property of
Ruth Hammontree and Rebecca Hawkins, about 13 miles East of
Madisonville, It may be reached by following the Povo Road
to road on West side of the Tellico River and there turning
down the river road. There are 18 inscriptions and possibly
fifty unmarked graves.

Mary Henry
Dec. 5, 1854
July 6, 1906
No, pain no griev no
anxious fear, can
reach our loved one
sleeping here.

------- Henry
Born (Unreadable)
Died (Unreadable)

GENTRY

Mary Gentry
Aug. 15, 1845
Aug. 1, 1883
May thy rest be sweet
until he bids thee
rise.

Nancy
Wife of
Allen D. Gentry
(No dates)

Allen D. Gentry
(No dates)

Pleas Gentry

Catherine E.
Wife of
James Gentry
Oct. 3, 1817
June 4, 1885
In God I Trust.

James Gentry.

WHITE

Margaret White
Oct. 30, 1845
Jan. 24, 1887
Sleep on blest saint
Until thy Savior bids
thee rise.

W. B. White
Mar. 5, 1842
July 22, 1908
In God I Trust.

Betsyan White
Died Feb. 4, 1852
(Note: The above was the wife
of James B. White. Death
date unreadable. L^{M}cC.)

2

HAWKINS CEMETERY

James B. White
Died Sept. 25, 1853
Age 77 years.

A. I. White
May 5, 1876
May 7, 1896
Do your work early,
life may not reach its
noon or setting sun.
No one can do the
work you leave undone.

HAWKINS

J. N. Hawkins
June 4, 1857
April 25, 1896

Joshua Hawkins

Polly
Wife of
E. C. Hawkins

E. C. Hawkins

Nancy Hawkins

MONROE COUNTY

DANIEL HEISKELL FAMILY CEMETERY

Copied by Lawrence McConkey, Englewood, Tennessee
Date: August 30-31, 1939

The family graveyard of Daniel Heiskell, a pioneer citizen
of Monroe County, Tennessee, and his descendants, is located
at the family homestead about a half mile East of Sweetwater
where the founder of this family originally settled where
he moved to Monroe County from upper East Tennessee. The
present owner is Bruner Axley.

Eight marked graves are found in the graveyard, and it is
possible that some of the slaves who belonged to the
Heiskell family prior to the Civil War are also inferred
here in the upper right hand corner.

For a history of this branch of the Heiskell family see
"History of the Sweetwater Valley by W. B. Lenoir, pages
159-175.

MONROE COUNTY

DANIEL HEISKELL FAMILY CEMETERY
TOMBSTONE INSCRIPTIONS

HEISKELL

Daniel Heiskell
March 7, 1799
Departed this life
July 22, 1875

Elizabeth Heiskell
Wife of
Daniel Heiskell
Died First of August 1841
Aged 37 years

Mary
Wife of
Daniel Heiskell
Born Jan. 1, 1819
Died June 4, 1888

GUINN

To my sister
Emily L. Guinn
Born Feb. 3, 1804
Died June 30, 1873

(Note: She was a cousin of
Daniel Heiskell and died
with cholera.)

HARRIS

Mrs. Sarah Harris
Born Oct. 1794
Died Dec. 11, 1885

(Note: She was related to
Daniel Heiskell, but the
relationship not known.)

SHRYOCK

Henry S. Shryock

(Note: The name Henry S. Shryock
was on the base of a monument, and
from indications the marker of
Emily L. Guinn that was not on a
base but iron rods in bottom
notched holes in the base of
where Shryock name was. Must
have been same marker.

SHELDON

James J. Sheldon
July, 1, 1829
Jan. 18, 1868

Mollie E. Sheldon
Jan. 20, 1856
Oct. 20, 1868

(Note: The two above were not
related to the Heiskell family
but neighbors and friends.)

MONROE COUNTY

TOMBSTONE INSCRIPTIONS

SAMUEL HENDERSON FAMILY CEMETERY

Copied by: Lawrence McConkey, Englewood, Tennessee
Date: Feb. 1, 1939.

The Samuel Henderson Family Cemetery is on the farm of Mrs.
Robert Burchfield, R. D. F. No. 4, Madisonville, Tennessee.
This is the old Henderson farm and is located about 3 miles
East of Madisonville, just off the road leading to Hopewell
Springs. There are 23 inscriptions and no unmarked graves.

HENDERSON

Samuel Henderson
Feb. 4, 1786
March 8, 1867

Nancy
Consort of
Samuel Henderson
Feb. 11, 1788
Sept. 2, 1866

Nannie C.
Daughter of
Samuel & Nancy Henderson
Feb. 19, 1830
Oct. 1, 1858

Martha E.
Daughter of
Samuel & Nancy Henderson
June 25, 1812
Dec. 19, 1873

Mary E.
Daughter of
Wm. & Amanda Henderson
Feb. 16, 1856
Nov. 22, 1858

William Henderson
Dec. 3, 1807
Aug. 8, 1859

Amanda L.
Wife of
Wm. Henderson
Mar. 30, 1912
July 30, 1876

Hattie A.
Wife of
Sam'l L. Henderson
May 20, 1842
Aug. 10, 1864

Oliver C. Henderson
July 14, 1828
Nov. 30, 1897

Margaret R. Henderson
Apr. 23, 1838
June 22, 1910
In memory of our
Father and Mother.
Blessed are the dead
which die in the Lord.

Frank C. Henderson
Sept. 16, 1862
Aug. 15, 1878

Sallie M. Henderson
Mar. 25, 1858
July 5, 1878

Joseph L. Henderson
Died Feb. 24, 1936
Aged 68 years.

2

SAMUEL HENDERSON FAMILY CEMETERY

Hugh K. Henderson

Eliza Castleberry
Wife of
Hugh K. Henderson

Herman Henderson
July 20, 1896
July 3, 1906

Sadie Henderson
Feb. 10, 1886
Aug. 14, 1905
Gone to rest.

Infant
Daughter of
G. L. & Carrie Henderson

Mary F.
Daughter of
S. P. & Sarah B. Henderson
July 11, 1854
March 31, 1865

Mattie E.
Daughter of
S. P. & Sarah B. Henderson
June 22, 1857
March 13, 1865

(Masonic Member)
S. P. Henderson
March 22, 1822
Feb. 22, 1865
At Rest.

George Lawrence Henderson
June 11, 1826
Sept. 17, 1916

Addie Kimbrough
Wife of
Lawrence Henderson
later
Addie H. Ward
July 2, 1856
Apr. 20, 1934

MONROE COUNTY

TOMBSTONE INSCRIPTIONS

DESCENDANTS OF COL. DAVID HENLEY CEMETERY

Copied by: Lawrence McConkey, Englewood, Tennessee
Date:

The Henley Cemetery was established on the Henley Plantation
on the Tennessee River but it is now known as the Bacon
Cemetery. The farm is owned by Mrs. James L. Bacon. It has
never been owned by anyone except the Henley family or their
descendants. It is located about 22 miles Northeast of Madisonville. To reach the cemetery go via highway to Knoxville, after
crossing Niles Ferry take the road up the Tennessee river to
Bacons Ferry. There are 3 unmarked graves.

HENLEY

Arthur H. Henley Sr.
Born Nov. 15, 1783
Died Feby 22, 1849
His part in advice to
his children,
Be virtious that you
may be happy.

Ann E. Henley
Wife of
A. H. Henley Sr.
Born --- 1860
Died Feb. 27, 1860

1st. Lt.
Arthur H. Henley
Co. E.
5 Tenn. Cav.
C. S. A.

Also a marker placed by the
Daughters of the Confederacy.)

Mother
Kittie Jones Henley
Nov. 13, 1841
Dec. 20, 1931

Father
Charles Fairfax Henley
Dec. 10, 1842
Mar. 30, 1926
2nd Lieut. Co. F.
26th Tenn. Reg.
C. S. A.

Also a marker placed by the
Daughters of the Confederacy.

BACON

Nona E. Bacon
May 4, 1883
Aug. 4, 1918

James L. Bacon
Sept. 7, 1847
Jan. 6, 1917
Father

Rosa H. Bacon
Dec. 9, 1880
June 1, 1906

Nathaniel L. Bacon
Nov. 16, 1885
Sept. 29, 1904

WILSON

Lena Moore Henley
Wife of
John Clinton Wilson
Nov. 4, 1883
Nov. 29, 1937

PARSHALL

John R. Parshall M. D.
Born 1827
June 17, 1854

DESCENDANTS OF COL. DAVID HENLEY CEMETERY

Ann E. Parshall
Sept. 6, 1829
July 27, 1896

MCGHEE

Elizabeth M. McGhee
January 26, 1819
August 23, 1844

Our Little Robert.

(Note: The grave of the
above named child is
at the head of Elizabeth
M. McGhee's grave and is
the nearest grave to it.
LMcC.)

COL. DAVID HENLEY FAMILY SKETCH

Col. David Henley of Georgetown, Mass., was a descendant of
King Egbert, the first king of England. The Henley's of the
early pioneer days of Knox, Blount and Monroe Counties were
very outstanding. Arthur H. Henley Sr., son of Col. David
Henley, married Ann Evelyn Moore. Their daughter, Ann,
married John Ross Parshall. He died and she married James
Lydall Bacon. The Bacons were related to General Robert E. Lee.
Elizabeth M. Henley married Barcley McGhee. She died and he
married her sister, Mary K. Barcley McGhee was a son of
John & Betsy McGhee. John McGhee owned approximately 78,000
acres of land in Western North Carolina and East Tennessee.
Charles Henley married Kittie, daughter of Joshua and Aphelia
Jones, of South Carolina.

TOMBSTONE INSCRIPTIONS

HIWASSEE HOLINESS CHURCH CEMETERY

Copied by: Lawrence McConkey, Englewood, Tennessee
Date: Feb. 16, 1940

The Hiwassee Holiness Church and Cemetery are located about 5 miles North of Madisonville and about 1 mile North of Hiwassee College. The church was established about 1918 on land given by Wm. Worthy.

The first burial that of Elisha T. Clowers, was December 26, 1937. Vester Green gave 1 acre of land for the cemetery. It is fenced and is in excellent condition and has a beautiful location. There are 6 inscriptions and no unmarked graves.

CLOWERS

Clowers
Elisha T.
Nov. 28, 1886
Dec. 26, 1937

Polly Green
Mar. 23, 1885
(Living)
Asleep in Jesus.

MOSER

Our darling
Wanda Christine Moser
May 9, 1938
June 19, 1938

Chas. Ivan Moser
Died Aug. 12, 1938
Aged 1 year 2 months & 15 days.

MORGAN

Roy Lester Morgan
Died Feb. 20, 1938
Aged 1 mo. 27 days.

DOCKERY

Mary Dockery
Died Feb. 14, 1938
Aged 21 years 10 months
& 23 days.

MONROE COUNTY

TOMBSTONE INSCRIPTIONS

GEORGE S. HOWARD FAMILY CEMETERY

Copied by: Lawrence McConkey, Englewood, Tennessee
Date:

T

The George S. Howard Family Cemetery is located about 18 miles
Northeast of Madisonville. The best route is the Niles Ferry
road. Do not cross the Tennessee river but take the Citico
road to the farm of Doctor Sharp. There are 8 inscriptions
and 2 unmarked graves in the cemetery.

HOWARD

Mother
Mattie A. Donohoo
Wife of
Geo. S. Howard
Jan. 9, 1849
Nov. 3, 1927
A tender and loving Mother
In after time we'll
meet her.

In memory of
George S. Howard
Born Jan. 22, 1848
Died Jan. 17, 1894
A precious one from us
has gone. A voice we
loved is stilled. A
place is vacant in our
home which never can be
filled. God in his wisdom
has recalled the boon his
loved had given, and though
the body slumbers now, his
soul is safe in Heaven.

Thomas C.
Son of
G. S. & M. A. Howard
Nov. 27, 1878
Mar. 17, 1902
His troubles are over.

Henry J. Howard
Born Jany 27, 1872
Died April 9, 1898
Weep not his is at rest.

Earnest G. Howard
Born Mar. 26, 1878
Died April 9, 1898
He was the sunshine of our home.

MOSER

Sallie S. Moser
Daughter of
G. S. & M. A. Howard
Sept. 17, 1882
Apr. 15, 1902
Asleep in Jesus.

Oscar J. Moser
Son of
J. B. & Sallie Moser
Dec. 17, 1901
Jan. 18, 1903
Budded on earth bloom in Heaven.

HITCH

Roy R.
Son of
A. L. & P. L. Hitch
Feb. 6, 1901
June 18, 1901
Only sleeping

2

GEORGE S. HOWARD FAMILY CEMETERY

GEORGE S. HOWARD FAMILY SKETCH

George S. Howard married Mattie A. Donohoo. They were the parents of: Thomas C., who married Alva, daughter of John B. and Sarah McGhee. They were the parents of Alliene born in 1897 and Irene born in 1895. She married Chas. Ray. Sallie S., married J. B., son of J. B. & Martha Moser. P. L. married A. L. Hitch. Henry J., never married; Earnost G., never married and George, married -----.

TOMBSTONE INSCRIPTIONS

HOYL CEMETERY

Copied by: Lawrence McConkey, Englewood, Tennessee.
Date: Nov. 1938.

John B. Hoyle and wife, Elizabeth, owned a farm. When they
died they were buried on their farm. John B. Hoyl was probably
the son of Thomas Hoyl. No dates or ages are given on the markers
of John B. & Elizabeth Hoyl. It is believed they were about
65 or 70 years of age and that they died about 1860. There are
only the two graves here. The cemetery is located 8 miles
Southeast of Athens, just below Piney Grove School and near
Longs Mill. It is on the farm of Walter Long.

HOYL

John B. Hoyl   Elizabeth Hoyl

MONROE COUNTY

PEYTON HUTSON FAMILY CEMETERY

Copied by Lawrence McConkey, Englewood, Tennessee
Date: August 23, 1939

The Peyton Hutson Family Cemetery is located on land
originally entered by Peyton Hutson, approximately one
and onehalf miles south of Madisonville.

Peyton Hutson and wife, Temperance, migrated from Virginia
to Tennessee, being among the first people to come to this
part of Monroe County. Nothing is known of their children
but there was a family of Hudson in the Rockville community
early. Although the name is spelled differently, it is
believed that the families are the same. Both have been
prominent in Monroe County.

Apparently there is but one unmarked grave. The graves are
along an old fence row, at a cedar tree and covered with
vines.

MONROE COUNTY

TOMBSTONE INSCRIPTIONS
PEYTON HUTSON FAMILY CEMETERY

HUTSON

Temperance Hutson
Was born Oct. the 4th. 1774
Died August the 2nd. 1850

Peyton Hutson

P. & T. Hutson

Note: Peyton Hutson it is
said died shortly after the
death of his wife. Also their
Child. It seems from the
sunken condition of the grave
to have been grown or about
grown.

DESCENDANTS OF JOSHUA JONES CEMETERY

Copied by: Lawrence McConkey, Englewood, Tennessee
Date:

The Descendants of Joshua Jones Cemetery is located about
22 miles North of Madisonville. To reach it take the road
leading to Knoxville. At Niles Ferry instead of crossing
the Tennessee river, turn up the river road known as the
Citico road, and go to the Jones farm near the Bacon Ferry.
The farm is now owned by J. P. Nance. There are 8 inscriptions and 3 unmarked graves.

Joshua and Aphelia Jones lived in South Carolina and never
moved to Tennessee. They were the parents of Thomas C.,
Joshua R., Charles C., O. L., William, John, Barrett, Sarah
and Kittie. Charles C. married Margaret McGhee and Joshua R.
married Lavenia McGhee. Margaret and Lavenia were daughters
of Barcley and Mary K. Henley McGhee. Kittie married Charles
Fairfax Henley. The McGhee's and Henley's were very wealthy
and prominent people of Monroe Co.

JONES

Thomas Jones
Co. F.
2 S. C. Inf.
(Also a Daughters of
the Confederacy marker
to above.)

At Rest.
J. R. Jones
Sept. 10, 1850
July 7, 1921

O. L. Jones
July 26, 1868
Sept. 8, 1906
At Rest.

In memory of
Charles C. Jones
Born Oct. 9, 1839
Died Sept. 18, 1900

Margaret McGhee Jones
Dec. 5, 1849
Apr. 25, 1925
Blessed are the pure
in heart for they shall
see God.

Helen Rollins
Daughter of
Moultrie & Sarah Jones
May 13, 1911
Nov. 23, 1913

Charles Jones Jr.
Died About 1928
Aged about 22 years.

John Wright

(Note: John Wright was not
related to the Jones family.
LMcC.)

Copied by: Lawrence McConkey, Englewood, Tennessee.
Date: Feb. 1, 1939.

The first Kimbrough to come to this country in colonial days
was John Kimbrough, of Irish descent.

The next record concerns Bradley Kimbrough Sr., who married
Sarah Thompson, a daughter of a wealthy planter of South
Carolina. Their third son, Duke, was born in Rowan Co.,
North Carolina Nov. 19, 1762.

At the age of 21 years he came to what is now Jefferson Co.
Tenn. He married Mary Gentry, a daugher of Robert Gentry,
who lived near Dandridge. Gentry gave them a fine farm there,
where they lived for some time. Then bought a farm near Mossy
Creek (now Jefferson City).

To this union was born one child, Mary Kimbrough, who married
William Chilton. Duke Kimbrough's wife having died, he then
remarried. His second wife was Susan Hunter, daughter of
Isaac Hunter of Washington County, Tennessee. To this union
was born four sons, William, Isaac, John and Elisha. Duke's
second wife died and he remarried again. His third wife was
Eunice Carlock daughter of Christopher Carlock of near Dandridge.
To this union was 9 children, 6 sons, and 3 daughters. Bradley
and Robert G. Kimbrough were two of them. Duke Kimbrough became
a Baptist in spite of his inherited prejudices which were
strongly Episcopolian. Joined Baptist church that later became
Dandridge church but then known as "Koonts Meeting House" 3
miles Northeast of Dandridge. Was 25th name on the membership
roll. In July 1793 he was a leading member of the church.
Ordained Aug. fourth Saturday 1797 at same church. He was
pastor at that church from July 1799 to his death Sept. 21,
1849 - over 50 years. Practically, Rev. Duke Kimbrough was a
man of only two books - Bible and Hymn book. These he kept
with him and constantly used - to young ministers especially
he was living concordance to the Scriptures.

Duke Kimbrough's son, Isaac, married Mary Randolph a daughter of
James Randolph of Dandridge. He was born April 26, 1788. Duke's
son, Bradley, Married Martha H., a daughter of John J. Whitaker of
Mulberry, Lincoln County, Aug. 31, 1837. He was born Nov. 3, 1799.
In 1822 he began reading law with Jacob Peck, who was a State
Supreme Court Judge. In 1824 the Supreme Court, which sat at
Rogersville, gave him license to practice. He then located at

KIMBROUGH FAMILY CEMETERY

Madisonville, where he practiced as a leading attorney for
10 years. He was a Representative of Monroe County in the
State Legislature and as a member, he was appointed a member
of the State Convention which remodeled the State Constitution
in 1834. He refused to be a candidate for reelection the
following year but chose to be a minister of the Gospel. He
was ordained a minister by the Madisonville Baptist church
in 1835. He later moved to Mulberry, in Lincoln County. He
died on June 30, 1874. Robert G., another son of Duke Kimbrough
was born July 24, 1806. Tutored some at a Methodist College
at New Market. On Jan. 23, 1836 he married Lemira A., a
daughter of Thomas & Elizabeth Wheeler of Campbell County
near Jacksboro. Moved there and in 1844 moved to Knox County.
Died at his farm in Marshall County near Mars Hill, on July
22, 1879. Dukes son, William, married Elizabeth Molder (or
Mohler) of Jefferson County. They moved to Monroe County in
the early 1820's on a farm. They were the parents of eight
children. Isaac Barton and John Mohler were two of them.
William and Elizabeth both died before 1833 leaving several
of their children quite young. Isaac Barton was only 7 years
of age and there was one younger than he. Isaac Barton
Kimbrough a grandson of Duke, was born Feb. 10, 1826 near
Madisonville on July 29, 1847 at the age of twenty one, he
married Mary J. Henderson. He was also ordained a Baptist
Minister in Autumn of 1852 by Shady Grove Church. In 1875 he
moved to what is now Jefferson City and became financial agent
of Mossy Creek College or Carson College. In 1876 Carson
College in recognition of his ability and merit, conferred
upon him the honorary title, Doctor of Divinity. In 1879
he moved with his family to Texas settling in Collin County. ⋇
He is buried at Plano, Texas. John Mohler Kimbrough, a
grandson of Duke and a son of William, was born Dec. 10, 1813.
He married Mary E. Ragon. The cemetery in question is his
families. The Kimbrough family has been and still is one of
Monroe County's outstanding families. There were several
preachers and doctors of note among the Kimbrough family.
The Kimbrough family is related to several influential families.
Among them are the Cooke, Peck, Kefauver, Henderson, Reagon,
Cantrell and other notable families. The Kimbrough Cemetery
was established about 1820 on the Coldwell family farm, either
as a Coldwell family or as a neighborhood cemetery. There
have been many burials in this cemetery, but none have tombstones except the Kimbroughs'. That is why it is known as
the Kimbrough Cemetery. There are about 100 unmarked graves.
The cemetery is located 3 miles East of Madisonville, on the
old Henderson farm, on the road leading to Povo.

3

KIMBROUGH CEMETERY

KIMBROUGH

Spencer H.
Son of
J. C. & M. A. Kimbrough
Feb. 7, 1856
May 24, 1875

William H.
Son of
J. C. & M. A. Kimbrough
May 26, 1847
May 30, 1885

Spencer Coke Kimbrough
June 22, 1889
July 10, 1890
Asleep in Jesus.

Jacob Kimbrough

Son
of
Mr. & Mrs. Ragon Kimbrough

John Mohler Kimbrough
Dec. 10, 1813
Jan. 30, 1891
At Rest.

Mary E. Ragon
Wife of
John Mohler Kimbrough
Apr. 10, 1823
June 14, 1893
At Rest.

(Note: The following named
people are buried in this
cemetery although they do
not have inscriptions on
their markers. LMcC.)

WOLDRIDGE

Elam Woldridge

1st wife of
Elam Woldridge

Manerva
2nd Wife of
Elam Woldridge

Dr. Hoyt Woldridge

Stella
Daughter of
Dr. Hoyt Woldridge

MONROE COUNTY

LINDSEY FAMILY CEMETERY

Copied by: Lawrence McConkey, Englewood, Tennessee.
Date:

This is a family cemetery but some persons other than members
of the family are buried here. All those whose graves have
markers are related to the Lindsey's except the Franklins.
There are 40 inscriptions and 21 unmarked graves. Location
is about 12 miles East of Madisonville on the Povo Road at
Lindsey Bridge over Tellico river on the farm of John Bright.

David M. Lindsey married Elizabeth Lucas. They were both
Kentuckians but moved to Monroe County in their early life
and also in the early days of the county, secured land on the
Tellico River.

They were the parents of 10 children; John, Wm., Isaac, Harvey,
Alexander, Pierce, Alabama, Harriet, Mary and David. John
married Josie Tallent; William married --- Millsaps and later
---- Vaughn; Isaac, married Elisabeth Burchfield; Harvey, never
married; Alexander, married Rachel Barnett; Pierce, married
Jane Rains, and died in Elk City, Okla.; Alabama, never married;
Harriet, married Henry Harris; Mary, married Sam Yates and
David married Melvina Tate.

GOURLEY

Lee
Son of
J. H. & Sallie Gourley
Born Apr. 25, 1904
Died Aug. 7, 1911
Asleep in Jesus.

John H. Gourley
Oct. 5, 1858
Apr. 4, 1936
Gone but not forgotten.

YATES

Mary Yates
Apr. 1, 1847
Mar. 9, 1898

Sam Yates
Nov. 2, 1842
Oct. 8, 1892

Liddie Yates
Born 1888
Died 1899

Garmley Yates
Age 5

GENTRY

Margaret Gentry
1899

READMON

Elvira J. Readmon
Daughter of
I. Lindsey
Dec. 21, 1869
June 22, 1899

MOSER

J. E. Moser
Jan. 10, 1883
Mar. 2, 1883

Josie P. Moser
Feb. 24, 1865
Mar. 22, 1907

J. F. Moser
June 13, 1858
Apr. 4, 1917

Luther I. Moser
June 3, 1881
Feb. 17, 1911
At Rest.

LINDSEY FAMILY CEMETERY

Ethel Mae Moser
Jan. 6, 1910
Aug. 6, 1911
At Rest.

Jesse Moser
Feb. 11, 1908
Feb. 17, 1931

Ross Moser
1911 - 1919
Gone but not forgotten.

MAYNARD

Rachel E. Maynard
Dec. 28, 1840
Jan. 14, 1885
Death is only a dream.

JACOBS

J. S. Jacobs
Oct. 25, 1854
July 8, 1898

LINDSEY

M. L. Lindsey
Aug. 2, 1872
Feb. 25, 1902
Resting with God.

Adline Lindsey
Dec. 18, 1860
July 25, 1879
Wife

James Lindsey
July 15, 1857
Oct. 28, 1880

J. H. Lindsey
June 13, 1876
Dec. 4, 1886

Infant
Daughter of
J. E. & Gertie Lindsey
Born & died
Jan. 23, 1912
Gone but not forgotten.

Infant
of
J. E. & Gertie Lindsey

Harvey Lindsey

Father
Isaac Lindsey
Sept. 30, 1840
Oct. 20, 1916

Elizabeth
Wife of
Isaac Lindsey
Oct. 12, 1859
Apr. 29, 1915

John H.
Son of
I & E. Lindsey
Mar. 9, 1882
May 4, 1883

James I.
Son of
I. & E. Lindsey
Oct. 3, 1879
Nov. 9, 1881

S. E. Lindsey
Age 11 months & 8 days
1878

C. H. Lindsey
Age 7 months 13 days
1875

A. Lindsey
Apr. 21, 1863
Apr. 17, 1776

Elisabeth Lindsey
Feb. 1, 1825
Sep. 28, 1889

Davied M. Lindsey
July 14, 1814
Feb. 11, 1896

David Lindsey
Nov. 15, 1848
Feb. 13, 1910
Gone but not forgotten.

LINDSEY FAMILY CEMETERY

Melvina Tate
Wife of
David Lindsey

(Note: The above are the
graves of Rachel Barnett
Lindsey's parents. LMoC.)

Infant
of
David & Melvina Lindsey

FRANKLIN

BARNETT

Rev. Henry Franklin

Barnett

Mrs. Henry Franklin

Barnett

MONROE COUNTY

TOMBSTONE INSCRIPTIONS

LITTLE TOQUA BAPTIST CHURCH CEMETERY

Copied by: Lawrence McConkey, Englewood, Tennessee
Date: Nov. 18, 1938

The tombstone of R. Mills, who died Dec. 7, 1864, records the
earliest date of a death, and possibly the first burial in
Little Toqua Baptist Church Cemetery. This was a neighbor-
hood cemetery many years before the church was established.
It is located 18 miles Northeast of Madisonville. To reach
the cemetery take the Niles Ferry road to intersection of
Vonore - Ball Play road, then Ball Play road to beyond
Mt. Zion section, then turn left onto road leading toward
Bacons Ferry. There are 105 inscriptions and approximately
100 unmarked graves in Little Toqua Cemetery.

SPRADLIN

Janie
Wife of
P. L. Spradlin
Oct. 6, 1892
May 5, 1920
At Rest.

P. L. Spradlin
Died July 21, 1936
Aged 42 yrs. 9 mos. 14 days.

Infant
Spradlin

Infant
Spradlin

WILLIAX

Lou Ella Williax
Died Feb. 7, 1930

-------- Williax

Williax

Williax

Williax

MILLS

Ambrose Mills
July 17, 1897
July 24, 1900

William T.
Son of
L. L. & M. L. Mills
Feb. 1, 1912
Feb. 21, 1912
We will meet again.

Annie May
Daughter of
T. H. & Laura Mills
May 21, 1910
May 22, 1910
Asleep in Jesus.

Aaron N. Mills
Apr. 15, 1850
June 15, 1902
He followed virtue as
his truest guide.
Lived as a christian
as a christian died.

Henry Mills
Aug. 25, 1852
Mar. 6, 1925

LITTLE TOQUA BAPTIST CHURCH CEMETERY

Mrs. Henry Mills

Infant
of
Mr. & Mrs. Henry Mills

Infant
of
Mr. & Mrs. Henry Mills

Lolie E.
Daughter of
A. N. & L. A. Mills
Dec. 30, 1886
Feb. 15, 1902
Gone in her young years
afar from lifes cares.

Mothers Angel
Author J. Mills
Son of
J. R.
Oct. 27, 1899
May 12, 1900

(Note: above as is, - but
suppose child to be son of
J. R. Mills. LMcC.)

Delilah Stuart
Wife of
Louis Mills
July 22, 1831
June 4, 1897
Gods finger touched
her and she slept.

Louis Mills

R. Mills
Born 1829
Died Dec. 7, 1864

LEMING

Roe Leming

Mary Leming

John Leming

------- Leming

(Note: No given name to last
inscription nor dates on any
of the Leming markers. LMcC.)

HENDERSON

Edward Henderson
Nov. 2, 1903
June 16, 1903

(Note: Above dates as are:
Error in years or dates rev-
ersed. LMcC.)

C. L. Henderson
June 28, 1901
Sept. 15, 1905

Mary
Wife of
Other Henderson
Feb. 14, 1884
Mar. 3, 1924

MILLSAPS

Arie Millsaps
July 16, 1918
Mar. 19, 1929
Be thou faithful unto
death and I will give
thee a crown of live.

JENKINS

Loyd Hubert Jenkins
July 24, 1923
Feb. 29, 1924
'Twas has to give thee
up but Thy will, O God be gone.
Our Baby.

Estie
Wife of
A. J. Jenkins
Jan. 16, 1882
June 3, 1911
(continued on next page)

LITTLE TOQUA BAPTIST CHURCH CEMETERY

Another link is broken
in our household Band
but a chain is forming
in a better land.

Andrew J. Jenkins
Sept. 14, 1871
Jan. 21, 1918
Gone but not forgotten.

Henry Jenkins
Mar. 12, 1892

Lora
Wife of
A. J. Jenkins
July 14, 1873
Jan. 3, 1899
Not lost blest thought
but gone before.

Infant
Jenkins

BIVENS

Joe Bivens
Dec. 18, 1886
Aug. 29, 1930
Gone but not forgotten.

Mother
Millie Bivens
June 23, 1859
Apr. 26, 1929

Father
B. F. Bivens
Feb. 5, 1858
Aug. 24, 1929

Baby Bivens
Born 1917
Died 1917

Nancy D. Bivens
Born Aprile 2, 1817
Died December 27.1878

Sallie
Wife of
Pink Bivens
July 10, 1884
Apr. 20, 1912
Not lost blest thought
but gone before.

Infant
Son of
Pink & Sallie Bivens
Born & died
Apr. 20, 1912
At Rest.

BRACKETT

L. A. Brackett
Aug. 23, 1855
Feb. 16, 1929
Gone but not forgotten.

JOHNSON

Onnie A.
Son of
J. R. & Mollie Johnson
Aug. 17, 1896
Mar. 13, 1897
At Rest.

J. R. Johnson

Mollie Johnson

BRIGHT

Nettie Bright
Mar. 10, 1906
June 18, 1907

Eseybel Bright
May 10, 1895
March 9, 1897

TALLENT

Samey Tallent
Dec. 25, 1894
Jan. 20, 1895

LITTLE TOQUA BAPTIST CHURCH CEMETERY

Worthey Tallent
Oct. 15, 1895
Jun. 15, 1896

Henry Tallent
Feb. 24, 1902
June 5, 1904

Julia Ann Tallent
Aug. 4, 1904
Apr. 10, 1907

Isey Tallent
Sep. 10, 1899
Oct. 3, 1899

John Oliver Tallent
June 30, 1907
July 16, 1907

WILLIAMS

Infant
Son of
C. L. & N. A. Williams
Born & died
Aug. 15, 1906
We will meet again.

Jesse
Son of
W. B. & Laura Williams
July 18, 1909
Jan. 30, 1910
Gone but not forgotten.

Annie May
Daughter of
W. P. & P. A. Williams
Sept. 21, 1915
Nov. 28, 1915
Safe in the arms
of Jesus.

Pollie An
Wife of
W. P. Williams
July 25, 1885
Jan. 22, 1918
She was a kind and
affectionate wife, a fond
mother and a friend to all.

Our darling
Irene Williams
Aug. 29, 1910
July 20, 1912
Baby

J. E. Williams

E. L. Williams

Williams

ROBERTS

James R. Roberts
Feb. 25, 1875
Jan. 26, 1877

Earnest H.
Son of
A. P. & M. A. Roberts
Sept. 15, 1904
July   6, 1909
Asleep in Jesus.

SKIDMORE

Turner
Son of
T. J. Skidmore
Jan. 16, 1878
April 16, 1879

Charles Skidmore
Died Nov. 17, 1877
Age 28 years.

Rufus Skidmore
Died July 11, 1876
Age 23 years.

Turner Skidmore
Died October 18, 1876
Age 72 years.

ADKINS

Pollie
Wife of
John Adkins
Died Feb. 14, 1900
Age 30 years.
May the Resurrection find thee
on the bosom of Thy God.

LITTLE TOQUA BAPTIST CHURCH CEMETERY

DEAN

Infant
of
Vinson & Wattace Dean
Died Sept. 11, 1926
Aged 1 day.

Bruce
Son of
J. J. & L. Z. Dean
June 12, 1916
Oct. 16, 1919
'Twas hard to give
thee up but Thy will
O God be done.

Wayne Dean
Dec. 17, 1903
Sept. 16, 1926
Gone, but not forgotten.

Boyd Dean
Apr. 30, 1906
Mar. 20, 1936
Gone but not forgotten.

COOPER

M. M.
Son of
J. A. & D. R. Cooper
Feb. 9, 1915
Oct. 14, 1919
At Rest.

MCMAHAN

Martha
Daughter of
H. M & D. E. McMahan

James Robert McMahan
Born (no date given)
Died Dec. 19, 1928

Ashley N. McMahan
Born ---- 18(no date given)
Died Dec. 7, 1921
Gone but not forgotten.

Veal Infant

Harvey M. McMahan
June 14, 1900
Jan. 5, 1936

Mellviney McMahan
Born (no date given)
Died Dec. -- 1923
At Rest.

WEST

Infant
Daughter of
Lewis & Mary West
Born & died
Jan. 29, 1907
At Rest.

VEAL

John Veal
Aug. 12, 1851
May 20, 1914

Clemma Veal
Oct. 8, 1881
Jan. 6, 1902

Medy Veal
Jan. 15, 1894
Aug. 10, 1902

Infant
Son of
Peyton & S. E. Veal
Born & died
Dec. 2, 1908
Gone but not forgotten.

COTRELL

Pearl D.
Daughter of
J. D. & Linnie Cotrell
Aug. 18, 1911
Sept. 12, 1911
At Rest.

J. B. Cotrell
June 22, 1878
Apr. 1, 1909
Gone but not forgotten.

LITTLE TOQUA BAPTIST CHURCH CEMETERY

LAUGHTER

Thomas H. Laughter
Infant of
J. W. & Sarah Laughter
Apr. 19, 1900
May 12, 1900

DEVINE

Clifford Devine
Died July 13, 1938
Aged 1 mo. 4 days.

AKINS

Earnest E.
Son of
Ed. & M. L. Adkins
Oct. 6, 1906
Nov. 18, 1906
Gone but not forgotten.

J------ B---- (broken)
Son of
Ed & M. L. Akins
Born ------------------
Died Feb. 18, ------
Gone but --- -----------

Ed & M. L. Akins
(Dates & name unreadable
is a small child's grave.
LMcC.)

Son of
Ed. & M. L. Akins
(Grave of another
small child)

Infant
Daughter of
B--- ------ Akins
Born ----------
Died June 12, 1911

(Note: All the markers of the
above are in bad shape. LMcC.)

Margaret L. Akins
Died Feb. 2, 1937
Aged 61 years 6 mos. 25 days.

Charlie Akins
1893 - 1934
Gone but not forgotten.

Johnfant Akins
Feb. 28, 1826
Feb. 18, 1897

Father
Ed Akins
At Rest.

VANCE

Floid Vance
Nov. 12, 1928
Feb. 12, 1933

GENTRY

Leney Gentry
June 3, 1896
Apr. 21, 1904

Jont L. Gentry
May 7, 1902
April 15, 1904

Infant
of
J. A. & W. J. Gentry
May 16, 1891
May 16, 1891

WATSON

C. C. Watson

MONROE COUNTY

TOMBSTONE INSCRIPTIONS

JAMES WRIGHT LONG FAMILY CEMETERY

Copied by: Lawrence McConkey, Englewood, Tennessee
Date: June 2 & 5, 1939

The James Wright Long Family Cemetery was established on the
farm of James Wright Long, who had entered the land. When
the County was first opened for settlement, or possibly before, several of his wife's first cousins also came to this
part of McMinn County and all lived within a radius of a few
miles of each other. Among them were Isham Reynolds and his
sisters; Elizabeth Reynolds who married William Maples; Alice
Reynolds who married David Cantrell; Anne Reynolds, who
married James Chesnutt; Jane Reynolds, who married Raleigh
Chesnutt. The James Wright Long Family Cemetery is owned by
Misses Nan and Grace Chestnutt, Route 2, Englewood, Tennessee.
It is on the Chestnutt Dairy farm 7 miles Southeast of Athens
just off the road leading from Athens to Etowah.

LONG

In Memory of
James W. Long
Died May 24, 1862
Aged 74 years
Died in the faith
of the Gospel.

In memory of
Nancy Long
Died Jan. 23, 1867
Aged 71 years
Died in the faith
of the Gospel.

Mahala J.
Wife of
Dr. J. A. Long
Born March 18, 1823
Died Sept. 6, 1870

Sarah T.
Daughter of
Dr. J. A. & M. J. Long
Born May 26, 1860
Died Nov. 29, 1861

Mahala K.
Daughter of
Dr. J. A. & M. J. Long
Born April 10, 1858
Died April 13, 1858

In Memory of
Nannie
Daughter of
C. & Nancy S. Long
Born May 28, 1852
Died Feb. 1, 1857
Of such is the Kingdom
of Heaven.

2

JAMES WRIGHT LONG FAMILY CEMETERY

JAMES WRIGHT LONG FAMILY SKETCH

James Wright Long was born in Rockingham County, Va., Sept.
21, 1788 and died May 24, 1862. He emigrated with his
parents to Hawkins Co., Tenn., when a small boy. He served
in two campaigns as a volunteer in the War of 1812. He
married Nancy Reynolds Aug. 18, 1814. Nancy Reynolds was a
daughter of William and --- Kestuton Reynolds. Her brothers
and sisters were: George R., born Feb. 7, 1787; John, born
May 6, 1791; Green, born Feb. 2, 1799, died Oct. 10, 1846 and
buried at Zion Hill Baptist Church Cemetery; William born
May 20, 1793, died Feb. 8, 1875; Hannah, born May 20, 1793
married Samuel Long, both buried at Zion Hill Baptist Church
Cemetery. Hannah died Jan. 8, 1875; Zilpha married -- Brown
and James.

Tradition has it that, two brothers, Isham and William (the
latter the father of Nancy) sons of the 1st Isham Reynolds,
born 1725, moved from Virginia to North Carolina, then to
Hawkins Co., Tennessee where they settled in Carmichael
Bottoms. Isham stayed in Hawkins County but William moved to
near Philadelphia, Tenn. They were the grandsons of William
Reynolds 1st, born in 1694. William Reynolds, it is believed
married Miss +--- Kestuton White in N. C. The children of
James Wright Long and Nancy Reynolds Long were as follows:
Lucy A. Long; Louisa Long; the Rev. William R. Long; Dr. John
A. Long; the Rev. Carroll Long; Nancy Long; the Rev. J. Rufus
Long; Dr. Albert Long; Mary Harriet Long; W. C. Long. Their
history is as follows: Lucy A., born June 23, 1815; Louisa,
born June 27, 1817; Rev. William R., born Feb. 18, 1819. He
married Elizabeth Atlee of Athens, Tenn. The Atlee's came
from Pennsylvania. Dr. John A. Long was born Nov. 29, 1820.
He was married three times. 1st time to Mahala Newman, 2nd
time to Alice Chesnutt, 3rd time to Ella Dunn. The Rev.
Carroll Long was born Nov. 26, 1823, married Nancy Sanders
Oury of Wytheville, Va., August 20, 1851. Both buried at
Wesleyann Southern M. E. Church Cemetery. He was for 20 years
a presiding elder of the Knoxville and Chattanooga District of
M. E. Church, South. Nancy Long born Jan. 10, 1826, married
John Goodner, of Cleveland, Tennessee. Rev. J. Rufus Long,
born June 19, 1828. He taught school in North Carolina,
married and moved North. Dr. Albert, born April 30, 1830,
married, lived and died in Cleveland, Tennessee. Mary Harriet
Long born Feb. 29, 1832, married William Shugart, of near her
home. W. C. born Jan. 9, 1834, died in youth. The children of
these children or the grandchildren of James Wright Long, are
as follows: Children of Rev. William R. Long are Sarah, who
married -- Sloan of Madisonville, Tenn., Rev. Carroll Long, a
missionary 8 years to Japan, married, he was born Jan. 3, 1850
and died Sept. 4, 1890; Dr. E. A. married twice, lived in
Johnson City, Tenn., died in Johnson City, Tenn. in 1936.
Dr. Albert, married, now dead.

JAMES WRIGHT LONG FAMILY CEMETERY

JAMES WRIGHT LONG FAMILY SKETCH

Eugenia, married the Rev. --- McIntire or McIntosh. Emma, married the Seymour, he died, then she married John Goodner, of Cleveland, Tenn. Belle, married Rev. Arnold of the Episcopal Church. Wilbur, married. Clara, married -- Durham of Atlanta, Ga. Atlee, Lawyer, married twice. Nannie, one party says she died in youth another says she did not. Children of Dr. John A. Long are as follows; R. Q. S. married Ellen Chesnutt, both are dead. W. C. C. was a merchant and died unmarried. Walter, living at old home place unmarried. Alice, married Edd Hall living at Rockwall, Texas. Oscar, married Eula Barnel living at Rockwall, Texas. Maude, married Dr. Eugene Phillips, lived at Rookwood, Tennessee. Bascombe, married --- Benton. Dudley, married -- McKinzie. Mary, married Chas. Newton. Mattie, married -- Standefer. Children of Rev. Carroll Long and Nancy Sanders (Oury) Long are as follows: Nancy Sanders, born May 26, 1852-died in infancy. Senah, and Elizabeth Frances both were born Sept. 9, 1855. James Carroll, born March 27, 1858. John Albert, born Feb. 17, 1860. Mary Louisa, born Nov. 23, 1862. George Rufus, born Feb. 10, 1866. Their history: Senah, married Dr. Benj. Cravey of Lowndesboro, Alabama. Elizabeth Frances, married William B. Blair of near Etowah. James Carroll, married Maggie Reynolds of near Etowah, Tenn. He was a merchant. John Albert, married Mary E. Painter of Bristol, Va. Mary Louisa, married A. B. Breeden of Decatur, Tenn. George Rufus, married Emma Reynolds of near Etowah, Tenn. Nancy Long, who married John Goodner, did not have any children. Children of Rev. J. Rufus Long are as follows: Rufus, no record; Pierce, no record; Sallie, no record; others also, no record. Children of Dr. Albert Long are as follows: no record. Children of Mary Harriet Long and husband William Shugart, are as follows: Nannie Shugart, married -- Boggess of Ten Mile, Tenn. Leslie Shugart, unmarried living near Athens, Tenn. James, died and buried at Chattanooga. Will, no record. Rev. E. A. of M. E. Church South, last of Marion, Va. No record of any children of W. C. Long. He died young. Great grandchildren of James Wright Long are as follows: Children of Sarah Long Sloan are: Molly, Carroll, Theadore; Children of Dr. E. A. Long are as follows: Mary, Dr. Carroll Long of Johnson City, Tenn., Frances, Eddie; Children of Emma Long Seymour are: Atlee Seymour, died in Philipine Island during the World War. Wingfield, married Mr. M. L. Harris. Living at Cleveland, Tenn. Children of Belle Long Arnold are: Paul, Pauline, George. Pauline married her cousin Mr. Durham, living in Atlanta, Ga., in 1936. Above great grandchildren of James Wright Long were also the grand children of Rev. William R. Long. The following are the grand children of Dr. John A. Long: Children of R. Q. S. Long. Mahala, married James Richardson, living near Etowah, Tenn., at Wesleyann. Children of Oscar Long are: Carroll, Fanny, Edith. Children of Mary Long Newton are: Maude, dead, Bessie, at Deckard, Tenn., Walter, at Chattanooga, Tenn. and Doc, dead at Chattanooga, Tenn.

JAMES WRIGHT LONG FAMILY CEMETERY

JAMES WRIGHT LONG FAMILY SKETCH

Mary Lee, at New York City. Children of Mattie Long Standifer
are: Will; Mae, at Chattanooga; Clyde, in Florida; Herman; Joe
in California and Harry in Florida. Grand children of Rev.
Carroll Long: Children of Senah Long Cravey are: Elizabeth
Cravey, living at Athens, Tenn.; William Benjamin, Pharmist
Died in Rockwall, Texas in 1911, buried at Athens, Tenn., un-
married. Carroll Long Cravey, Pharmist also Postal Clerk at
Etowah, Tenn., for about 25 years, died at Foree Hospital,
Athens, Nov. 18, 1937, buried at Athens, was unmarried.
Nannie Laura Cravey, married Fritz Long, living at Athens,
Tenn.; Sallie Penelope Cravey, married Bryan Clark, living at
Athens, Tenn.; James Cravey, merchant, married Alice MacKenzie
of Decatur, Tenn., and parents of Alice Vandine, born Apr. 6,
1938. Children of Elizabeth Frances Long Blair are: Ben C.
Blair, died 1910, buried at Weslyann M. E. Church Cemetery.
Flora Blair, living at Athens, Tenn.; Albion Blair, died in
youth buried at Wesleyann Cemetery; William B. Blair, Salesman
and merchant, married Nina Farley of Virginia and parents of
Betty Catherine. They lived at Athens, Tenn.; Carroll K. Blair,
Civil Engineer, served in World War, died 1929 buried at
Athens, Tenn. Children of James Carroll Long & Maggie Reynolds
Long are: Carroll Long, conductor on L. & N. Railroad, married
Ocie Barnett they are parents of J. C. & Katherine. They live
at Etowah, Tenn.; James B. Long, married and living at Nashville,
Tenn.; Charles Long, deceased buried at Etowah, Tenn.; Jewell
Long, deceased, buried at Etowah, Tenn.; Dr. Clarence Long,
Pharmist, married and have two children. They live at Knoxville,
Tenn. Children of Mary Louisa Long Breeden are: Carroll C.
Breeden, merchant married Kate --- and parents of Katherine and
Carroll Jr. They live at Los Angeles, Calif.; Sam Breeden,
Salesman lives at Memphis, Tenn.; Edna Breeden, married ----
Murphy, lives at Atlanta, Ga. Frank Breeden, Salesman, deceased;
Paul Breeden, Salesman, living at Memphis, Tenn., and George.
Children of George R. Long are: Dr. Robert R. Long, Pharmist
married Ruby ----. They are parents of: Robert Jr. and George.
They live at Maryville, Tenn. Oury Long, married, deceased -
no children. Sidney Long, married twice, living in Montana;
Ben C. Long, deceased; Emma Long, living at Knoxville, Tenn.
Children of John Albert Long are: Kate Foster Long married
Fred Stone of Athens, Tenn., living at Beckley, West Va.;
Nancy Sanders Long, married Frank B. Bell of Bristol, Virginia.
They were parents of: Mary Jean Bell and Nancy Bell. They live
at Knoxville, Tenn.; John Carroll Long, died in the World War in
France. Children of Nannie Shugart Boggess are: Willie, Frank,
of Sweetwater, Tenn., and Mary Lee. As the record shows quite
a few of the Long family have been doctors, preachers or some
other skilled profession. They have been leaders all along.

TOMBSTONE INSCRIPTIONS

LULA M. E. CHURCH CEMETERY

Copied by: Lawrence McConkey, Englewood, Tennessee
Date:

Lula Methodist Episcopal Church Cemetery was established about
50 years ago and discontinued about 45 years ago. Lula M. E.
Church was constituted about 1880. Land for both church and
cemetery was secured from Ferring Milligan. The location is
five miles down the Tellico river road, from Tellico Plains,
on the bank of the river. Tellico Plains is 16 miles South
of Madisonville. The cemetery is grown up with bushes and
trees and there does not seem to have been but two graves.

SELF   CAUGHRON

Infant   Infant
of   of
Mr. & Mrs. Newton Self   Terrell & Callie Caughron
  1889

MONROE COUNTY

TOMBSTONE INSCRIPTIONS
MADISONVILLE M. E. (SOU.) CHURCH CEMETERY

When the town of Madisonville was laid off in 1832, the Methodist Denomination was given a grant for the plot where the church and cemetery are located. When part of the Methodist churches in 1848 seceded, then soon the Madisonville Church was organized into the Southern Methodist Church organization. There have been four church buildings on this location. Dr. D. B. Carter whose wife is buried in this cemetery was one of the founders of Hiwassee College. A. T. Hicks was for years, Clerk of the County Court. District Judge Hicks and the Hicks buried here are descendants of the same family that came to this country in the early settlement days. Some of the members of the Hicks' family, as well as many others have been removed to other cemeteries on account of widening of streets, etc. Three southern (Confederate) soldiers were killed and buried here, but is said that their markers have been removed to make room for street widening. It is also said that (Miss) Sue Meek and possibly other members of the Meek family are buried here. Also seems that there are graves under the church, therefore it is impossible to closely estimate the number of unmarked graves, however there are possibly fifteen unmarked graves. The location is three blocks south of the court house in Madisonville.

Sacred to the memory of
Margaret L. H. Billingsley
Wife of
B. F. Billingsley
And daughter of
F. and S. Orr
Aug. 4, 1833
Dec. 3, 1854
"Blessed are the dead
which die in the Lord."

Jessie E. Hicks
Daughter of
G. W. and Martha Hicks
May 29, 1854
March 18, 1876

Our Baby -
Son of
J. C. and F. Hicks
Sept. 29, 1886
Dec. 15, 1886

Sacred to the memory of
Cynthia C. Carter
Wife of
Rev. D. B. Carter
And daughter of
S. P. and F. Burnett
Sept. 19, 1815
July 27, 1846
"Blessed are the dead
which die in the Lord."

Maggie R. Hicks
Wife of
J. C. Hicks
May 23, 1856
Feb. 17, 1877

A. T. Hicks
——

M. F. Hicks
——

M. H. Hicks
——

MONROE COUNTY

TOMBSTONE INSCRIPTIONS

MCCROSKEY FAMILY CEMETERY

Copied by: Lawrence McConkey, Englewood, Tennessee
Date: Oct. 28, 1938

Two brothers, John and Samuel McCroskey, who were born in
Virginia, entered two adjoining tracts of land in Monroe County
on which they later established their family cemetery. They
owned several slaves and some of them are buried in this cemetery. The McCroskeys were prominent people. Thomas and his
son, Barrett McCroskey, were lawyers. All graves that have
markers are graves of members of the family. There are 13
inscriptions, approximately 30 unmarked graves. The cemetery
is located 7 miles North of Madisonville via Hiwassee College
and Rockville section. It is between Rockville and Burton Hill
School on the farm of Arthur Borden.

MCCROSKEY

Pricilla McCroskey
Born Dec. 28, 1808
Died Nov. 23, 1879

John McCroskey
Born Mar. 17, 1788
Died Nov. 10, 1866

To the memory of
Mrs. Lucinda Ann McCroskey
Born Aug. 15, 1799
Died Mar. 21, 1833
Mors Omnibus Communis.

To the memory of
Franklin K. McCroskey
Born Oct. 17, 1824
Died Aug. 8, 1853

In memory of
James F. G. McCroskey
Born Nov. 8, 1826
Died Sept. 4, 1828

Erected to the memory of
Patrick H. McCroskey
Born at Rockville E. Tenn.

Dec. 2nd 1830
Died of Cholera on board
the Steamship Cortez, on
her passage from Panama
to San Francisco, Cal., the
5th of Dec. 1852
Age 22 yrs. 23 days
His body was committed
to the Pacific Ocean in
Lat. 11° 12 N.
Long. 88° 58 W from
Greenwich.

In memory of
Mary Irene
First born of
B. B. & Irene McCroskey
Born Aug. 3, 1875
Died Feb. 21, 1876

In memory of
Nancy T. McCroskey
Born Jan. 27, 1823
Died Aug. 16, 1824

In memory of
Elizabeth McCroskey
Born March 19, 1804
Died Aug. 23, 1824

MCCROSKEY FAMILY CEMETERY

In memory of
Sarah McCroskey
Born Nov. 1, 1808
Died Aug. 28, 1841

In memory of
Samuel McCroskey
Born July 24, 1782
Died Sept. 28, 1848

GALLAHER

Infant
Daughter of
A. H. & F. L. Gallaher
Born & Died
July 22, 1881

MAGILL

Joseph
Son of
W. N. & S. H. Magill
Born Feb. 14, 1882
Died Mar. 9, 1882
Asleep in Jesus.

MONROE COUNTY

TOMBSTONE INSCRIPTIONS

MCCULLOCH & HARDIN CEMETERY

Copied by: Lawrence McConkey, Englewood, Tennessee.
Date:

The McCulloch and Hardin Cemetery was established years ago
before these families owned the farm on which it is located.
The McCulloch children buried here are the children of T. D.
& M. L. McCulloch. W. W. Hardin is a great grandson of J. C. R.
& Polly Hardin. The families are related. Several members of
each family are buried at Mt. Zion Baptist Cemetery. The cemetery is about 15 miles Northeast of Madisonville. It may be
reached by taking the highway toward Niles Ferry and at Vonore
taking the road known as the Vonore Ballplay road to Mt. Zion
Baptist Church. There go left to the farm of Ben Davis. There
are 5 inscriptions and 8 unmarked graves.

MCCULLOCH

W. T. McCulloch
Mar. 27, 1899
Oct. 9, 1901

Thomas D. McCulloch
Born Dec. 19, 1895
Died Jan. 21, 1899

HARDIN

Vicie
Wife of
W. A. Hardin
Died Feb. 21, 1912
Aged 36 years.
Not lost blest thought
but gone before where
we shall meet to part
no more.

W. W. Hardin
Born June 9, 1884
Died Oct. 16, 1902

1899   L.

(Note: Inscription as
is. LMcC.)

MONROE COUNTY

TOMBSTONE INSCRIPTIONS

MCSPADDEN FAMILY CEMETERY

Copied by: Lawrence McConkey, Englewood, Tennessee.
Date: Feb. 1939.

The Hannibal McSpadden Family Cemetery is about 5 miles
Northeast of Tellico Plains on the road leading down the
East side of the Tellico River. Tellico Plains is 16
miles South of Athens.

The Cemetery was established by Hannibal McSpadden at the
death of his wife, Nicy, on June 2, 1901. An iron fence
surrounds the cemetery which covers a space of about 12X15
feet. Hannibal McSpadden was the son of Samuel McSpadden.
Hannibal had two brothers, Teed and Tine. Hannibal and Nicy
did not have any children but raised Grace Giles, a daughter
of Horace and ----- Giles. She married ------ Patterson.
Most of the older members of Hannibal McSpadden's family
are buried at Tellico Baptist Church, farther down the
Tellico River.

MCSPADDEN

Hannibal McSpadden
Oct. 27, 1825
Jan. 26, 1913

Nicy McSpadden
March 6, 1827
June 2, 1901

PATTERSON

William Frank Patterson
June 14, 1902
June 28, 1904

MONROE COUNTY

TOMBSTONE INSCRIPTIONS

MILLSAPS FARM CEMETERY

Copied by: Lawrence McConkey, Englewood, Tennessee
Date:

The Millsaps Farm Cemetery is about 27 miles up the Little
Tennessee river from Vonore on the river road leading into
the Unicoi Mountains.   It is over one ledge of the mountain
from the river about 2 miles and on the nearest public road
to the river.   The cemetery was established at the time of
the Civil War.   Persumably the Millsaps family entered this
land.   It is now owned by Mrs. Mary Millsaps.   The cemetery
has been discontinued for over 50 years.   It is in the woods
and covers about 50X30 feet of ground.   Vonore is 9 miles
North of Madisonville.   There are 2 inscriptions, 6 graves
marked with field stones and 4 or more unmarked graves.

DAVIS   KEENER

John Davis   Jon F. Keener
                               June 22, 1840
                               June 26, 1879

MONROE COUNTY

TOMBSTONE INSCRIPTIONS

JOSHUA MOSES FAMILY CEMETERY

Copied by: Lawrence McConkey, Englewood, Tennessee
Date:

The Joshua Moses Family Cemetery is located about 7 miles Southeast of Madisonville. It may be reached by taking the road
leading to Tellico Plains to the road leading to Big Creek, then
the road via Hicks School to the farm of Joseph Moses on
Laurel Mt. The cemetery is not reserved in deed. The first
person buried in this cemetery was Andrew, a son of Joshua
Moses. The grave was on the Joshua Moses farm before the Civil
War. The cemetery is still in use and contains ¼ acre of land.
The following do not have dates as to when they were born or
died. Most of the other members of the Moses family are buried
at Big Creek Baptist Church Cemetery except possibly about 20
that are buried here that don't have inscriptions. This cemetery
has 6 graves with inscriptions, 11 marked with field stones and
8 unmarked graves.

Joshua Moses

(Note: He was born
before 1800. LMcC.)

Sarah Sample
Wife of
Joshua Moses

James Moses

(Note: He was a
son of above and
died about 1931. LMcC.)

Martha Dulin
Wife of
James Moses

Andrew Moses

(Note: 1st burial in cemetery.
Andrew Moses was 45 years
old. He died before the
Civil War. LMcC.)

Nancy Moses
Wife of
Henry Breeden

(Note: She was daughter
of James & Martha Moses. LMCC.)

JOSHUA MOSES FAMILY SKETCH

Joshua Moses was possibly from S. C. He entered a tract of land
in Monroe County Northeast of this place along the Tellico river
and sold it and entered or bought 120 acres at this location.
He married Sarah Sample. They were the parents of: John, James,
Anderson, Edward, Samuel, Jessee, Nancy and Andrew. They married
as follows: John married Pollie Morgan; James married Martha
Dulin; Anderson married Gadd then -- Hicks and (name not known);
Edward married --- Hicks; Samuel married Sussie McKinney; Jessee
married Texie Walker; Nancy married Thomas Saffles; Andrew never
married. James and Anderson Moses were confederate soldiers
according to statement of Joseph Moses.

MONROE COUNTY

TOMBSTONE INSCRIPTIONS

MT. ISABELL BAPTIST CHURCH CEMETERY

Copied by: Lawrence McConkey, Englewood, Tennessee
Date: Feb. 5, 1940

The Mt. Isabell Baptist Church Cemetery is located 6 miles East
of Tellico Plains on the road leading to Rafter. Tellico Plains
is 16 miles South of Madisonville. The church was constituted
in 18--. William Williams gave approximately one acre of land
for space for a school house, a church house and a cemetery but
later the church was moved across the road on to land secured
from John Freeman. Now the cemetery covers land where the church
once was located. The cemetery covers one half acre approximately.
There are no Negroes buried here. Cemetery is still in use. There
are 61 graves with inscriptions; 54 marked with field stones and
6 unmarked graves.

DUCKETT

Jessie Duckett
Nov. 23, 1861
Dec. 29, 1926

(Note: At North side of
above is grave of his
wife, M. E., and also two
other unmarked graves.
LMcC.)

Sintha J.
Daughter of
W. J. & M. E. Duckett
July 8, 1898
Apr. 15, 1910
We will meet again.

(Masonic Emblem)
Jane Hamilton
Wife of
John Duckett
Feb. 22, 1816
Jan. 22, 1905

(Note: The above masonic
emblem on marker either
means that she belonged to
Eastern Star or that her
husband was a mason. LMC.)

1st Sgt.
Robert C. Duckett
Co. H.
10 Tenn. Cav.

(Note: The above grave has a
regulation government soldier
marker. It is and believed
Duckett was in Civil War. LMcC.)

Arizonia Duckett
Died Feb. 12, 1936
Aged -------------

Sarah
Wife of
J. J. Duckett
Sept. 1, 1875
Apr. 17, 1907
We will meet again.

(Note: An infant of the Sarah &
J. J. Duckett born & died in 1907,
is buried beside above grave. Also
3 field stones on South and 2 on
North without inscription. LMcC.)

Fannie
Wife of
D. M. Duckett
May 10, 1881
Oct. 31, 1901
We will meet again.

2

MT. ISABELL BAPTIST CHURCH CEMETERY

Anderson
Son of
M. H. & Adra Duckett
Oct. 15, 1897
Nov. 22, 1897
We will meet again.

5 field stones North and 4
South.

SMITH

Rosten
Son of
Charley & Minnie Smith
July 29, 1916
Apr. 15, 1919
Safe in the arms of Jesus.

1 field stone North of above
and 4 South of above.

H. L. Smith

POWERS

Infant
of
Z. B. & M. A. Powers
May 15, 1911

1 field stone North of above.
1 field stone South.

ROBERTS

Twin
Children of
W. M. & Harriet Roberts
April 8, 1909
April 9, 1909
Asleep in Jesus.

BOLIX

Mrs. W. E. Bolix
Sept. 30, 1866
Sept. 16, 1936
Gone but not forgotten.

LEDFORD

Miss D. B. Ledford
Daughter of
J. B. Ledford
Born May 22, 1895
Died Nov. 11, 1902

G. L. Ledford
Son of
J. B. Ledford
Oct. 22, 1902
Nov. 7, 1908

Jasper Ledford
Dec. 26, 1845
May 9, 1904
Not lost blest thought
but gone before where
we shall meet to part
no more.

W. C. Ledford
Son of
J. B. Ledford
Sept. 11, 1884
Dec. 7, 1885

Janie
Daughter of
B. A. Ledford
Born July 23, 1910
Died Jan. 1, 1911
From mothers arms to
the arms of Jesus.

Florence
Daughter of
B. A. Ledford
Oct. 5, 1912
Mar. 1, 1913
From mothers arms to
the arms of Jesus.

George Ledford

(Note: At North of George Ledford's
grave is grave of infant son of
above and one other grave, believed
to be his wife, with only field
rocks as markers. LMcC.)

MT. ISABELL BAPTIST CHURCH CEMETERY

Ethel Ledford

SHAW

Infant
of
J. & F. Shaw
Born & died Sept. 11, 1901

Rebeckah Shaw
Wife of
B. Shaw
Jan. 1, 1919
Aug. 5, 1898

Nellie
Daughter of
B. B. & Jane Shaw
Nov. 15, 1890
Apr. 19, 1892
We will meet again.

4 field stones North
of above.

LYNN OR LINN

Sire
Son of
J. B. & Margarett Lynn
Sept. 24, 1903
Sept. 25, 1904
At Rest.

4 field stones South of
above and 1 field stone
North of above.

Infant
of
W. B. & Mattie Lynn
Born & died
Sept. 21, 1911
We will meet again.

4 field stones North
5 field stones South of above.

(Note: Following graves are at
another location but are graves
of same family. LMcC.)

Wm. H. Linn
Co. A.
17 Ind. Inf.

Elizabeth A. Linn
Nov. 17, 1834
May 5, 1922

(Note: Wm. H. Linn was a
Civil War Soldier according
to Mrs. Jane Odell. He also
has a regulation Governement
soldier tombstone. LMcC.)

Elizabeth Lynn
Dec. 23, 1863
Dec. 14, 1904
Member of the Missionary
Baptist Church.

. H. Lynn
Died Aug. 15, 1938
Aged 64 years, 4 months
& 29 days.

(Note: The above two graves
are not together. LMcC.)

J. W. Lynn
Son of
Mr. & Mrs. W. H. Lynn
Oct. 11, 1900
July 13, 1936
Gone to rest.

2 field stones South of above.

FISHER

Martha A.
Wife of
B. F. Fisher
Nov. 15, 1836
May 20, 1909

DOCKREY

Rebecca J.
Wife of
Noah Dockrey
Sept. 25, 1877
Nov. 10, 1909
Asleep in Jesus.

MT. ISABELL BAPTIST CHURCH CEMETERY

3 Field Stones N. of above.

TALLENT

C. H. Tallent
Died Jan. 30, 1893
Age 45 years
Not lost blest thought
but gone before where we
shall meet to part no more.

4 Field Stones S. of above.

VEAL

J. H. Veal
May 5, 1859
Apr. 18, 1920
Thy life was beauty, truth
goodness and love.

2 Field Stones S. of above.

Mother
Cyntha
Wife of
James Veal
Died Nov. 10, 1939
Faithful to her trust
even unto death.

William H.
Oct. 27, 1890
Jan. 13, 1891

John B.
Born & died
Mar. 15, 1903

Lee
Aug. 18, 1892
Dec. 18, 1904
Children of
J. H. & C. J. Veal

KIRKLAND

Clara
Wife of
C. M. Kirkland
Dec. 3, 1887
July 19, 1928

Note: 3 graves North of above,
one said to be the grave of
an infant of Clara Kirkland.
Died in 1928.   LMcC.)

AKINS

Fred Akins
Son of
Henry Akins
June 18, 1899
Oct. 22, 1902
At Rest.

Molly Akins
Wife of
H. N. Akins
Born Mar. 31, 1874
Mar. 8, 1917
Gone but not forgotten.

Henry Akins
Mar. 30, 1867
July 27, 1927
And if this earthly
tabernacle besolved I
have a home eturnal
in the Heavens.

Venia Akins
June 14, 1928
Jan. 26, 1929
Daughter of
Lida Oley Akins
At Rest.

MASON

Tommie
Son of
W. M. & Nellie Mason
July 6, 1926
Mar. 29, 1929
He was the sunshine
of our home.

FREEMAN

John A. Freeman
Co. E.
6 Ind. Cav.

MT. ISABELL BAPTIST CHURCH CEMETERY

(Note: 1 grave North of above
said to be grave of Jane
Williams Tallent wife of John
A. Freeman. Died 1933 aged
75 yrs. LMcC.)

TUCKER

Burlin
Son of
Oscar & Kate Tucker
April 13, 1923
Sept. 24, 1924
He was the sunshine
of our home.

1 unmarked grave.

FARNER

L. P.
Wife of
W. I. Farner
Born Sept. 15, 1871
Aug. 11, 1917
Beloved one farewell.

Grady
Son of
C. W. & I. D. Farner
Dec. 1, 1913
Feb. 12, 1914
From mothers arms to
the arms of Jesus.

WATSON

Osie
Wife of
C. J. Watson
Nov. 3, 1894
May 4, 1914
She was an affectionate
daughter and a faithful
friend.

(Note: 1 grave North of
above said to be grave of
an infant of the above.
LMcC.)

1 unmarked grave

UNDERWOOD

John Underwood

HARRIS

Dorthie M.
Daughter of
Will & Carrie Harris
July 17, 1902
Oct. 17, 1909
We will meet again.

PLASTER

William E.
Son of
W. M. & Clara Plaster
Nov. 23, 1910
Feb. 28, 1911
At Rest.

THOMPSON

Varia Thompson
Wife of
R. O. Thompson
Oct. 17, 1890
Jan. 31, 1933
At Rest.

3 graves S. of above.

BELCHER

H. A.
Son of
A. R. & M. J. Belcher
July 31, 1918
Aug. 24, 1918
Gone but not forgotten.

3 Field stones South of above.

THOMPSON

Martha J.
Dau. of
(continued on next page)

MT. ISABELL BAPTIST CHURCH CEMETERY

H. F. & R. L. Thompson
Oct. 6, 1916
Nov. 9, 1916
God gave, He took
He will restore.

(Note: 5 field stones North
of above. H. F. & R. O.
Thompson are brothers but
graves of their families
are in separate locations.
LMcC.)

ROBERTS

Bob
Son of
W. M. & Harriet Roberts
May 11, 1890
--- 29, 1909
At Rest.

KIRKLAND

Mrs. L. C. Kirkland
Wife of
C. W. Kirkland
May 21, 1892
Dec. 29, 1913
She's at Rest in
Heaven.

GILES

Giles
Gertie
Daughter of
Frank Giles
Oct. 17, 1915
Apr. 22, 1925

COLEMAN

John W. Coleman
Son of
J. A. & L. A. Coleman
Mar. 13, 1883
July 1, 1907
May the resurrection
find thee on the bosom
of thy God.

(Note: 5 field stones South
of above. One said to be
grave of Jesse Coleman. LMcC.)

HARRIS

Lizzie
Daughter of
J. M. & Cyntha Harris
April 20, 1899
Oct. 17, 1903
We will meet again.

(Note: Above may be related
to the Ledford family, as
grave was between Miss D. B.
Ledford and G. L. Ledford. LMcC.)

MONROE COUNTY

TOMBSTONE INSCRIPTIONS
MOUNT LEBONON CUMBERLAND PRESBYTERIAN CHURCH CEMETERY

WRIGHT

Infant
Daughter of
J. A. & M. A. Wright
Born & died
Aug. 14, 1852

TATE

Samuel W. Tate
Feb. 24, 1842
April 6, 1845

Thomas C. Tate
Nov. 24, 1851
Sept. 6, 1854

GERDING

Edward Montegre Gerding
Aged 8 years

JOHNSTON

Clarissa
Wife of
Josiah K. Johnston
April 23, 1811
April 9, 1864

Josiah K. Johnston
Feb. 10, 1805
Dec. 12, 1861
"A peaceful rest in Heaven
By your loving children."

Sue E.
Daughter of
J. K. & C. Johnston
Dec. 15, 1845
Aug. 8, 1867

SNEAD

Nancy P.
Wife of
Wm. E. Snead
and daughter of
J. K. & C. Johnstone
April 3, 1833
Dec. 31, 1853

GRUBB

Derias Grubb

Sophia A. Grubb

Martha C. Grubb

(Note: The three above inscr.
were on nice markers. A member
of the Grubb family has been
Sheriff of Monroe County.)

MONROE COUNTY

TOMBSTONE INSCRIPTIONS

MT. ZION BAPTIST CHURCH CEMETERY

Copied by: Lawrence McConkey, Englewood, Tenn.
Date:

The Mt. Zion Baptist Church was organized in or about 1840.
It has been at three locations but all within a radius of less
than one mile. The cemetery was established possibly about
the same date on the farm of William Gray either as a family
or community cemetery, later changing to a community cemetery.
The inscriptions indicate the graveyard was established at a
much later date than 1840, as the oldest section of the cemetery
has very few markers. It is noted that a large majority of
persons buried here died when young. It is estimated that there
are 400 or 500 unmarked graves. Mt. Zion Cemetery is about 15
miles Northeast of Madisonville. To reach it take highway to
Knoxville but when even with Vonore, take the Vonore to Ballplay
road. The cemetery is located about $\frac{1}{8}$ mile in front and across
the road from the church. There are 262 inscriptions.

GENTRY

E. C. Gentry
B. May 27, 1933
D. June 22, 1933

R. N. Gentry
B. Oct. 3, 1928
D. Nov. 1, 1928

M. M. Gentry
B. Nov. 18, 1929
D. Dec. 25, 1933

Martha Miltildy Gentry
June 18, 1869
July 21, 1931
Married
July 26, 1888

E. J. Gentry
May 8, 1838
Dec. 24, 1927

Alsie Ann
Daughter of
W. N. & Martha Gentry
Nov. 8, 1903
Oct. 26, 1918
At Rest.

W. A. Gentry
Nov. 22, 1927
Feb. 2, 1928

D. M. Gentry
Dec. 24, 1924
Jan. 19, 1925

Viola
Daughter of
W. M. Gentry
Apr. 15, 1916
June 22, 1917

Unis Gentry
Mar. 7, 1914
Apr. 17, 1924
At Rest.

E. H. Gentry
Oct. 14, 1872
Jan. 10, 1922
Farewell my wife and
children all, from you a
father Christ doth call.

Effie M. Gentry
July 7, 1920
June 14, 1921

MT. ZION BAPTIST CHURCH CEMETERY

Nellie M.
Daughter of
E. H. & E. M. Gentry
Feb. 25, 1908
Feb. 25, 1910

William A.
Twin son of
E. H. & E. M. Gentry
Born Nov. 14, 1902
Died --- -- 190-

Alles Gentry
Died June 3, 1885

Nearvy Gentry
Sept. 21, 1855
Sept. 29, 1893

Maryellie Gentry
Apr. 8, 1910
May 30, 1910

Arvale Gentry
Oct. 11, 1906
Jan. 7, 1907

Joe Allen Gentry
Died March 6, 1938

Mr. Ell Gentry
Died July 8, 1937
Aged 92 yrs. 9 mos. 21 days.

Our Baby
Infant
of
E. & J. Gentry

Joseph E.
Twin Son of
E. H. & E. M. Gentry
Nov. 14, 1902
Jan. 28, 1908

J. M. Gentry
Mar. 4, 1870
May 1, 1921
Gone but not forgotten.

W. H. Gentry
Jan. 25, 1890
Dec. 15, 1910

John Gentry
Feb. 10, 1901
May 11, 1904

George Gentry
Mar. 12, 1907
May 12, 1907

Sarah Gentry
Died May 19, 1887

SUMMEY

Sallie Summey
Died June 5, 1935
Gone but not forgotten.

Rosco Summey
Sept. 7, 1933

Fanney Means Summey
Feb. 1, 1905
Oct. 30, 1925
Mother
Gone but not forgotten.

Horles D. Summey
Nov. 5, 1912
Jan. 2, 1921

Pete Summey
July 5, 1858
Apr. 5, 1924
Twas hard to give thee
up but 'thy will'
O God be done.

Fannie Summey

James M.
Son of
Pete & Tex Summey
Born & died
Mar. 6, 1887

Walter
Son of
Pete & Tex Summey
June 3, 1889
Jan. 21, 1891

FARR

MT. ZION BAPTIST CHURCH CEMETERY

J. A. Farr
Died Feb. 16, 1938
Aged 84 yrs. 4 mos.

BURTON

Nellie Burton
Died Aug. 13, 1926

HOWARD

D. B. Howard
April 18, 1878
Jan. 21, 1917
Gone but not forgotten.

Earnest R.
Son of
D. B. & L. E. Howard
Sept. 9, 1900
Mar. 18, 1910
He was the choice of
the family.

J. B. Howard
Nov. 2, 1846
Feb. 15, 1917
Not dead but asleep in Jesus.

Infant
of
J. H. & M. Howard
Sept. 1, 1893
Sept. 9, 1893

Infant
of
J. B. & A. D. Howard
Nov. 3, 1885
Nov. 9, 1885

L. M. Howard
Sept. 1, 1882
Aug. 4, 1892

W. M. R. Howard
July 22, 1875
Oct. 20, 1892

Sgt.
J. B. Howard
Co. D.
11th Tenn. Cav.
Born Oct. 22, 1830
Died Mar. 8, 1901

Howard
J. B. Howard
Oct. 22, 1830
Mar. 8, 1901
His wife
Adeline D. Howard
Mar. 4, 1844
Sept. 15, 1935
At Rest.

Sallie Howard
Mar. 2, 1896
Apr. 24, 1910

Lucy L. Howard
July 16, 1879
July 19, 1879

B. Howard
Died Mar. 16, 1870

Fannie L. Howard
Nov. 23, 1817
June 27, 1905
Our kind Mother at rest.

Walter
Son of
W. B. & Ina Howard
Nov. 6, 1895
Dec. 16, 1915

Oscar
Son of
B. & I. Howard
July 17, 1900-Aug. 28, 1902

TUCKERS

Evie Summey
Wife of
J. B. Tuckers
Aug. 23, 1889
Jan. 23, 1930

MT. ZION BAPTIST CHURCH CEMETERY

THOMAS

Floyd Thomas
Died July 30, 1933
Aged 28 yrs. 6 mos. 29 days.

BRIGHT

Father
L. L. Bright
Oct. 1, 1883
(still living)

Mother
C. C. Bright
May 25, 1885
Jan. 16, 1923
May the resurrection
find thee on the
bosom of thy God.

Worth Bright
Nov. 12, 1884
Nov. 2, 1927
Remember friends as you
pass by, as you are now
so once was I. As I am now
so you must be, so be prepared for death and
follow me.

Iney May
Daut. of
J. H. & H. E. Bright
Oct. 31, 1909
Jan. 22, 1910

Nancy A.
Wife of
W. L. Bright
Jan. 25, 1860
Feb. 2, 1911
Erected by our son
W. C. Bright

W. L. Bright
Apr. 26, 1856
Aug. 16, 1905

J. H. Bright
Oct. 18, 1880
Aug. 19, 1905

Myrtis
Daughter of
J. H. & E. M. Bright
July 27, 1906
Jan. 9, 1910

Hattie
Daughter of
Mr. & Mrs. J. L. Bright
Feb. 11, 1914
May 4, 1914

Geneva Ree
Daughter of
W. J. & Josie Bright
June 10, 1921
Oct. 25, 1922

BORDEN

Anna Reba Borden
Died Feb. 3, 1937
Aged 21 yrs. 4 mos. 20 days.

GRAY

Mart Gray
June 25, 1910
Jan. 18, 1932
Resting in hope of a
Glorious Resurrection.

W. W.
Son of
Wm. & Maggie Gray
Dec. 22, 1918
Our darling

Nellie Reba Gray
Mar. 24, 1905
Sept. 21, 1917

Lawson Gray
Sept. 13, 1903
Dec. 10, 1915
Weep not father and mother.

Infant
of
Mr. & Mrs. Joseph Gray
Mar. 23, 1913
Apr. 20, 1913

MT. ZION BAPTIST CHURCH CEMETERY

William Gray
Jan. 26, 1831
Dec. 1, 1902

Mary Jane Gray
Wife of
W. M. Gray
July 30, 1835
Jan. 25, 1897
Blessed are they which
have a part in the
first Resurrection.

Infant
of
Joe & Bessie Gray

Infant
of
Joe & Bessie Gray

Infant
of
Sam & Sallie Gray

Infant
of
Sam & Sallie Gray

Lawson Gray
Jan. 8, 1899
Oct. 31, 1902

Modeania
Wife of
Samuel Gray
Oct. 27, 1851
May 23, 1893

W. R. Gray
Jan. 26, 1883
Jan. 23, 1884

Sam Gray
Aug. 9, 1851
Mar. 10, 1927
Blessed are they that die
in Christ.

Luther
Jan. 1, 1891
June 6, 1907

Addie
May 10, 1899
Sept. 30, 1904
Children of
Sam & Modena Gray

Warren Gray
Feb. 6, 1822
Aug. 15, 1897

S. C. Gray
July 23, 1830
June 30, 1905

DILLS

Allie Dills
B. Jan. 17, 1918
D. Apr. 31, 1919

DIAL

Rev. James Lee Dial
May 15, 1871
Dec. 26, 1935

SHIRK

Mr. W. G. Shirk
Died Dec. 13, 1934
Aged 70 yrs. 2 mos. 26 days.

Bruce Boot Shirk
Feb. 22, 1896
Dec. 26, 1934
Gone but not forgotten.

Johnnie R.
Son of
W. J. & Ida Shirk
May 16, 1901
Jan. 18, 1902

Modean
Daughter of
W. J. & Ida Shirk
Dec. 18, 1910
Jan. 9, 1911

MT. ZION BAPTIST CHURCH CEMETERY

M. L. Shirk
Oct. 21, 1890
July 5, 1900

MORGAN

John Jordan Morgan
Died Mch. 6, 1937
Aged 49 years.

MCINTURFF

Norma L.
Daughter of
Mr. & Mrs. G. A. McInturff
Mar. 15, 1925
Nov. 6, 1926
Our darling has gone
before to greet us on
that blissful shore.

ARDEN

G. W. Arden
1842- (buried no date)

Susie Arden
1845 - 1926
Father - Mother
Gone to rest.

Mamie
Daughter of
G. W. & S. C. Arden
Mar. 23, 1890
Feb. 28, 1909
Asleep in Jesus.

Julia
Dau. of
G. W.& S. C. Arden
Born --- --- ----
Died Oct. 9, ----

Noah J.
Son of
G. W. & S. C. Arden
Nov. 10, 1879
Mar. 23, 1908

Infant
Daughter of
John & Mollie Arden
Mar. 21, 1903
Mar. 27, 1903

COOK

Vinie Cook
Dec. 10, 1876
April 26, 1896

HUNT

W. M. Hunt
May 8, 1894
July 7, 1937
Asleep in Jesus.

Bessie Hunt
June 21, 1897
Apr. 29, 1921

Virgil Hunt
Nov. 20, 1914
Mar. 9, 1915

Rubie
Daughter of
E. D. & Vinie Hunt
Sept. 4, 1916
Dec. 12, 1916

Infant
of
E. D. & Vinie Hunt
July 27, 1915

Vinie
Wife of
E. D. Hunt
Dec. 19, 1896
Sept. 16, 1918

Calvin Hunt
Died Sept. 9, 1908
Age 63 years.

Susie Hunt
Died May 3, 1895

MT. ZION BAPTIST CHURCH CEMETERY

Barbara Hunt
Nov. 13, 1877
July 13, 1931
Mother

Darthula K.
Wife of
M. L. Hunt
1859 - 1895

HODGE

Nellie B. Hodge
Mar. 20, 1908
July 21, 1908

Elbert W. Hodge
Nov. 5, 1899
Oct. 6, 1904
Father will you meet me.

Lolie De Lilian Hodge
Died Dec. 17, 1937
Aged 5 months 6 days.

Sellis P. Hodge
Sept. 18, 1908
May 21, 1908

Earnest Hodge
Jan. 3, 1878
June 10, 1900

Anderson Hodge
Nov. 30, 1846
Jan. 27, 1913
At Rest.

William A. Hodge
Sept. 1, 1876
Nov. 24, 1904

Adaline Hodge
July 22, 1850
Sept. 11, 1892

SMALLING

Mrs. Dossie Smalling
Was born Dec. 11, 1900
Died Feb. 4, 1930

WADE

M. C. Wade

DOTSON

J. E. Dotson
Nov. 14, 1889
May 6, 1922
Don't weep after me
there is a place
with Jesus for me.

W. T. Dotson
June 4, 1862

His wife
Julia Ann
June 18, 1869
Trusting in Jesus.

Infant
Daughter of
Ike & Ludie Dotson
Nov. 5, 1923
Nov. 6, 1923
Sleeping in the arms
of Jesus.

SINGLETON

Arthur
Son of
W. E. & S. E. Singleton
Oct. 26, 1892
Nov. 1, 1892

WHITE

Thomas H.
Son of
T. E. & M. L. White
Oct. 14, 1907
Feb. 12, 1908

Bertha
Daughter of
T. E. & M. L. White
Feb. 24, 1902
Apr. 26, 1902

MT. ZION BAPTIST CHURCH CEMETERY

Rachel White
May 15, 1854
Nov. 21, 1897
The Lord calls me and I
am willilg and ready to go.

J. H. White
Apr. 17, 1854
Apr. 29, 1921
Gone to live with Jesus.

Wm. White
Feb. 14, 1858
Oct. 28, 1895

Infant
of
Mr. & Mrs. J. C. White
Sept. 27, 1916

Randa
Wife of
Joe White
Jan. 20, 1895
Mar. 29, 1913
Gone to rest.

Walter
Son of
Mr. & Mrs. Joe White
Jan. 7, 1919
Mar. 27, 1919

Martha White
Daughter of
S. Gray
Jan. 18, 1878
Feb. 28, 1898

Martha White
Apr. 1, 1820
July 1, 1887

B. L. White
Sept. 1, 1817
Feb. 19, 1864

TYLER

Nora Glan
Daughter of
Mr. & Mrs. Sam Tyler
Nov. 28, 1931
Jan. 9, 1937

J. C. Tyler
Apr. 1, 1851
Feb. 17, 1926

Samantha Tyler
Apr. 2, 1853
(Date of death not given)

HARDIN

Wm. E. Hardin
Co. B.
3 Tenn. Mt'd Inf.

Mary E. Hardin
Jan. 26, 1846
Aug. 30, 1902

Thomas J. Hardin
July 31, 1871
Aug. 11, 1871

Polly L. Hardin
Oct. 2, 1872
Aug. 7, 1874

Fanny M. Hardin
Dec. 26, 1874
Nov. 28, 1875

Polly Hardin
Wife of
J. C. R. Hardin
June 9, 1810
Died July 21, 1894

J. C. R. Hardin
Dec. 25, 1775
Jan. 3, 1881

SHADDEN

A. A. Shadden
Sept. 22, 1885
Jan. 19, 1888

Louis S. Shadden
Jan. 16, 1894
Mar. 5, 1904
Hee is waiting at the gate.

LOWERY OR LOWRY

MT. ZION BAPTIST CHURCH CEMETERY

Madge Jeanette
Dau. of
S. F. & M. R. Lowery
Apr. 6, 1924
Jan. 20, 1926
Our darling

Lee
Infant son of
J. A. & M. C. Lowry
Mar. 5, 1902
Aug. 3, 1902
Suffer little children
to come unto me.

Dorcas Emma
Daughter of
J. A. & M. C. Lowry
Nov. 9, 1895
Sept. 26, 1905
Gone but not forgotten.

SNYDER

Florence Snyder
Sept. 6, 1910
Jan. 17, 1936
Gone but not forgotten.

Fannie Gray
Wife of
Fred Snyder
July 8, 1895
June 20, 1918
Only sleeping.

TOWNSON

Mary
Wife of
C. Townson
Died April 10, 1909
Age 52 years.

Maggie Mays
Wife of
John Townson
May 22, 1873
Aug. 24, 1903

S. E. Townson
Feb. 9, 1842
Apr. 22, 1891

Bertha Townson
Jan. 12, 1898
Feb. 5, 1899

Lula Townson
May 27, 1907
May 27, 1907

CLINE

Mother
Carra Cline
Dec. 15, 1887
Aug. 27, 1932

READMOND

G. W. Readmond
Nov. 2, 1903
Nov. 17, 1903

S. M. Grason
Wife of
Bart Readmond
June 7, 1865
Aug. 22, 1909
Gone but not forgotten.

John H. Readmond
Aug. 25, 1889
Jan. 16, 1907
Gone to rest.

KENNEDY

Eunice Lee
Daughter of
J. M. & Artie Kennedy
Aug. 5, 1908
Nov. 2, 1908

Mary Kennedy
May 9, 1867
(Date of death not given)

MT. ZION BAPTIST CHURCH CEMETERY

C. A. Dennedy
Dec. 9, 1852
Feb. 8, 1921

Eunice L.
Daughter of
C. A. & Mary Kennedy
Nov. 3, 1905
June 27, 1906

Neoma I.
Daughter of
C. A. & Mary Kennedy
Aug. 21, 1904
May 9, 1906

Infant
Son of
C. A. & Mary Kennedy
Born & died
Oct. 12, 1894

Infant
Son of
C. A. & Mary Kennedy
Born & died June 10, 1897

Flora E.
Daughter of
C. A. & Mary Kennedy
Born Apr. 1, 1889-Died June 10, 1890

R. L. Kennedy
Apr. 12, 1884
Aug. 4, 1886

P. F. Kennedy
Jan. 29, 1890
July 9, 1891

J. F. Kennedy
U. S. Navy
Sept. 16, 1880
Apr. 13, 1904
Asleep in Jesus.

Father
William M. Kennedy
Nov. 8, 1842
Oct. 17, 1921

Mother
Chelnelsey Kennedy
Dec. 6, 1848
(Date of death not given.)

Cicero A. Kennedy Jr.
Mar. 31, 1905
Mar. 18, 1919
Gone but not forgotten.

Infant
of
J. P. & E. Kennedy
Jan. 17, 1908

Ulis Kennedy
May 22, 1907
Our Babies

WELLS

William Jr.
Son of
W. W. & M. D. Wells
May 11, 1918
June 19, 1919

McKEEHEN

Nancy
Wife of
W. M. McKeehen
Died Mar. 16, 1901
Age 20 years.

M. C. McKeehen
Aug. 24, 1898
Sept. 17, 1899

Jimmie
Mar. 5, 1902
July 10, 1902

Peter
June 6, 1905
Aug. 20, 1905
Children of
W. M. & Annie McKeehen

MT. ZION BAPTIST CHURCH CEMETERY

IVY

James B. Ivy
June 19, 1833
Feb. 12, 1899

Elizabeth Ivy
Feb. 26, 1834
Oct. 5, 1912

LEMING

Ethellone Leming
July 10, 1888
Oct. 12, 1903
Erected by W. H. Kirkland

KIRKLAND

Nonie Kirkland
Wife of
W. H. Kirkland
Daughter of
W. D. & Sarah E. Leming
Apr. 27, 1876
Apr. 22, 1901
I lived and died
for God.

Will Kirkland
July 4, 1888
Feb. 14, 1907
Gone but not forgotten.

Sammie W.
Son of
W. D. & M. A. Kirkland
Aug. 26, 1904
Oct. 3, 1904

James T.
Son of
W. D. & M. A. Kirkland
May 18, 1900
May 20, 1900

DEVINE

Thomas L. Devine
Sept. 6, 1885
Feb. 28, 1934
The rose may fade, the
lily die, but the flowers
immortal bloom on high.

MOSER

Father
J. B. Moser
Oct. 5, 1858
Sept. 27, 1925

Mother
Martha Moser
May 22, 1864
July 31, 1929
Gone but not forgotten.

BURCHFIELD

Infant
of
Mr. & Mrs. Edd Burchfield
Jan 7, 1929
Our darling

Robert C. Burchfield
Died June 29, 1938
Aged 65 yrs. 4 mos. 26 days.

Odis N. Burchfield
Died Sept. 19, 1938
Aged 33 yrs. 3 mos. 29 days.

BROWN

Harrison Brown
Died Nov. 20, 1935
Aged 19 yrs. 11 mos & 27 days.

HARRIS

Oscar
Son of
Boyd & Ida M. Harris
Born Aug. 15, 1908
Died Sept. 5, 1909

W. C. Harris
Mar. 19, 1890
Dec. 1, 1905

H. H. Harris
Apr. 1, 1855
Apr. 27, 1918

Martha Bly
Wife of
L. Harris
Dec. 30, 1879
Mar. 4, 1909

MT. ZION BAPTIST CHURCH CEMETERY

WATSON

Maggie
Daughter of
J. A. & M. E. Watson
Oct. 29, 1903
Mar. 22, 1912
Weep not she is at rest.

CURTIS

Gonia
Our darling
Daughter of
John & Jennie Curtis
Nov. 6, 1904
Aug. 27, 1907

Isaac Curtis
Nov. 3, 1885
Aug. 20, 1906
At Rest.

William Garrett Curtis
Feb. 19, 1897
Oct. 28, 1915
Dear boy gone but
not forgotten.

F. C. Curtis
Sept. 3, 1889
Feb. 9, 1891

Ines Curtis
Dec. 9, 1903
Jan. 3, 1904

Lizzie B.
Dau. of
R. F. & Ella Curtis
Feb. 16, 1907
July 29, 1907

Ella
Wife of
R. F. Curtis
Feb. 7, 1885
Dec. 20, 1908

Wince Curtis
Mar. 14, 1899
Nov. 21, 1926
Gone but not forgotten.

HICKS

Vena Hicks
1913--1926
In the arms of Jesus.

John Hicks
1873 - 1923
Gone but not forgotten.

WAYMAN

Mary Nell
Dau. of
C. W. & M. L. Wayman
Mar. 8, 1922
Oct. 15, 1928
Meet me in Heaven.

Susan
Wife of
N. F. Wayman
Sept. 26, 1862
Sept. 1, 1896

Reagan Siles Wayman
Son of
Mr. & Mrs. C. W. Wayman
Mar. 1, 1924
Sept. 1, 1925
A little time on earth
he spent till God for
him his Angels sent.

Walter Otto Wayman
Son of
Mr. & Mrs. C. W. Wayman
June 10, 1930
Dec. 9, 1930

CROWDER

Infant
of
E. & J. Crowder

NELSON

W. L. Nelson
Sept. 17, 1886
Aug. 19, 1888
Gone so soon.

MT. ZION BAPTIST CHURCH CEMETERY

M. Nelson
Dec. 16, 1887
June 1, 1888
Gone so soon.

MILLER

D. D. Miller
Jan. 11, 1925
Mar. 16, 1925

Hubert D. Miller
Jan. 9, 1918
June 17, 1919
Gone but not forgotten.

J. T. Miller
June 22, 1855
Nov. 8, 1921
Gone to rest.

CHASTAIN

A. B.
Son of
Guss & Mary E. Chastain
Born & died
Apr. 19, 1912

Thomas J. Chastain
Feb. 11, 1877
May 30, 1917

Nancy
Dau. of
A. B. & Elizabeth Chastain
Sept. 29, 1904
Aug. 24, 1906

SMILEY

Smiley
W. P.
Infant of
W. G. & A. M. Smiley
Nov. 24, 1916
Feb. 8, 1917
Darling we miss Thee.

FELTY

Eliza Felty
Nov. 22, 1841
May 29, 1908
Asleep in Jesus.

DUN OR DUNN

Jane Dun
Wife of
Arch Dun
Oct. 14, 1863
Aug. 15, 1900
At Rest.

Arch Dunn
Oct. 13, 1855
Sept. 11, 1934
Beloved how we miss you.

RUSSELL

Hannah
Wife of
Cal Russell
Died July 10, 1905
Age 29 years.
Asleep in Jesus.

Mamie
Daughter of
Cal and Catherine Russell
Oct. 10, 1907
Oct. 15, 1908

YATES

Malisa D. Yates
Nov. 20, 1882
Dec. 8, 1901
Gone but not forgotten.

MILLSAPS

Fannie Millsaps
Apr. 17, 1865
June 17, 1884

MT. ZION BAPTIST CHURCH CEMETERY

W. A. Milsaps
Born June 13, 1834
Died Dec. 24, 1889

LINDSEY

Mary Jane Lindsey
Nov. 26, 1873
Mar. 16, 1894

Martha Lindsey
1854 - 1914
At Rest.

Isaac Samuel Lindsey
Sept. 15, 1889
Feb. 17, 1907

W. B. Lindsey
Feb. 17, 1899
Sept. 11, 1905

HENDERSON

Infant
Son of
M. L. & Sarah Henderson
Born & died
May 8, 1908

Infant
Son of
M. L. & Sarah Henderson
Born & died
May 10, 1904

John E.
Son of
M. L. & Sarah Henderson
Dec. 29, 1909
Jan. 13, 1910

Infant
Daughter of
M. L. & Sarah Henderson
Born & died
Dec. 18, 1910

Georgia A.
Son of
M. L. & Sarah Henderson
Born & died
Jan. 12, 1912

Sarah Henderson
Feb. 11, 1874
Dec. 23, 1913

WILLIAMS

H. Williams
Mar. 31, 1896
June 16, 1899

GOODEN

J. H. Gooden
Feb. 14, 1859
Jan. 23, 1922

Bettie Gooden
Died June 18, 1938
Age 68 years 5 mos. 9 days.

BRADLEY

James Bradley
Mar. 8, 1836
July 20, 1905

Elizabeth
Wife of
James Bradley
Dec. 1, 1836
Oct. 10, 1911

Vinie
Wife of
Lafayette Bradley
May 12, 1869
Jan. 1, 1897
As a wife devoted
As a mother kind and
as a friend ever true.

Lafayette Bradley
Feb. 10, 1866
Oct. 20, 1901
Another link is broken
in our household band
but a chain is forming in
a better land.

MCCULLOCH

MT. ZION BAPTIST CHURCH CEMETERY

Gracy Mae McCulloch
Aug. 25, 1901
Apr. 4, 1913

Infant
of
T. D. & M. L. McCulloch
Nov. 18, 1904
Nov. 18, 1904

Mary L. McCulloch
May 19, 1869
Jan. 28, 1905

BRACKETT

John W.
Son of
N. D. & F. P. Brackett
July 30, 1908
Sept. 16, 1911

Horace N.
Son of
T. G. & Sarah Brackett
July 18, 1892
May 1, 1912

CRAIG

Infant
of
F. G. & L. Craig
May 29, 1906
May 30, 1906

Lusinda
Wife of
F. G. Craig
Apr. 23, 1865
June 5, 1906
At rest in peace.

CHAMBERS

Lassie R.
Daughter of
W. T. & R. R. Chambers
Feb. 14, 1909
Apr. 1, 1909
Asleep in Jesus.

DYER

Margaret Dyer
Nov. 8, 1836
May 8, 1906

BRYSON

Nervey E.
Wife of
J. H. Bryson
Dec. 22, 1860
Dec. 19, 1885
Blessed are the dead
which die in the Lord.

Mary -- Bryson
Born March 2, 1799
Died Feb. 10, 1885

BROOKS

Delena E. Brooks
July 26, 1885
Nov. 14, 1908

Infant
of
J. F. & D. E. Brooks

BROWN

Joseph Brown
Oct. 1, 1843
Jan. 12, 1847

Sarah Brown
July 17, 1844
Sept. 11, 1845

SELF

Self

Self

C. W. Ba
1929

(Note: Above inscription
as is. LMcC.)

MONTOE COUNTY

TOMBSTONE INSCRIPTIONS

MULLINS CEMETERY

Copied by: Lawrence McConkey, Englewood, Tennessee.
Date:

The Mullins Cemetery is on the farm of Robert Mullins about
12 miles East of Madisonville. It may be reached by following
the Povo Road to edge of farm of Russell Lindsey, then turn
left.

This is a neighborhood cemetery and there are 38 graves with
inscriptions and approximately one hundred unmarked graves.

MCLEMORE

Donie
Daughter of
W. M. & Margaret McLemore
Aug. 1, 1888
July 10, 1910

William Ira McLemore
Died July 30, 1938
Aged 3 years & 4 days.

Mary Jane McLemore
Feb. 11, 1933
Mar. 15, 1935
At Rest.

Marry McLemore
Died June 12, 1931

L. L. McLemore
Died Feb. 23, 1936

-------- McLemore

MULLINS

Lewis L.
Son of
J. R. & A. L. Mullins
June 27, 1904
Dec. 21, 1911
We will meet again.

Infant
Mullins.

Kittie
Daughter of
J. R. & A. L. Mullins
Aug. 27, 1900
Nov. 28, 1904

WHITE

Hugh Clenton White
June 13, 1912
Oct. 24, 1912

J. N. White
Jan. 29, 1863
Aug. 5, 1898

Eve White
May 25, 1879
Dec. 3, 1893
At Rest.

Nervie White
June 21, 1906
May 10, 1908

William Gath White
June 27, 1916
Aug. 1, 1916

Esther White
Sept. 5, 1842
Jan. 3, 1910

Allen N. White
Dec. 22, 1842
Oct. 26, 1906

- 2

MULLINS CEMETERY

A. L. White

Mary White

HICKS

Elbert Hicks
Aug. 27, 1907
June 11, 1908

Pheba
Wife of
Ed Hicks
Sept. 16, 1879
July 25, 1933

E. Hicks

Maggie Hicks
Nov. 27, 1898
Jan. 7, 1899

WILBURN

M. J. Wilburn
Infant of
P. A. & E. J. Wilburn
Mar. 8, 1880
Mar. 16, 1880

Infant
of
P. A. & E. J. Wilburn

P. A. Wilburn

E. J. Wilburn

HENRY

James Henry
Died Oct. 11, 1937
Aged 1 yr. 5 mos. 13 days.

Addie Henry
March 5, 1928
Aged 43 yrs. 1 mo. 16 days.

Paul Henry
Jan. 26, 1909
Jan. 1, 1910

Infant
of
W. C. & A. D. Henry
Feb. 17, 1903

Infant
of
----- Henry

JENKINS

Mary Jenkins

James Jenkins

JONES

E. S. Jones

A. J. Jones

Infant
Jones

Betty Jones

Mandy --------
Born Apr. 16, 1872
Died Jan. --, ----

C. J.

B. C. M.

HAMMONTREE

Hammontree
Hiram
Jan. 2, 1843
Mar. 24, 1917

Phoebe
Oct. 8, 1859
June 26, 1938

MONROE COUNTY

TOMBSTONE INSCRIPTIONS

NEW BETHEL HOLINESS CHURCH CEMETERY

Copied by: Lawrence McConkey, Englewood, Tennessee
Date:

New Bethel Holiness Church and Cemetery are located 9 miles
South of Madisonville. To reach them take Tellico Plains
road to Hauns or Watkins Mill then road leading to McConkeys
School; or, go 1½ miles down the L. & N. Railroad from Mt.
Vernon to the farm of Henry Harris. The land for both the
church and cemetery were furnished by Henry Harris in 1923.
The earliest inscription is dated Oct. 2, 1923. The graves
cover about ¼ acre but the cemetery comprises 1 acre. There
is no fence. The church is practically abandoned but the
cemetery is still used. There are 10 inscriptions; 12 graves
marked by field stones & 18 unmarked graves.

CROFT

Infant
of
A. -- Croft
Born Oct. 18, 1935

MOSES

Annie Moses
Died June 28, 1938
Aged 35 years 2 months
& 24 days.

(Note: There are other
graves nearby. LMcC.)

WATSON & NEWMAN

Willie Watson
March 11, 1927
March 16, 1927

J. C. Newman
Mar. 18, 1924
Mar. 19, 1924
Gone but not forgotten.

Winnie Mae Bille Newman
April 13, 1921
Oct.   2, 1923
She was the sunshine
of our home.

Father
Sam W. Newman
Nov. 3, 1888
Jan. 4, 1933

Mother
Ervin Newman
Mar. 13, 1895
(Living)
Gone but not forgotten.

(Note: There are several
unmarked graves here but
some of them may not be
graves of this family. LMcC.)

LEE

Hubert Lee

HARRIS

S. T. Harris
Nov. 11, 1928
Nov. 11, 1928

Mrs. Fanna M. Harris
Died June 21, 1934
Aged 68 yrs. 3 mos. & 7 days.

Eliga Harris
Died May 14, 1934
Aged 76 years, 10 months & 24 days.

MONROE COUNTY

TOMBSTONE INSCRIPTIONS

MARY ANN NICHOLDS GRAVE

Copied by: Lawrence McConkey, Englewood, Tennessee
Date: Jan. 1939

The grave of Mary Ann Nicholds is located on the farm of
Nancy Cable. The farm is near Mt. Pleasant School or about
7 miles up Citico Creek near where the creek road and the
Little Tennessee river roads intersect, and about 35 miles
Northeast of Madisonville.

She and her husband entered a large tract of this mountain
land. He died several years before she did. They were the
parents of several children.

NICHOLDS

Mary Ann Nicholds
Born Oct. 5, 1799
Died Jan. 14, 1877

Copied by: Lawrence McConkey, Englewood, Tennessee.
Date:

In 1853 William Watson and his wife, Rebecca, gave a three
acre plot of land as follows: One acre for school grounds,
one acre for church grounds and one acre for a cemetery.
The Notchey Creek Baptist Church was established that year.
The cemetery had already been established for several years
on the Watson farm. The burial of Hughes Torbett, who died
Aug. 11, 1844, is the oldest one indicated by markers, but
George Crofts was buried about the same date.

William Watson entered and acquired over 800 acres of land
surrounding the cemetery. It is believed that one fourth of
those buried in this cemetery were descendants of William
Watson. Also a majority were relatives of each other.

The cemetery is at Notchey Creek 4 miles South of Madisonville
on the Tellico Plains Pike.

There are 331 inscriptions and 300 or more unmarked graves in
this cemetery. Many buried here were 70 years or older when
they died and many were parents of from 8 to 19 children.

PATTERSON

Nannie C. Henderson
Wife of
Charlie Patterson
Dec. 22, 1873
Apr. 1, 1920
We miss the voice of
one we loved.
A precious one from us
has gone. A voice we
loved is stilled. A
place is vacant in our
home that never can be
filled.

Patterson
Easter Patterson
Sept. 12, 1891
June   6, 1926
She was the sunshine
of our home.

Vestie Patterson
Aug. 17, 1907
Apr. 18, 1915
Safe in the arms
of Jesus.

Rachel Patterson
Oct. 26, 1857
Apr. 27, 1915

Susan Patterson
Jan. 1, 1810
July 30, 1898

George Patterson
May 17, 1868
Aged 65 years.

Chas. Patterson
Died Feb. 22, 1936
Aged 66 years

Lee Patterson
Died May 14, 19--
Aged 33 years.

NOTCHEY CREEK BAPTIST CHURCH CEMETERY

WATSON

Mother
Fannie
Wife of
J. N. Watson
Sept. 6, 1869
Dec. 25, 1936
Asleep in Jesus.

Father
J. N. Watson
Apr. 15, 1873
June 15, 1929
Asleep in Jesus.

Mr. B. Watson
Died Nov. 28, 1935
Aged 16 years.

Holston Watson
Died --- 17, 1935
Aged 17 yrs. 6 days.

Johnie Watson
Died July 13, 1928
Aged 59 yrs. 10 mos. 9 days.

Rebeckey Watson
June 26, 1849
Feb. 12, 1927
She was a kind and
affectionate wife, a
fond mother and a
friend to all.

R. B. Watson
Died Nov. 29, 1934
Aged 10 yrs. 1 mo. & 23 days.

Phebie Watson
Feb. 11, 1858
Mar. 25, 1932
Gone but not forgotten.

Mrs. Lochie Watson
Died June 16, 1931
Aged 32 yrs. 10 mos. 21 days.

Flossie Mae Watson
July 29, 1909
Mar. 20, 1926
Prepare to meet me
in Heaven.

Phebe
Daughter of
Sam & Titia Watson
July 16, 1906
Nov. 2, 1906

William Watson
(Born About 1790
(Died about 1860
(Note: Above dates are not
on marker. LMcC.)

Rebecca
Wife of
William Watson

Robert Watson
Born 1830
Aged 74 years.

Mary Ann
Wife of
Robert Watson
Died 1875
Aged about 72 years.

Janie Watson
Daughter of
W. H. & Mary A. Watson
Born 1876
Died 1926

Berdie Watson

Thomas Watson

James Watson

Charlotte Watson
Died Nov. 29, 19(can't read)
Aged 58 yrs. 8 months.

Verna Sue Watson
June 4, 1923
Dec. 12, 1924

Joe Watson
Aug. 1, 1891
July 5, 1917
Gone to rest.

NOTCHEY CREEK BAPTIST CHURCH CEMETERY

Hartwell
Son of
Marion & Josie Watson
Died 1918

James Watson

Lottie Newman
Wife of
James Watson

Chas E.
Son of
Mr. & Mrs. J. W. Watson
Oct. 21, 1925
June 4, 1927

Rufus Watson
Feb. 14, 1852
Sept. 11, 1935
and Children

Berdie
Dau. of
Rufus & Frances Watson
Born 1896
Died 1906

Effie
Daughter of
Rufus & Frances Watson
Born 1898
Died 1904

Sarah A.
Wife of
Uriah Watson
Sept. 4, 1863
Nov. 23, 1923
We join Thee in that
Heavenly Land, no more
to take the parting
hand.

Uriah Watson
Nov. 6, 1858
Apr. 2, 1935
Gone beyond the skies.

Austin C. Watson
Dec. 22, 1888
Sept. 21, 1934
To live in hearts
we leave behind
is not to die.

(Note: He had been County
School Superintendant and
interested in Civics. LMcC.)

Archie Watson
April 22, 1882
Oct. 8, 1893,

Elihu Watson
Mar. 21, 1893
Oct. 2, 1893

Tennessee Watson
Sept. 23, 1886
Oct. 12, 1893

Infant
Watson

Ethleen Watson
Dec. 12, 1921
Jan. 3, 1922
Daughter of
Starling Watson.

Beddie
Wife of
Tom Watson
Jan. 4, 1890
Sept. 26, 1920
Gone but not forgotten.

J. B. Watson
Jan. 29, 1915
Jan. 26, 1934
We will meet again.

David Watson

Bettie Jane Watson
Died July 11, 1937
Aged 6 days.

NOTCHEY CREEK BAPTIST CHURCH CEMETERY

Nellie Watson
Apr. 23, 1903
Aug. 14, 1904

Mattie
Daughter of
John & Mary Watson

Father
John Watson
Feb. 8, 1864
Sep. 21, 1916
A precious one from
us is gone. A voice we
loved is stilled. A place
is vacant in our home
that never can be filled.

Josie Watson

Henry Watson

William Watson
Born About 1831
Aged about 80 yrs.

Mollie
Wife of
William Watson
Born about 1835
Aged about 65 yrs.

George Watson

Rachel Watson

Willie Merle
Daughter of
Mr. & Mrs. B. W. Watson
Nov. 26, 1922
May 14, 1924
She was the sunshine
of our home.

Rev. James E. Watson
May 7, 1839
May 14, 1882

Infant
of
S. M. & Elsie Watson
Feb. 12, 1924
Feb. 12, 1924

Albert Hoyet
Son of
Mr. & Mrs. I. H. Watson
Apr. 17, 1933
Apr. 28, 1934
Asleep in Jesus.
J. S. Watson

E. L. Watson

B. C. Watson

Cricket
Wife of
W. H. Watson
1883 - 1938
At Rest.

Mary A.
Wife of
W. H. Watson
Aug. 20, 1853
Aug. 12, 1916
A true wife and
a dear mother.

Alice Raper
Wife of
Marion Watson
1865 - 1885

Mary Watson
Feb. 3, 1882
Apr. 9, 1916

Martha Watson

Taylor Watson

Adline Watson
1876 - 1910

Lethia Watson

NOTCHEY CREEK BAPTIST CHURCH CEMETERY

MOSES

Henry Moses
Dec. 10, 1875
Feb. 10, 1913

Samuel Moses
Aug. 10, 1844
Feb. 11, 1922
At Rest.

Alta Morrow Moses
Feb. 24, 1842
Feb. 17, 1924
At Rest.

LAND

William E. Land
July 11, 1906
Dec. 4, 1909

JONES

Benjamin Fred Jones
Died Jan. 23, 1931
Aged 3 days.

RAPER

Lena Raper

Caroline
Wife of
J. M. Raper
Mar. 18, 1870
Apr. 4, 1932
Our mother at rest.

Riley Raper

Mary Gibson
Wife of
Riley Raper

----- Watson
Wife of
Riley Raper

J. R. Raper
Apr. 8, 1899
Feb. 19, 1900
Our darling baby
has gone before.

Martha A. Watson
Wife of
J. H. Raper
May 10, 1856
Feb. 3, 1882
At Rest.

J. H. Raper

Mary A. Raper
Oct. 9, 1824
Oct. 16, 1897

J. S. Raper
Oct. 11, 1821
Feb. 14, 1898

Infant
of
----- Raper

W. J. Raper

Sarah Raper

John Raper

MASON

Mary Sue Mason
Died Oct. 10, 1919

MULLENS

Zymblee Mullens
July 31, 1910
Aug. 2, 1911
Our darling baby
We miss Thee.

DYER

Casper Dyer
1885 - 1908

Marvin Dyer
1895 - 1916

Grady Dyer
1893 - 1920

Arthur Dyer
1890 - 1920

NOTCHEY CREEK BAPTIST CHURCH CEMETERY

Infant
Dyer

ATKINS

Carl Atkins

Infants
Son
and
Daughter
of
Mr. & Mrs. R. W. Atkins
Aug. 13, 1937

Willie Atkins
Born Mar. 2, 1913
(all that was on marker)

Robert Atkins

John
Son of
J. N. & M. E. Atkins
July 27, 1896
Aug. 3, 1896
Our Baby

M. J. Atkins

Annie
Daughter of
  John & Mary Watson
Wife of
Thomas R. Atkins
Born 1888
Aged about 21 years.

Willard
Daughter of
Alex. & Tildia Belcher
Wife of
T. R. Atkins
June 20, 1871
Apr. 18, 1902
At Rest.

Thomas Atkins
Oct. 30, 1877
June 9, 1910
At Rest.

Cora Atkins
Sept. 8, 1895
Sept. 29, 1898
At Rest.

Infant
of
J. W. Atkins
Apr. 2, 1918

Dollie Watson
Wife of
Joe Atkins
Daughter of
John & Mary Watson
Sept. 29, 1890
Apr. 22, 1918
At Rest.

Andy Atkins
May 25, 1852
June 11, 1937

Juretta Tallent
Wife of
Andy Atkins
Nov. 24, 1860
Apr. 12, 1924

(Note: The above were the
parents of 17 children and
all lived to be grown. LMcC.)

Eligah Atkins
Born about 1848
Aged about 75 yrs.

Caroline
Wife of
Eligah Atkins
Born about 1850
Aged about 71 yrs.

Sarah Atkins

J. E. Atkins

Infant
of
J. N. & Luda Atkins
Born & died April 9, 1892
At Rest.

NOTCHEY CREEK BAPTIST CHURCH CEMETERY

Luda Ervin
Wife of
J. N. Atkins
Jan. 22, 1874
April 22, 1892
Aged 18 yrs. & 3 mos.
She is in Heaven.

Sarah Jane Malone
Wife of
Worth Atkins
Born about 1865
Aged about 30 yrs.

Josie Malone
Wife of
Worth Atkins
Born about 1874 - aged 28 yrs.

SLOAN

Daisy
Inf. of
Mr. & Mrs. J. C. Sloan
Nov. 14, 1907
Dec. 3, 1907
Our darling baby.

J. C. Jr.
Inf. of
Mr. & Mrs. J. C. Sloan
Apr. 4, 1915
Apr. 9, 1915
Our darling baby.

TALLENT

Fanney Tallent
June 14, 1822
Oct. 11, 1887

James Tallent
Oct. 20, 1824
June 8, 1906

T. R. Tallent
Mar. 28, 1845
Apr. 20, 1893

Nancy Jane Tallent
Wife of
T. R. Tallent
Feb. 14, 1845
(Date of death not given)

(Note: Tallent was killed
and Nancy Jane Tallent
married Ham Wimberley and
this grave is between their
graves. LMcC.)

John Tallent
1870 - 1892

Carrie Tallent
Aug. 3, 1903
Apr. 10, 1904
With Angels above.

Vesta
Daughter of
Mr. & Mrs. J. C. Tallent
Jan. 7, 1902
Nov. 3, 1918
Gone but not forgotten.

Tallent
Jasper C.
June 10, 1865
Mar. 19, 1936

Eliza J.
Nov. 13, 1869
Jan. 10, 1929
At rest, with Thee.

Malinda C. Tallent
Died Nov. 11, 1926
Aged 69 years.

Carrie Viola
Daughter of
John & Myrtle Tallent
Mar. 30, 1917
Apr. 12, 1921
We miss Thee.

NOTCHEY CREEK BAPTIST CHURCH CEMETERY

Dixie Ila
Daughter of
J. H. & M. Tallent
Feb. 20, 1912
July 21, 1912
We miss Thee.

Bud Tallent
Born About 1851
Aged about 50 yrs.

Savilla Tallent
1843 - 1911
Second wife of James Tallent.

Cate
Daughter of
Geo. & Elizabeth Tallent
Aged about 4 yrs.

AKINS

L. C. Akins
Mar. 9, 1869
(Date of death not given)

J. H. Akins
June 28, 1857
May 25, 1921
Mother & Father
Gone to rest.

WILSON

Hairse
Son of
I. N. & Bettie Wilson
Sept. 30, 1905
May 29, 1920

Bettie
Daughter of
I. N. & Bettie Wilson
Feb. 5, 1902
Apr. 19, 1904
She was the sunshine of
our home.

Inis
Daughter of
I. N. & Bettie Wilson
June 17, 1898
Jan. 6, 1901
Asleep in Jesus.

Alice Haun
Wife of
I. N. Wilson
June 3, 1850
June 14, 1892

I. N. Wilson
Sept. 12, 1848
May 6, 1910

BALL

Cornellius Ball

Mollie Ball
Born July 23, 1882
Died Dec. 31, 1903

Infant
of
Mr. & Mrs. Isaac Ball

Infant
of
Mr. & Mrs. Isaac Ball

Louisa Mason
Wife of
H. Ball
Apr. 10, 1838
Feb. 5, 1900
At Rest.

Henry Ball
Born about 1833
Aged about -- yrs.

Infant
of
J. D. & Nanie Ball

Infant of
of
J. D. & Nanie Ball

Infant
of
J. D. & Nanie Ball

Bernard Isham Ball
Aug. 11, 1907
Oct. 13, 1910
Gone but not forgotten.

NOTCHEY CREEK BAPTIST CHURCH CEMETERY

Beatrice Ball
Died Jan. 30, 1907
Age 1 yr. 2 mos.
Gone but not forgotten.

John E. Ball
June 19, 1893
 Jan. 16, 1911

C. W. Ball
Died Oct. 10, 1903
Age 53 yrs.

Isham Ball

Minnie Lowery
Wife of
I. E. Ball

Ball

Ball

DAILEY

Infants of
Mr. & Mrs. C. W. Dailey
Lena Merele
Aug. 8, 1916
June 16, 1918

Carrie Mae
June 5, 1920
Gone but not forgotten.

BIBEE

Ruthey E. White
Wife of
R. B. Bibee
Dec. 19, 1855
July 2, 1925
She was a kind and
affectionate wife a fond
mother and a friend
to all.

Pleasley
SSon of
R. B. & R. E. Bibee
May 1, 1901
June 1, 1920
Just asleeping until
the Resurrection Morn.

MCCONKEY

Enos C. McConkey
Nov. 30, 1889
Nov. 6, 1918
Gone but not forgotten.

McConkey
Joh J.
1859 - 1937

Mary E.
1862 - (Still living)
Awaiting the Resurrection.

GIBSON

Dorthey E. Bibee
Wife of
Jim Gibson
Nov. 19, 1896
Jan. 8, 1925
Gone but not forgotten.

Elige Gibson
Died Sept. 27, 1929
Aged 37 yrs. 8 mos. 6 days.

Martha M. Gibson
Jan. 26, 1864
Aug. 18, 1930
She was too good, too gentle
and fair to dwell in
this cold world of care.

Eligah Gibson
Oct. 12, 1861
Feb. 13, 1926
Father let thy grace
be given that we
may meet in Heaven.

Earl
Son of
Eliga & M. Gibson
Aug. 15, 1902
Sept. 8, 1902

Lucresie Gibson
Born 1827
Died Feb. 14, 1907
Sleeping in the arms of
Jesus in Heaven. We hope
to meet her.

NOTCHEY CREEK BAPITST CHURCH CEMETERY

John Gibson
Born About 1820
Aged about 45 years.

Frank Gibson

G. W.
Son of
Eliga & M. Gibson
Jan. 4, 1888
July 4, 1888

Maranda McConkey
Wife of
George Gibson
1870 - 1935

Alice Atkins
Wife of
John Gibson
Died Nov. 19, 1936
Aged 66 yrs. 6 mos. 1 day.

John Gibson
Born about 1865
Aged about 53 years.

John Wesley
Son of
J. W. & A. L. Gibson
April 20, 1905
Aug. 20, 1905

Bernard Earl Gibson
Mar. 13, 1919
Mar. 7, 1937
The Lord hath need
of him.

KEY

Wesley Edward Key
Died Sept. 22, 1936
Aged 19 yrs. 3 mos. 13 days.

LEE

Alice
Wife of
Neal Lee
Sept. 28, 1860
Oct. 8, 1930
Gone but not forgotten.

Neal Lee

Rachel Stephens
Wife of
A. R. Lee
May 19, 1885
Sept. 26, 1914

Father
(Masonic member)
I. C. Lee
Apr. 4, 1846
Nov. 12, 1919

Martha
Wife of
I. C. Lee
Jan. 3, 1849
June 21, 1869
Blessed are the dead
which die in the Lord.

Jas. W. Lee
June 18, 1861
Sept. 18, 1869

Infant
daughter of
I. C. & L. Lee
June 5, 1873
Aug. 24, 1873

Infant Daughter
of
I. C. & L. Lee
Nov. 2, 1882
Nov. 2, 1882

Troy Blane
Son of
Charlie & Buna Lee
Apr. 18, 1914
Apr. 24, 1914

BELCHER

At Rest
Charlie Belcher
Son of
J. B. & Nancy Belcher
Oct. 28, 1907
Oct. 30, 1907
Gone so soon

NOTCHEY CREEK BAPTIST CHURCH CEMETERY

Beuna
Daughter of
J. H. & M. Belcher
Dec. 25, 1909
Jan. 1, 1910

ARDEN

At Rest
Nannie
Daughter of
J. H. & Mollie Belcher
Wife of
Frank Arden
Oct. 29, 1895
Aug. 24, 1915

MITCHELL

Mary Sue Mitchell
Dau. of
Ira Mitchell & wife
Born Sept. 18, 1933
and died in Infancy

Malinda
Wife of
J. W. Mitchell
July 29, 1829
Nov. 17, 1896
Blessed are the
dead which die
in the Lord.

J. W. Mitchell
Husband of
M. J. Mitchell
Apr. 22, 1822
Aug. 2, 1869
Blessed are the dead
which die in the Lord.

Lizzie H. Mitchell
July 17, 1851
June 27, 1935

Lewis A. Mitchell
Aug. 20, 1856
(Still Living)

HAUN

F. L. Haun
Aug. 24, 1905
Oct. 27, 1923
Gone but not forgotten.
Leslie

(Note: Leslie is the given
name. LMcC.)

Earl
Infant of
Mr. & Mrs. Luther Haun
June 7, 1923
At Rest.

Ora
Daughter of
J. L. & J. C. Haun
Jan. 25, 18--
Nov. 14, 1897

A. W. Haun
Aug. 29, 1858
Mar. 18, 1924
At Rest.

Callie Mitchell
Wife of
A. W. Haun
Aug. 7, 1858
Jan. 19, 1892
At Rest.

Infant
of
A. W. & C. Haun

Infant
of
A. W. & C. Haun

Infant
of
A. W. & Callie Haun

Infant
of
A. W. & Callie Haun

Infant
of
A. W. & Callie Haun

Infant
of
A. W. & Callie Haun

Mary A. Haun
Born Jan. 1, 1826
Died Apr. 20, 1904

S. M. Haun
Nov. 20, 1820
Nov. 21, 1899
Ordained a Baptist
Minister Jan. 10, 1852
Masonic member.

(Note: The above was the
first pastor of Notchey
Creek Baptist Church.
LMcC.)

GARREN

Leander Garren
May 8, 1818
Jan. 27, 1865

STEPHENS

Gordon H. Stephens
Oct. 7, 1925
Aug. 15, 1928
Now thou art gone
beyond the reach
of woe.
Where sorrow tears
shall ever cease to flow.
Our Baby.

J. T. Stephens
June 19, 1923
Nov. 27, 1923
Gone but not forgotten.

Annie Biboe
Wife of
Robert Stephons
July 4, 1894
July 3, 1927
She was the Sun-
shine of our home.

L. A. Stephens
Apr. 29, 1892
Oct. 4, 1893
Our Darling Baby.

J. H. Stephens
Sept. 19, 1897
Oct. 24, 1898
Our Darling Baby

S. I. Stephens
May 9, 1894
Mar. 9, 1905
We miss Thee.

PRESSWOOD

Rev. J. H. Presswood
Feb. 16, 1812
Feb. 20, 1900

NEWMAN

M. M. Newman
Died Feb. 2, 1937

J. W. Newman
Feb. 24, 1895
July 22, 1924
It was hard indeed
to part with thee
but Christ's strong
arm supported me.

Mother
Marinda
Wife of
L. C. Newman
Jan. 4, 1842
May 29, 1919
Gone to rest.

Father
Cleve Newman
May 3, 1837
Mar. 30, 1922
Discharged from U. S.
Service Nov. 30, 1864

Cleve Newman
Co. G.
Tenn. Mtd. Inf.
May 3, 1837
Mar. 30, 1922

(Note: Above is an
extra marker. LMcC.)

NOTCHEY CREEK BAPTIST CHURCH CEMETERY

HARRIS

On Wings of love
To a Heavenly Home
Archie Harris
Oct. 14, 1892
Jan. 23, 1914

Ezekiel Harris
Oct. 15, 1845
Dec. 21, 1912
Gone to Rest.

Fanney Harris

DUGGAN

J. A. Duggan
June 10, 1847
Mar. 17, 1912
Father gone but
not forgotten.

CROFTS

James Crofts

Nancy Jane Watson
Wife of
James Crofts

Artie Crofts
Died May 31, 1936
Aged 60 years, 15 days.

Nancy Jane Crofts

R. F. Crofts

Ellen Crofts

William Crofts
Sept. 11, 1904
Oct. 12, 1904

Viola Crofts
Sept. 22, 1912
Sept. 11, 1913

Luther M. C. Crofts
Jan. 8, 1898
Feb. 21, 1915
Gone but not forgotten.

George Crofts

Mrs. George Crofts

(Note: the above two persons
were born before 1800 and
died about 1844. LMcC.)

Hazel Crofts
Son of
James & Nancy Jane Crofts
Killed July 6, 1901
Aged about 18 yrs.

Infant
of
G. W. & Elizabeth Crofts

Andrew Crofts

Bettie Watson
Wife of
Geo. Crofts
Born 1830
Died 1935

Betty Crofts

Rufus Crofts

S. E. Crofts

J. R. Crofts

Mary Crofts

IRONS

Martha A. Irons
Died Jan. 26, 1912
Aged 26 yrs.

Mattie L. Irons
Born Nov. 3, 1908
Died May 15, 1909
Our darling.

NOTCHEY CREEK BAPTIST CHURCH CEMETERY

Raymond R. Irons
June 21, 1907
Jan. 2, 1908
Our darling.

Alvin Irons

TORBETT OR TORBET

Rock of Ages
S. H. Torbett
July 3, 1881
(Still Living)

Callie
Wife of
S. H. Torbett
Nov. 15, 1887
May 31, 1919
Awaiting The Resurrection.

Troy William Torbett
Feb. 6, 1917
Sept. 30, 1918
Gone to rest.

Infant
of
Mr. & Mrs. Joe V. Torbett

Susie Ann Torbett
Died Dec. 1st 1935

Hughes Torbett
Died Aug. 11, 1944
Aged 42 years.

Mary Torbett
Died May 27, 1879
Aged 81 years
Father & mother

Uriah H. Torbett
Dec. 25, 1832
June 17, 1852
Our loved one has gone.

Nancy Ann Torbett
Nov. 25, 1827
Aug. 26, 1905

Lucinda Torbett
May 10, 1832
June 30, 1897
(Continued on next page)

One by one our hopes
grow brighter as we
near the shining shore.

David A. Torbett
Feb. 22, 1831
Jan. -- 1873
One by one our hopes
grow brighter as we
near the shining shore.

Mary Jane Torbett
Aug. 6, 1856
Mar. 6, 1909

Edith Torbett
Dec. 8, 1916
Oct. 15, 1920

Luther Torbett
Died Nov. 4, 1932
Aged 33 yrs. 6 mos. 26 days.

John Torbett
Aug. 11, 1870
May 8, 1932

Marget Torbett
Aug. 14, 1873
June 7, 1921
A precious Mother
and Father
At Rest.

Edward Torbet
Apr. 9, 1915
July 3, 1916
Gone but not forgotten.

Roy Torbett
Mar. 27, 1915
Dec. 19, 1933
Gone but not forgotten.

Lucy Torbett
Jan. 1, 1901
June 13, 1905

Mary Lou Torbett

RODGERS OR ROGERS

NOTCHEY CREEK BAPTIST CHURCH CEMETERY

Susan Rodgers
May 10, 1857
Mar. 29, 1883
Resting with Thee.

J. M. Rogers
May 10, 1853
July 1, 1919

Louisa E. Rogers
Oct. 28, 1852
Dec. 12, 1936
At Rest.

Infant
of
Mr. & Mrs. A. A. Rogers
Born & Died
Oct. 22, 1927
Gone to a better land.

Thomas Rogers

Tennessee McDaniel
Wife of
Geo. Rogers
Died Sept. 26, 1936
Aged 64 yrs. 8 days.

George Rogers
Born 1870
Aged about 63 yrs.

WATKINS

Martha J. Tallent
Wife of
Henry Watkins
Feb. 11, 1855
Oct. 19, 1924
At Rest.

Father
Henry C. Watkins
Feb. 13, 1852
Aug. 18, 1894
At Rest.

(Note: The above were the
parents of 19 children. LMcC.)

SHARP

Sharp
Erma Geraldine
Dau. of
H. H. & Lena Sharp
Jan. 18, 1925
Apr. 20, 1925
Darling we miss Thee.

KING

Carl T.
Infant son of
Mr. & Mrs. C. B. King
Oct. 23, 1897
Jan. 2, 1898
Of such is the
Kingdom of Heaven.

(Mason member)
W. B. King
Nov. 1, 1836
Feb. 1, 1901

Callie
Daughter of
J. K. & Sarah King
1873 - 1889

Nancy Jane
Dau. of
J. K. & Sarah King
1870-1888

Mollie Rice King
Daughter of
W. B. & S. M. King
July 16, 1891
Mar. 31, 1893
Our dear baby

S. M. King
July 18, 1852
Feb. 4, 1927

J. K. King
Jan. 8, 1847
Feb. 6, 1883
Awaiting a glorious
Resurrection.

MALONE

NOTCHEY CREEK BAPTIST CHURCH CEMETERY

Mollie
Wife of
James Malone

S. B. Malone
June 22, 1854
May 16, 1889
With Jesus.

Ida Atkins McConkey
Wife of
James Malone
Born 1870
Aged about 30 yrs.

Malone
W. Z. Malone
Feb. 8, 1851
June 12, 1931

His wife
Vinie Morgan
Feb. 28, 1850
Feb. 6, 1919

My darling child
Lola May Malone
Aug. 22, 1908
Apr. 19, 1913

MCDANIEL

Josie May
Wife of
L. F. McDaniel
Aug. 26, 1874
Mar. 24, 1900
A dear wife.

Berdie Watson
Wife of
Thomas McDaniel
Mar. 18, 1865
Feb. --, 1927

PETTITT

Earl
Son of
B. C. & Ida Pettitt
Dec. 4, 1902
Apr. 20, 1904

MCDONALD

Alie N. McDonald
Died June -- 19--
Aged -----------
(faded out)

RATLEDGE

Ben Ratledge
Born about 1821
Aged about 66 years.

Sallie
Wife of
Ben Ratledge
Born about 1826
Aged about 64 yrs.

BOOKOUT

Bell Sneed
Wife of
David Bookout

David Bookout

CARDIN

Infant
of
Jack & Mollie Cardin

Infant
of
Jack & Mollie Cardin

SMITH

Frank Smith
May 10, 1857
June 16, 1922
At Rest.

Mrs. Frank Smith

David Smith
Born about 1854
Aged about 81 yrs.

NOTCHEY CREEK BAPTIST CHURCH CEMETERY

Margaret Stalcup
Wife of
David Smith
Born about 1858
Aged about 76 yrs.

HICKS

Wesley Hicks
His wives
Mary ———
and
Julia Watson

Berry Hicks

Mariah
Wife of
Berry Hicks

COOPER

Minerva E.
Wife of
C. P. Cooper
Died Jan. 27, 1900
Aged 65 yrs. 8 Mos. 7 days.
Awaiting the Resurrection.

C. P. Cooper
Born Feb. 20, 1827
Died Apr. 11, 1900
Awaiting the Resurrection.

BOGART

John T. Bogart
May 13, 1867
 May 31, 1894
Gone but not forgotten.

MANIS

Myrtle Josephine
Daughter of
Mr. & Mrs. Strode Manis
Jan. 15, 1927
June 24, 1935
Sister

Carrie Manis
Apr. 28, 1873
Dec. 26, 1932
A precious Mother

Robert L. Manis
Feb. 19, 1866
Mar. 21, 1925
A Noble father

Virgie E. Manis
May 5, 1897
July 13, 1907
A precious one from
us has gone.

Betty
Daughter of
Geo. & Callie Manis
Aged about 4 yrs.

HENDERSON

William Henderson
Dec. 10, 1833
Jan. 20, 1901

Mary E. Henderson
Mar. 16, 1837
(date of death not given)
We shall meet again.

WIMBERLY

Ham Wimberly
Apr. 13, 1839
Dec. 1, 1914
At Rest

BROOM

Zebbie Francie Broom
June 1, 1892
July 9, 1905

SUTTON

Martha Alsa Sutton
Mch. 26, 1864
Jan. 26, 1896
At Rest.

BOATNER

Amos Boatman

HAMILTON

Edith
Infant dau. of
Lon. & Josie Hamilton
1892

MONROE COUNTY

TOMBSTONE INSCRIPTIONS

OLD SWEETWATER BAPTIST CHURCH CEMETERY

Copied by: Lawrence McConkey, Englewood, Tennessee
Date: Feb. 12, 1940

The Old Sweetwater Baptist Church and Cemetery are located 2
miles South of Philadelphia or about 5 miles North of Sweetwater
and on highway between the two above towns.

According to the Baptist minutes this is the oldest Baptist Church
in the County having been constituted in 1820.

The oldest inscriptions is that of Alie Cleveland who died
Nov. 3, 1821.

A book, "Sketches of Tennessee's Pioneer Baptist Preachers", by
J. J. Burnett states the following in substance: The Rev.
Eli Cleveland moved to the Sweetwater Valley in 1821. He united
with the church at Sweetwater the fourth Saturday in Jan. 1822.
He gave the ground for the meeting house and cemetery of the Old
Sweetwater Church and largely built the house, boarding the hands
and furnishing teams and Negroes to drive them as well as to do
other work in connection with the building. The house was of
brick. It is supposed to be same building as is there now.

The cemetery covers about 3 acres and is on the Equitable Life
Insurance Company farm, but supposedly deeded by the Rev. Eli
Cleveland to the church, which is on a different plot about ¼
mile North. The cemetery is still in use. The Southwest corner, is the Negro section. Very few, if any, Negroes will in
the future be buried here.

As the Rev. Eli Cleveland was possibly the most prominent
person buried in the Old Sweetwater Baptist Church Cemetery
there is a history of the Cleveland family given following the
inscriptions.

MCINTOSH

David M.
Feb. 19, 1924
Mar. 24, 1925
Son of
Andrew & Myrtle McIntosh
God carries the little
ones in his bosom.

In memory of
My daughter
Florence Jones
Born Feb. 19, 1859
Died June 1, 1876

In memory of
My husband
Jessee F. Jones
Born Aug. 9, 1808
Died Dec. 31, 1868

2

OLD SWEETWATER BAPTIST CHURCH CEMETERY

Our Mother
Clarissa H.
Wife of
Jessee F. Jones
Sept. 6, 1815
May 11, 1880

L. C. Jones
Wife of
Chas. Cannon
Oct. 6, 1831
June 30, 1862

J. B.
Son of
Chas. & L. C. Cannon
Feb. 3, 1858
Oct. 10, 1863

Robert R. Cleveland
Sept. 15, 1808
Apr. 7, 1868
I will lift up mine eyes
to the hills from whence
cometh my help. Psalms 121: 1

Sydney G. Nelson
Wife of
R. R. Cleveland
July 5, 1811
Oct. 23, 1884

In memory of
Rev. Eli Cleveland
Born Oct. 1, 1781
Died Nov. 23, 1859
Saved by grace.

Our dear Mother
Polly Cleveland
Born July 30, 1786
Died Jan. 21, 1862

John Shearman
Son of
D. H. & M. N. Cleveland
Oct. 21, 1885
Sept. 26, 1891

Elizabeth A.
Wife of
D. H. Cleveland
Jan. 5, 1827
Dec. 31, 1882

E. C.

(Note: Above was at foot of a
grave. No head stone. LMcC.)

Emma S.
Wife of
E. C. Jones
Aug. 31, 1857
Jan. 8, 1878

Nellie J.

(Note: Suppose above J. stands
for Jones as it marks grave side
of Emma S. Jones' grave. LMcC.)

Our Father
Daniel Ragan
July 6, 1792
July 26, 1860

Our Mother
Elizabeth
Consort of
Daniel Ragan
Sept. 18, 1793
Dec. 29, 1861

Clarissa E.
Daughter of
J. E. & L. J. Ragon
Mar. 10, 1864
July 3, 1865

(Note: Name is spelled both
Ragan and Ragon. LMcC.)

Jesse J.
Son of
W. H. & A. M. Ragon
Nov. 7, 1873
Sept. 15, 1874

Albert
Son of
W. H. & A. M. Ragon
Sept. 18, 1883
Nov. 16, 1884

Thy will be done
M. A. Ragon
Dec. 1, 1826
Apr. 23, 1909

OLD SWEETWATER BAPTIST CHURCH CEMETERY

J. E. Ragon
Sept. 6, 1828
Nov. 22, 1906
Dear is the spot where
christians sleep, and
sweet the stranes that
angels pour.

L. J. Ragon
Mar. 28, 1838
Mar. 17, 1917

Dora A.
Daughter of
W. H. & A. M. Ragon
April 27, 1867
Jan. 21, 1891

Bettie C.
Daughter of
W. H. & A. M. Ragon
Jan. 2, 1866
Oct. 23, 1885

Mary B.
Daughter of
L. E. & L. J. Ragon
May 1, 1854
Sept. 6, 1871

Lodusky Jones
Wife of
Joseph Walker
Oct. 20, 1820
Sept. 15, 1875

Joseph Walker
Sept. 10, 1813
Dec. 30, 1862

In memory of
Elizabeth J.
Wife of
Joseph Walker
July 25, 1825
Feb. 14, 1846

Intered here an
Infant
Child of
J. D. & A. M. Jones

J. F. Cleveland
Son of
D. H. & E. A. Cleveland
July 11, 1845
Oct. 27, 1846

Louis J. Cleveland
Son of
S. H. & E. A. Cleveland
Feby 17, 1853
Oct. 4, 1853

Aley M. Cleveland
Wife of
J. D. Jones
May 7, 1813
May 30, 1855

Aley Mathis
Daughter of
J. D. & A. M. Jones
Jan. 8, 1840
March 3, 1857

Mary L. Jones
Wife of
S. Y. B. Williams
Dec. 16, 1836
Nov. 18, 1858

Barbara
Wife of
S. Y. B. Williams
Died July 2, 1866
Aged 25 yrs. 9 mos. & 11 days.

James H.
Son of
S. Y. B. & B. Williams
Died Sept. 15, 1864
Aged 1 yr 3 mos & 13 days.

Martha Ann Cleveland
May 23, 1838
April 18, 1839

Eli Nelson Cleveland
June 8, 1836
Oct. 12, 1836

4

OLD SWEETWATER BAPTIST CHURCH CEMETERY

Polly
Daughter of
Eli & Polly Cleveland
April 17, 1827
Sept. -- 1831

Alie Cleveland
Oct. 14, 1816
Nov. 3, 1821

Wm. Cleveland
Oct. 11, 1820
Apr. 22, 1835

A. M. Cleveland
Sept. 26, 1833
July 25, 1854

H. H. Cleveland
March 18, 1830
Sept. 1, 1854

Elizabeth Cleveland
Feb. 17, 1792
Nov. 20, 1854

Presley Cleveland
Sept. 16, 1779
May 31, 1861

BLACK

Mother
Annie L. Black
Nov. 24, 1859
May 19, 1895

Father
William T. Black
Sept. 1, 1859
Dec. 10, 1917

Infant
Daughter of
W. T. & A. L. Black
1886

MCGUIRE

D. J. McGuire
Mar. 20, 1833
July 8, 1904

(Mason Emblem)
Nicholas McGuire
Mar. 25, 1831
June 5, 1891
Blessed are the dead wh'ch
die in the Lord.

LILLARD

Lillard
Joseph Berry Lillard
March 1, 1843
June 1, 1920

His wife
Margaret Harrison
Dec. 6, 1863
Nov. 13, 1932

JOHNSON

Carrie Otto Pearce
Wife of
Ben L. Johnson
Sept. 27, 1866
Nov. 26, 1906
At Rest.

James R. Johnson
Dec. 31, 1836
Mar. 21, 1919

His wife
Mary E. King
Mar. 16, 1849
May 22, 1920

Nancy Carrie Johnson
Apr. 17, 1876
May 22, 1920

Katie C. Johnson
Jan. 20, 1875
May 22, 1920

John K. Johnson
Oct. 17, 1882
May 22, 1920

(Note: The four above died -
all same day - May 22, 1920.
LMcG.)

OLD SWEETWATER BAPTIST CHURCH CEMETERY

William E. Johnson
Apr. 28, 1823
Sept. 17, 1909
A soft answer turneth
away wrath.

Eliza Ann Johnson
Jan. 17, 1823
Oct. 3, 1908
Blessed are the pure in
heart for they shall
see God.

Son of
J. R. & M. E. Johnson
Dec. 3, 1887

W. S.
Son of
J. R. & M. E. Johnson
Apr. 18, 1885
Oct. 28, 1889

Catherine
Wife of
Lewis Johnson
May 29, 1805
Sept. 5, 1865

Louis Johnson
Jan. 29, 1799
Apr. 17, 1890

Wm. Johnson
Mar. 21, 1766
Dec. 27, 1837

BALLARD

Callie S.
Daughter of
W. L. & M. R. Ballard
Mar. 10, 1882
July 31, 1891

OSBORNE

Joseph R. Osborne
July 5, 1812
March 10, 1870
Blessed are the dead which
die in the Lord.

JONES

Nannie A.
Wife of
R. A. Jones
June 7, 1846
Feb. 22, 1882

LILLARD & HARRISON

William Lillard
Aug. 14, 1798
Dec. 18, 1844

Mary Caroline Lillard
Aug. 20, 1835
Jan. 12, 1922

William W. Lillard
Feb. 7, 1831
Nov. 16, 1883

In memory of
Our mother
Nancy Lillard
Aug. 28, 1807
July 27, 1809

Jane Harrison
Died Apr. 28, 1882

Nathaniel Harrison
Died Nov. 23, 1875
Dear is the spot where
christians are buried.

RUTH

Sacred to the
memory of
Mrs. Elizabeth Ruth
Oct. 30, 1780
Sept. 26, 1826

HOGUE

Nancy E. Hogue
Dec'd 15 Jany 1835
Aged 4 years, 9 months
& 21 days.

6

OLD SWEETWATER BAPTIST CHURCH CEMETERY

SANDS

Ann Sands
Wife of
Joseph Sands Sr.
Born   1793
Died Jan. 20, 1848

LETTERMAN

Father
W. J. Letterman
Jan. 1, 1841
Feb. 8, 1910

Mother
S. M. Letterman
Feb. 2, 1847
(Date of death not given.)

Tennie C. Letterman
Aug. 23, 1891
July 26, 1922

RINES

At Rest
(Odd Fellow Emblem)
J. H. Rines
Dec. 6, 1859
Feb. 20, 1915

Sidney Rines
Mar. 26, 1911
Aug. 26, 1911

GRAYSON & ROYLSTON

Linnie Belle
Daughter of
T. A. & C. M. Boylston
Born May 8, ----
Died Sept. 24, 1905

John Calvin Grayson
Oct. 5, 1849
Feb. 7, 1912
Asleep in Jesus
Blessed thought.

Lena M.
July 5, 1902
Dec. 21, 1902

Ethel C.
Oct. 10, 1895
Feb. 24, 1899

Sidie Grayson
Wife of
Bob Roylston
Nov. 25, 1874
Feb. 13, 1913
She has gone to the
mansions of rest.

Ethel C.
Daughter of
T. A. & C. M. Roylston
Oct. 10, 1895
Feb. 24, 1899

MARTIN

S. J. Martin
Died Jan. 31, 1912
Aged 79 years.
Faithful through life.
At rest in Jesus.

Caroline Martin
Nov. 25, 1827
Nov. 10, 1896

SHULTS

Sallie Shults
July 15, 1861
May 27, 1889

MORRIS

Sallie Lucile Morris
Died May 15, 1938
Aged 4 yrs, 9 months
& 11 days.

CHESNUTT

James Chesnutt
April 15, 1808
July 31, 1854

OLD SWEETWATER BAPTIST CHURCH CEMETERY

Henry Chesnutt
Died Nov. 5, 1854
Aged 74 years.

(Note: About 65 yrs. ago,
3 members of the Chesnutt
family died from poison.
They made either peach or
apple butter one day and it
being late when done, they
died not empty it all from
a brass kettle. The next
morning they ate some of
the butter and were brass
poisoned. They lived nearby the cemetery and pres-
umably are buried here.
LMcC.)

PENNINGTON

Lucinda E. Pennington
July 4, 1823
Dec. 9, 1828

Wm. Pennington
Dec. 13, 1777
Apr. 22, 1838

Elizabeth Pennington
Oct.   1778
Dec. 7, 1844

Sarah Pennington
April 23, 1848
Dec. 3, 1848

TREW

In memory of
Our Uncle
John Trew, Sr.
Died Sept. 14, 1870

CHAFFIN

Alford Chaffin
Died March 12, 1892
Aged 69 years
Gone to rest.

UPTON

C. A. Upton
Mar. 21, 1879
July 3, 1904

Samuel Upton
Died Jan. 14, 1903
Age about 63 years.

Hennie
Daughter of
J. F. & Maggie Upton
April 25, 1896
Sept. 14, 1901
Only sleeping.

PASCHAL

Gussie B.
Wife of
T. G. Paschal
Jan. 28, 1889
Oct. 7, 1906
Darling we miss thee.

(Note: The above person possibly was related to the Upton
family. LMcC.)

JOHNSON

Harvey Johnson
Died June 10, 1926
Aged 66 years.

SLEDGE

Chas. F. Sledge
Died Dec. 9, 1935
(No age given.)

MORELAND

Moreland Monument

Charles O.
May 25, 1879
June 6, 1900

OLD SWEETWATER BAPTIST CHURCH CEMETERY

Samuel L.
April 6, 1876
May 11, 1900

Mary Malinda
Feb. 19, 1846
Jan. 8, 1895

William H.
Dec. 25, 1833
Jan. 20, 1894

WILSON

Mary Louise
July 24, 1899
Aug. 28, 1899

Eugene
April 11, 1900
Children of
W. P. & E. F. Willson
Budded on earth to
bloom in Heaven.

Earl Henry
Son of
W. P. & E. F. Willson
Sept. 22, 1888
July 2, 1889

LILLARD

Nancy E.
Daughter of
J. B. & M. J. Lillard
March 12, 1888
June 10, 1889
With folded wings she
now her little sonet
sings safe at home.

THOMPSON

Mason Emblem
John H. Thompson
Apr. 29, 1872
June 16, 1934

William H.
Son of
J. H. & Theodoshie Thompson
Oct. 12, 1901
Oct. 28, 1915

May
Daughter of
J. H. & Dosie Thompson
May 27, 1898
Dec. 31, 1911

Dosie
Wife of
J. H. Thompson
Oct. 16, 1876
Mar. 6, 1904
How desolate our
home bereft of her.

John Thompson
Born & died
May 1894

James Thompson
June 25, 1844
Dec. 29, 1893

LEONARD

Matty Leonard
Died July 28, 1888

Several unmarked graves nearby.

BYRUM

Joel Byrum
Co. A.
5 Tenn. Inf.

Mary J. Byrum
Oct. 29, 1857
Aug. 8, 1886

John J. Byrum
Apr. 5, 1858
Nov. 26, 1888

Martha Byrum
July 18, 1856
July 8, 1888

OLD SWEETWATER BAPTIST CHURCH CEMETERY

BREWER

Mary Alice
Little daughter of
M. R. & M. T. Brewer
Jan. 22, 1893
Oct. 4, 1897

MCCROSKEY

Masonic Emblem
Ben Alexander McCroskey
Born   1847
Died April 23, 1892

BILLINGSLEY

Mary E.
Wife of
John P. Billingsley
June 24, 1831
Aug. 14, 1881

BROWDER

Matilda Jane Browder
Died Jan. 1909
Aged about 70 yrs.

STEPP

Sgt.
William Stepp
1st Ga. Mtd Inf.
Ind. War.

Elizabeth P. Stepp
June 28, 1842
Aug. 22, 1900
Gone to rest.

BURNS & SCOTT

Lucy A. Burns
June 24, 1878
April 13, 1901

Nannie R. Scott
Aug. 16, 1870
Jan. 14, 1900

Louisa E. Scott
Wife of
G. W. Scott
Dec. 24, 1850
Dec. 1, 1902

PITTMAN

Martha Sledge Pittman
Born   1843
Died Nov. 9, 1916
A precious one from us has
gone. A voice we loved is
stilled. A place is vacant
in our home that never can
be filled.

BREWER

Father
Joseph Brewer
Sept. 22, 1844
Mar. 3, 1937

Katherine Wyett
Wife of
Joseph Brewer
Jan. 31, 1842
Apr. 18, 1910

JOHNSON

Wm. L. Johnson
Jan. 7, 1850
May 5, 1856

PENNINGTON

W. J. Pennington
July 10, 1827
Oct. 27, 1854

EDWARDS

James C. Edwards
Oct. 30, 1869
Aug. 29, 1876

Infant
Son of
W. T. & Sarah J. Edwards
Born & died
Sept. 8, 1888

OLD SWEETWATER BAPTIST CHURCH CEMETERY

Sarah J. Edwards
Nov. 25, 1840
Aug. 17, 1890

Several unmarked graves
nearby.

MCGUIRE

Sarah McGuire
Born   1799
Died May 17, 1879
Aged 79 years.

Cy McGuire
Born   1794
Died Aug. 8, 1860

PARKS

Laura C. Parks
Died July 25, 1928
Aged 51 yrs. 7 days.

C————

Dr. C. ————

(Note: This marker is real
old. It is located near
the center of the cemetery
LMcC.)

REYNOLDS

Sallie Reynolds
Died July 8, 1936
Aged 41 years, 3 months
& 23 days.

This cemetery being such an
old one, is covered with grass,
weeds, bushes etc. There are
149 inscriptions; about 75
graves marked by field stones;
221 unmarked graves and 4
whose inscriptions have been
destroyed.

ELI CLEVELAND FAMILY SKETCH

The Clevelands are a numerous and noted family, both in England
and in the United States. A book has been written which gives
the history of the family as far back as the year 1200, showing
various spellings of the name to be Cliffland, Clyveland,
Cliveland, Clieveland, Cleaveland and Cleveland.

Eli Cleveland, born in Wilkes County N. C., was a son of Capt.
Robert Cleveland and a nephew of Col. Benj. Cleveland, both of
Revolutionary fame. It is thought that their father settled in
Orange County, Va., about the year 1700.

Eli Cleveland married Mary Ragon of Ashe Co., N. C. They were
parents of four sons and four daughters. They moved to Knox
Co., Tenn., in 1817 and to Sweetwater Valley in Monroe Co., in
1821. He owned a fine farm, many slaves and thirty thousand
dollars on interest at his death. It is said that Cleveland,

11

OLD SWEETWATER BAPTIST CHURCH CEMETERY

ELI CLEVELAND FAMILY SKETCH

Tennessee was named for him, at any rate for the Cleveland family.

MONROE COUNTY

TOMBSTONE INSCRIPTIONS

PINEY KNOB PRIMITIVE BAPTIST CHURCH CEMETERY

Copied by: Lawrence McConkey, Englewood, Tennessee.
Date: December 1, 1939.

In 1908 one acre of land was given by Charles S. Sawinson for a
church and cemetery. The church was established that year but the
first burial was that of Estell E., daughter of J. A. & L. E.
Coleman, who died April 23, 1910. The church was discontinued
about 1919 but the cemetery is still in use and consists of about
⅓ acre of land. The cemetery is located about four miles East of
Tellico Plains near the road leading to Rafter. Tellico Plains
is 16 miles South of Madisonville. The cemetery is mostly known
as the Hard Shell Cemetery, very few know its real name, Piney
Knob Primitive Baptist Cemetery. There are 20 inscriptions, 42
graves marked by field stones and 16 unmarked graves.

ODELL

Dortha Odell
Dau. of
John & Jane Odell
July 3, 1925
Sept. 22, 1939

Ella Mae
Daughter of
John & Jane Odell
July 15, 1939
July 15, 1939

Lucile
Daughter of
John & Jane Odell
Aug. 24, 1934
July 22, 1935

(Note: At head of above
grave is the grave of
Louis Odell. He was a
brother of John Odell.
LMcC.)

LYNN

Letha Odell
Wife of
Wince Lynn
Born 1900
Died 1929

Emma
Daughter of
Wince & Letha Lynn
April 1925
July 1927

(Note: At North of above grave
is the grave of Nelson Carver
aged about 85 years
Died About 1926
He was a Federal Soldier in
Civil War, according to Mrs.
Jane Odell, but as yet he has
no tombstone: LMcC.)

(Note: The following are at a
different location in the
cemetery. LMcC.)

Joe B. Lynn
Dec. 8, 1875
June 18, 1935

2 stones North of above
1 South of Above.

Susan
Wife of
Base Lynn
March 15, 1851
Jan. 21, 1917
We will meet again.

2

PINEY KNOB PRIMITIVE BAPTIST CHURCH CEMETERY

1 field stone North of
above 2 South of above.

Son
and
Daughter
of
Wince & Ida Lynn
Born & died
Jan. 5, 1916
Gone but not forgotten.

(Note: Ida Lynn and Bige
Lynn are buried near the
above marker. LMcC.)

AKINS

Virda Akins
Daughter of
A. L. & C. Akins
Born & died
Aug. 12, 1927

Clersa Akins
Jan. 30, 1894
Oct. 1, 1937
Gone but not forgotten.

ROBERTS

Joe Roberts
Died Dec. 3, 1939

(Note: Frances Roberts
also an infant of Howard
Roberts are buried here
without markers. LMcC.)

WALKER

Troy Walker
June 15, 1917
June 15, 1917
In Heaven.

Roy Emerson Walker
Jan. 17, 1912
Jan. 7, 1920
At Rest.

BELL

Wash Bell
Born Nov. 3, 1901

SELF

Tedd
Son of
John S. & Mary Self
Sept. 23, 1909
April 15, 1911
We will meet again.

COLEMAN

Estell E.
Daughter of
J. A. & L. E. Coleman
Sept. 8, 1909
Apr. 23, 1910
We will meet again

Jessie Anderson Coleman
March 7, 1888
July 13, 1918
Weep not he is at Rest.

TRUE

Junior True

Minnie True

MONROE COUNTY

TOMBSTONE INSCRIPTIONS

PRESWOOD CEMETERY

Copied by: Lawrence McConkey, Englewood, Tennessee
Date: Jan. 1939

The Preswood Cemetery was started as a family burial ground
on the land of Augustine Preswood June 17, 1842 at the death
of Sarah, wife of Michael Widner. Sarah Widner, Polly Callam
and the Preswoods were related and their graves are enclosed
in a heavy iron fence. This soon became a community cemetery.

It is on the farm of Rosco Green, about 25 miles South of
Madisonville and may be reached by going via Mt. Vernon,
Jalapa and Brown Hill School, then to Ivy, then on road leading
to Starr Mountain.

There are 66 inscriptions and 125 unmarked graves approximately
in this cemetery. Many of them are very old.

SCOGGINS

M. J.
Mar. 28, 1854
(Date of death not given)

R. L. Scoggins
Apr. 24, 1854
Oct. 17, 1912
Blessed are the dead
which die in the Lord;
Yea, saith the spirit, that
they may rest from their
labors and their works
do follow them.

B. E. Scoggins
Apr. 4, 1898
Sept. 4, 1914

Lovey Scoggins
Jan. 1, 1896
July 28, 1913
We miss the bright
eyes of our darling children
and the sweet rosy lips
that so oft on us smiled.

GROVES

W. E. Groves

M. L. Groves

HICKS

Roe Hicks
Aug. 26, 1825
May 16, 1916
Gone but not forgotten.

Lillia
Wife of
C. A. Hicks
Dec. 20, 1883
Apr. 3, 1917
Gone but not forgotten.

HAMPTON

Viola
Daughter of
J. B. & S. C. Hampton
Dec. 31, 1904
June 18, 1906

PRESWOOD CEMETERY

John Hampton

Callie Hampton

SMITH

Edith Ednia Smith
Oct. 24, 1905
Feb. 27, 1907
Suffer little children
to come unto me.

L. H. Smith

E. C. Smith

PRESWOOD

Marthy
Wife of
Augustine Preswood
Born Dec. 19, 1809
Died July 25, 1897
A treasure in Heaven
to beckon us all to
a higher life.

Augustine Preswood
Died Oct. 14, 1872
In his 96th year.
This marble is devoted
to his memory by her
who best knew his merits
and most deplores his loss.

WIDNER

Sarah
Wife of
Michael Widner
Died June 17, 1842
Aged 75 years.

CALLAM

(Polley Callam)
Born Sept. 19, 1805
Died Dec. 19, 1854

BOWMAN

A. M. Bowman
Co. B.
6th Tenn. Inf.

------- Bowman
Wife of
A. M. Bowman
Born ---- ---
Died --------

L. A. Bowman

CANE

W. Charles
Son of
James & Tempy Cane
Jan. 22, 1896
June 29, 1896
A little voice of love.

Cora Bell
Daughter of
Jacob & E. K. Cane
Aug. 13, 1886
June 14, 1888
Our loved one

(Note: Jacob & Elizabeth
Cane are buried in Bullet
Creek Baptist Church
Cemetery and name is spelled
Cain. LMcC.)

James Cane
Born (unreadable)
Died (

Tempy Cane
Born (
Died (unreadable)

Mary Jane Cane

LINGERFELT

Elijah Lingerfelt
May 8, 1836
Feb. 15, 1916
Gone to a better land.

3

PRESWOOD CEMETERY

Mary Ann Lingerfelt
Mar. 2, 1835
Oct. 1, 1916
She is safe at home.

COWDEN

L. Cowden

Mary Cowden

C. W. Cowden
Apr. 5, 1828
Apr. 24, 1910

Lucinda Cowden
July 9, 1828
Sept. 24, 1901

Martha Jane
Dau. of
C. W. & Lucinda Cowden
Nov. 23, 1851
Apr. 13, 1899

J. C. Cowden

CARDIN

James Cardin

Nancy M.
Wife of
J. J. Cardin
Aug. 3, 1823
Apr. 6, 1913
Sleep mother dear and
take thy rest God
for you his Angels sent.

Charles C.
Son of
Jas. & Nancy Cardin
Mar. 16, 1875
Sept. 17, 1902
Peace be thy sweet slumber.

Joseph Cardin

Alex Cardin

M. E. Cardin

S. L. Cardin

WILLIAMS

Infant
of
L. D. & F. P. Williams

Jane Williams

BUCKNER

Henry Buckner
Feb. 12, 1836
Dec. 18, 1859

Amanda Buckner
July 14, 1840
Sept. 23, 1868

Geo. Buckner
Mar. 27, 1838
Aug. 16, 1871

Cordelia Buckner
Oct. 19, 1841
Jan. 6, 1869

Delia Buckner

Jane Buckner

Horace Buckner

E. H. B.

KILBY

J. M. Kilby
Dec. 4, 1865
May 29, 1867

E. J. Kilby
Mar. 7, 1863
Nov. 11, 1866

FREEMAN

Mary Freeman

4

PRESWOOD CEMETERY

H. C. Freeman

L. S. Freeman

P. Freeman

DUGGAN

M. R. Duggan

D. B. Duggan

George Duggan

EATON

John Eaton
12 - 3 - 1838
 4 - 9 - 1864

Nancy Eaton
7 - 18 - 1841
9 - 17 - 1867

M. E.

H. E.

LIMTNER

Limptner

ERVIN

Albert Ervin

MONROE COUNTY

TOMBSTONE INSCRIPTIONS

PROSPECT CEMETERY

Copied by: Lawrence McConkey, Englewood, Tennessee
Date:

John H. Hankins gave two acres of land to the Baptist
denomination to be used for church and cemetery grounds.
The date was between 1840 and 1850. The church was
constituted in 1850 and named Prospect Baptist Church. About
1890 the church was removed approximately 1 mile to a new
location and renamed Rocky Springs Baptist Church.

The cemetery name has been known all along as Prospect, or
as some call it now, "Old" Prospect Baptist Church Cemetery.

John H. Hankins was a prominent early settler and also owned
a considerable acreage of land.

William P. Mullins, buried here, was likewise a prominent man,
served as Esquire etc.

The cemetery is joined by the farm lands of the Jenkins,
Crowder and Miller families. It is about $4\frac{1}{2}$ mile East of
Madisonville and about 1 mile beyond Rocky Springs.

There are 75 or more unmarked graves.

SAMPLES

A. H. Samples

L. S. Samples

M. J. Samples

E. Samples
John
John Samples

Martha Samples
1856

M. E. Samples

W. Samples

John Samples
L. E. S.

(Note: John Samples is
buried beside Lucinda and
it is believed that L.E.S.
are her initials on his
Marker. LMcC.)

Lucinda Samples
Died June 19, 1889

H. M. --------
Dec. Feb. 4 -------

(Note: It is believed the
above party was a Samples as
the grave is bes'de the Samples
graves. The Rock was chipped.
LMcC.)

J. E. S.

M. J. S.

T. H. S.

B. G. S.

(Note: Above also must be Samples
family graves. All their markers
are homemade or field rocks and
hard to read. LMcC.

PROSPECT CEMETERY

HANKINS

John H. Hankins
Born Feb. 3, 1799
Died Sept. 5, 1856

Cornelious
Son of
E. E. & J. A. Hankins
Jan. 5, 1853
Aug. 27, 1857

Capt. E. E. Hankins
Jan. 4, 1827
Dec. 9, 1866
Held in fondest re-
memberance by his
children.

JONES

Hattie
Daughter
of
Newton & Mary Jones
Born 1890
Died 1918

Mary Isbill
Wife of
Newton Jones
Died 1934
Aged about 65 years.

Newton Jones
Died 1936
Aged about 70 years.

ISBILL

Ida King
Wife of
G. W. Isbill
Feb. 9, 1868
Jan. 31, 1906

Mary J. Webb
Wife of
G. W. Isbill
April 14, 1854
Jan. 30, 1890
My love is gone to rest.

Isaac Isbill

Father
At Rest
G. W. Isbill
Sept. 2, 1851
Oct. 24, 1917
Gone but not forgotten.

Infant
of
G. W. & M. J. Isbill
Died Jan. 27, 1890

Callie D.
Daughter of
G. W. & M. J. Isbill
May 11, 1874
Nov. 9, 1875

Eula
Daughter of
G. W. & M. J. Isbill

Ota Lou
Daughter of
G. W. & Ida Isbill

Etta Sue
Daughter of
G. W. & Ida Isbill

CROWDER

Rachel
Wife of
J. T. Crowder
Dec. 25, 1830
Nov. 25, 1903
Gone where life is
eternal.

J. T. Crowder
Feb. 14, 1827
Dec. 13, 1893
Gone to rest.

A. O. Crowder

J. E. Crowder

M. L. Crowder

PROSPECT CEMETERY

S. -. Crowder

HUNNICUTT

P. H. M. Hunnicutt

Joseph B. Hunnicutt
Jan. 22, 1806
May 19, 1884
Gone to rest.

Mary Stephens
Wife of
Joseph B. Hunnicutt
Aug. 22, 1808
Aug. 1, 1877
Gone to rest.

Ethel Hunnicutt
Sept. 11, 1877
Sept. 27, 1877
Aged 16 days
Gone to rest.

Infant
-------- Hunnicutt

Maggie A. Crippen
Wife of
L. D. Hunnicutt
Oct. 12, 1856
Oct. 27, 1887
Gone to rest.

E. L. Hunnicutt
W. Hunnicutt

J. D. Hunnicutt
Died Feb. 10, 1863

H. G. Hunnicutt
Born & died Dec. 18, 1861

Margaret Hunnicutt

LEDFORD

Nora Wood
Wife of
G. W. Ledford
Jan. 1, 1880
Dec. 29, 1902
At Rest

G. W. Ledford
Dec. 27, 1876
Apr. 25, 1916

J. T. Ledford
Mar. 30, 1868
May 6, 1892
At Rest.

D. O. Ledford

M. A. Ledford
Sept. 12, 1865
June 6, 1884
With Jesus.

J. M. Ledford
Aug. 12, 1837
June 6, 1905
A life well spent.

John Ledford
Died 1879
Aged 20 yrs.

Callie Ledford

Ed. - Ledford

DENTON

John Denton
Died Aug. 12, 1912
Age 70 years.
Dear Uncle you have
left us. left us yes
for ever more but we
hope to meet you on
that bright and happy
shore.

MULLINS OR MULLENS

Beulah Mullins
Dau. of
Mr. & Mrs. J. C. Mullins
May 1, 1919
Dec. 7, 1927
Gone to be an Angel.

George
Son of
Mr. & Mrs. Jake Mullins
Feb. 22, 1917
Nov. 22, 1918
Budded on earth to
bloom in Heaven.

Mullens
Clarence
Son of
Mr. & Mrs. J. C. Mullens
July 1, 1912
Jan. 8, 1929
Weep not, father and
Mother, for me for, I
am waiting in Glory
for thee.

Bertha Webb
Wife of
Joe H. Mullins
Died Jan. 1928
Aged 43 years 5 months

Joe H. Mullins

Our Darling
Ilamae
Daughter of
J. H. & B. E. Mullens
Aug. 27, 1905
May 26, 1907
Baby

In memory of mother
Margaret Mullins
Mar. 2, 1850
Dec. 24, 1927

In memory of father
William P. Mullins
Nov. 5, 1852
Nov. 29, 1919
Peace be thy silent slumber,
Peaceful in thy grave so
low. Thou no more will
join our number.
Thou no more our sorrows
know, yet again we hope
to meet thee when the day of
life is fled and in Heaven
with joy to greet thee
where no farewll tears
are shed.

CANTRELL

M. M. Cantrell
Died June 14, 1929
Aged 73 yrs. 11 mos. 26 days.

Mrs. M. M. Cantrell

Joe Cantrell

H. D. Cantrell

COWDEN

Sophronia Henry
Wife of
J. R. Cowden
Feb. 14, 1878
May 14, 1920
Heaven now is
mothers home.

GREGORY

Easter E. Gregory
Jan. 10, 1857
Feb. 20, 1906

C. W. Gregory
Mar. 12, 1847
(Date of death not given.)
Gone but not forgotten.

C. Walter Gregory
Son of
C. W. & E. E. Gregory
Aug. 8, 1897
Apr. 3, 1898
Our babe at rest.

Two
Infants of
S. W. & Jennie Gregory
Erected Apr. 16, 1912

C. L. Gregory

S. E. Gregory

WILBURN

Bettie King
Wife of
F. A. Wilburn
Sept. 8, 1845
Nov. 29, 1914

PROSPECT CEMETERY

P. A. Wilburn
Apr. 6, 1845
Nov. 30, 1915

Elbert F. Wilburn
Dec. 15, 1877
June 5, 1938

Dorcas Mullins
Sept. 7, 1880
(Still Living)
Resting till the Res-
urection Morn.

George
Son of
Mr. & Mrs. E. F. Wilburn
Feb. 24, 1907 - Feb. 24, 1918

CLAYTON

Margaret
Wife of
Frank Clayton

PITTMAN

Walter Worth
Son of
H. & S. E. Pittman
Mar. 10, 1895
June 9, 1895
He is gone to rest.

WOOD

Retta
Wife of
G. W. Wood
May 6, 1884
May 4, 1910
Asleep in Jesus.

Effie Wood
Jan. 20, 1902
May 7, 1911
Budded on earth to
bloom in Heaven.

WEBB

Easter Webb
Sept. 18, 1801
Apr. 26, 1870
In God we trust.

William Webb

James Howard Webb
Died Nov. 21, 1937
Aged 48 yrs. 6 mos. 29 days.

Eligah Webb

Josie Burleson
Wife of
Eligah Webb

Isabella Webb
Mar. 31, 1868
Nov. 11, 1897

James Webb
Oct. 17, 1866
Feb. 13, 1917
In memory of mother and
father.

Asther
Daughter of
James & Isabella Webb

Lu---- Webb

B. Webb

M. S. Webb
Aug. 15, 1912
Nov. 14, 1913

M. A. Webb
May 27, 1834
Sept. 8, 1911
At Rest.

M. R. Webb
Aug. 8, 1829
June 4, 1896
At Rest.

W. C. Webb
Age 14

TOMBSTONE INSCRIPTIONS

REEDS SPRINGS BAPTIST CHURCH CEMETERY

Copied by: Lawrence McConkey, Englewood, Tennessee
Date:

Reeds Springs Baptist Church was established in 1912 at
Sunnyside near the Sunnyside County school.   J. M. Reed, a
relative of Ex-Senator J. M. Reed of Missouri, gave 2 acres of
land for the church and cemeterh.

The Reeds Springs Baptist Church Cemetery was established in
1912 when Henry Cook died.   James Harrison died Dec. 24, 1909
and was buried on his farm but was removed to this cemetery.
The graveyard is 9 miles North of Madisonville on the road
leading from Madisonville to Philadelphia, via Hiwassee
College and Rockville.   There are 53 inscriptions and approximately 38 unmarked graves.

MILLER

Stell Miller

Teddy
Infant son of
Stella Miller

Robert M. Miller
Feb. 22, 1857
May 31, 1921
Beloved how we miss you.

Amos K. Miller
Died Dec. 19, 1932
Aged 48 yrs. 4 mos. 22 days.

Mary Helen Miller
Died Nov. 14, 1935
Aged 1 yr. 3 mos. 19 days.

Kinwood F. Miller
Died Dec. 20, 1932
Aged 5 mos. 16 days.

William Hardin Miller
Died May 16, 1938
Aged 1 yr. 9 mos. 17 days.

MCBROOM

Dora McBroom
Died Aug. 23, 1938
Aged 58 yrs. 7 mos 8 days.

HARRISON

Charity A. Harrison
Died Dec. 2, 1931
Aged 87 yrs. 2 mos.

Louise J. Harrison
Died Sept. 28, 1832
Aged 82 yrs. 7 mos. 25 days.

James Harrison
Jan. 17, 1834
Dec. 24, 1909

Edward M. Harrison
Died May 30, 1938
Aged 12 yrs. 10 mos.

WARD

Isaac A. Ward
Died May 6, 1936
Age 81 yrs. 1 mo. 7 days.

REEDS SPRINGS BAPTIST CHURCH CEMETERY

HUGHES

Fannie Hughes
Died Jan. 9, 1937
Aged 42 yrs. 6 mos. 19 days.

Robert C. Hughes
Died Sept. 20, 1935
Aged 69 yrs. 6 mos. 25 days.

RINES

Martha Belle
Wife of
S. M. Rines
Jan. 5, 1881
Apr. 15, 1936
Gone but not forgotten.

Infant
Son of
Mr. & Mrs. H. H. Rines
Apr. 16, 1923
June 23, 1923

GREEN

John Green

ALMON-ALLMAN

Joe Clyde Almon
Died Aug. 13, 1923
Aged 1 yr.

Fay Allman
Died April 6, 1936
Aged 1 yr. 21 days.

LETTERMAN

Roscoe
Son of
Frank & Effie Letterman
Died Oct. -- 1936
Aged 1 yr.

Jessee M. Letterman
Died Oct. 19, 1930
Aged 40 yrs. 11 mos. 18 days.

OLIVER

Carnell Oliver
Died Nov. 23, 1937
Aged 8 yrs. 11 mos.

SKINNER

William Kenneth Skinner
Died July 4, 1935
Aged 2 yrs. 5 mos. 11 days.

MCCALLIE

Jack McCallie

MOORE

Infant
of
------- Moore

JOHNSON

Mary Dean Johnson
Died May 23, 1935
Aged 16 yrs. 10 mos. 22 days.

EDWARDS

Bulah
Wife of
Robert Edwards
Jan. 24, 1898
Mar. 16, 1925
Gone but not forgotten.

James Everett
Son of
Mr. & Mrs. Sam Edwards
Feb. 9, 1923
Feb. 25, 1923

Sam Edwards
Sept. 15, 1898
Aug. 9, 1924
Gone but not forgotten.

Edna R. Edwards
Sept. 21, 1903
Sept. 24, 1913
At Rest.

REEDS SPRINGS BAPTIST CHURCH CEMETERY

Erven Edwards
Born Feb. 24, 1908
Died Mar. 16, 1920
At Rest.

Lessie Edwards
Born Sept. 1, 1889
Died Mar. 21, 1920
Gone but not forgotten.

Frank Edwards
Born Aug. 27, 1909
Died Oct. 8, 1923

Robert Edwards
Oct. 13, 1895
Feb. 15, 1938

LAUDMILK

Robert Franklin Laudmilk
Died Feb. 11, 1923
Aged 21 yrs. 8 mos. 2 days.

COOK

Henry Cook
Died 1912
Aged about 50 years.

JONES

Lenard Jones
Died July 25, 1928
Aged (fadedout)

ESTES

Kermit B. Estes
Died June 15, 1938
Aged 12 days.

HENSLEY

Lela Fay Hensley
Dec. 5, 1915
Dec. 12, 1915
She's safe at home.

Julia Mae Hensley
Died May 3, 1936
Aged 2 days.

MCCULLEY

Mrs. E. McCulley.

VAUGHN

Roy Vaughn
Died Aug. 31, 1937
Aged 45 yrs. 10 mos. 13 days.

KINSER

J. H. Kinser
Mar. 17, 1869
Feb. 18, 1930
At Rest.

HENSLEE

F. H. Henslee
Born in Union Co. Ga.
June 19, 1842
Died in Monroe Co. Tenn.
July 20, 1914

Mary A. Peagle
Wife of
F. H. Henslee
Born in Cherokee Co. N. C.
Oct. 9, 1843
Feb. 5, 1930

BRAY

Lois Lee Bray
May 9, 1920
Mar. 28, 1922
A precious one from
us is gone.

Charles F. Bray
Died July 15, 1935
Aged 10 yrs. 4 mos. 22 days.

4

REEDS SPRINGS BAPTIST CHURCH CEMETERY

Willie
Son of
Charles & Catherine Bray

GUNTER

Clorence T. Gunter
Died May 30, 1937
Aged 1 yr. 7 mos. 18 days.

BAILEY

Lucile Inman
Daughter of
Lillie Bailey
June 14, 1924
June 16, 1924
At Rest.

JENKINS

Lois Jenkins
Died May 16, 1938
Aged 1 yr. 9 mo. 17 days.

LANGLEY

Frank M. Langley
Born Aug. 28, 1919
Gone but not forgotten.

Charlie J. Langley
Died July 30, 1937
Aged 27 yrs. 10 mos. 28 days.

Copied by ; Lawrence McConkey, Englewood, Tennessee
Date:

The Rocky Springs Baptist Church or McClellan Cemetery was
established on the farm of Thomas McClellan Sept. 26, 1896
as a family burial ground, when his son, W. M. died. Later
the farm was owned by J. B. and Sallie McClellan Isbill and
relatives of the Isbill family were buried here. Later John
and Callie McClellan Atkins owned the farm and relatives of
the Atkins family were also buried here. In 1930 the Rocky
Springs Baptist Church secured a deed for the cemetery. It
is situated about 2½ miles Southeast of Madisonville. It may
be reached by going via Kefauver on Tellico Plains road then
Rocky Springs road. There are 53 inscriptions and 3 unmarked
graves.

MCCLELLAN

W. M. McClellan
Oct. 8, 1892
Sept. 26, 1896

Mariah McClellan
April 12, 1829
July 27, 1904
There are no partings
in Heaven.
Mother

Vista Clark McClellan
May 8, 1857
Apr. 19, 1935

Thomas McClellan
July 15, 1848
Dec. 18, 1933
Mother and Father
Gone but not forgotten.

Infant
of
Mr. & Mrs. Thos McClellan
June 28, 1901

HAWKINS

Come Ye blessed
Annie McClellan
Wife of
A. R. Hawkins
Aug. 18, 1896
Mar. 30, 1919

ISBILL

John Ross
Son of
Mr. & Mrs. J. B. Isbill
Oct. 1, 1905
May 26, 1921
Asleep in Jesus.

Elizabeth Isbill
Aug. 2, 1835
Mar. 26, 1916

Wash Isbill
Apr. 28, 1832
Nov. 7, 1910
Blessed are the dead
which die in the Lord.

Artie Isbill
Sept. 15, 1880
Aug. 14, 1910
Asleep in the arms
of Jesus.

ROCKY SPRINGS BAPTIST CHURCH OR MCCLELLAN CEMETERY

Ida Mae Isbill
May 11, 1867
Apr. 6, 1922
Asleep in Jesus.

LAY

W. B. Lay
Apr. 9, 1864
July 19, 1936

JONES

Ralph
Son of
Mr. & Mrs. Bert Jones
July 26, 1917
Jan. 1, 1918

Infant
of
Mr. & Mrs. Bert Jones

Infant
of
Mr. & Mrs. Bert Jones

ATKINS

Easter Tallent
Wife of
J. M. Atkins
June 14, 1844
Jan. 9, 1925
Gone but not forgotten.
Mother

J. M. Atkins
July 8, 1842
Aug. 22, 1917
Gone but not forgotten.
Father

Alex Sanders Atkins
Apr. 20, 1900
July 21, 1920
Dear brother you have
left us, left us for ever
More but we hope to
meet you on that bright
and shining shore.

James N. Atkins
Apr. 14, 1867
Nov. 9, 1927
Gone but not forgotten.

R. B. Atkins
Son of
Mr. & Mrs. W. L. Atkins
Feb. 9, 1922
Mar. 18, 1925
Darling we miss thee.

WATSON

Madilene Watson
July 18, 1930
Feb. 4, 1933
Budded on earth to bloom
in Heaven.

Josie Tallent
Wife of
R. D. Watson
Nov. 27, 1864
Mar. 30, 1934
Mother, at rest.

Gordon Watson
Dec. 16, 1924
Jan. 26, 1931

Infant
of
Mr. & Mrs. Willie Watson

Elbert
Son of
J. W. & Berdie Watson
July 13, 1918
Nov. 18, 1927
Gone but not forgotten.

Sarah Geneva Watson
Nov. 1930
Nov. 1930
Daughter of
Mr. & Mrs. Mack Watson
Gone but not forgotten.

Father
Marian Watson
Born Aug. 26, 1866
Died Dec. 21, 1927
As my friends pass my
body by a layen buye
with the clay remember
you will bee place the same
waye sum day. Papy will no
more on aurth joine air number.
(continued on next page.)

ROCKY SPRINGS BAPTIST CHURCH OR MCCLELLAN CEMETERY

Papy gone but not
forgotten.
Made bye William Watson.

RAPER

Callie Watson
Wife of
Wom Raper
Mar. 19, 1883
Aug. 20, 1927
Gone but not forgotten.

M. C. Raper
Dec. 9, 1859
Aug. 24, 1927
Gone but not forgotten.

Fannie Atkins
Wife of
M. C. Raper
July 5, 1863
Sept. 4, 1925
Gone but not forgotten.

ARNOLD

Junior Ray Arnold
Died Dec. 21, 1937
Aged 9 yrs. 5 mos. 22 days.

George E. Arnold
Died Feb. 11, 1938
Aged 87 yrs. 1 mo. 2 days.

LUMKINS

Georgia Ellen Lumkins
Died July 21, 1937
Aged 6 mos. 10 days.

GREEN

Lillian Faie Green
Daughter of
Mr. & Mrs. William Green
Sept. 16, 1937
May   30, 1938

PEEPLES

D. M. Peeples
Feb. 4, 1884
Jan. 22, 1930

COLEMAN

John B.
Born Aug. 11, 1923
Died Jan. 1, 1924
and
Fredrick Mills
Born July 9, 1924
Died Aug. 14, 1924
Sons of
Mr. & Mrs. W. A. Coleman
A little while on earth
they spent till God
for them his angels sent.

MILLS

George Lee
Son of
Mr. & Mrs. A. H. Mills
Oct. 25, 1926
July 28, 1927
Our darling gone
but not forgotten.

GIBBY

J. T. Gibby
Jan. 30, 1865
Sept. 18, 1936

Florence Gibby
Nov. 3, 1864
(Still living)
Gone but not forgotten.

Gibby
George
Son of
Mr. & Mrs. G. T. Gibby
Oct. 17, 1932
Oct. 18, 1932
Asleep in Jesus.

ROCKY SPRINGS BAPTIST CHURCH OR MCCLELLAN CEMETERY

GILREATH

Nancy A. Gilreath
Feb. 23, 1861
Jan. 10, 1923
Was a member of Mt.
Pleasant Baptist Church
Gaddis town Ga.
until death.

BELCHER

Our darling
Bernice
Daughter of
Mr. & Mrs. J. A. Belcher
Dec. 24, 1934
Oct. 25, 1936
Asleep in Jesus.

ROSS

Mary Ross
Age 61
Died Aug. 11, 1932
Gone but not forgotten.

COLE

Mrs. A. S. Cole
Died Dec. 11, 1937
Aged 65 yrs. and 9 mos.

JENKINS

Grace Jenkins
Nov. 30, 1917
Oct. 3, 1920
Gone to be an Angel

Blanche Jenkins
June 6, 1913
Apr. 9, 1928
Gone to be an Angel.

MILLER

Alex Miller
1852 - 19(not yet)

His wife
Rachel Miller
1854 - 1932
Gone but not forgotten.

Annie May Miller
Was born Oct. 26, 1914
Died July 6, 1920
Darling how we miss you.
Gone but not forgotten.

KIMBLE

Infant
of
John & Nannie Kimble

MANIS

George R. Manis
Jan. 21, 1869
Feb. 4, 1936

Mrs. George R. Manis
July 4, 1878
(not buried)
Gone but not forgotten.

MONROE COUNTY

TOMBSTONE INSCRIPTIONS

RURAL VALE BAPTIST CHURCH CEMETERY

Copied by: Lawrence McConkey, Englewood, Tennessee
Date:

The Rural Vale Baptist Church Cemetery is 17 miles South of
Madisonville. It may be reached by going to Mt. Vernon, thence
to Jalapa, thence following the Ivy road to the Rural Vale
Community. The old Rural Vale Church build'ng was used by
both the Methodist and Baptist Denominations. It was also
used as a school house. The first Church building was possibly
erected about 1840. On January 31, 1880 the Baptist organized
in a new building with C. H. Eaton as pastor and G. W. Harris
as church clerk. The oldest date on a marker in this cemetery
records the death of Sarah G., mother of S. P. Hale, on Oct.
5, 1858. The cemetery possibly was established at an earlier
date. There are 61 inscriptions and approximately 100 unmarked
graves.

PIKE

W. K. Pike
Aug. 4, 1910
Mar. 22, 1934
Gone but not forgotten.

HAMBY

K. E. Hamby
Aug. 8, 1861
Aug. 7, 1921
Asleep in Jesus
Peaceful sleep.

KILBY

Come Ye blessed
Oct. 3, 1884
June 5, 1916
Gods ways are just.

Inf.
of
Mr. & Mrs. J. S. Kilby

J. S. Kilby
Died April 12, 1936
Aged 56 yrs. 5 mos. 28 days.

GREEN

Loice K.
Infant of
V. R. & I. F. Green
Oct. 8, 1918
Jan. 5, 1919

Ida F. Green
Aug. 15, 1892
Feb. 16, 1920
Meet me in Heaven.

ROMINGER

Thy will be done
Samantha Rominger
July 25, 1869
May   4, 1912

Henry Rominger
Infant

Infant
of
W. E. & S. E. Rominger
Born & died
July 25, 1910

RURAL VALE BAPTIST CHURCH CEMETERY

JENKINS

Sarah J. Jenkins
Apr. 10, 1821
Feb. 19, 1907
Erected by her son
J. C. Jenkins
Our mother.

In memory of
W. A.
Son of
J. C. & Cardelia Jenkins
Aug. 10, 1875
July 4, 1904

J. C. Jenkins
Nov. 17, 1843
Sept. 15, 1913
Gone but not forgotten.

Cordelia
Wife of
J. C. Jenkins
Aug. 22, 1846
Dec. 19, 1909

SMITH

Pearl Smith
Died Feb. 12, 1930
Aged 16 yrs. 3 mos. 22 days.

Texie
Wife of
I. A. Smith
Feb. 20, 1890
Feb. 24, 1910
Thy will be done.

Horace Smith
Feb. 22, 1903
June 27, 1907
We miss thee so
very much.

W. H. Smith

Grace Ritchie
Wife of
W. H. Smith
July 19, 1867
Mar. 26, 1912
Our loved one gone
but to a brighter land.

Infant
of
W. H. & Grace Smith

Infant
of
W. H. & Grace Smith

COFFEY

John G. Coffey
1897 - 1938

Buckner

Mrs. Ruby Buckner
Died July 8, 1927
Aged 29 yrs. 6 mos. 9 days.

Infant
Buckner

Infant
Buckner

FRYE

Sept. 3, 1901
Nov. 16, 1901
Our sweet baby.

LEE

Lester Lee
Son of
Edward & Amanda Lee
Dec. 8, 1910
Aug. 4, 1920
Asleep in Jesus.

RURAL VALE BAPTIST CHURCH CEMETERY

Edward Lee
Aug. 5, 1883
Dec. 4, 1918
Not dead but sleepeth.

Hubert Ross Lee
Died Oct. 31, 1937
Aged 21 yrs. 4 mos. 26 days.

Mary
Wife of
Calvin Lee
Oct. 31, 1815
June 20, 1887

Calvin Lee
Aug. 16, 1816
May 20, 1880

James M.
Son of
C. & M. Lee
Oct.   7, 1839
Sept. 18, 1863
A precious on from
us has gone, a place is
vacant in our home
that never can be filled
but a chain is forming
in a better land.

Amanda Rice
Wife of
T. J. Lee
Apr. 16, 1857
Jan. 6, 1928
At Rest.

In my fathers house are
many mansions.
Thomas J. Lee
Nov. 30, 1847
Aug. 4, 1911
Asleep in Jesus.

HALE

In memory of
My mother
Sarah G.
Born July 8, 1807
Died Oct. 5, 1858
This stone is erected
by her son S. P. Hale.

INGRAM

Marybell Ingram
July 23, 1916
Aug. 11, 1916

Susie Ingram
July 2, 1917
Nov. 3, 1918

TIPTON

Tipton
Mother
Eglantine Tipton
1855 - (dead no date)

Father
Joseph M. Tipton
1853 - 1923

George W. Tipton
Mar. 28, 1882
July 29, 1905
Peaceful be thy
silent slumber.

LOVINGOOD

Max Lovingood
June 15, 1915
Dec. 27, 1918
Our Darling not lost
but gone before.

CUNNINGHAM

Father
C. C. Cunningham
Apr. 27, 1838
Jan. 1, 1928

Mother
Mary Russell
C. C. Cunningham
May 8, 1841
May 30, 1917
A tender mother and
faithful father.

John Cunningham
Died Feb. 8, 1938
Aged (not given but grave
is a long one.)

RURAL VALE BAPTIST CHURCH CEMETERY

NORWOOD

Sarah Norwood
June 25, 1861
 (Living)

J. C. Norwood
July 10, 1860
Mar. 4, 1928

Florence
Wife of
John Norwood
Mar. 19, 1892
July 11, 1923

Lee Vestal Norwood
July 25, 1921
Apr. 18, 1923
Gone to rest.

M. G. Norwood
Apr. 18, 1895
June 3, 1923
Gone but not forgotten.

Cora Gardner
Wife of
Frank Norwood
Oct. 18, 1885
May 30, 1919
Gone but not forgotten.

Anelandee Norwood
Nov. 9, 1833
July 21, 1885
Gone but not forgotten.

F. A. Norwood

EDMONSON

Reece Edmonson
Died June 6, 1937
Aged Inf.

Infant
Edmonson

TORRENCE

In memory of
W. Aa Torrence
Apr. 5, 1826
Dec. 3, 1904

SEAGLE

Mrs. Lou Jane Seagle
Oct. 6, 1855
May 10, 1930

J. S. Seagle

Louiza Seagle

Mary Seagle

BROWN

James Brown
July 12, 1868
Aug. 7, 1872

Sarah Brown
Jan. 29, 1870
Sept. 14, 1870

MONROE COUNTY

TOMBSTONE INSCRIPTIONS

ST. PAUL EVANGELICAL LUTHERN CHURCH (OLD) CEMETERY

Copied by: Lawrence McConkey, Englewood, Tennessee.
Date:

The St. Paul Evangelical Lutheran Church was organized by the
Rev. Adam Miller about the year 1812. The Governor of the
State granted four acres to be used for the church and a
cemetery. The first church, built of logs, stood where a
part of the cemetery is now located. The church building
was also used for the school. In 1868-1869 a frame building
size 60 feet by 46 feet took the place of the old building and
was placed just outside of the cemetery. On Sunday May 7th
1869 the Rev. J. C. Barb preached the dedication serman from
Ephesians 2nd chapter 20th verse.

The church was removed about one mile to Lakeside in 1920.

The church and cemetery are about 8 miles North of Madisonville and may be reached by taking road via Oak Grove County
School. About 1 mile beyond, at the Ivins farm, turn right
and follow road leading to Lakeside. Just ½ mile before
reaching Lakeside turn to the right. The cemetery is on the
farm of John W. Wright.

There are 103 inscriptions and between 200 and 300 unmarked
graves.

GASTON

Peggy
Daughter of
J. & M. Gaston
Born Aug. 25, 1829
Died Apr. 28, 1830

MOSER

Francis Moser
Died Oct. 22, 1836
Aged 76 years.

Francis Moser
Born Jany 31 1812
Died Oct. 30, 1865

John Fox Moser
Born April 1, 1845
Died Mar. 7, 1864

James C. Moser
Born Oct. 31, 1853
Died Sept. 9, 1861

Infant
of
Francis & E. Moser

Infant
Daughter of
Philip & J. A. Moser
Born & died Nov. 4, 1858

Infant
of
Philip & Julia Moser
(No dates)

Noah Moser
Born Apr. 20, 1856
Died Oct. 9, 1861

ST. PAUL EVANGELICAL LUTHERAN CHURCH (OLD) CEMETERY

A. Lafayette Moser
Born Apr. 28, 1860
Died Apr. 13, 1867

John H.
Son of
Philip & Julia A. Moser
Born Feb. 3, 1849
Died Oct. 11, 1869

C. L. Moser
Son of
P. & J. A. Moser
Born Jan. 6, 1867
Died Sep. 2, 1887

Philip Moser
Born April 15, 1820
Died Aug. 14, 1895
Blessed are the dead
which die in the Lord.

Julia Ann Carey
Wife of
Philip Moser
Oct. 4, 1828
Aug. 29, 1905

Henry Moser
Born Oct. 22, 1830
Died May 18, 1854

William C.
Son of
Noah & Mary A. Moser
Died Feb. 9, 1848
Aged 2 yrs. 7 mos. 16 days.

Eliza J.
Daughter of
Noah & Mary A. Moser
Died Nov. 2, 1847
Aged 1 year & 2 ds.

Infant
Of
N. & M. A. Moser

John H.
Son of
F. M. & M. A. Moser
Died Jan. 23, 1852
Aged 2 mos. & 7 days.

Mary C.
Daughter of
F. M. & M. A. Moser
Died July 19, 1857
Aged 2 yrs. 6 mos. 16 da's.

Infant
of
D. M. & E. Moser

Magdoline
Wife of
John Moser
Oct. 3, 1803
May 28, 1877

John Moser
Aug. 18, 1793
Jan. 2, 1882
He giveth his beloved sleep.

Noah Moser
Born Apr. 9, 1822
Died Oct. 13, 1885

Mary A.
Wife of
Noah Moser
Born Mar. 10, 1824
Died Aug. 23, 1903

Philip Moser
Born Aug. 2, 1857
Died Dec. 24, 1913

John F. Moser
Born Dec. 22, 1851
Died Jan. 12, 1903
Asleep in Jesus
blessed sleep.

ST. PAUL EVANGELICAL LUTHERAN CHURCH (OLD) CEMETERY

Infant
Son of
J. & S. Moser
Born & died
Jan. 13, 1887

Simply to thy cross I cling.
Ivan Moser
Apr. 3, 1894
Dec. 21, 1915
Gone but not forgotten.

Harold Hugh
Son of
J. M. & A. M. Moser
Born Sept. 12, 1895
Died Aug. 29, 1900

DELASHMITT

Isaiah Delashmitt
Died May 31, 1896
Aged about 63 years.
At Rest.

TERRY

Here lies the body of
William J. Terry
Was born May 13, 1841
Died   July 15, 1841

SUMMITT OR SUMMIT

Lula Mae
Wife of
W. L. Summitt
Died Oct. 4, 1911
Aged 22 yrs.
Resting in the hope of
a glorious Resurrection.

John S. Summitt
Aug. 16, 1845
Apr. 6, 1916

His wife
Mary E. Moser
March 22, 1852
August 18, 1933

Denver W.
Son of
J. S. & M. E. Summitt
Born Apr. 30, 1894
Died June 23, 1896
Suffer little children to come
unto me. Asleep in Jesus
Blessed sleep.

Joseph Summitt
Born May 17, 1824
Died June 6, 1896

Jacob E.
Son of
J. & L. Summitt
Born Sept. 20, 1853
Died June 1, 1891

David L.
Son of
J. & L. Summitt
Born June 15, 1858
Died Oct. 2, 1882
Death is a debt thats
justly due. That I have
paid and so must you.
This I own is justly
due and I have come
to sleep with you.

E. Summitt
Born Feb. 10, 1815
Died Mar. 25, 1893

Sarah Summitt
Wife of
E. Summitt
Born Jan. 29, 1822
Died Sept. 11, 1891

J. W.
Son of
M. L. & M. C. Summitt
Born June 19, 1872
Died June 12, 1890

Mary T.
Daughter of
M. L. & M. C. Summitt
June 6, 1880
Oct. 9, 1887

ST. PAUL EVANGELICAL LUTHERAN CHURCH (ODD) CEMETERY

Darius E.
Son of
M. L. & M. C. Summitt
July 29, 1882
Dec. 22, 1882

M. C.
Wife of
M. L. Summitt
Born Nov. 25, 1853
Died Feb. 20, 1884

Martin Luther Summitt
Died Dec. 5, 1927
Aged 79 years 1 day.

Mrs. Callie Summitt
Died Dec. 4, 1930
Aged 83 yrs. 9 mos. 25 days.

Ella F.
Daughter of
M. L. & R. C. Summitt
Oct. 10, 1886
Oct. 13, 1886

Robert D.
Son of
M. L. & R. C. Summitt
Sept. 28, 1885
Sept. 28, 1885

Nancy Jane Summitt
Nov. 27, 1835
Aug. 31, 1915
She was the sunshine
of our home.

Peter Summitt
Feb. 11, 1833
June 5, 1910
He was beloved by
God and man.

In loving Remembrance of
Jonathan Summit
Born Jan. 26, 1817
Died June 17, 1896
A precious one from us has gone
A voice we loved is stilled.
A place is vacant in our home
that never can be filled.

Daniel Summit
Born Apr. 5, 1795
Died Sept. 30, 1838

Sarah
Wife of
Daniel Summit
Born May 24, 1796
Died June 30, 1856

Hetty Ann
Wife of
Joseph Summit
Died Nov. 24, 1846
Aged 22 yrs. 8 mos. & 12 days.

Philip
Son of
Joseph & H. A. Summit
Born Apr. 29, 1845
Died Nov. 13, 1845

VINCENT

G. W. Vincent
Born Nov. 19, 1822
Died Jan. 9, 1892

MOREE

M. M. Moree
Born May 1, 1889
Died May 29, 1890

SHIELDS

Jacob Shields
Nov. 23, 1840
Aug. 15, 1917

Father
Joseph Shields
Born June 17, 1809
Died Aug. 22, 1831

Mother
Margaret Shields
Born 1811
Died July 18, 1901

ST. PAUL EVANGELICAL LUTHERAN CHURCH (OLD) CEMETERY

Sarah A.
Wife of
J. D. Shields
Born June 23, 1863
Died June 8, 1888

Lucinda J. Shields
Feb. 17, 1834
Dec. 15, 1909
Our beloved sister.

Cook

John Cook
Born Mar. 1807
Died Aug. 28, 1860

John Wesley Cook
Died Aug. 17, 1840
Aged 2 months & 23 days.

SAMPLES

S. H. Samples
Born Aug. 6, 1886
Died Dec. 27, 1910
At Rest.

J. H. Samples
Dec. 1, 1858
Apr. 9, 1924
Asleep in Jesus.

Savior lead me.
S. R. Samples
Dec. 18, 1835
        19--

Savior lead me
S. A. Samples
Aug. 15, 1833
June 20, 1893

J. S. Samples
Apr. 13, 1874
May 5, 1914
At rest.

BURTON

Alice M.
Wife of
David Burton
Born Nov. 1, 1859
Died June 10, 1893

STEPHENS

Jordan Stephens
Died July 12, 1923
Aged 11 years 1 month & 4 days.

DAVIS

Nora Isabelle
Wife of
C. R. Davis
Dec. 23, 1881
Oct. 17, 1902
All who knew thee loved thee.
Many friends now mourn they
death. We will set our hearts
to meet thee in the land of
sweetest rest.

Nellie Louise Davis
July 25, 1909
Jan. 7, 1919

Wm. Henry Davis
July 8, 1850
Dec. 31, 1902

Margarett D. Davis
Sept. 21, 1850
Aug. 16, 1915
Dead unto sin but alive
unto God.

CRAIG

A. G. Craig
Sept. 26, 1858
Sept. 3, 1906
At Rest.

BIRCHFIELD

ST. PAUL EVANGELICAL LUTHERAN CHURCH (OLD) CEMETERY

Isabella Summitt
Wife of
Henry Birchfield
Born Feb. 14, 1829
Died June 19, 1910
Blessed are they which
die in the Lord.

MCAFFERY OR MCAFFREY

Margaret McAffery
Born Oct. 9, 1798
Died Feb. 9, 1885
Dearest one thou art gone
but not forgotten.

John T. McAffrey
Born June 17, 1829
Died Feby 16, 1895

MOODY

Carl Moody
Son of
L. B. & M. T. Moody
Aug. 28, 1892
July 8, 1908

Myrtle Moody
Mar. 5, 1899
June 27, 1899

John Moody
May 24, 1897
June 30, 1897

Josephine Moody
June 24, 1891
July 27, 1891

Fletcher Moody
Oct. 21, 1888
Apr. 21, 1889

SMYER

Sacred to the memory of
Rev. E. E. Smyer
Who was born in Catawba County,
N. C. Sept. 15th A. D. 1831
Baptised in Infancy and confirmed
May 12th A. D. 1855. He entered

the ministry in the Lutheran
Church A. D. 1858 and departed
this life in hope of a blessed
immortality Aug. 16th A. D.
1869. Blessed are the dead
which die in the Lord from henceforth; yea saith the Spirit
that they may rest from their
labors and their works do
follow them.

JOHNSTON

In memory of
Nancy Ann Johnston
Was born Feby 13, 1825
Died July 16, 1871

In memory of
Margarett J. Johnston
Was born Jan. 11, 1827
Died Novr 25, 1861

J. N. Johnston
Oct. 14, 1828
Nov. 12, 1908

SHAFFER

W. ------ Shaffer
Born Dec. 27, 1793
Died July 18, 1864

HICKS

Mary C.
Daughter of
S. & S. Hicks
Born Aug. 9, 1855
Died Oct. 30, 1855

HARRISON

G. W. Harrison
May 28, 1854
June 11, 1911

At Rest
Maggie Moser
Wife of
G. W. Harrison
Nov. 19, 1854
Dec. 22, 1898

ST. PAUL EVANGELICAL LUTHERAN CHURCH (OLD) CEMETERY

SHEETS

John C.
Son of
Jacob & Mary J. Sheets
Born Oct. 26, 1854
Died Nov. 3, 1855

(Masonic)
Jacob Sheets
Born June 14, 1822
Died May 15, 1873

Mary Jane
Wife of
Jacob Sheets
Born Feb. 14, 1828
Died July 20, 1876

HARTSOOK

James A.
Son of
G. L. & N. G. Hartsook
Born June 16, 1879
Died Feb. 27, 1880

Nannie G.
Wife of
G. L. Hartsook
Born Dec. 6, 1845
Died May 3, 1880
Gone but not forgotten.

CLONINGER

Jacob Cloninger
Oct. 3, 1826
May 29, 1904

Margaret E. Cloninger
Sept. 25, 1824
Nov. 29, 1904

John W. Cloninger
Born Nov. 10, 1821
Died Oct. 6, 1905
(Double marker see top page)

Catharine
Wife of
J. W. Cloninger
Born May 13, 1830
Died (Date of death not given.)

BRAKEBILL

Martha Brakebill
Mar. 7, 1843
Aug. 18, 1860
Remember friends as you
pass by, as you are now,
so once was I. As i am
now so must you be, so
be prepared for death and
follow me.

In memory of
Sarah Isabelle
The beloved wife of
J. E. Brakebill
Born May 10, 1852
Departed this life
Sept. 20, 1873
Blessed are the dead which
die in the Lord.

PHILLIPS

Phillips
Martha E.
Wife of
T. L. Phillips
July 8, 1865
Apr. 27, 1918
She was the sunshine
of our home.

B. S.M.

The above, initials only.

TOMBSTONE INSCRIPTIONS

ST. PAUL LUTHERN CHURCH (NEW) CEMETERY

Copied by: Lawrence McConkey, Englewood, Tennessee
Date:

St. Paul Luthern Church was removed in 1920 to Lakeside, a
distance of about 1 mile from where it was first established
96 years before.   One acre of land was purchased from Frank
Lee Johnston for the church site and cemetery which are
located 8 miles Northeast of Madisonville.

The Rev. Walter C. Davis dedicated the new church and the
Rev. F. M. Harr was the first pastor. Henry Moser, who died
in 1922, was the first one buried in the new cemetery.

There is only one unmarked grave here.

CLEMMER

James I. Clemmer
Died April 19, 1936
Aged 56 yrs. & 29 days.

DAVIS

Mother
Minnie E. Summitt
Wife of
C. F. Davis
Mar. 14, 1879
Dec. 6, 1928
At Rest.

SUMMITT

Summitt
Joseph C.
Oct. 19, 1857
Nov. 3, 1929

Susie
July 26, 1873
(Still living)
Beloved one farewell.

SAMPLES

Virginia L. Samples
May 16, 1874
July 26, 1934
At Rest.

Samples
Deva Samples
July 8, 1917
Oct. 24, 1931
At Rest.

MCLENDON

Roxie Samples
wife of
I. H. McLendon
Feb. 2, 1904
June 18, 1935
Gone but not forgotten.

MCSPADDEN

Harvey L. McSpadden
Tennessee Pvt. 17 Engrs.
Sept. 2, 1931

Baby
Son of
H. L. McSpadden
1928-1928
Our darling

MOSER

W. H. Moser
Sept. 22, 1847
Aug. 6, 1922

A. A. Moser
Aug. 4, 1845
June 25, 1931

2

ST. PAUL LUTHERN CHURCH (NEW) CEMETERY

Our Baby Boy
Born Dec. 27, 1888
Died Jan. 1, 1889

(Note: Above child is the
son of W. H. & A. A. Moser
and remains were removed
from another cemeter. LMcC.)

MONROE COUNTY

TOMBSTONE INSCRIPTIONS

STEPHENS CEMETERY

Copied by: Lawrence McConkey, Englewood, Tennessee
Date: February 12, 1940

The Stephens Cemetery is located on the farm of Archie Roy
6 miles West of Madisonville on road leading to Athens via
Craighead Springs & Christianburg.

The cemetery was established when George Stephens owned the
farm, possibly as a Stephens family cemetery. It later became
a community cemetery. The earliest inscription of a death is
that of Wm. S. Jarvis who died Jan. 13, 1848 but the cemetery
was undoubtedly established earlier. It covers a space fenced
of about three-fourths of an acre, and is said to be full of
graves. The last inscription is that of Orisia Thomas who
died Sept. 10, 1877 and is also about the time the cemetery
was discontinued.

JARVIS

Wm. S. Jarvis
Aug. 29, 1828
Jan. 13, 1848

Note: There are many other
graves nearby but it is
not know if of same family.

THOMAS

Anderson Thomas
Dec. 25, 1836
June 27, 1859

Haywood Thomas
April 14, 1843
Oct. 30, 1857

Orisia Thomas
Oct. 18, 1859
Sept. 10, 1877

(Note: There are many
unmarked graves nearby the
above Thomas tombstone and
may and may not be of same
family.)

SANDS

Judy A.
Daughter of
Joe & E. Sands
March 6, 1854
Aug. 23, 1854

(Note: Also many unmarked
graves by above-but may not be
of same family.)

ROY

Susan
Wife of
Jos. A. Roy
June 19, 1829
Jan. 10, 1852
Aged 22 years 6 months & 21 days.

Note: It seems that her husband
is buried in the Christianburg
Baptist Cemetery only a short
distance away. - but possibly
some of the many unmarked graves
are of some relatives. -don't know)

LONG

2

STEPHENS CEMETERY

Long
George
Died March 1853

Nan C. Long
Bo. Aug. 13, 1850

(Note: Balance of above
inscription chipped off.
Also unmarked graves near the
Long markers.)

CUNNINGHAM

Phoebe
Wife of
Joseph Cunningham
Aged 67 years.

Joseph Cunningham
Nov. 3, 1768
May 21, 1858
Aged 89 years, 6 months
& 18 days.

(Note: Like around other
markers these also have
nearby unmarked graves.)

(Note: Graves without
inscriptions are as follows

60 Field Stones Approximately
2 Inscriptions destroyed
238 unmarked graves.

TOMBSTONE INSCRIPTIONS

SHADY GROVE BAPTIST CHURCH CEMETERY

Copied by: Lawrence McConkey, Englewood, Tennessee
Date: June 21-23, 1939

The Shady Grove Baptist Church Cemetery was established soon
after establishment of the Shady Grove Baptist Church near
Tellico Plains in 1842. The first burial inscription is
1848. The land for both the church and the cemetery was
given by James Williams. The section of the cemetery between
the church and the graves of Wiley Ray family, that are in
a brick house, was reserved for the Williams family and
relatives. Years ago Negroes were buried in one section of
the cemetery, but Negroes are not being buried there now.

There are 276 unmarked graves. Including the Negro burials,
there are as many unmarked graves as there are those with
inscriptions. Shady Grove Baptist Church Cemetery is located
about one mile West of Jalapa on the road leading to Etowah.
Jalapa is about 18 miles South of Madisonville.

ALLEN

Dorothy Ann Allen
Died June 6, 1938
Aged 88 years, 2 days

NEWMAN

A. R. Newman
Born May 12, 1850
Died July -- ----

Johnnie Williams Newman
1855 - 1930
At Rest.

BORING OR BORIN

A. Borin
Nov. 25, 1846
Sept. 15, 1904
Father

Mattie A. Borin
Sept. 3, 1852
June 2, 1906
Mother
At Rest.

Sarah A.
Wife of
John Boring
Dec. 14, 1835
Nov. 22, 1879

John M.
Son of
Nick & E. J. Borin
May 21, 1860
Nov. 23, 1860

J. A. Borin

Borin
Emma Borin
Jan. 14, 1869
(not buried)

E. W. Borin
Jan. 25, 1862
Jan. 28, 1929
Prepare to meet
me in Heaven.

SHADY GROVE BAPTIST CHURCH CEMETERY

Mary E.
Wife of
Jacob Boring
Died April 16, 1910
Age 83 years
Not lost blest thought
but gone before where
we shall meet to
part no more.

(Note: Several of the family
drop the "g" from their name.
All are descendants of John
D. and Mary J. Boring. Family
Cemetery about 2 miles South-
east. LMcC.)

SMALLIN

At Rest
Daisy Dean
Wife of
W. O. Smallin
June 3, 1874
Apr. 8, 1920

Willie D.
Son of
W. O. & Daisy D. Smallin
Died Sept. 29, 1902
Aged 2 years, 5 months
and 25 days.
Our sweet darling.

E. J. Smallin
Oct. 22, 1834
Apr. 6, 1915

Jeff Smallin
Feb. 24, 1827
Nov. 29, 1911
At Rest.

LOFTISS

Joseph Loftiss
Co. E.
7th Tenn. Mtd. Inf.

Mrs. Joseph Loftiss

Jackson Loftiss
Co. E.
7th. Tenn. Mtd. Inf.

Mrs. Jackson Loftiss

PERRINE

Perrine
Essie
Mar. 15, 1881
Aug. 10, 1909
At Rest.

Perrine
Lizzie
Apr. 22, 1874
Sept. 25, 1907
At Rest.

Husband
John H. Perrine
Feb. 2, 1876
July 12, 1937

Wife
Martha E. Perrine
Oct. 30, 1878
(not yet buried)
Prepare to meet us
in Heaven.

Perrine
Mother
N. A. Perrine
Mar. 19, 1849
July 1, 1914

Father
W. H. Perrine
Nov. 11, 1838
Nov. 29, 1910
Prepare to meet us
in Heaven.

WEAR

Lelia May
Wife of
Homer Wear
1902 - 1928
Thy life was beauty
Goodness and love.

SHADY GROVE BAPTIST CHURCH CEMETERY

VAUGHN

Mary Anise Vaughn
Died April 28, 1938
Aged 59 years, 5 months
& 28 days.

Wm. Vaughn
Died Jan. 1890
Aged about 60 years.

WHITE

J---- White
Died Aug. 17, 1931
Aged 17 years, 1 month
& 6 days.

Mary White

DAUGHERTY

Susan Cordelia Dougherty
Died March 1, 1937
Aged 68 years & 2 months

William Daugherty
Mar. 7, 1852
May 30, 1923
At Rest
Gone but not forgotten.

Nannie Daugherty
Dec. 7, 1854
June 7, 1925
At Rest
Gone but not forgotten.
Father and mother.

Asleep in Jesus
Ralph Daugherty
Mar. 20, 1891
Apr. 18, 1920
Gone but not forgotten.

Asleep in Jesus
Donnie Wear
Wife of
Ralph Daugherty
Sept. 2, 1898
Mar. 5, 1924
Just when we learned to
love her most, God called
her back to Heaven.

(Note: The above had at the
base "Wear" but as she was
the wife of the deceased
Ralph Daugherty I am placing
her inscription in the
Daugherty list.) LMcC.

Bettie Daugherty
Nov. 21, 1874
July 18, 1903
At Rest
We shall meet thee.

John Daugherty
June 3, 1860
(Not buried)

Sallie
Wife of
John Daugherty
June 13, 1867
Oct. 8, 1910
At Rest.

Brazeal Daugherty
May 10, 1834
July 31, 1911

Margret Daugherty
Jan. 1, 1839
May 28, 1903
We will be waiting above.

Eliza Daugherty
Feb. 24, 1869
Apr. 5, 1899
At Rest.

Linda Daugherty
Oct. 16, 1864
Aug. 6, 1894
At Rest.

Spicie G. (or C.)
Wife of
Alex. Daugherty
Aug. 10, 1829
Apr. 8, 1877
Here lies one who in this
life was a kind mother
and a true wife.

(Note: Another inscription
of above.) LMcC.

SHADY GROVE BAPTIST CHURCH CEMETERY

Spicy C. Daugherty
Aug. 10, 1829
Apr. 8, 1877

Alexander Daugherty
Jan. 22, 1831
June 22, 1909
At Rest.

Kate
Daughter of
Alex. & S. C. Daugherty
July 8, 1866
Sept. 3, 1871
A little time on
earth she spent till
God for her his Angel sent.

T. A. Daugherty
Aug. 1, 1831
Sept. 14, 1902
At Rest.

Nancy J. Daugherty
Oct. 7, 1833
Aug. 13, 1916
Gone Home to
die no more.

ROY

Phebe
Wife of
William Roy
Dec. 16, 1830
Apr. 15, 1881
Awaiting the Resurrection.

William M. Roy
July 9, 1841
Oct. 31, 1913
At Rest.

Carrie Daugherty
Wife of
W. M. Roy
July 14, 1859
Oct. 31, 1910

Wiley Roy

(Note: He does not have an
inscription but he, his wife
and several of his family
have a brick house over
them. He was an early
settler. LMcC.)

TATE

Tate
Mary J. Smallin
Sept. 1, 1854
May 13, 1937

Isaac
May 3, 1851
May 6, 1920
At Rest.

Daisy
Wife of
John A. Tate
Sept. 4, 1880
Apr. 2, 1910
Beloved one farewell.

Ada E.
Wife of
John A. Tate
May 13, 1880
May 10, 1908

John A. Tate
April 26, 1875
Feb. 12, 1915
After the days
of sadness, hope
sheds her brightest rays.

UNDERWOOD

Carlin Underwood
Dec. 25, 1842
Apr. 4, 1892
Safe at home with Jesus.

KING

Elizabeth Hawkins King
Born   1781
Died June 29, 1870

SHADY GROVE BAPTIST CHURCH CEMETERY

In memory of
H. L. King
Oct. 10, 1796
Sept. 28, 1855

Rev. J. H. King
May 26, 1821
Apr. 13, 1897

Mary King
Oct. 27, 1830
June 4, 1912
Lives well spent.

King
John C.
1856 - 1901

Sarah J.
1863 - 1926
At Rest.

Rebecca King

MYERS

Jesse Myers
Dec. 25, 1827
Oct. 1, 1907
Asleep in Jesus.

SMITH

At Rest
Charlotta Smith
July 3, 1830
June 30, 1912

J. J. Smith
Jan. 1, 1820
Sept. 5, 1911

William Henry Smith
Died April 13, 1938
Aged 90 years, 4 months
& 1 day.

Smith
Nancy Jane
July 3, 1861
Dec. 24, 1882

James L. Smith
Jan. 1, 1872
Jan. 14, 1930
Our father
At rest.

Our father and mother
Wm. R. Smith
Born Tues.
Jan. 10, 1817
Died Feb. 24, 1894

Mary E. Smith
Born Wedns.
Feb. 26, 1824
Died Aug. 10, 1897

In memory of
Asenith A. Smith
Born Jan. 10, 1852
Died Aug. 4, 1854

BRIANT

N. C. Anna Bell Brient
Sept. 22, 1877
Sept. 19, 1885

ADAMS

Wash Adams
Died April 30, 1926
Aged 69 years, 8 months
& 12 days.

EDINGTON OR EDDINGTON

Walter Edington
June 18, 1902
June 12, 1903

M. J. Eddington
Nov. 15, 1834
(Buried no date)

A. A. Eddington
June 9, 1826
Mar. 22, 1893

LEE

SHADY GROVE BAPTIST CHURCH CEMETERY

Our darling
Robert E. Lee
June 22, 1920
Jan. 31, 1921
Baby
A little time on earth
he spent till God for
him his Angel sent.

Our darling
Sue Ella Bernice Lee
Aug. 17, 1918
June 13, 1919
Baby
A little time on earth
she spent till God for
her his Angel sent.

Ida
Wife of
G. C. Lee
Oct. 7, 1860
Sept. 22, 1882

Infant
of
G. W. & H. E. Lee
June 26, 1882
July 15, 1882

Father
John Lee
(no dates but seems he
is buried)

Mother
Margaret
Wife of
John Lee
Feb. 29, 1837
Mar. 16, 1910
At Rest.

Marshall
Son of
Robt. & Sarah Lee
Mar. 27, 1891
Nov. 9, 1896
Asleep in Jesus.

Wm. Lee
Co. K.
3rd Tenn. Cav.

Emmaline
Wife of
William Lee
Dec. 7, 1821
Sept. 22, 1881
Asleep in Jesus.

Bob Lee
Oct. 21, 1909
May 27, 1910
At Rest.

Sue Lee
Feb. 12, 1886
Nov. 6, 1902
She was too good and
too gentle to dwell in
this cold world of care.

Roxie Lee
Nov. 20, 1900
Sept. 17, 1902

Ethel Lee
Feb. 5, 1888
Apr. 25, 1893
Sleep on sweet children
and take your rest, God
called thee home he thought
it best.

Kittie Lou Lee
Dec. 9, 1904
May 31, 1908
Asleep in Jesus.
Blessed sleep.

Edward Lee
June 30, 1824
Jan. 15, 1871
We know no sorrow,
Knew no grief Till thy
bright face was missed

Esther A. Lee
Feb. 29, 1832
Sept. 14, 1904
Her spirit smiles from
that bright shore and
softly whispers, weep no
more.
Father & mother

SHADY GROVE BAPTIST CHURCH CEMETERY

Maud Lee
Oct. 1, 1885
Dec. 28, 1885
Sleep on and take
thy sweet rest, God
called thee home
he thought it best.

Edd Lee
Died April 16, 1939
Aged 82 years, 4 months
& 15 days.

Mrs. Edd Lee

CURTIS

Lonna V.
Son of
T. J. & Emma E. Curtis
May 15, 1883
July 4, 1885

Harless
Son of
T. J. & Emma E. Curtis
Feb. 8, 1885
Mar. 14, 1886

Thomas
Infant of
J. R. & Mattie Curtis
Apr. 10, 1898
Apr. 22, 1898

DEAN

Come ye blessed
Dr. David Dean
Nov. 6, 1799
Feb. 8, 1885
Gone but not forgotten.

WILLIAMS

Millie
Wife of
H. P. Williams
June 1, 1862
July 21, 1929

Lee
Son of
J. & Barbara Williams
Jan. 12, 1886
June 5, 1912

Nancy Jane Williams
Wife of
H. P. Williams
Sept. 9, 1836
April 24, 1885
Age 48 years 7 months
& 15 days.

H. P. Williams
Nov. 1, 1834
Oct. 7, 1918

In memory of
Margaret F.
Daughter of
H. P. & N. J. Williams
Sept. 16, 1865
Sept. 3, 1871

Etta
Daughter of
H. P. & N. J. Williams
Feb. 20, 1874
April 4, 1875

Infant
of
Mr. & Mrs. W. W. Williams
March. 18, 1917
March 20, 1917
Our darling.

George W. Williams
June 18, 1870
Jan. 8, 1918
At Rest.

James Williams
Husband of
Elizabeth Williams
May 14, 1799
April 14, 1876
Aged 76 years, 8 months.

SHADY GROVE BAPTIST CHURCH CEMETERY

Elizabeth Williams
Wife of
James Williams
Jan. 23, 1804
Aug. 29, 1878
Aged 74 years, 7 months
& 6 days.

Melissa C.
Wife of
Samuel Williams
April 16, 1844
Sept. 15, 1869

Louisa J. King
Wife of
Samuel Williams
Aug. 10, 1849
Dec. 31, 1898

Samuel Williams
Dec. 10, 1829
(Buried no date given)
At Rest.

Mary J. Williams
April 2, 1831
(Buried no date)
Mother

G. W. Williams
Sept. 22, 1822
Mch. 16, 1904
Father

Samuel R. Williams
Jan. 28, 1854
Aug. 25, 1855

Lady Kate
Daughter of
George & Nannie Williams
May 12, 1902
Feb. 24, 1903
Our darling has
gone before.

Infant son
of
George & Nannie Williams
March 14, 1905
July 8, 1905

James H. E. Z. Williams
Son of
G. W. & M. J. Williams
Aug. 16, 1852
Aug. 7, 1854

In memory of
James F. Williams
Son of
M. & V. Williams
Dec. 6, 1846
Dec. 3, 1848

In memory of
Georgia M.
Daughter of
G. W. & M. J. Williams
Mar. 7, 1865
Oct. 4, 1871

In memory of
Edward Martin
Son of
G. W. & M. J. Williams
Sept. 27, 1872
Nov. 25, 1873

J. A. Williams
Sept. 29, 1832
May 14, 1892

Elizabeth
Wife of
J. A. Williams
Oct. 23, 1832
Sept. 7, 1875

Annie
Daughter of
J. A. & B. W. Williams
Aug. 28, 1880
Aug. 28, 1880

Nanie Pirl Williams
Jan. 7, 1910
May 21, 1911
Our darling.

Infant daughter
of
Sam & Nettie Williams
Dec. 2, 1908
Dec. 2, 1908

SHADY GROVE BAPTIST CHURCH CEMETERY

RITCHIE

Husband
At Rest
Alex. Ritchie
(Mason member)
Born Oct. 26, 1843
Died Mar. 10, 1912

Wife
Margaret Ritchie
June 20, 1835
Jan. 26, 1910

Husband
W. C. Ritchie
Mar. 26, 1832
Aug. 19, 1909

Synthie Ritchie
March 17, 1840
Jan.   8, 1913

MCCLELLAN

Sarah E. McClellan
Oct.   3, 1871
Sept. 21, 1922
She is safe at Home.

W. B. McClellan
June 28, 1858
Sept. 21, 1914
At Rest.

J. A. McClellan
Oct. 18, 1866
Nov. 3, 1899
At Rest.

S. L.
Son of
W. B. & J. A. McClellan
July 31, 1885
Apr. 4, 1904
Asleep in Jesus.

McClellan
(Mason member)
Thos. A. McClellan
Jan. 21, 1883
Jan. 31, 1923
Asleep in Jesus.

(Note: The following inscription of "Mc" were at another
location in the cemetery
than those above but they are
believed to be members of
same family, as above.

P. Mc

J. M. Mc

D. F. Mc

GRAVES

Graves
Fredie
Sept. 2, 1895
Oct. 24, 1908

Mary Katherine Graves
Died Oct. 14, 1926
Aged 63 years

CARDIN OR CARDEN

Stonewall Cardin
Died April 1927
Aged 69 years

Nancy Jane
Wife of
Jordan Cardin
June 6, 1826
Feb. 26, 1900
Prepare to meet
me in Heaven.

L. Carden
Aug. 20, 1853
Dec. 16, 1919
At Rest.
Gone but not forgotten.

James C. Cardin
Aug. 26, 1889
Feb. 28, 1920
Gone to rest.

Ruby Cardin
Mar. 6, 1891
Apr. 7, 1910
Gone to rest.

SHADY GROVE BAPTIST CHURCH CEMETERY

Desie Cardin
May 27, 1915
June 8, 1917
Our darling.

Carden
Fayett
May 5, 1890
Apr. 29, 1909

Sarah
June 29, 1893
Apr. 29, 1909

Joseph Cardin

MCDANIEL

Birdy
Daughter of
G. & R. McDaniel
Nov. 27, 1902
Dec. 10, 1904
Asleep in Jesus.

James
Son of
G. & R. McDaniel
Sept. 21, 1892
Asleep in Jesus.

Jessy
Son of
G. & R. McDaniel
Sept. 17, 1893
June 27, 1896
Asleep in Jesus.

J. McDaniel

Mary D.
Daughter of
G. & R. McDaniel
July 9, 1890
Apr. 12, 1892
Asleep in Jesus.

Johnie R. McDaniel
May 1, 1889
Aug. 16, 1902
Budded on earth to
bloom in Heaven.

BLANTON

Ethel
Daughter of
J. B. & N. J. Blanton
Aug. 6, 1888
Oct. 14, 1903
Gone but not forgotten.

ROGERS

Mother
Ora Rogers
Aug. 5, 1887
May 15, 1929

Father
(Mason member)
Luther Rogers
July   3, 1886
Sept. 12, 1928
Gone but not forgotten

COPPENGER

Flossie
Daughter of
W. H. & Maggie Coppenger
Dec. 17, 1904
Dec. 19, 1904
Gone but not forgotten.

DUGGAN

Mrs. W. H. L. Duggan

Henry Duggan

W. H. L. Duggan
July 20, 1852
June 28, 1913
At Rest.

GAINES

Sarah J. Gaines
July 22, 1834
Apr. 28, 1900
At Rest.

Thomas H. Gaines
Mar. 24, 1826
Nov. 26, 1909
At Rest.

SHADY GROVE BAPTIST CHURCH CEMETERY

ROSE

Amelia Rose
May 28, 1845
Oct. 21, 1892
Erected by
J. D. Crofts and wife.

Hick
Son of
G. W. & Mealie Rose
May 13, 1879
July 23, 1920
A loved one gone.

FLOYED

Richard Floyd
Dec. 16, 1877
Nov. 28, 1901
Gone but not forgotten.

Joseph Floyed
March 16, 1827
December 24, 1898
At Rest.

CUNNINGHAM

David Cunningham
July 12, 1804
Feb. 13, 1887

Adaline Cunningham
April 11, 1810
Dec. 1, 1889
Aged 79 years, 7 months
and 19 days.

Mahala C.
Daughter of
D. & A. Cunningham
Sept. 2, 1835
Feb. 5, 1882

Robert Cunningham
Aug. 19, 1800
Jan. 12, 1885
Aged 84 years, 4 months
and 24 days.

Rutha Cunningham
May 21, 1800
Aug. 7, 1891
Aged 91 years, 2 months
and 17 days.

Earl W. Cunningham
Nov. 3, 1902
Dec. 21, 1902
Aged 1 mo. 18 days
Gone but not forgotten.

M. C.
Wife of
M. Cunningham
Apr. 3, 1861
May 28, 1901
Just how changed that
lovely flower, which
bloomed and cheered
my heart.

MURPHY

Rowena M. Murphy
Aug. 31, 1915
June 28, 1916
He took, He will
restore.

HARRIS

Harris
Husband
John J. Harris
Jan. 5, 1873
(not buried)

Wife
Mary R. Harris
July 7, 1867
Apr. 2, 1929
Asleep in Jesus.

William O. Harris
April 11, 1857
July 15, 1865
Of such is the
Kingdom of Heaven.

SHADY GROVE BAPTIST CHURCH CEMETERY

John C. V. Harris
July 19, 1864
July 8, 1865
Of such is the
Kingdom of Heaven.

George C. Harris
Oct. 6, 1850
Dec. 11, 1850
Of such is the
Kingdom of Heaven.

ROBERTS

Mother
Delena Evaline Roberts
Oct. 12, 1868
June 23, 1933
She was the sun-
shine of our home.

Father
Joseph L. Roberts
Feb. 19, 1860
(not buried)
Life's work well
done, he rests in peace.

KILBY

W. G. Kilby
June 10, 1893
June 17, 1918

BAREFIELD

Amos Barefield
Apr. 27, 1900
Apr. 9, 1919
Gone to rest.

Thomas Barefield
Oct. 4, 1869
Sept. 18, 1902
Gone Home.

Lina
Wife of
J. B. Barefield
July 23, 1832
Aug. 11, 1918
Her spirit smiles from
that bright shore and
softly whispers weep no more.

M. L. J. Barefield
May 11, 1882
Sept. 19, 1897

Ethellean
Daughter of
Mr. & Mrs. J. S. Barefield
Sept. 25, 1910
Oct. 2, 1912
Our darling gone to rest.

Colonel J. Barefield
Dec. 20, 1870
Sep. 10, 1903
At Rest.

EVERHART

Lillie V.
Wife of
N. G. Everhart
Sept. 26, 1881
Oct. 1, 1909
With Thee.

Jessie B. Everhart
Aug. 22, 1902
Sept. 9, 1902

CLINE

Prof. James S. Cline
Oct. 24, 1837
Aug. 6, 1918
The Lord is my Keeper.

Elizabeth M. Cline
Apr. 4, 1843
June 8, 1913
Blessed are the
dead who die in
the Lord.

Lenora Arista Cline
Nov. 19, 1872
Apr. 25, 1918
And God shall
wipe away all tears
from their eyes.

SHADY GROVE BAPTIST CHURCH CEMETERY

James A. Cline
1869 - 1931
My trust is in God.

Elizabeth
Daughter of
J. S. & E. M. Cline
Dec. 17, 1874
Dec. 4, 1893
Gone but not forgotten.

Henry
Son of
J. S. & E. M. Cline
Oct. 20, 1868
Mar. 19, 1894
Asleep in Jesus.

Reuben
Son of
J. S. & E. M. Cline
Aug. 12, 1877
Mar. 10, 1912
Sleep on dear loved
ones and take thy rest
God hath called thee
home. He thought it best.

LAND

At Rest
Thomas S. Land
Mar. 4, 1860
Nov. 4, 1894
It was hard indeed
to depart with thee,
but Christ's strong
arm supports me.

Isaac S. Land
Feb. 1, 1834
Aug. 13, 1911
Gone to rest.

Elizabeth J.
Wife of
Isaac S. Land Sr.
March 12, 1837
June 23, 1886
Gone to rest.

Elizabeth Land
July 8, 1873
July 10, 1911

Maggie
Daughter of
I. S. & E. J. Land
Mar. 28, 1865
Oct. 22, 1878

William
Son of
I. S. & E. J. Land
July 8, 1873
Dec. 16, 1873

Dora
Daughter of
I. S. & E. J. Land
Nov. 29, 1878
Dec. 31, 1895

HUES

Rachiel Hues
Feb. 9, 1844
Oct. 18, 1908
At Rest.

MCBRAYER

Father
Wm. Ervin McBrayer
Feb. 24, 1840
May 22, 1914
An honest man is
the noblest work of God.

James F.
Son of
E. D. & F. P. McBrayer
Mar. 11, 1896
Mar. 12, 1896
Budded on earth to
bloom in Heaven.

Jennie E. McBrayer
Daughter of
E. D. & F. P. McBrayer
Dec. 29, 1898
Nov. 4, 1908
Budded on earth to
bloom in Heaven.

GARREN

H. G. Garren
Mar. 15, 1893
Feb. 23, 1923
Gone but not forgotten.

SHADY GROVE BAPTIST CHURCH CEMETERY

Fredie Garren
Nov. 25, 1900
Oct. 2, 1902
Our Darling.

Elizabeth
Wife of
J. A. Garren
May 31, 1857
Nov. 30, 1904
In God we trust.

Mrs. Lee Garren
Died Dec. 10, 19--
Aged 44 years.

Murtle Garren
Apr. 6, 1908
June 14, 1908
Our darling

Lizzie Garren
July 7, 1909
Oct. 30, 1912
Our darling.

KIRKLAND

J. A. Kirkland
Co. H.
3rd Tenn. Mtd. Inf.

Kirkland
Nellie Kirkland
May 2, 1885
March 31, 1918
She is safe at Home.

HUNT

Oren L.
Son of
C. & C. Hunt
Mar. 20, 1916
Mar. 21, 1916
Gone to be with Jesus.

N. C. King
Wife of
W. A. Hunt
Oct. 14, 1850
June 7, 1873

WILLIAMSON

Maggie Tate
Wife of
R. F. Williamson
July 10, 1887
Apr. 28, 1921
At Rest.

W. H. Williamson
Mar. 21, 1905
Feb. 4, 1907
Our darling

Infant
of
Mr. & Mrs. W. W. Williamson
Mar. 18, 1917
Mar. 20, 1917
Our darling

RUTHERFORD

Mother
Malinda J. Rutherford
Mar. 7, 1856
June 28, 1918
At Rest.

King
Son of
J. F. & M. J. Rutherford
April 5, 1883
Aug. 3, 1887
At Rest.

Father
John F. Rutherford
Oct. 30, 1837
Aug. 12, 1912
At Rest.

O'NEAL

Alice May
Daughter of
A. M. & E. V. O'Neal
Feb. 20, 1885
Oct. 27, 1890
Our darling.

SHADY GROVE BAPTIST CHURCH CEMETERY

Kate
Daughter of
A. M. & E. V. O'Neal
May 20, 1880
Aug. 28, 1890

NEWKIRK

Joseph H. Newkirk
Apr. 28, 1904
May 4, 1927

LEWIS

Lewis
Fannie Lewis
Wife of
N. B. Lewis
Sept. 29, 1866
Sept. 23, 1915
Our dear departed one
Gone to the land of
love. We shall meet
her again some
bright day.

NORWOOD

Kittie Norwood
Apr. 11, 1897
Nov. 4, 1897

SHADDEN

Father
(Jr. O.U.A.M. Member)
J. A. Shadden
Oct. 8, 1860

In Christ he lives.

Mother
Spicie Shadden
Sept. 4, 1877
Feb. 9, 1926
Gone but not forgotten.

Mary
Wife of
J. A. Shadden
Dec. 30, 1861
Nov. 21, 1902
Gone but not forgotten.

Infant
of
J. A. & Mary Shadden
Feb. 26, 1901, May 2, 1901

Little Maggie
Child of
J. A. & Mary Shadden
Nov. 10, 1892
Sept. 1, 1902

J. O. Shadden
Oct. 1, 1879
Oct. 27, 1906
At Rest.

Dora Shadden
Mar. 6, 1858
May 6, 1913

G. C. Shadden
Apr. 2, 1856
Jan. 5, 1928
At Rest.

Shadden
William H. Shadden
July 23, 1858
Oct. 24, 1929

Shadden
Nina Deloris Shadden
June 7, 1897
Oct. 6, 1902
At Rest.

Amos P.
Son of
A. D. & Lyda Shadden
Dec. 29, 1912
Jan. 17, 1923
Not our will but
thine be done.

SHADY GROVE BAPTIST CHURCH CEMETERY

MORGAN

Morgan
Father
James R. Morgan
Mar. 3, 1872
Dec. 10, 1934

Mother
Mary J. Morgan
Apr. 4, 1876
(not buried)
Gone but not forgotten.

LESLIE

In memory of
Sue L.
Wife of
Thomas Leslie
Mar. 17, 1855
Jan. 31, 1875

Susan L. Leslie
Mar. 17, 1855
Jan. 31, 1875
She was too good and too
gentle to dwell in this
cold world of care.

Thomas Leslie
Apr. 22, 1845
Aug. 20, 1902
Living, he made the
poor mans heart be
glad and at his death
the sorrowing ones
more sad.

STILWELL OR STILLWELL

J. M. Stillwell
July 1, 1805
June 28, 1882

Rebeca S.
Wife of
J. M. Stilwell
Mar. 31, 1808
Feb. 25, 1891

BAKER

Thomas Baker
Feb.   1823
Sept. 5, 1890
At Rest.

HIGHTOWER

T. H. Hightower
Nov. 29, 1825
June 29, 1891
Husband of
Margaret Hightower

Margaret H.
Wife of
Thos Hightower
Mar. 5, 1830
Jan. 14, 1895
Blessed are the
pure in spirit.

DUCKETT

Father
J. J. Duckett
Born 1875
Died March 12, 1918
Rest in peace.

Elizabeth Duckett
Feb. 2, 1824
Oct.   1888
Age 64 years.

GHORMLEY

James Ghormley
Dec. 7, 1798
Jan. 25, 1867

Elizabeth Ghormley
Dec. 16, 1804
Sept. 19, 1871

Amanda E. Ghormley
Apr. 4, 1835
Aug. 27, 1862

SHADY GROVE BAPTIST CHURCH CEMETERY

Lorenzo Ghormley
Apr. 25, 1812
Jan. 6, 1862
Erected by will of
Mrs. A. Ghormley
1917

Mary Ann
Daughter of
Jas. & Elizabeth Williams
Wife of
W. H. Ghormley
Son of
Jas. & Elizabeth Ghormley
June 25, 1842
Feb. 10, 1876

MILLER

Genevra V.
Daughter of
L. L. & S. A. Miller
Apr. 27, 1884
May 4, 1884

E. S. Miller

HOLDER

Lee Orie Holder
Sept. 11, 1916
Nov. 24, 1916
In after time we
will meet her.

MILSAPS OR MILLSAPS

Thelma Milsaps
Oct. 27, 1914
May 9, 1917
Just when we
learned to love her
most, God called
her back to Heaven.

Lillie Ann Millsaps
Jan. 24, 1893
Oct. 17, 1896
Just when we learned
to love her most,
God called her back to Heaven.

NILES

Phillys H.
Daughter of
W. H. & E. L. Niles
June 7, 1923
May 25, 1925
God gave, He took,
He will restore.

John D.
Son of
W. H. & E. L. Niles
Aug. 8, 1921
Oct. 10, 1922
In Heaven there's
one Angel more.

GARLAND

Idia Norwood
Wife of
R. L. Garland
Nov. 10, 1891
May 4, 1914

WATSON

Baby Erastus
Son of
J. A. & Laura Watson
Sept. 24, 1900
Dec. 8, 1905

Henry Watson
1896 - 1898
Our baby.

S. F. Watson
May 17, 1889
Sept. 10, 1894
Beyond the shadows of tears.

SHULTZ

R. Shultz
Died Sept. 13, 1935
Aged 48 years

BROWN

James Brown

Henry Brown

TOMBSTONE INSCRIPTIONS

SINK PRESBYTERIAN CHURCH CEMETERY

Copied by: Lawrence McConkey, Englewood, Tennessee.
Date:

Sink Presbyterian Church and Cemetery are 4 miles Northeast of
Tellico Plains. They may be reached by taking the road to
Big Creek for 3 miles then turning left. The road is known
as Sink road. Tellico Plains is 14 miles South of Madisonville.

The Cumberland Presbyterian Denomination established a church
at this location, probably about 1830 and named it Sink. About
1910 it was changed from a Cumberland Presbyterian to a
Presbyterian Church. The land for both the cemetery and the
church was given by a Mr. Smith but the deed was lost and in
1930 the church paid Sam Patterson $300.00 for the church and
cemetery land which comprises approximately 5 acres. The
cemetery occupies about 4 3/4 acres. The oldest inscription
is that of Harvey M. Weldin who died Nov. 24, 1838. It is
probable that the first burial was still earlier.

There is a marker at the grave of Jacob Franklin Peck placed
by Alexander Doran Chapter U. S. D. 1812, Cleveland Tennessee,
indicating that Peck was a soldier of the War of 1812.

Maj. Robert T. Ghormley, buried here, was a Civil War Soldier
on the authority of Guss Hunt, who also says that William S.
Wear, interred in Sink Cemetery, was a World War Soldier.

Dr. H. G. Carter, at the death of his second wife, Lena Sloan
Carter, deeded or willed to the church 30 acres of land adjacent
to Hensley Springs at Ball Play. Members of the Henderson,
Carter, McSpadden, Ghormley, Peck, and other families buried
here, were prominent in this section.

The cemetery is still used. The lower side has some unmarked
Negro graves.

In the Sink Presbyterian Church Cemetery there are 60 field stone
markers; 2 markers unreadable; 77 inscriptions and approximately
200 unmarked graves. There is no way even to estimate the
unmarked graves as most of the ground is smooth and people
disagree as to the number of burials here. Some say the old
part of the cemetery is full of graves and if so there are 500
or more unmarked graves, some say old part does not contain
many graves.

SINK PRESBYTERIAN CHURCH CEMETERY

GAY

William Walker
Son of
Wm. R. & E. J. Gay
Sept. 29, 1866
Jan. 25, 1892

William R. Gay
Feb. 22, 1829
Nov. 6, 1883

(Note! The graves of William
Walker & William R. Gay are
2 rows apart. Beside each
of them are unmarked graves,
probably family burials.
LMcC.)

HENDERSON

Thomas A. Henderson
Sept. 28, 1818
July 31, 1871

Rachel Allison
Wife of
Thomas Anderson Henderson
Mar. 3, 1822
Sept. 15, 1891
Age 69 yrs. 6 mos. & 12 days.
Here I lay my burden
down change the cross
into the crown.

(Note! There are 3 graves at
North of Thomas Anderson
Henderson and 1 grave at
South of Rachel Allison
Henderson. From their
location it is probable that
they are graves of the
same family. LMcC.)

(Note! The following are
at another location in the
cemetery but are same
family. LMcC.)

Darcus
Wife of
John Henderson
Born Feb. 10, 1772
Died Sept. 14, 1869
Blessed are the dead
which die in the Lord.

John Henderson
Sept. 26, 1790
Aug. 23, 1871
Blessed are the dead which
die in the Lord.

Benjamin P. Henderson
Jan. 21, 1821
Apr. 27, 1893
Oppressed by grief
yet cherished by faith
and hope.

PECK

Nervey Alice Peck
Daughter of
Joseph A. & Minerva A. Peck
July 24, 1866
July 29, 1867

James M. Peck
Infant Son of
Joseph & Minervia Peck
April 18, 1859
April 18, 1859

Sacred to the memory of
Minervia A. Peck
Wife of
Joseph A. Peck
March 24, 1832
Novr. 18, 1866

1 grave at South of above.

Mrs. Jane Peck
Feb. 11, 1795
Feb. 16, 1870

(above marker broken)

SINK PRESBYTERIAN CHURCH CEMETERY

Jacob F. Peck
Born Jan. 31, 1793
Died Aug. 22, 1871

A slab over this grave
bears the inscription:
Jacob Franklin Peck
Bolted on above slab is
another marker made of
marble and inscribed
as follows:
Descendant of
Benj. Franklin
U. S. D.
1812
Placed by
Alexander Doran
Chapter U. S. D. 1812
Cleveland, Tennessee.

ROMAN

Children of
F. A. & S. A. Roman
Edgar H.
Oct. 12, 1886
July 11, 1887

Bertha E.
Oct. 12, 1886
July 14, 1887

L. L.
T. H.
and
Z. R.
Born & Died
Dec. 15, 1885

(Note: The first two Roman
children were twins.
The last three were
tripletts. IMcC.)

Elisha Roman
Aug. 26, 1894
Aug. 27, 1894
Cold in the grave the
perished heart may be
but that which warmed it
once can never die.

Noble Peace Roman
July 20, 1880
Apr. 2, 1885
Cold in the grave the
perished heart may be but
that which warmed it
once can never die.

CURD

Susan Peck
Wife of
Richard Curd
Dec. 13, 1819
Feb. 7, 1900
Blessed are the dead
who die in the Lord.

EDINGTON

Asenith J. Edington
Daughter of
P. C. & E. E. Edington
Feb. 17, 1849
Oct. 29, 1855

1 grave to North of above
3 graves to South of above.

GHORMLEY

Come ye blessed
Robert T. Ghormley
Aug. 5, 1858
Dec. 17, 1926
He died as he lived
a Christian.

At Rest
Lillie L Ghormley
July 21, 1865
Mar. 14, 1921
Sweetly sleeping

At Rest.
Robert T. Ghormley III
Aug. 14, 1907
Oct. 14, 1934

SINK PRESBYTERIAN CHURCH CEMETERY

James L. Ghormley
Mar. 3, 1833
May 26, 1911
May the resurrection
find thee on the bosom
of thy God.

Elizabeth
Wife of
J. L. Ghormley
Born Feb. 3, 1829
(date of death not given)
Gone to a brighter home
where grief cannot come.

J. H. Ghormley
June 12, 1854
June 10, 1938

Maj. R. T. Ghormley
Oct. 27, 1827
June 27, 1900

Nancy K.
his wife
Nov. 1, 1828
May 13, 1899
How firm a foundation.

HAWKINS

Mrs. Bettie Hawkins
Died Nov. 27, 1930
Aged 67 years.

Thomas Porter
Son of
J. M. & Bettie Hawkins
Nov. 12, 1894
July 25, 1907
Age 12 yrs. 8 mos & 13 days.
He was a kind loving son
and an affectionate brother.

J. M. Hawkins
Nov. 14, 1859
Apr. 2, 1917
It was hard to give thee
up but thy will of God
be done.

LANKFORD

Infant
of
D. H. & M. L. Lankford
Dec. 15, 1907
Dec. 16, 1907

STEPHENS

Charles W. Stephens
Mar. 25, 1885
Aug. 6, 1903

Henry Clay Stephens
May 20, 1854
Apr. 12, 1921
His works do follow him.

Sallie L. Stephens
Wife of
H. C. Stephens
Oct. 25, 1854
Mar. 4, 1899
Age 44 yrs. 4 mos. & 9 days.
Blessed are the pure in
heart for they shall see God.

HARRISON

E. W. Harrison
Died Aug. 4, 1928
Aged 74 years.

Annie Harrison
Sept. 30, 1868
May 26, 1903

Infant Child
of
E. W. Harrison
Sept. 2, 1893
Sept. 2, 1893

Lizzie J.
Wife of
E. W. Harrison
Oct. 25, 1852
Sept. 5, 1893
Here I lay my burden down.
Change the cross into the crown.

SINK PRESBYTERIAN CHURCH CEMETERY

SATTERWHITE

Virginia Evelyn
Daughter of
W. A. & F. G. Satterwhite
Oct. 19, 1915
Apr. 4, 1919

Satterwhite
Sarah Frances Lee
Wife of
Robert Satterwhite
Dec. 16, 1849
Nov. 25, 1892

Robert Tate Satterwhite
Jan. 16, 1851
Jan. 27, 1916
At Rest.

F. M. Satterwhite
Born   1820
Died July 8, 1870

WELDIN

In memory of
Harvey M. Weldin
June 30, 1823
Nov. 24, 1838

In memory of
Ann Weldin
Jan. 7, 1790
Dec. 18, 1851

2 graves with field stones
North of above.

(Note: The grave of
Lucinda McNabb is between
Weldin graves. LMcC.)

MCNABB

In memory of
Lucinda McNabb
Dec. 25, 1816
July 12, 1840

MCSPADDEN

Mandy Satterwhite
Wife of
James McSpadden
Born   1855
Died Dec. 1878

S. K. McSpadden
Jan. 30, 1798
June 7, 1883

CANTRELL

Mary Cantrell
Aug. 29, 1855
Nov. 14, 1887

DAUGHERTY

W. A. Daugherty
Sept. 29, 1854
Jan. 22, 1886

CARTER

P. P. Carter
Sept. 15, 1841
Oct. 26, 1881

Anna
Wife of
Dr. N. G. Carter
Sept. 9, 1856
Feb. 2, 1884
In God I trust.

Dr. N. G. Carter
Dec. 31, 1833
June 20, 1902
My Lord calls me
an I am ready and
willing to go.
Gone but not forgotten.

HELEMNS

John A.
Husband of
M. A. Helemns
Aug. 14, 1830
Jan. 7, 1886
Not lost blest thought
but gone before

SINK PRESBYTERIAN CHURCH CEMETERY

MCDERMOTT

Jane E. McG. Henderson
Wife of
Wm. P. H. McDermott
Feb. 14, 1812
May 8, 1862

Wm. P. McDermott
Dec. 17, 1800
Aug. 3, 1854

6 stones South and 1
stone North of grave
of Jane E. McDermott,
1 stone at head of
her grave and 1 stone
at head of grave of
Wm. P. McDermott.

SHADDEN OR SHADDON

In memory of
William A. Shadden
Aug. 9, 1822
July 2, 1856

A. W. Shaddon
Mar. 14, 1832
April 25, 1889
Aged 57 yrs. 1 mo & 11 days.
Thou art gone but
not forgotten.

Mary Leslie
Wife of
A. W. Shaddon
Oct. 3, 1842
Nov. 26, 1902
Blessed are the pure
in heart for they shall
see God.

LESLIE OR LESLEY

(Note: The Leslie and
Shadden graves are in
the same plot. The
families are related.
LMcC.)

Leslie
James Leslie
Apr. 23, 1702
Oct. 23, 1854

1 unmarked grave

Thomas Lesley
Jan. 27, 1805
Sept. 29, 1881

Nancy
Wife of
Thomas Lesley
Aug. 2, 1804
Feb. 15, 1867

8 stones North in
same row as above.

RHEA

Margaret Rhea
Died June 10, 1851
Aged 61

Jesse Rhea
Died July 10, 1859
Aged 80

1 stone North of
Margaret Rhea's grave.

FERGUSON

Bartlett N.
Son of
W. H. & Margaret Ferguson
Jan. 7, 1888
July 2, 1888

Margaret
Wife of
W. H. Ferguson
Dec. 29, 1845
Sept. 13, 1888

WEAR

SINK PRESBYTERIAN CHURCH CEMETERY

William S. Wear
Co. D. 318 M. G. Bn.
November 30, 1888
June   16, 1922
Rest soldier rest thy
warfare is over.
Jr.O.U.A.M. Emblem
and American flag.

1 stone marker

Jesse Wear
Dec. 25, 1859
Mar. 17, 1908
He followed virtue
as his truest guide.
Lived as a christian
as a christian died.

EDICK

Samuel R. Edick
Sept. 20, 1805
Nov. 10, 1853
Beneath this stone I've
placed in trust, not the
immortal but the dust
of one on earth to me
most dear, who learned
in youth his God to fear.

OGS

----omhi Ogs
died April 21 ----
at Tellico
Age 22 years.

(Note: Stone chipped badly
and stone North unreadable.
LMcC.)

YOUNG

In memory of
Robert R. Young
June 11, 1856
Jan. 8, 1858

CARMICHAEL

------ Carmichael

(Note: The above grave has
a hewn slab over it with
much inscription but chipped
off too badly to read. LMcC.)

SMITH

Thomas M.
Son of
P. M. & M. A. Smith
Aug. 9th. 1856
Aug. 1st. 1858

1 grave to North of above.

J. H. Smith

L. E. Smith

M. J. Smith

Copied by: Lawrence McConkey, Englewood, Tennessee
Date: Nov. 1938

The Sunset Cemetery was established in 1931 by the late
B. F. White, Sr., as a public burial ground. It is now
controlled by the B. F. White, Estate. Bodies of 3 members
of the White family were removed from other cemeteries to
this one. It is a beautiful location and mostly used by
prominent families.

Among persons buried in Sunset Cemetery are Emerson O. Luther,
a former County Representative; C. A. Kennedy, a former Justice
of the Peace and County Judge; Rex Lee, a former Circuit Court
Clerk; N. M. McDaniel, prominent Attorney, also County Attorney;
James Axley, former County Trustee; Boyd Upton, son of former
Sheriff Upton; Rankin and Jennie Tallent, children of former
Sheriff Hugh Tallent; John C. Candler, son of a prominent
Georgia State Official.

The cemetery is located on the East side of Madisonville. There
are no unmarked graves.

INGRAM

Jimmie Edward Ingram
Died May 25, 1937
Aged 15 days.

SLOAN

Sloan
Hugh L. Sloan
  1874 - 1936

Louise A. Sloan
1877 - 19(Date not complete)

Sloan
Thomas F. Sloan
1866 - 19--

His wife
Oma Elizabeth Mason
1893 - 1936
At rest in him.

LEE

Rex Lee
Jan. 28, 1889
Jan. 24, 1937

Claude Franklin Lee
Died Sept. 18, 1934
Aged 11 years, & 27 days.

AXLEY

James Axley
Sept. 14, 1862
Dec. 31, 1931

MCCONKEY

Helen K. McConkey
May 1, 1918
June 3, 1934

McConkey
Carl E. McConkey
Dec. 30, 1896
Jan. 3, 1934

SUNSET CEMETERY

MCDANIEL

N. M. McDaniel
May 13, 1872
May 29, 1937

TALLENT

Rankin Tallent
July 4, 1934
Aged 23 years 8 mos. 22 days.

Miss Jennie Tallent
Oct. 6, 1909
Feb. 22, 1925

KENNEDY

Kennedy
C. A. Kennedy
1873 - 1938
(Mason)

Joe E. Kennedy
1904 - 1934

YOUNG

Young
James C. Young
1888 - 1933

His wife
Esta Forrester
1888 - (Still living)

MULLINS

Hartsell R.
Mar. 17, 1879
(Still living)

Edith Martin
Jan. 31, 1889
July 25, 1937

WILLIAMS

Andrew J. Williams
Feb. 27, 1865
Nov. 17, 1937

LAYMAN

Layman
Albert C.
Nov. 9, 1862
(Still Living)

Sarah A.
July 19, 1868
Sept. 8, 1936

BIVENS

Mary Etta Bivens
Died Nov. 11, 1935

CARROLL

Stella Carroll
Dec. 10, 1887
(Still Living)

George R. Carroll
Oct. 11, 1882
Nov. 30, 1935

Rev. M. B. Carroll
Sept. 17, 1852
Dec. 30, 1934

WINTERS

Mrs. Lillian Winters
Died May 17, 1934

LONG

Bud Long
June 4, 1884
Nov. 21, 1937

WHITE

White
B. F. White Sr.
1871 - 1935

Martha Lindsey
Wife of
B. F. White Sr.
1879 - 1935

John White
1879 - 1910

SUNSET CEMETERY

John A. White
1848 - 1920

Belle Moser
Wife of
John A. White
1850 - 1890

CANDLER

John C. Candler
Died Dec. 10, 1936

SHEETS

John Aiken Sheets
Oct. 9, 1865
Oct. 8, 1938

UPTON

Boyd Upton
July 8, 1906
Sept. 3, 1934

LUTHER

Luther
Emerson O. Luther
1878 - 1937

ANDERSON

Minnie Caroline Anderson
Dec. 26, 1933
Sept. 19, 1936

LOWRY

Marshall Reed Lowry Jr.
Sept. 18, 1935
Sept. 19, 1935

ADAMS

Maud Ilene Adams
Died Jan. 18, 1938
Aged 18 yrs. 3 mos. 22 days.

DAVIS

Andrew Davis
Aug. 23, 1887
June 1, 1934

MITCHELL

Mitchell
Aubrey Alfred Mitchell
Jan. 22, 1915
Oct. 27, 1937

HENRY

Mrs. Calvin Henry
1936

Infant
of
Ira Henry
1934

Infant
of
Ira Henry

CAGLE

Mrs. Amanda Rogers Cagle
Aug. 27, 1879
June 27, 1933

CHAMBERS

Infant
of
Ralph & S. Chambers

MONROE COUNTY

TALLASSIE QUAKER CHURCH CEMETERY

Copied by Lawrence McConkey, Englewood, Tennessee
Date:

The Tallassie Quaker Church Cemetery is located 2 miles
from Calderwood on a farm owned by Mrs. Sam Millsaps. The
cemetery comprises approxminately 1 acre and is fenced.
The earliest inscription of a death is that of A. E. Lackey,
July 19, 1886.

The Quaker or Friends Denomination over fifty years ago
established a church at the Tallassie location as well as
several others in the mountain section of Monroe County.
The land for the church and cemetery was secured from the
Millsaps family, but it was to fall back to the owner of
the farm if not used. The church has been discontinued
for about 20 years but the cemetery is still in use.

It is presumed that Mrs. Millsaps owns the cemetery and
church building as well as the farm. Calderwood, the
nearest town, is 2 miles over the mountain and Little
Tennessee river in Blount County or the cemetery is 9
miles South of Citico, up Citico Creek. Citico is approximately 27 miles East of Madisonville up the Little Tennessee
River.

Tallassie Quaker Church Cemetery contains 45 inscriptions
and 27 field stones. There are no broken tombstones and no
ummarked graves.

MONROE COUNTY

TOMBSTONE INSCRIPTIONS
TALLASSIE QUAKER OR FRIENDS CHURCH CEMETERY

CLINE

J. E.
Son of
Willie & Carrie Cline
Jan. 1, 1913
Jan. 3, 1913

(Note: 7 stones at side
may be of same family.)

Lee Cline
Oct. 23, 1893
Oct. 28, 1918
"Not lost blest thought
but gone before."

Viola
daughter of
A. B. Cline
Apr. 1, 1901
July 11, 1901

Vira
Wife of
A. D. Cline
Died June 17, 1901
Aged 35 years
"In love she lived
In peace she died,
Her life was craved
but God denied."

(Note: 1 stone at side
of above.)

BOWERS

Nelson Bowers

Eliza Bowers

(Note: They were 80 years
approx. old.)

NELSON

Mother
Sarah E. Nelson
Feb. 18, 1831
Jan. 2, 1931
"Beyond the Sunset."

Father
James L. Nelson
Apr. 15, 1833
Apr. 17, 1911
"Earth has no sorrow
that Heaven cannot heal."

SMITH

George Jr.
Son of
George R. & C. D. Smith
May 4, 1914
Oct. 22, 1918
"Gone but not forgotten."

(Note: 4 stones at left.)

Irene
daughter of
Judson & Mary Smith
Jan. 10, 1900
Sept. 10, 1900

Herman
Son of
Judson & Mary Smith
Jan. 24, 1896
Nov. 26, 1896

Mary Smith
May 28, 1875
Aug. 6, 1906
"Tho' lost to sight to memory dear."

FARR

Lucinda
Wife of
J. A. Farr
July 15, 1853
July 8, 1902
"As a wife, devoted; as a
Mother, affectionate; as a
friend, ever kind and true."

James Farr

(Note: at left side of wife.)

TALLASSIE QUAKER OR FRIENDS CHURCH CEMETERY

FARR

Louis
Son of
J. A. & Lucinda Farr
April 13, 1878
Aug. 8, 1902
"Another link is broken in
our household band but a
chain is forming in a
better land."

Myra E.
Daughter of
J. A. & Lucinda Farr
June 24, 1879
July 12, 1893
"May the Resurrection
find thee on the Bosom
of thy God."

Robert
Son of
J. A. & Lucinda Farr
Mar. 16, 1885
Nov. 11, 1890
"At Rest."

(Note: 2 stones but may
not be same family as above.)

STRATTON

Arminda
Dau. of
R. R. & Susan Stratton
Feb. 12, 1891
Nov. 15, 1892
"At Rest."

Manda
Daughter of
R. R. & Susan Stratton
Feb. 23, 1879
June 9, 1903
"In love she lived, In peace
she died, Her life was craved
but God denied."

Kair
Son of
R. R. & Susan Stratton
Oct. 30, 1872
Feb. 14, 1906
"He followed virtue as his
truest guide. Lived as a
Christian as a Christian died."

Susan
Wife of
Richard R. Stratton
Mar. 5, 1847
June 8, 1911
"May the resurrection find thee
on the bosom of thy God."

Richard R. Stratton
Apr. 9, 1842
Oct. 15, 1915
"A friend to his country and
a believer in Christ."

Roscoe
Son of
A. J. & M. C. Stratton
Sept. 28, 1901
July 3, 1903
"Christ loved him and took him
home."

DALE

Virgil A.
Son of
W. M. & M. E. Dale
Aug. 8, 1889
Oct. 3, 1907
"We will meet again."

M. E. Dale
Wife of
W. M. Dale
May 17, 1863
Dec. 20, 1901
"At Rest."

W. M. Dale

TALLASSIE QUAKER OR FRIENDS CHURCH CEMETERY

LAKEY

Ora Lakey
Wife of
N. W. Lakey
Mar. 8, 1852
Jan. 4, 1887

A. E. Lakey
June 27, 1886
July 19, 1886

Rachel A. Lakey
Nov. 13, 1822
Dec. 23, 1909
"Blessed are the dead
which die in the Lord."

TURNER

Lizzie
Wife of
T. F. Turner
Oct. 24, 1870
Nov. 3, 1904
"The Golden Gates were
opened wide a gentle
voice said come."

MILLSAPS

Elcie Millsaps
Sept. 22, 1902
Oct. 3, 1902
"Asleep in Jesus O
how sweet."

Cathern
wife of
Rance Millsaps
June 10, 1834
Sept. 25, 1919
"We trust our loss will
be her gain and that with
Christ shes gone to reign."

Samantha
Wife of
Wm. Millsaps

WILLIAMS

Eugene
Son of
L. H. & Finia Williams
Jan. 11, 1911
July 3, 1911
"At Rest."

Oma
Daughter of
L. H. & Finia Williams
May 11, 1902
July 19, 1903
"At Rest."

Birtha Williams
Ma 7, 1892

(Note: Above was an Inf or
a child.)

Edward Williams

Finia
Wife of
L. H. Williams
Apr. 15, 1879
Mar. 2, 1920
"She was a kind and
affectionate wife, a
fond mother and a friend to all."

Malowiney Williams
Dau of
J. A. & C. Millsaps
Dec. 17, 1861
Feb. 25, 1893
"She believed and sleeps in
Jesus."

(Note: 1 stone by above.)

COPPOCK

A Baby

"At Rest."
E. Coppock

J. H. Coppock

4

TALLASSIE QUAKER OR FRIENDS CHURCH CEMETERY

JOHNSON   ANDERSON

R. J. Johnson   Mollie Anderson

Mrs. R. J. Johnson

TOMBSTONE INSCRIPTIONS

TELLICO BAPTIST CHURCH CEMETERY

Copied by: Lawrence McConkey, Englewood, Tennessee.
Date:

The oldest date of a death noted in Tellico Baptist Church
Cemetery is that of Sarah A. Sloan who died Dec. 4, 1863. The
cemetery was possibly started sooner as the church was there
several years prior to this date. The land was given by
Zachariah Givens. The Tellico Baptist Church Cemetery is
located on the Ball Play road, 9 miles East of Madisonville.
There are 236 inscriptions and approximately 180 unmarked graves.

SLOAN

Father
James Riley Sloan
June 28, 1831
Oct. 8, 1904

Mother
Mary Caroline Sloan
June 7, 1838
July 11, 1916

Sloan
John A. Sloan
1840 – 1927

Sarah L. Sloan
1851 – 1926
Awaiting the Resurrection.

In my fathers house
are many mansions
Robert Carroll
Son of
J. A. & S. L. Sloan
Oct. 27, 1880
Feb. 7, 1904

Boyce
Son of
Mr. & Mrs. E. L. Sloan
Aug. 26, 1926
Oct. 29, 1926
Our darling is gone
but not forgotten.

Zelma
Daughter of
Mr. & Mrs. E. L. Sloan
Feb. 4, 1913
Jan. 23, 1925
A little while on earth
to give us joy but now in
Heaven where joy is supreme.

Lucile
Daughter of
Mr. & Mrs. E. L. Sloan
Our darling gone but
is not forgotten.

In memory of
Carl
Son of
Mr. & Mrs. E. L. Sloan
Nov. 1, 1911
Dec. 16, 1917

Infant
of
O. B. & Mattie Sloan
Sept. 4, 1914

Callie
Wife of
Floyd Sloan
Oct. -- 1873
Nov. 2, 1899

Sloan
John R.
Oct. 11, 1856
Mar. 3, 1937

TELLICO BAPTIST CHURCH CEMETERY

Martha L.
Jan. 8, 1884
(Still Living)
Awaiting the Resurrection.

Ruth Ellen Sloan
Aug. 4, 1913
Dec. 15, 1914
Our darling is
at rest.

Our darling
At Rest
Gillis Sloan
July 2, 1917
July 3, 1917

Sloan
William H. Sloan
1839 - 1917
E. Saphrona Sloan
1846 - 1922

Father
M. J. C. Sloan
June 27, 1830
Sept. 8, 1914

Mother
Josie P. Sloan
Oct. 30, 1837
Mar. 14, 1915

Arrie Sloan
July 3, 1888
July 2, 1889

Nettie Sloan
Sept. 30, 1890
Apr. 29, 1898

S. Sloan
Born Feb. 4, 18--

Oston
Son of
Mr. & Mrs. Frank Sloan
Oct. 3, 1922
Mar. 11, 1924
Darling we miss thee.

George W.
Son of
Mr. & Mrs. C. W. Sloan
Apr. 24, 1908
Mar. 14, 1929
Gone but not forgotten.

Infant
of
----- Sloan

Edna Mae
Daughter of
K. A. & Bertha Sloan
Apr. 30, 1910
Oct. 15, 1913
Our darling, we miss thee.

Ray
Son of
Fred & Nellie Sloan
Feb. 27, 1927
Apr. 26, 1936

Sloan
W. R. Sloan
Feb. 2nd. 1858
Nov. 30th. 1922

His wife
Emma Ghormley
Sept. 21st 1865
Feb. 4th 1897
At peace with God.

Isaac Sloan
Died 1910
Aged about 55 years.

Bruscilla Cagle
Wife of
Isaac Sloan
Died 1910
Aged ----

William Sloan

Robert Sloan

TELLICO BAPTIST CHURCH CEMETERY

Boyce
Son of
W. R. & Emma Sloan
April 30, 1893
Dec. 28, 1896
Gone to rest.

Amanda A. Rains
Wife of
T. B. Sloan
Jan. 30, 1865
July 2, 1885

Archibald Sloan
Born Apr. 15, 1796
Died Apr. 13, 1868

Susanah Sloan
Born Apr. 2, 1800
Died Mar. 28, 1887
In memory of our
Father and mother
'Tis hard to break
the tender cord but
thy memory will be
cherished Till we see
thy heavenly faces.

Robert Sloan
Born May 10, 1800
Died Nov. 13, 1870

Elizabeth
Wife of
Robert Sloan
Born Oct. 2, 1810
Died July 5, 1901

James S. Sloan
Apr. 3, 1879
May 6, 1890

Apch. M. Sloan
Mar. 1, 1860
Apr. 26, 1879

(Note: The above name
may be Arch.   LMcC.)

Catherine S. Sloan
Aug. 10, 1835
Jan. 1, 1875

Mason Sloan
July 16, 1868
July 25, 1868

Sarah A. Sloan
Feb. 12, 1858
Dec. 4, 1863

Elizabeth Sloan

George Sloan

M. M. Burris
Wife of
R. B. Sloan
Oct. 9, 1852
Apr. 20, 1919

R. B. Sloan
Jan. 31, 1849
Apr. 28, 1913
Gone to rest.

In memory of
Our mother
Marry C. Sloan
Feb. 10, 1845
June 13, 1889
This is the love we
have for mother

Neoma
Daughter of
Mr. & Mrs. T. C. Sloan
Jan. 21, 1914
Oct. 25, 1918

T. C. Sloan
Died Feb. -- 1934
Aged 52 yrs. 8 mos. 14 days.

Sloan
G. W. Sloan
Aug. 14, 1835
Mar. 22, 1909
I did this for the love of
my husband that I might mark
his last resting place.

Mrs. G. W. Sloan

Carroll Sloan

Sloan
Erskine Lowry Sloan
May 9, 1906
Apr. 24, 1924
Gone but not forgotten.

RAINS

Mack Rains
Aug. 16, 1874
Dec. 22, 1920
Gone but not forgotten.

Vergil Rains
June 12, 1912
Mar. 26, 1915
Gone to rest.

Mary L. Rains
Sept. 23, 1909
May 27, 1914
At Rest.

James A. Rains
Jan. 31, 1914
Sept. 24, 1914
At Rest.

D. A. Rains
Jan. 1, 1848
Mar. 19, 1922

(Note: Double marker-

J. E. Rains
Sept. 17, 1846
Apr. 11, 1914
Gone to rest.

Infant
of
J. M. & L. Rains
May 16, 1905
Age 1 day

Lina Rains
Died May 19, 1908
Age 28 yrs.

BEST

Will Best
Died Jan. 8, 1935
Age (not given)

A Twin
Gearldine Best
May 19, 1931
Oct. 14, 1931

James Ernest
Son of
W. L. & S. F. Best
Feb. 14, 1903
Jan. 1, 1916
Gone to a bright home
where grief can
not come.

Carrie Jane
Daughter of
W. L. & S. F. Best
Mar. 5, 1892
Aug. 27, 1895
From mothers arms
to the arms of Jesus.

Infant
of
W. L. & S. F. Best
Feb. 4, 1889
Feb. 7, 1889
From mothers arms
to the arms of Jesus.

Sarah Best

Rev. John Best
June 23, 1827
Nov. 18, 1894

Martha J. Best
Dec. 30, 1832
Mar. 31, 1908
In memory of
Father & Mother

Sitia Best

Henry Best

TELLICO BAPTIST CHURCH CEMETERY

Kathrine Best
Mar. 18, 1821
Aug. 24, 1895
Sweet be thy slumber

John C. Best
Born June 27, 1817
Died (no date given)

(Note: Believed to be husband
of Kathrine and to have died
after 1895. Tombstones are
identical. LMcC.)

Bettie Best
Mar. 1, 1844
May 10, 1919

Clara Best
Feb. 12, 1888
May 27, 1890

Sina Best
June 10, 1889
May 29, 1890

Elizabeth Best

William Best

HENRY

Flora Henry
Nov. 4, 1896
Jan. 17, 1897

Sarrah A. Henry
Apr. 3, 1837
Dec. 18, 1910
Married Apr. 3, 1853
Joined church 1887

Infant
Sister
1906

Sister
1904

Eula Raymond Henry
1904

L. T. Henry
1864 - (Living)

Nancy Corlion
1872 - 1937
At Rest.

Hugh L. Henry
Dec. 18, 1886
Feb. 7, 1930
At Rest.

Sarah Ann Henry
Died Mar. 20, 1931
Age 70 yrs. 4 mos. 18 days.

Wm. T. Henry
Died Aug. 2, 1937
Aged 83 yrs. 4 mos. 1 day.

RODGERS

Nellie Ann Rodgers
Died Sept. 23, 19--
Aged 40 yrs. 13 days.

GIVENS

Hence Givens
Feb. 3, 1865
May 3, 1920

Zachariah Givens

James Givens

BOATMAN

Thurman
Son of
J. S. & Ellen Boatman
Mar. 21, 1908
Mar. 29, 1909

STAPP

Amanda
Wife of
Wm. Stapp
Oct. 22, 1826
July 31, 1911

TELLICO BAPTIST CHURCH CEMETERY

Wm. Stapp
Oct. 16, 1826
Dec. 14, 1900

MCSPADDEN

Henry M. McSpadden
Jan. 2, 1842
May 28, 1885
(Masonic member)

Sarah Maude
Daughter of
W. H. & Nellie McSpadden
Nov. 9, 1912
Feb. 11, 1924
At Rest.

Mary A. McSpadden
1877 - 1951

Ollie McSpadden
Dec. 2, 1873
Dec. 21, 1918

Peace Perfect Peace
Martha McSpadden
Dec. 12, 1805
Feb. 8, 1899
Asleep in Jesus.

Infant
Daughter of
Henry M. & M. A. McSpadden
Born Aug. 24, 1885
Died Aug. 25, 1885
Gone to fairer land.

Infant
Son of
Henry M. & M. A. McSpadden
Born Mar. 23, 1884
Died (unreadable)

Martha J.
Daughter of
Henry M. & M. A. McSpadden
Oct. 29, 1871
Sept. 20, 1874
Gone to a fairer land.

Henry M. McSpadden
Jan. 2, 1842
May 28, 1885

Margaret A. McSpadden
Aug. 12, 1847
Aug. 16, 1912
Awaiting the Resurrection.

Viola
Daughter of
Hobart & Nellie McSpadden
Feb. 4, 1916
Nov. 19, 1918
Asleep in Jesus.

Mother
Sarah McSpadden
Oct. 15, 1859
Nov. 15, 1918

Father
T. T. McSpadden
Dec. 30, 1860

Gone but not forgotten.

Fletcher McSpadden
Dec. 7, 1892
Dec. 7, 1895
Our darling we
loved so much

Melven McSpadden
Aug. 5, 1891
May 18, 1893
Our Darling we
loved so much.

Arnold McSpadden
May 10, 1827
Dec. 11, 1900

Margaret L. McSpadden
July 23, 1837
(Death date not given)
Awaiting the Resurrection.

TELLICO BAPTIST CHURCH CEMETERY

Sallie L.
Daughter of
Arnold & Margaret L. McSpadden
Jan. 9, 1857
Mar. 2, 1876
Asleep in Jesus
blessed sleep.

HURST

John Hurst

Nancy Hurst

Charles Hurst

TALLENT

Opha Marie
Daughter of
Mr. & Mrs. E. C. Tallent
Dec. 2, 1914
Mar. 30, 1916
Gone but not forgotten.

Mother
Jane Tallent
Aug. 29, 1853
Oct. 15, 1880

Father
M. D. L. Tallent
March 13, 1849
May 10, 1880

Infant
Daughter of
Jane & M. D. L. Tallent
Oct. 6, 1880

Sam H. Tallent
Died March 21, 1934
Aged 83 yrs. 1 mo. 25 days.

Margaret Humphrey
Wife of
S. H. Tallent
Born July 18, 1852
married Aug. 19, 1874
Died Apr. 10, 1898
Gone but not forgotten.

Katie Tallent
April 1, 1898
April 2, 1898
Gone but not forgotten.

GAMBLE

J. H. Gamble
Co. I.
37 U.S.V. Inf.
Aug. 1, 1823
Dec. 5, 1905

Sarrah Gamble
Feb. 10, 1833
Feb. 3, 1912
Gone home to live
with Jesus to doe no more.

Henry Gamble

Joseph Gamble

Elizabeth Gamble

MASON

J. C. Mason
Died Feb. 28, 19--
Age 65 years

Rena Best
Wife of
J. C. Mason
June 7, 1868
Feb. 7, 1912
I have fought a good
fight I have kept the faith.

Frank M. Mason
Jan. 11, 1840
Feb. 28, 1912

Sarah E. Mason
Aug. 25, 1843
(Date of death not given)

Rastus Mason
Nov. 11, 1888
Jan. 3, 1913
Gone but not forgotten.

TELLICO BAPTIST CHURCH CEMETERY

Luther Ragon Mason
Died April 18, 1928
Age 38 yrs. 1 mo. 25 days.

Our Mother
Nancy Mason
Died Dec. 22, 1878
Aged about 70 years.

William Mason
Nov. 25, 1801
Aug. 14, 1884
Age 82 yrs. 8 mos. 19 days.

Nancy Jane Mason
Sept. 5, 1855
Aug. 16, 1912

Henry Mason

FREEMAN

Roe Freeman
Oct. 3, 1902
Apr. 3, 1909
Our Darling

WHITE

I. W. White
Nov. 14, 1908
July 15, 1914

Mrs. Maggie White
Died May 28, 1933
Aged 66 yrs. 4 mos. 24 days.

I. S. White
Died Nov. 26, 1932
Aged 74 yrs. 26 days.

Frankey Mason
Wife of
I. S. White
Oct. 2, 1849
Feb. 1, 1906
Our beloved mother.

Worth White

John White

HARRIS

Come ye blessed
John Akin Harris
May 18, 1880
Oct. 19, 1918
Gone but not forgotten

Manda Dye
Wife of
J. A. Harris
Feb. 15, 1878
May 24, 1913

Beuna Harris
July 3, 1887
Sept. 26, 1887
Our darling baby.

John F. Harris
Nov. 11, 1849
Sept. 8, 1921
Gone but not forgotten.

In memory of
Mary Jane
Wife of
J. F. Harris
Sept. 3, 1846
Aug. 29, 1906
At Rest.

HELMS OR HELMES

Henry Helms

Annie Harris
Wife of
Henry Helms
Aug. 18, 1862
Nov. 16, 1913

Lithie
Daughter of
Henry & Annie Helmes
June 19, 1895
Aug. 26, 1896
Gone but not forgotten.

TELLICO BAPTIST CHURCH CEMETERY

Luther
Son of
Henry & Annie Helmes
July 2, ----
May 12, ----
At Rest.

(Note! This child is buried
between Walter and Lithie
and seems to have died after
Lithie died but before Walter
died. LMcC.)

Walter
Son of
Henry & Annie Helmes
Sept. 3, 1902
Aug. 27, 1910
At Rest.

STRATTON

Nelson Stratton
Died 1930
Aged about 65 yrs.

Nancy
Wife of
Nelse Stratton
Died 1925
Aged about 58 yrs.

Steve Stratton

John R.
Infant of
Mr. & Mrs. L. O. Stratton
Oct. 3, 1927

HAMBEY

Leurise Hambey
Died Dec. 5, 1929
Age 36 yrs. 5 mos. 21 days.

DYE

Jane
Wife of
Wm. Dye
Feb. 5, 1852
Jan. 5, 1908
At Rest.

William Dye
Aug. 4, 1841
May 3, 1918
At Rest.

BIVINS

James Bivins
Jan. 8, 1865
(Still living)

His wife
Margaret Giles
Apr. 4, 1869
Feb. 18, 1933

SHEETS

Martha J. Sheets
Mar. 3, 1859
Dec. 9, 1920
At Rest.

Robert T. Sheets
Nov. 1, 1850
Dec. 16, 1888
At Rest.

Frank Sheets
Nov. 1, 1881
Jan. 1, 1899
At Rest.

Infant
Daughter of
Mr. & Mrs. T. F. Sheets
Mar. 17, 1927

HUFF

Margaret Best
Wife of
George Huff
Daughter of
John & Martha Best
Died 1935
Aged -------

George Huff

ANDERSON

Francis Paul
Son of
W. P. & M. Anderson
May   4, 1914
Sept. 17, 1914

ROSS

John C. Ross
    1873

GRIFFITH

Sina Sheets
Wife of
E. L. Griffith
Oct. 29, 1876
Mar. 21, 1914

ERVIN OR ERWIN

Mary Ervin
1856 - 1930

Dee Erwin
June 30, 1891
Mar. 27, 1922
A. E. F.

(Note: The above soldier
is buried between Mary
and Steve Ervin and is
possibly their son. LMcC.)

Steve Ervin
1857 - 1929

CARDIN

Correne Cardin
Died June 1, 1938
Aged 10 yrs. 6 mos. 9 days.

Roy Cardin

Richard Cardin

BROOKS

Emmaline Brooks
May 20, 1822
Oct. 6, 1901

Hiram Brooks
Died Dec. 2, 1901
Age 70 years.

William
Son of
J. J. & J. A. Brooks
Feb. 18, 1894
May 25, 1896

HUMPHREYS

Washington Humphreys
Dec. 31, 1847
Mar. 4, 1912
Gone but not forgotten.

WEAR

James P.
Son of
W. J. & Salena Wear
Mar. 15, 1890
Nov. 3, 1890
Gone to a better land.

William J. Wear
May 7, 1875
June 8, 1896

Salena Wear

W. J. Wear

MCMULLIN

Sarah A. McMullin
Nov. 27, 1839
Apr. 23, 1904
Gone to rest.

Jason McMullin
Feb. 22, 1813
Dec. 15, 1881
He wrought well.

MAHAN

At Rest
Manda E. Mahan
Mar. 10, 1850
July 8, 1923
Sister gone to rest.

TELLICO BAPTIST CHURCH CEMETERY

At Rest
Jariah
Wife of
R. S. Mahan
Apr. 16, 1817
Apr. 3, 1875
Mother gone to rest.

JONES

Father
Ephraim G. Jones
Apr. 2, 1847
Jan. 29, 1926

Mother
Martha C. Jones
Sept. 17, 1858
(Death date not given)
At Peace with God.

COLEMAN

J. C. Coleman
Sept. 30, 1865
June 26, 1926

Walter Coleman
Dec. 6, 1893
Nov. 24, 1897
Our Darling Baby

Mrs. J. Coleman

WEBB

Sallie Stapp
Wife of
T. N. Webb
May 4, 1862
Sept. 5, 1906

Willie
Son of
T. N. & S. Webb
Sept. 29, 1884
Aug. 3, 1885

Nelse Webb
1860 - 1924

BYRUM

1837 - 1911

GHORMLEY

Louie
Wife of
W. A. Ghormley
May 21, 1875
Sept. 21, 1897
She's gone to worlds above
where Saints and Angels
meet to realize our
Saviours love and
worship at his feet.

WRIGHT

In memory of
Josie
Beloved wife of
R. M. Wright
Daughter of
Geo. W. Sloan
Died Feb. 9, 1905
Aged 24 years
Her life was
pure and spotless.

George Anna
Infant Daughter of
R. M. & Josie Wright
Mar. 1, 1904
June 15, 1905

CROWDER

In loving remembrance of
Elisebeth Crowder
Aug. 29, 1850
Mar. 17, 1900

STEED

Sarah Jane
Wife of
John Steed
Jan. 1, 1858
Mar. 20, 1917
Not lost blest thought
but gone before.

TELLICO BAPTIST CHURCH CEMETERY

John Steed
1852 - 1927

STRICKLAND

James Robert
Son of
Mr. & Mrs. J. F. Strickland
Dec. 22, 1911
Jan. 2, 1912
Our darling.

FORRIESTER

Mother
B. A. Forriester
Dec. 14, 1846
(Death date not given.)

Father
W. M. Forriester
Feb. 2, 1846
Jan. 27, 1915
Sweet be thy slumbers.

James
Son of
W. M. & B. A. Forriester
Mar. 4, 1871
Oct. 27, 1872

HITSON

Nellie J. Ray
Wife of
B. C. Hitson
May 19, 1908
June 8, 1926
Gone but not forgotten.

TEAGUE

Infant
of
W. H. & Susan Teague
Apr. 29, 1904
Apr. 30, 1904
At Rest.

H. H. Teague
Nov. 25, 1841
Aug. 26, 1913
At Rest.

Mary Ann Teague
Dec. 14, 1840
Sept. 28, 1901
At Rest.

SAMPLES

Bertha Samples

Roy Samples

Mary Samples

John Samples

Hattie Samples

Joe Samples

Henry Samples

Sallie Samples

Betty Samples

Dixie Samples

(Unknown)

S. E. C.

E. L. C.

W. N. T.

J. O. T.

MONROE COUNTY

TELLICO PLAINS BAPTIST CHURCH CEMETERY

Copied by Lawrence McConkey, Englewood, Tennessee
Date: September 21-22, 1939

The Tellico Plains Baptist Church Cemetery is in Tellico
Plains, a community about 14 miles South of Madisonville.
The Tellico Plains Baptist Church was established in 1900
and about the same time the Tellico Iron and Slate Company,
owned by the Swainson Brothers, gave the land for a
cemetery. The property comprises approximately 3 acres.
The earliest date of death found on an inscription is that
of E. M. White, August 29, 1904.

A number of prominent persons are buried in the Tellico
Plains Baptist Cemetery. Among them are Charles A. Scott,
sawmill owner; L. W. Cathey, Superintendent of the Babcock
Lumber Compnay; Charles S. Swainson, land operator; Dr. C. S.
Jenkins, physician; John A. McConkey, druggist and merchant;
James Cable and Virgil F. Wall. Mr. Scott owned a number of
sawmills. He bought timber from thousands of acres of
mountain land and built railroads to haul the lumber out of
the mountains. He willed $25,000 for a school at Tellico
Plains. It is known as the C. A. Scott Memorial High School.

MONROE COUNTY

TOMBSTONE INSCRIPTIONS
TELLICO PLAINS BAPTIST CHURCH CEMETERY

HARRIS

Laura Harris
Wife of
J. H. Harris
July 4, 1883
June 16, 1939
"Gone but not forgotten."

HALL

Lester Faree
Son of
Chas. & Alice Hall
July 12, 1910
Nov. 5, 1910

Georgia A.
Wife of
James K. Hall
Mar. 10, 1839
Mar. 6, 1913
"Her spirit smiles from
that bright shore and
softly whispers weep
no more."

In Memoriam
Lula Mae
Infant daughter of
H. E. &. S. B. Hall
June 8, 1912
June 5, 1913
"From mothers arms to the
Arms of Jesus."

Alice Hall
Daughter of
C. L. & O. E. Lester
Oct. 29, 1892
Sept. 4, 1910

Note! She was also wife of
Chas. Hall

PEARSON

Lula M. Pearson
Age 6 yrs. & 15 days
Died Nov. 27, 1909

William L. Pearson
Age 22 mos.
Died Nov. 22, 1909

Mollie Pearson
1850--1929

W. H. Pearson
1848--1916

MCCONKEY

Father
John A. McConkey
Feb. 12, 1868
Apr. 15, 1928
"There is rest in Heaven."

Rayner J. McConkey
Oct. 14, 1901
Dec. 25, 1925
"Gone but not forgotten."

Raymond D. McConkey
Nov. 7, 1890
Nov. 29, 1914
"Gone but not forgotten."

Marion
Daughter of
Mr. & Mrs. R. McConkey
June 30, 1920

CRAWFORD

Infant
of
J. B. & M. C. Crawford
Apr. 4, 1911
May 26, 1911
"Gone but not forgotten."

Infant
of
J. B. & M. C. Crawford
July 8, 1913
July 28, 1913
"Gone but not forgotten."

TELLICO PLAINS BAPTIST CHURCH CEMETERY

CATHEY

(Masonic Emblem)
L. W. Cathey
Jan. 7, 1869
Feb. 19, 1930
"He died as he lived
a Christian."

WILLIAMS

Rev. W. H. Williams
Feb. 9, 1870
Jan. 22, 1923
"At Rest."

Oralee
Daughter of
Mr. & Mrs. J. N. Williams
July 28, 1922
June 21, 1923
"Gone but not forgotten."

BURCHFIELD or BIRCHFIELD

W. E. Burchfield
July 17, 1885
March 11, 1935

Georgie Burchfield
Feb. 17, 1892
(Not buried.)

J. B. Birchfield
Apr. 24, 1920
Jan. 24, 1936

Willa Ree
Infant of
Mr. & Mrs. Loyd Birchfield
Sept. 18, 1922
"Our loved One."

WATSON

Eva E.
Daughter of
Mr. & Mrs. Walter Watson
Sept. 29, 1919
Oct. 20, 1924
"Darling we miss thee."

Gilford C. Watson
Died Nov. 20, 1935
Aged 23 years 5 months & 4 days.

BEIGHTOE

Infant
Son of
H. E. & H. L. Beightoe
Born & Died
July 23, 1911
"Asleep in Jesus."

HICKS

Daughter
Ruby May Hicks
May 27, 1912
Dec. 18, 1930
"At Rest."

Son
Willie Lee Hicks
Feb. 21, 1908
Dec. 2, 1934
"At Rest."

ALEXANDER

Nelson Alexander
July 18, 1912
March 11, 1927
"Gone but not forgotten."

Fay Elexander
Sept. 7, 1906
Apr. 29, 1928
"Gone but not forgotten."

Delie S. Alexander
Sept. 27, 1909
May 20, 1912
"At Rest."

COPPINGER

Bettie Coppinger
Feb. 25, 1880
Aug. 6, 1917
"A tender mother and a
faithful friend."

TELLICO PLAIN BAPTIST CHURCH CEMETERY

WILSON

Sam Wilson
Sept. 1, 1867
Feb. 19, 1928
"A kind loving companion
and father."
"Gone but not forgotten."

Mrs. Sam Wilson

HUGHS or HUGHES

Bettie Hughs
May 10, 1889
June 18, 1919
"Faithful to her trust
even unto death."

Judy Hughs
July 6, 1909
July -- 1910
"Darling we miss Thee."

Edward P. Hughes
Died Jan. 3, 1932
Aged 17 years, 11 months
& 1 day.

Washington Hughes
May 6, 1891
Feb. 2, 1918
"A precious one from us
has gone. A voice we loved
is stilled. A place is
vacant in our household
that never can be filled."

Earnest Hughes
Dec. 16, 1911
Mar. 23, 1915
"Our darling we miss Thee."

BELL

Dorthy C. Bell
Aug. 18, 1922
July 13, 1924
"At rest in Heaven."

Emeline
Wife of
John Bell
July 18, 1864
July 6, 1909
"Gone but not forgotten."

John Bell

ROPER

Laura Roper
Died Aug. 24, 1938
Aged 82 years 4 mos & 5 days.

MCDANIEL

Christeena Millsaps
Wife of
Ross McDaniel
Aug. 30, 1907
Jan. 23, 1929
"Asleep in Jesus."

Peter McDaniel
June 16, 1848
Aug. 27, 1906

His Wife
Callie McDaniel
June 15, 1849
Mar. 1, 1929
"I have fought a good fight,
I have finished my course, I
have kept the faith."

MOSIER

Phoebe Mosier
Died Sept. 4, 1928
Aged --------------

HAMBY

Charles B.
Infant of
Richard & Boois Hamby
July 11, 1913
July 13, 1913

TELLICO PLAINS BAPTIST CHURCH CEMETERY

HAMBY

Cordelia Hamby
Nov. 12, 1915
Jan. 14, 1916

PAYNE

Wm. W. Payne
Dec. 2, 1904
March 11, 1931
"He rests from his labors."
(Jr. O. U. A. M. Emblem)

BROWN

Narcissas Brown
Aug. 31, 1862
Aug. 31, 1930
"Asleep to Wake again."

Berlin W. Brown
Jan. 31, 1897
Aug. 2, 1933
"Blessed are the pure
in heart."

Sergt. Berlin Wesley Brown
Co. M. 117th Inf.
Distinguished himself by ex-
traordinary heroism in
connection with military
operations against armed
enemy of the United States
at Busigng, France on Oct.
18, 1918 and in recognition
of his gallant conduct, I
have awarded him in the
name of the President the
distinguished service cross.

Vesta
Wife of
Zenes Brown
Daughter of
Mr. & Mrs. W. N. Burger
Jan. 16, 1892
June 1, 1913
"Blessed are the pure in
heart for they shall see
God."

BURGER

Lucious C. Burger
Feb. 22, 1886
Mar. 14, 1910

BARNNARD

Mattie Hunt
Wife of
W. L. Barnnard
Dec. 3, 1875
Jan. 12, 1930   Mother

HAMILTON

Ira Cliford
Son of
R. M. & M. A. Hamilton
July 22, 1913
July 12, 1914
"Budded on earth to bloom in Heaven."

Father
Thomas Hamilton
(not buried)

Mother
Martha E. Hamilton
1882--1928
"Gone but not forgotten."

HUTSON

R. N. Hutson
Died March 15, 1939
Aged 66 years

TAYLOR

L. W. Taylor
Dec. 17, 1857
June 10, 1926
"At Rest."

Mother
Mollie D.
Wife of
L. W. Taylor
Jan. 29, 1861
Mar. 8, 1923
"At Rest."

TELLICO PLAINS BAPTIST CHURCH CEMETERY

TAYLOR

J. H. Taylor
Son of
M. D. Taylor
Nov. 28, 1886
Oct. 11, 1918
"Died at West Point,
N. Y. In U. S. service
10 years."

Myrtle M.
Daughter of
F. F. & M. C. Taylor
Mar. 28, 1908
Jan. 10, 1916
"Gone but not forgotten."

C. H Taylor
Died Nov. 3, 1927
Aged 45 years

KING

(W. O. W. Memorial)
E. L. King
May 19, 1876
Aug. 26, 1927
"Father is gone but
not forgotten."

M. N. King

NELMONS

Floyd Nelmons
Nov. 18, 1913
July 11, 1922
"Suffer little children
to come unto Me."

MILLSAPS

Clinton Millsaps
Aug. 24, 1848
Jan. 20, 1930
"Gone but not forgotten."

TRUE

Charles M. True
Died July 28, 1932
Aged 58 years, 6 months,
& 10 days.

MCNABB

Jake McNabb
April 4, 1880
April 28, 1932
(Masonic Emblem)

TALLENT

Rachel White
Wife of
I. M. Tallent
July 12, 1888
May 1, 1919
"Gone to Rest."

Lizzie Tallent
Mar. 22, 1860
Sept. 25, 1915
"Gone to Rest."

Hommer
Infant of
I. M. & Rachel Tallent
Nov. 6, 1913
Apr. 29, 1914
"Our darling
Asleep but not forgotten."

Bessie
Daughter of
W. P. & A. B. Tallent
Sept. 5, 1905
Jan. 19, 1911
"Our darling
Asleep but not forgotten."

S. L. Tallent

HARRISON

Sarah Ann Harrison
1878--1931

BARRETT

Infant, U. W. Barrett
Son of
G. W. & L. E. Barrett
May 14, 1915
May 16, 1915
"Asleep in Jesus."

TELLICO PLAINS BAPTIST CHURCH CEMETERY

CROFTS

Walter
Son of
Dr. B. T. & S. C. Crofts
Nov. 26, 1907
Dec. 25, 1907
"Darling we miss Thee."

Infant
of
Dr. B. T. & S. C. Crofts
Jan. 9, 1910
Jan. 10, 1910
"Plucked like a rose."

(Jr. O. U. A. M. Emblem)
Dr. B. T. Crofts
Feb. 4, 1879
Mar. 28, 1926
"When the pearly gates
unfold, we hope to clasp
glad hands once more."

COMBS

Ruby L.
Daughter of
M. E. &. T. C. Combs
May 11, 1911
May 29, 1911
"Our darling."

LETHCOE

George R.
Son of
G. W & F. H. Lethcoe
July 24, 1902
July 12, 1909
"Darling we miss thee."

WATTS

In memory of
Mother
Margaret Watts
Sept. 24, 1870
Dec. 19, 1909

NEWMAN

Jessie Samuel Newman
Died Oct. 13, 1931
Aged 26 years, 5 months & 13 days.

Husband
John F. Newman
June 14, 1864
May 11, 1916
"He is not dead but
sleepeth. The angels called him."

Sarah J. Newman

Sarah C.
Daughter of
John F. & Sarah J. Newman
Oct. 12, 1895
Nov. 22, 1905
"At Rest."

CAUGHRON

Ailsa Tipton
Wife of
John H. Caughron
Jan. 2, 1851
July 15, 1925

John H. Caughron
May 1, 1849
Dec. 11, 1935
"At Rest."

(Masonic Emblem)
Wade H. Caughron
Nov. 2, 1871
May 5, 1922
"Gone but not forgotten."

GREEN

Joseph Green
Died Aug. 1921
Aged (faded out)

Harreld
Son of
N. T. & M. L. Green
Aug. 21, 1912
Sept. 5, 1912
"Budded on earth to
bloom in Heaven."

TELLICO PLAINS BAPTIST CHURCH CEMETERY

GREEN

Infant
of
Mr. & Mrs. N. T. Green
Jan. 10, 1916
Jan. 11, 1916
"Gone but not forgotten."

Infant
of
Mr. & Mrs. N. T. Green
Jan. 10, 1916
Jan. 11, 1916
"Gone but not forgotten."

"Blessed are they that
die in the Lord."
Mary J. Green
Oct. 11, 1848
Dec. 17, 1907

HENSLEY

Mary E. Hensley
---- -- 1929

ARP

Roy Arp
Died May 7, 1914
Born Dec. 21, 1913
16 months Old

Note: Either mistake on
the marker or mistake in
copying inscription as
age and dates don't tally.
Child might have been 6
months Old.

LEE

Bell Lee
Died Jan. 21, 1936
Aged 24 years

W. W. Lee
Died July 13, 1936
Aged 77 years, 2 months
& 27 days.

WALLACE

Mary Wallace
Dec. 15, 1895
Mar. 30, 1916
"Gone but not forgotten."

SHAW

Mary Noal Shaw
May 14, 1918
July 3, 1919

Ethel
Oct. 1, 1884
(Not buried)

Luther
May 24, 1887
Apr. 27, 1929

BRITTON

Reed Verlin Britton
May 6, 1919
March 4, 1920
"Our darling babe."

James Jr. Britton
July 27, 1921
Aug. 14, 1925
Our darling son."

MILLER

Jas. W. Miller
Co. M
4 Tenn Cav.

Richard W. Miller
July 25, 1900
Jan. 21, 1919
"Mother's darling baby."

R. V.
Son of
L. J. Miller
April 5, 1895
July 26, 1913
"From Mothers arms to the arms
of Jesus."

TELLICO PLAINS BAPTIST CHURCH CEMETERY

MITCHELL

J. E. Mitchell
June 22, 1881
Nov. 12, 1918
"At Rest."

Esquire Jas. G. Mitchell
1848----1929

His wife
Catherine Mitchell
1855--(Buried No date given)
"At Rest."

GUNTER

Gladys
Daughter of
C. T. & D. L. Gunter
Feb. 14, 1920
July 13, 1920
"My darling baby
Asleep with Jesus."

Dovie Lee
Wife of
C. T. Gunter
May 5, 1850
July 14, 1920
"At Rest with Jesus."

Glen Albert
Son of
Fred & Annie Gunter
July 28, 1913
Feb. 1, 1919

BLACKWELL

Maydell
Wife of
A. M. Blackwell
Jan. 23, 1885
Dec. 28, 1917

Note: The above two
inscriptions of--Glen Albert
Gunter and Maydell Blackwell
were on the same marker.

HAWKINS

Reed Hawkins
July 24, 1899
June 25, 1928

JOHNSON

Addie Johnson
Died Nov. 16, 1938
Aged 60 years & 8 months.

L. S. Johnson

J. Johnson

BURNETT

Willie Burnett
Died March 7, 1938
Aged 42 yrs. 8 Mos. & 18 days

Jack Burnett

Mary Burnett

KEENER

Maud
Daughter of
Amos & Rachel Keener
Aug. 5, 1909
Nov. 24, 1910
"Gone but not forgotten."

HYDE

Nora Myrtle
Daughter of
J. M. & M. E. Hyde
Apr. 19, 1897
Nov. 10, 1911
"At Rest."

J. M. Hyde

RUTHERFORD

Infant
of
Mr. & Mrs. A. C. Rutherford
Nov. 16, 1923

TELLICO PLAINS BAPTIST CHURCH CEMETERY

WALKER

Father
John H. Walker
Dec. 9, 1852
Mar. 22, 1927
"Gone but not forgotten."

Mrs. Cora Lee Walker
Died June 15, 1933
Aged 23 yrs. 1 Mo. & 10 days

PENNINGTON

B. J. Jr.
Son of
B. J. & Florence Pennington
March 23, 1915
Sept. 2, 1915

JONES

Lillie
Daughter of
D. W. & Nellie Jones
Sept. 9, 1906
May 13, 1910
"We will meet again."

Lennie
Daughter of
D. W. & Nellie Jones
Oct. 21, 1908
Sept. 5, 1911
"We will meet again."

Mother
Nellie
Wife of
D. W. Jones
Apr. 28, 1884
Apr. 28, 1922
"At Rest."

William Jones

BURGESS

(Masonic Emblem)
Samuel Luther Burgess
1875---1930

LANCE

Bob Lance
1884---1934

Loucase Lance
Apr. 26, 1906
Sept. 19, 1909
"Our darling."

John W. Lance
July 28, 1877
(Not buried)

His wife
Laura Lance
Feb. 20, 1878
Jan. 30, 1935

SCOTT

Scott (on large Marker)
Charles A. Scott
1866--1930

CAVENDER

M. E. Cavender

JENKINS

Dr. C. S. Jenkins
Oct. 6, 1872
Aug. 29, 1923
(also large marker with
(Masonic Emblem.)

Infant
Son of
Dr. & Mrs. C. S. Jenkins
Feb. 17, 1915

HAMMOND

(Masonic Emblem)
Dr. W. J. Hammond
Feb. 18, 1858
Sept. 10, 1936

JORDAN

TELLICO PLAINS BAPTIST CHURCH CEMETERY

JORDAN

Infant
of
J. T. & M. O. Jordan
Mar. 10, 1910
Mar. 11, 1910
"The sweetest flowers are
gathered first."

MASON

Earnest B. Mason
Oct. 17, 1891
July 23, 1918
"Blessed are the dead which
die in the Lord."

J. D. Mason
Mar. 23, 1918
Jan. 4, 1920
"Darling we miss Thee."

Mrs. Julie Mason
Died May 23, 1932
Aged 71 yrs. 1 Mo.&
13 days.

ASHE

Mrs. Lonesome S. Ashe
Died Dec. 15, 1932
Aged 57 yrs. 4 Mos. &
17 days.

WRIGHT

Clarence A.
Son of
Wm. & N. S. Wright
Feb. 5, 1910
Feb. 10, 1911

CABLE

James Arthur Cable
Mar. 25, 1873
Sept. 19, 1920

SWAINSON

Of such is the Kingdom of Heaven.
Mary Gladys
Daughter of
Charles & Mary Swainson
July 22, 1906
May 14, 1906

Charles S. Swainson
Sept. 9, 1865
Sept. 9, 1933

MAYFIELD

"Our darling
Walter Mayfield
Son of
H. & G. F. Mayfield

"Our darling"
Lee Olis Mayfield
Son of
H. G. F. Mayfield

"Our darling."
Minnie Lou Mayfield
Daughter of
H. & G. F. Mayfield

BLACK

Daughter of
J. M. & A. M. Black
July 23, 1907
July 23, 1907

BEAVERS

Alice
Wife of
Joe Beavers
Mar. 22, 1887
June 11, 1910
"At Rest."

GRIFFIN

Mary Lea
Wife of
J. T. Griffin
Aug. 25, 1848
Aug. 13, 1913

TELLICO PLAINS BAPTIST CHURCH CEMETERY

TOWNSEND

Ralph
Son of
W. P. & Mary Townsend
July 4, 1908
Nov. 22, 1909
"Asleep in Jesus."

James G. Townsend
Apr. 18, 1846
May 29, 1919

Serena J. Townsend
June 14, 1850
Dec. 25, 1911
"In Memory of
Father & Mother

W. P. Townsend
Died Dec. 27, 1936
Aged 64 yrs. 3 Mos. &
1 day.

Mary Townsend

PORTER

A. J. Porter
1914

RUNION

T. L. Runion
Died Oct. 28, 1915
Born Feb. -- 18--

WAYMAN

William Thomas Wayman
July 3, 1913
July 11, 1913
"Little children are
His jewels."

SHEPARD

Earnest
Son of
J. W. & Dollie Shepard
May 23, 1913
Feb. 13, 1917

WALL

WALL

(Masonic Emblem)
Virgil F. Wall
July 28, 1879
Feb. 19, 1923
"Death is eternal life
why should we weep."

BATES

Infant
Son of
Robert & Mamie Bates
Aug. 7, 1910
Aug. 7, 1910
"Gone to be an Angel."

CHRISTOPHER

In Memoriam
Baby John
Son of
J. H. & I. L. Christopher
Feb. 25, 1915
May 25, 1916

CURTIS

Glian
Son of
J. A. & A. G. Curtis
June 16, 1910
June 29, 1910

RHEA

William R. Rhea
Died June 26, 1929
Aged 50 years

THOMAS

Grace Lee Thomas
Died March 20, 1938
Aged 31 years & 5 days

Bessie L.
Daughter of
James & Sarah Thomas
Dec. 11, 1905
Apr. 20, 1908
"Our darling."

TELLICO PLAINS BAPTIST CHURCH CEMETERY

THOMAS

James Thomas
Oct. 24, 1850
May 20, 1908
"May the resurrection
find thee on the
bosom of thy God."

GRAY

Rafe Gray
Feb. 20, 1880
Sept. 12, 1933
"Asleep to wake again."

Mary Nell
Daughter of
R. W. & Zadie Gray
May 26, 1910
March 28, 1911
"Darling we Miss Thee."

Clarence
Son of
R. W. & Zadie Gray
1907--1932
"Gone but not forgotten."

WHITE

Aroel
Son of
Wyatt & Iva White
Nov. 15, 1919
Dec. 18, 1919
"Our darling baby."

James White

Tracy
Son of
Mr. & Mrs. L. E. White
Sept. 9, 1920
Feb. 9, 1930
"Shouting on the hills
of glory."

Vernon Doyle
Son of
E. L. & E. A. White
Died Sept. 6, 1910
"Asleep in Jesus."

E. M. White
Sept. 4, 1903
Aug. 29, 1904
"I know that my redeemer liveth."

RODERS

S. G. Hoyt Rogers
1894--1924

Josie Rogers
1879--1932
"At Rest."

COLLINS

J. E. Collins
Son of
Mr. & Mrs. J. H. Collins
Nov. 28, 1902
Nov. 18, 1924
"He was the sunlight
of our home."

J. H. Collins
Oct. 15, 1879
Dec. 18, 1934
"And if this earthly tabernacle
be disolved, I have a home
eternal in the Heavens not
made with hands."

CROWE Or CROW

William Thomas Crowe
Feb. 24, 1876
Jan. 13, 1936

Marie Crowe
Feb. 11, 1911
Apr. 10, 1930

TELLICO PLAINS BAPTIST CHURCH CEMETERY

CROW

Lena E.
Wife of
W. T. Crow
Oct. 22, 1879
Dec. 21, 1920
"She was a kind and
affectionate wife a
fond mother and a
friend to all."

HUNT

Mrs. Walter Hunt
Died July 27, 1933
Aged 34 years & 10 months.

Roy Hunt
Apr. 3, 1914
Mar. 10, 1936
"At Rest."

MCNUTT

Johnnie McNutt
Apr. 12, 1919
Dec. 8, 1928
"A little time on earth
he spent, till God for
him his angel sent."

RYMER

Letha Rymer
Feb. 4, 1870
July 9, 1911
"We shall remember you
Mother."

SUTTON

J. L. Sutton
Died Mch. 10, 1938
Aged 65 years. 9 months
& 18 days.

RICHESON

Margaret S.
Wife of
H. B. Richeson
Died Dec. 14, 1910
Aged 65 years.

DAVENPORT

Clarence Davenport
Died Nov. 26, 1931
Aged 21 years, 7 months &
28 days.

CARTER

Ben
Son of
R. T. Carter
Aug. 21, 1907
Sept. 11, 1924

Fannie
Wife of
R. T. Carter
March 26, 1876
Dec. 28, 1927

BLAIR

"Come unto Me."
Laura E. Blair
Nov. 22, 1891
June 5, 1906
"Like the stars, she looks
down from the skies."

LESTER

Howard Lester
July 13, 1895
Sept. 24, 1916
"Asleep in Jesus."

GRAVES

Bessie Graves
Died July 22, 1938
Aged 35 years

TELLICO PLAINS BAPTIST CHURCH CEMETERY

GRAVES

Samuel Graves
Co. G
3 Tenn Mtd Inf.

HAMPTON

Lonie
Daughter of
W. M. & Nancy Hampton
Dec. 6, 1908
Aug. 30, 1911
"Gone but not forgotten."

WILLIAMSON

Wella Nell Williamson
Apr. 11, 1912
June 22, 1912
"Of such is the Kingdom
of Heaven."

BARNETT

J. R. Barnett
Dec. 18, 1859
Feb. 13, 1914

MOSES

James R. Moses
1933--1934

Henry Moses

Joe Moses

STEPHENS

Infant
of
Mr. & Mrs. R. E. Stephens
Feb. 4, 1924
Feb. 4, 1924
"Gone so soon."

SYLVESTER

Nanie S.

Bob S.
Brother

S. S.
Father

L. S.
Mother

Note: It is said that the
four above were members of
the Sylvester family, listed
as are.

MONROE COUNTY

TOMBSTONE INSCRIPTIONS

TOQUA PRESBYTERIAN CHURCH CEMETERY

Copied by: Lawrence McConkey, Englewood, Tennessee
Date: Feb. 15, 1940

Toqua Presbyterian Cemetery is located 11 miles Northeast of
Madisonville or 2 miles East of Vonore, via Citico road. The
church is 1 mile further East on the road leading to Citico.
The cemetery was established July 12, 1932 at the death of Carl
Millsaps. Mrs. H. G. Hutchison gave about 2 acres for this
cemetery. The 8 graves are widely scattered over the cemetery.
There is 1 grave marked by a field stone and 1 unmarked grave.
H. G. Hutchison gave the land and helped financially in build-
ing the church. The cemetery and church are both used.

STAMEY

Mrs. Alice Stamey
Died Oct. 26, 1937
Aged 60 years.

Millsaps

Baby
Carl Clinton
Son of
Tom & Reba Millsaps
Feb. 26, 1932
July 12, 1932
For such is the Kingdom
of God.
The first body to be
placed in this cemetery.

BINGHAM

Martha Bingham
Aged 70
Died May 1938

GRIFFITH

Rahett Griffith

James Griffith

WARD

Mrs. Isaac Ward
Died   1937
Aged about 30 years.

MONROE COUNTY

UNICOI BAPTIST CHURCH CEMETERY

Copied by Lawrence McConkey, Englewood, Tennessee
Date:

Unicoi Baptist Church Cemetery is 1½ miles South of Tellico
Plains near the church and Hunts School house.

The Hunts buried here were of prominent county families.

The Unicoi Baptist Church was established in 1873 about
2 miles South of Tellico Plains on the road leading to
Ironsburg. It was removed to its present location, where
2 acres of land was bought from Willie Jones for the
cemetery.

Several members of the Hunt family, prominent in Monroe
County, are buried here.

MONROE COUNTY

TOMBSTONE INSCRIPTIONS
UNICOI BAPTIST CHURCH CEMETERY

LOVE

D. H. Love
Died Oct. 24, 1937
Aged 81 years, 7 months
& 4 days.

DAVIS

J. L. Davis
Died Sept. 5, 1936
Aged 62 years, 6 months
& 24 days.

PLEMMONS

Died Nov. 20, 1936
Aged 36 years, 1 month
& 15 days.

HUNT

Louis H. Hunt
Died Jan. 15, 1936
Aged 60 years.

G. W. Hunt
Died April 27, 1937
Aged 78 years, 5 months
& 26 days.

GRAVES

Allen Graves
Died July 4, 1937
Aged 32 years, 8 months
& 2 days

FARMER

Benjamin Fred Farmer
Died Oct. 20, 1937
Aged 45 years, 11 months
& 30 days

MCJUNKIN

Mary Bryant
Wife of
G. M. McJunkin
Jan. 11, 1866
Aug. 9, 1937
"At Rest."

SYLVESTER

Texie Sylvester
1879--(not buried)

Sam Sylvester
1870--1929
"Asleep in Jesus."

Mother & Father

TOMBSTONE INSCRIPTIONS

UNION HALL PRESBYTERIAN CHURCH CEMETERY

Copied by: Lawrence McConkey, Englewood, Tenn.
Date:

Union Hall Presbyterian Church was the first church established
in this section of Monroe County. Ex-Sheriff Sloan, who is an
old man, thinks it was among the first churches in the county.
The cemetery is thought to have been established about the
same time as the church although the inscriptions do not date
back that far. The Presbyterian Denomination in early days had
a large shed that they used for camp meetings. The name Union
Hall seems to have derived from the fact that it was the only
meeting place in that section of the county.

The graveyard is 7 miles East of Madisonville on the Ball Play
road. There are 34 inscriptions and approximately 100 unmarked
graves.

LONG

Geo.W. Long
Died Mar. 9, 1929
Aged 63 yrs. 11 mos. 27 days.

Mrs. Geo. Long

STAMEY

Charles D. Stamey
Born Jan. 7, 1936
Died Feb. 11, 1936
Our darling has gone
before and we aim
to meet him in that
bright land above.

TALLENT

Vaddie Tallent
May 1, 1911
May 13, 1911

A. R. Tallent
June 3, 1909
June 12, 1909
Our darling baby at rest.

Our darlings together
in Heaven.
Samie Tallent
May 30, 1907
June 2, 1907

Jackie Tallent
May 30, 1907
May 31, 1907

Juritta A. Tallent
May 8, 1848
Nov. 17, 1869

Tallent

Tallent

Tallent

(Note: Above are real old
markers. LMcC.)

SANDERS-SAUNDERS

Margaret Crowder
Wife of
A. J. Sanders
Jan. 27, 1836
Sept. 15, 1882

UNION HALL PRESBYTERIAN CHURCH CEMETERY

(Masonic)
A. J. Saunders
Feb. 16, 1829
Nov. 27, 1889
Aged 60 years 9 months &
11 days.

Nancy A. Sanders
 Feb. 14, 1831
Jan.   7, 1894
At Rest.

Margaret I. Sanders
July 11, 1857
Feb. 13, 1885
Sweetly Resting.

(Note: Margaret I. Sanders
was buried between Samuel &
Mary Mason and possibly was
a Mason before marriage.
LMcC.)

MASON

Mary J. Mason
Jan. 20, 1850
Jan. 15, 1933
I know my redeemer
liveth.

Mary J. Mason
Apr. 5, 1828
Feb. 7, 1899
In God I trust.

(Masonic member)
Archibald Mason
July 20, 1820
June 8, 1894
An honest man is
the noblest work of God.

Samuel H. Mason
June 1, 1860
Feb. 11, 1894
Thy work is done
rest in peace.

Charles Mason
May 1, 1852
Aug. 11, 1856

Ere sin could blight
or sorrow fade, Death
came with friendly
Care. The opening bud
to Heaven conveyed and
bade it bless on there.

FRYE

John Frye

Mrs. John Frye
Died 1925

Samuel Frye

Caroline Frye

Betty Frye

MOSES

Daniel Moses

John Moses

Catherine Moses

Sarah Moses

Mary Moses

WHITE

Amanda
Wife of
J. E. White

James
Son of
J. E. & A. White

Mary White

Serena White

Joseph White

MONROE COUNTY

VONORE BAPTIST CHURCH CEMETERY

Copied by Lawrence McConkey, Englewood, Tennessee
Date: September 8, 1939

The Vonore Baptist Church Cemetery was established about
25 years ago. The church was constituted in 1907. Land
for both the church and cemetery was given by Mrs. George
W. Ray.

The earliest tombstone inscription is that of Charlotte
B., daughter of H. E. and R. M. Swabe, who died April
12, 1919.

There are approximately 25 unmarked graves.

MONROE COUNTY

TOMBSTONE INSCRIPTIONS
VONORE BAPTIST CHURCH CEMETERY

LAYNE

Vina Rasar
Feb. 22, 1884
Nov. 14, 1923
Mother

Carl R.
March 24, 1880
(not buried)
Father

Earl Layne
Sept. 1923
June 1924

ARP

Mrs. Bettie Arp
Died Feb. 11, 1939
Aged 84 years

KEYES

Miss Viola Keyes
Died Nov. 29, 1931
Aged 29 years, 1
Month & 29 days

WILLIAMS

Marcus
Nov. 3, 1871
July 19, 1931

Vada Lea
April 23, 1879
Aug. 15, 1931
"Saved by Grace."

TALLENT

Jep H.
Aug. 12, 1869
Dec. 25, 1938

Florida
Aug. 7, 1869
(buried no date)
"I am satisfied in Jesus."

CHAMBERS

Joseph Oliver Chambers
Nov. 18, 1867
Feb. 4, 1934

Mattie Caroline Chambers
Aug. 30, 1876

W. L. Chambers
Sept. 2, 1929
Feb. 3, 1936
"Weep not he is at rest."

MOSER

J. O. Moser
Mar. 12, 1890
(Not buried)

Nova Moser
Oct. 24, 1901
Apr. 6, 1934
"Death is eternal life
why should we weep."

Henry Moser Jr.
Sept. 30, 1866
(not buried)

Vera Moser
Jan. 19, 1872
Sept. 12, 1935

LEMING

Cora Leming
Feb. 4, 1897
Jan. 28, 1921
"Darling we miss thee."

W. G. Leming
Died Jan. 10, 1932
Aged 81 years, 6 days

D. F. Leming
Feb. 7, 1893
July 27, 1932
"Gone but not forgotten."

VONORE BAPTIST CHURCH CEMETERY

DAVIS

Robert R. Davis
Died Oct. 27, 1937
Aged 67 years, 1 Month
& 11 days.

JOHNSON

F. B. Johnson
1916--1928

HAMPTON

Bettie Hampton
Died April 14, 1937
Aged 85 years, 9 Months
& 15 days

LOMAX

In memory of
Mother
Nancy Isbill Lomax
May 16, 1868
Dec. 23, 1930

Father
J. B. Lomax
Sept. 23, 1860
(Not buried)

CANNON

Addie Ray Cannon
Mar. 13, 1852
Mar. 19, 1920
"At Rest."

WHITE

"Gone to Rest."
James C. White
April 27, 1884
Feb. 18, 1935

His wife
Bulah Moser
May 6, 1890
(Not buried)

MCSPADDEN

Tom McSpadden
1881--1931
"Our darling one hath gone
before to greet us on the
blissful shore."

GRAYSON

In memory of
Our darling
Annie Lawson Grayson
Mar. 11, 1922
Mar. 20, 1922

TYLER

Marion J. Tyler
Mar. 2, 1925
Sept. 5, 1925

W. J. Tyler
1840---19(not buried)

His wife
Martha Ann Poplin
1847--1929

CURTIS

Faber R. Curtis
1883-1931
"Asleep in Jesus."

FARMER

J. R. Farmer
1903--1932

His wife
Viola Curtis
1905--(not buried)
"At Rest."

CAREY

John Fowler Carey
March 9, 1857
Feb. 1, 1938
"Gone but not forgotten."

VONORE BAPTIST CHURCH CEMETERY

SNIDER

Paul W. Snider
Dec. 17, 1915
July 2, 1922
"Darling we miss thee."

AXLEY

Mrs. A. L. Axley
Died April 24, 1937
Aged 61 years, 5 months
& 12 days.

BORDEN

Sam Borden
Died Jan. 20, 1932
Aged 50 years, 11 months
& 26 days.

GRAY

Mrs. H. B. Gray
Died Dec. 30, 1931
Aged 47 years, 3 Months &
21 days.

INGRAM

Miss Emma Jane Ingram
Died May -- 19--
Age 11 years, 5 months.

MONROE COUNTY

VONORE SOUTHERN M. E. CHURCH CEMETERY

Copied by Lawrence McConkey, Englewood, Tennessee
Date: September 12, 14, 1939

Vonore Southern M. E. Church Cemetery is near the L. & N.
Railroad on the Southwest side of Vonore. It seems to have
been established when Wm. S. & Mahala Blair owned the farm
on which the graveyard is located. The first burial, that
of Isaac Upton, was on August 19, 1848. Isaac Upton had
married Bettie, daughter of Wm. S. & Mahala Blair, who later
owned the land. It was used as a community cemetery until
about 35 years ago, when James C. Hall deeded it to the
Vonore Southern Methodist Church.

Among the prominent persons buried in Vonore Southern M. E.
Church Cemetery are William H. Dawson, Joseph Starritt,
Monroe Starritt and Brice Williams.

William H. Dawson, was a Justice of the Peace and County
Representive for several years, and was very prominent in
the county. He was over 100 years old when he died.

Joseph Starritt was likewise a Justice of the Peace and a
member of the Tennessee State Legislative and very prominent in the county. His father, Monroe Starritt, was also
prominent. Neither one has a marker at his grave.

There are approximately 125 unmarked graves in Vonore
Southern M. E. Church Cemetery.

MONROE COUNTY

TOMBSTONE INSCRIPTIONS
VONORE SOU. M. E. CHURCH CEMETERY

SMITH

John Smith
July 10, 1861
Nov. 26, 1915
"Let our Fathers will
be done."

Sarah Smith

Henry Smith

A. L. Smith

MOREE

Ransom Moree
Aug. 29, 1835
Sept. 4, 1918
Father

Sarah Moree
Aug. 16, 1861
(Buried no date.)
Mother

Father
Erskin Moree
May 8, 1884
Dec. 25, 1922

Mother
Nannie Moree
Dec. 30, 1883
(Not buried.)

BORDEN

Infant
Son of
A. R. & Lucy Borden
Born & died
Dec. 19, 1913

SLOAN

Mary J. Hensley
Wife of
Lee R. Sloan
April 13, 1872
Feb. 19, 1903
"A devoted wife and a
loving Mother."

Arnold
Son of
Lee & Mary Sloan
Dec. 24, 1905
Aug. 30, 1906
"Gone but not forgotten."

Hilda Mary
Daughter of
Ben & Kada Sloan
June 27, 1909
Feb. 2, 1912
Age 2 years, 7 months & 6 days.

Infant
Son of
Ben & Kada Sloan
Sept. 25, 1910
Sept. 25, 1910

ISBILL or ISBELL

Rosa
Wife of
G. C. Isbell
Apr. 2, 1897
Apr. 26, 1916
"At Rest."

Lee Isbill
Jan. 10, 1891
Sept. 26, 1911
"Dearest loved one we
have laid Thee in the
peaceful grave.-------
--------------------."

STEEL or STEELE

James F. Steel
Died June 23, 1894
Age 21 years & 15 days

Margarette A. Steele
Died April 25, 1931
Aged 81 years, 7 months
& 17 days.

MONROE COUNTY

TOMBSTONE INSCRIPTIONS
VONORE SOU. M. E. CHURCH CEMETERY

BRAKEBILL

Milburn C. Brakebill
April 16, 1906
Feb. 5, 1925
"Darling We miss Thee."

BLAIR

William S.
Son of
Wm. S. & Mahala Blair
Nov. 28, 1825
Nov. 4, 1849
Aged 23 years, 11 months
& 24 days.

BOWERS

J. Bowers
Oct. 14, 1876
June 9, 1894

McKEEHAN or McKEEHEN

G. W. McKeehan
June 14, 1861
Sept 17, 1936
"At Rest."

Missouri Ann Isabel
Wife of
W. M. McKeehen
Mar. 1, 1861
Apr. 4, 1906

Revebell
Daughter of
Charlie & Mary McKeehen
Jan. 9, 1914
May 23, 1914

Nellie A. McKeehan
Nov. 22, 1902
June 24, 1908
"Our darling One."

RAY

Stella Samples
Wife of
J. B. Ray
Nov. 24, 1903
July 30, 1926
"None knew thee but to
Love thee."

Geo. W. Ray
May 13, 1859
(buried no date)

His wife
Sallie A. Ray
Apr. 4, 1868
Nov. 6, 1924

Frank A
Son of
G. W. & S. A. Ray
Aug. 19, 1897
Nov. 4, 1918
"Once a soldier of his Country
Now a soldier of his Country."

WILLIAMS

Ruth Lee Williams
Mar. 1, 1920
Mar. 3, 1920
"Asleep in Jesus."

Eugene Williams
Dec. 4, 1916
Feb. 3, 1917
"Asleep in Jesus."

Ada Pearl Williams
Aug. 19, 1915
June 19, 1916
"Our little darling."

W. B. Williams
Feb. 4, 1856
Oct. 1, 1932
"At Rest."

MONROE COUNTY

TOMBSTONE INSCRIPTIONS
VONORE SOU. M. E. CHURCH CEMETERY

WILLIAMS

Robert Williams

Ruth S. Click Williams
June 20, 1863
Jan. 21, 1938

WEAR

Jean Lea
Daughter of
F. B. & R. J. Wear
Feb. 16, 1911
Jan. 1, 1912
"Suffer little Children to
Come unto Me."

MCCULLOCH

Bessie Blankenship McCulloch
Dec. 18, 1900
Nov. 21, 1924
"At Rest."

Nancy A.
Wife of
William McCulloch
Oct. 10, 1843
May 6, 1911
"May the resurrection find
thee on the bosom of thy God."

MARSHALL

Wm. Marshall
Died Sept. 21, 1935
Aged 72 years, 9 months &
5 days.

Nancy E.
Wife of
R. G. Marshall
Mar. 8, 1842
Apr. 24, 1906
"Gone but not forgotten."

R. G. Marshall
March 15, 1830
July 7, 1902
"Gone but not forgotten."

Harriet
Wife of
Jas. Marshall
Apr. 5, 1868
Nov. 14, 1903
"We will meet again."

James Marshall

Algia
Daughter of
J. H. & Emma Marshall
Feb. 28, 1912
June 5, 1913
"Gone so soon."

Charles Wilford
Son of
Charlie & W. Marshall
Aug. 30, 1914

Elisha R. Marshall
Died March 3, 1937
Aged 67 years, 3 months & 10 days.

CLINE

Martha J. Lowry
Wife of
J. L. Cline
Aug. 1, 1858
Feb. 25, 1893
Aged 34 yrs, 6 mos, 24 days.
"Blessed are the dead which die
in the Lord."

HALL

Nick B. Hall
Aug. 7, 1873
(not dead)

Maggie Henley Hall
Feb. 18, 1875
June 17, 1936

Lou O. Hall
Aug. 9, 1842
Mar. 15, 1924

MONROE COUNTY

TOMBSTONE INSCRIPTIONS
VONORE SOU. M. E. CHURCH CEMETERY

HALL

James C. Hall
Jan. 13, 1824
June 11, 1910

Artie Lou
Daughter of
N. B. & Maggie Hall
May 12, 1908
Sept. 8, 1909

James C. Hall
Jan. 3, 1898
Jan. 3, 1929

HORNER

Lottie Q Hall
Wife of
P. H. Horner
Mar. 13, 1896
Dec. 20, 1921
"She was a kind and
affectionate wife and
Mother, and a friend
to all."

SWANEY

Laura Josephine Griffiths
Wife of
Albert M. Swaney
Oct. 29, 1871
Sept. 9, 1915
Crown Chapter No. 91
Eastern Star

DAWSON

Henry F. Dawson
June 14, 1853
Dec. 4, 1935

Mary M. Dawson
Sept. 24, 1875
(Not buried)

"The Righteous shall be in
everlasting remembrance."
Lavenia Tipton Dawson
Nov. 12, 1826
Aug. 8, 1902

William H. Dawson
March 12, 1827
Aug. 28, 1927
"At Rest."

Betty E. Dawson
Mar. 2, 1859
Dec. 2, 1918
"Faithful to her trust
even unto her death.

JOHNSON

Earl Johnson
Nov. 18, 1896
Aug. 6, 1915

Frank Lee Johnson
Died ------1939
Aged 73 years.

B. S. Johnson
Oct. 5, 1848
May 28, 1922
"Death is the crown of life."

Margaret J. Johnson
Feb. 24, 1852
June 8, 1920
"She was the sunshine of our
home."

RODGERS

N. J. McKeehen
Wife of
T. J. Rodgers
Mar. 15, 1859
May 4, 1922
"At Rest."

5

MONROE COUNTY

TOMBSTONE INSCRIPTIONS
VOMORE SOU. M. E. CHURCH CEMETERY

RODGERS

James L. Rodgers
Died March 29, 1935
Aged 1 day.

Dave Rodgers
June 19, 1857
Sept. 25, 1915
Father

Laura B. Rodgers
Apr. 11, 1900
May 13, 1900
"Our Darling."

BLUFORD

James Bluford
Jan. 18, 1838
Nov. 23, 1922
"Gone but not forgotten."

Sarah C.
Wife of
James Bluford
Feb. 2, 1860
Dec. 5, 1930
"Gone but not forgotten."

Mrs. Anderson Bluford
Sept. 30, 18-9
Aug. 21, 1900

SNIDER

Infant
of
J. A. & A. H. Snider
Oct. 31, 1909
Oct. 31, 1909

MOSER

Austin Moser
Sept. 18, 1898
Feb. 10, 1899
"Gone to Rest."

Infants
of
C. V. & G. L. Moser
Born May 10, 1900
Died May 10, 1900 and
May 11, 1900

Annie Bell
Infant of
C. V. & G. L. Moser
Dec. 18, 1905
June 23, 1906
"Only sleeping."

Croft V. Moser
Died Feb. 15, 1938
Aged 72 years, 11 months &
21 days.

Lindell H.
Son of
Mr. & Mrs. Carl Moser
Nov. 28, 1916
Aug. 14, 1917
"Our darling One."

L. S. Moser
1851--1929
"At Rest."

Elizabeth Bingham Moser
1856--1929
"At Rest."

"Asleep in Jesus
Come unto Me."
Neppie Bell
Wife of
L. W. Moser
Mar. 23, 1885
Mar. 18, 1912

Infant
daughter of
Denver & Nellie Moser
May 28, 1912
May 28, 1912
"Budded on earth to
bloom in Heaven."

MONROE COUNTY

TOMBSTONE INSCRIPTIONS
VONORE SOU. M. E. CHURCH CEMETERY

MOSER

Annie L.
Wife of
L. Moser
Aug. 15, 1867
Aug. 12, 1886
"At Rest."

L. Moser

SAMPLES

Mrs. Mary Lou Samples
Died July 19, 1925
Aged 50 years

S. E. Samples

BRANNON

F. Brannon
June 23, 1892
June 23, 1892

M. A. Brannon
Apr. 26, 1893
July 22, 1895

Mattie Lee Brannon
Nov. 11, 1900
Sept. 14, 1902
Aged 22 Mos & 3 days.

Father
G. A. Brannon
Aug. 30, 1838
Jan. 3, 1922
"At.Rest."

Infant
Daughter of
I. A. & Annie Brannon
Oct. 7, 1904
Oct. 9, 1904
"Our little angel."

Joe Reed
Son of
I. A. & Annie Brannon
June 22, 1903
June 23, 1904
"Only sleeping."

CLEMMER

Gratus Dale
Son of
J. E. & P. P. Clemmer
Feb. 2, 1903
June 24, 1904
"Gone to be an angel."

HAWKINS

Earl
Infant son of
J. R. & Parley Hawkins
Feb. 4, 1901
July 26, 1901
"Our darling."

Barbara
Dau of
J. R. & Parley Hawkins
July 10, 1902
Aug. 22, 1903
"Asleep in Jesus."

To my Wife
Mattie
Wife of
R. A. Hawkins
Oct. 20, 1875
Apr. 10, 1903
"To live in hearts we leave
behind is not to die."

Anilea
Daughter of
R. A. & Mattie Hawkins
Jan. 22, 1902
Oct. 1, 1902
"Our darling one, we miss thee."

MONROE COUNTY

TOMBSTONE INSCRIPTIONS
VONORE SOU. M. E. CHURCH CEMETERY

STARRITT

Helen Margarite Starritt
Oct. 24, 1921
Mar. 23, 1925
"She was the sunshine of
our home."

Tye Starritt
Died Aug. 17, 1931
Aged 58 years, 4 months
& 7 days.

Lilly Starritt
Died Jan. 17, 1929
Aged 50 years

Mary
Wife of
J. M. Starritt
Born   1823
Died Mar. 16, 1882

BERRY

W. A. Berry
Dec. 26, 1829
Feb. 5, 1903
"Gone but not forgotten."

Joseph W. Berry
Apr. 11, 1879
Mar. 24, 1907
"I will arise the
judgement day."

DITMORE

H. M. Ditmore
Apr. 10, 1841
Apr. 15, 1910
"At Rest."

HARVEY

Willie Irine Harvey
Born Dec. 2, 1934
Aged 13 years & 12 days

N. L. Harvey
Nov. 16, 1843
Apr. 27, 1915

M. J. Harvey
Nov. 10, 1844
May 20, 1932
Father & Mother

Infant
of
G. S. & E. E. Harvey
Dec. 9, 1912
Dec. 10, 1912
"We Miss thee."

MILLIGAN

John Harrison Milligan
Died May 15, 1930
Aged 75 years, 4 months & 10 days.

(Masonic emblem)
William Homer
Dear Son of
J. L. & Addie Milligan
Oct. 23, 1895
Nov. 5, 1918
"A soldier for his Country."
Died in France.
Co. K. 6 Inf. A. E. F.

James L. Milligan
Feb. 18, 1844
Aug. 1, 1927

Addie Milligan

COPPINGER

Mr. & Mrs. John Careys'
Grandson
Thomas Floyd Coppinger
Apr. 28, 1911
June 6, 1912
"Asleep in Jesus."

MONROE COUNTY

TOMBSTONE INSCRIPTIONS
VONORE SOU. M. E. CHURCH CEMETERY

BELCHER

Father
Alex Belcher
Feb. 22, 1845
Feb. 27, 1930

Mother
His Wife
Tilda Belcher
Oct. 26, 1855
Jan. 26, 1930
"At Rest."

Lillard
Son of
Mr. & Mrs. M. C. Belcher
May 14, 1926
Jan. 9, 1930
"Asleep in Jesus."

Horace Ray
Son of
Mr. & Mrs. M. C. Belcher
Dec. 1, 1929
Oct. 18, 1937
"Asleep in Jesus."

FLETCHER

Ethel L. Brakebill
Wife of
B. W. Fletcher
June 10, 1897
Jan. 2, 1923
"Gone so soon."

PRESLEY

Glenn B.
Son of
R. M. & Nellie Presley
Jan. 26, 1920
May 17, 1936
"Gone but not forgotten."

Billie W. Presley
July 27, 1919
July 18, 1922
"Asleep in Jesus."

LOWRY

Joseph H. Lowry
Apr. 13, 1853
July 7, 1915
"Asleep in Jesus."

Fannie Fowler Lowry
Oct. 13, 1858
(not dead)

Annie Lowry
Feb. 16, 1861
Jan. 10, 1937
"Gone to Rest."

Thomas J. Lowry
Aug. 6, 1866
Sept. 13, 1932
"At Rest."

David Lowry
Jan. 6, 1823
April 12, 1899
"At Rest."

Mary Lowry
Wife of
David Lowry
June 8, 1822
Nov. 6, 1893
"We trust our loss will
be her gain and that with
Christ she's gone to reign."

Arthur H. Lowry
June 27, 1899
July 13, 1899
"At Rest."

Samuel
Son of
D. & M. Lowry
Aug. 23, 1854
Aug. 20, 1857

Elizabeth A
Daughter of
D. & M. Lowry
Nov. 13, 1856
Sept. 8, 1857

MONROE COUNTY

TOMBSTONE INSCRIPTIONS
VONORE SOU. M. E. CHURCH CEMETERY

LOWRY

Isaac Lowry
Oct. 25, 1848
June 8, 1870
"Farewell until we meet
again."

James C. Lowry
Aug. 11, 1865
July 14, 1923

Maggie A. Lowry
Jan. 5, 1868
Apr. 2, 1928

Albert Lowry
Died Dec. 25, 1920
Aged------

Helen Parker Lowry
Sept. 29, 1916
Feb. 28, 1919
"Budded on earth to
bloom in Heaven."

UPTON

Aunt Bettie Upton
July 15, 1824
June 5, 1916
"Not my will but
Thine be done."

In Memory of
Isaac Upton
Who departed this life
10th of Aug. 1848
In the 30th year of his life.

MCCAULEY

Neva B. McCollum
Wife of
R. P. McCauley
Apr. 5, 1903
Sept. 28, 1929

KINSER

N. I. Kinser
Jan. 11, 1850
(Burried no date.)

F. J. Kinser
Dec. 14, 1850
Feb. 14, 1924
"At Rest."
Father & Mother

STEPHENS

Infant
Son of
Anderson & Edna Stephens
1930--1930

BURGIN

John Burgin
Oct. 18, 1905
Oct. 27, 1923
"Gone but not forgotten."

STRICKLAN

Mary J. Stricklan
Aug. 2, 1902
July 28, 1919

Manda H. Stricklan
Feb. 27, 1895
Aug. 16, 1921

GERDING

Mar. 18, 1934
May 1, 1934
"At Rest."

HENRY

"Rock of Ages."
Nola Isabell Rodgers
Wife of
S. C. Henry
Oct. 1, 1892
Apr. 2, 1919
"Faithful to her trust even unto
death."

MONROE COUNTY

TOMBSTONE INSCRIPTIONS
VONORE SOU. M. E. CHURCH CEMETERY

UNDERWOOD

Louisa Underwood
Died July 13, 1929
Aged 70 years

S. L. Underwood

M. L. Underwood
June 13, 1835
Sept. 18, 1836

Infant
Son of
Ed. & Martha Underwood
Aug. 5, 1910
Aug. 18, 1910
"Asleep in Jesus."

Arkel
Son of
Ed & Martha Underwood
Aug. 3, 1911
Aug. 6, 1911
"Asleep in Jesus."

Mr. Elic Underwood
Died Sept. 10, 1937
Aged (not given)

George Howard Underwood
Nov. 23, 1918
June 4, 1920

Henry M.
Son of
D. M. & Mary Underwood
May 5, 1921
May 5, 1921
"Gone so soon."

SARTON

T. C. Sarton
Husband of
M. E. Sarton
July 2, 1854
Mar. 26, 1886
Aged 51 years, 8 Months
& 24 days.

NILES

J. W. Niles
Died Dec. 29, 1936
Aged 74 years

Orra Wesley Niles
Dec. 17, 1910
Sept. 24, 1911
"Our loved one."

STRATTON

"Our darling."
M. D.
Son of
W. A. & M. V. Stratton
Oct. 30, 1909
Dec. 22, 1909

H. A. Stratton
Mar. 20, 1917
June 19, 1917
"Budded on earth to
bloom in Heaven."

RUSSELL

David W. Russell
Son of
J. B. & J. W. Russell
Who died Feb. 24, 1855
Aged 6 years, 10 months & 21 days.

ROBISON

W. B. Robison
May 10, 1909
March 4, 1920
"Asleep in Jesus."

WAYMAN

"Come ye blessed."
Howard Wayman
Aug. 8, 1905
March 26, 1913
"Gone to a better land."

MONROE COUNTY

TOMBSTONE INSCRIPTIONS
VONORE SOU. M. E. CHURCH CEMETERY

TYLER

Annie M. Tyler
Died April 14, 1929
Aged 28 years 5 months
& 28 days

John Tyler

Mary Tyler

BROOKSHEAR or BROOKSHIRE

Finley Ross
Son of
A. W. & Birdie Brookshear
Feb. 14, 1916
Oct. 19, 1918
Gone but not forgotten.

Mary Belle Brookshear
Jan. 29, 1903
May 15, 1907
"Safe in the Arms of Jesus."

John Wesley Brookshire
Died Dec. 5, 1931
Aged 6? years, & 19 days

Nancy Brookshire
Died March 5, 1932
Aged 77 years & 13 days.

(Note: The last two were
undertaker markers and
name may have been spelled
incorrectly.)

WRIGHT

Dorthy Wright
Died Feb. 2, 1934
Aged 1 day

Howard Wright
Died Jan. 3, 1938
Aged 8 days

Horless Wright
Oct. 19, 1892
July 17, 1893
"At Rest."

ANDERSON

Elmer
Son of
George & Ida Anderson
July 6, 1902
Oct. 14, 1906

BINGHAM

Harriet S. Bingham
Aug. 23, 1829
Mar. 13, 1918
"Dear Mother gone but not
forgotten."

Infant
daughter of
W. B. & M. E. Bingham
Born & died
Feb. 4, 1908
"We will meet again."

Billie S
Son of
W. B. & M. E. Bingham
Feb. 19, 1894
Dec. 18, 1909
"The Lord is my light."

MELTON

Leona
Daughter of
C. E. & Callie Melton
May 6, 1904
July 3, 1915
"Darling we miss thee."

WIGGINS

George W. Wiggins
Sept. 26, 1861
Aug. 8, 1914

MONROE COUNTY

TOMBSTONE INSCRIPTIONS
VONORE SOU. M. E. CHURCH CEMETERY

WIGGINS

Maggie Wiggins
May 10, 1864
Aug. 10, 1903
"They have gone to
that home in Heaven."

Nancy
Wife of
O. H. Wiggins
Nov. 8, 1863
Feb. 28, 1912
"Gone but not forgotten."

Annie F.
Daughter of
G. W. & Maggie Wiggins
Aug. 13, 1902
Aug. 23, 1902
"Only sleeping."

COOK

In Memory of
Louisa Cook
Born 1827
Died Dec. 12, 1903
Age 77 years "
"At Rest."

CANTREE

Lillie Arp
Wife of
S. I. Cantree
Mar. 1, 1881
Jan. 19, 1920

PETTETT or PETTIT

Cecil C
Son of
Rufe & Mollie Pettett
May 29, 1908
Jan 31, 1914
"Our darling gone but
not forgotten."

Edith Aline
Daughter of
Mr. & Mrs. Oscar Pettit
Nov. 15, 1913
Oct. 31, 1916

MOSES

W. A. Moses
Age 56

To My wife
Margaret Moses
Aug. 15, 1810
Jan. 13, 1908

John Moses

KENNEDY

Dr. W. B. Kennedy
Jan. 10, 1850
Oct. 26, 1912

FAGG

Nellie
Wife of
J. W. Fagg
Feb. 11, 1865
Nov. 3, 1918
"Gone but not forgotten."

Helen
Daughter of
J. W. & N. M. Fagg
April 6, 1913
Oct. 25, 1914

HUMES

In Memory of
T. W Humes
Son of
A. & N. Humes
Nov. 1, 1900
June 16, 1901
"Our darling baby."

HITCH

Josie M.
Daughter of
J. A. & A. J. Hitch
Feb. 15, 1902
July 8, 1903
"The Angels called her."

MONROE COUNTY

TOMBSTONE INSCRIPTIONS
VONORE SOU. M. E. CHURCH CEMETERY

HITCH

(Jr. O. U. A. M. Emblem)
James A. Hitch
Nov. 16, 1848
Mar. 5, 1908
"Thy will be done."

GRIGSBY

Mrs. Thomas Grigsby
Died June 24, 1936
Aged 42 years, 10
months & 13 days

GRAYSON

John Grayson
Jan. 29, 1833
Sept. 1, 1902
"Sweet peace the gift
of God's love.

Louisa Grayson
Nov. 24, 1843
July 4, 1903
"At Rest."

WOODY

Mother
Martha J. Woody
Mar. 22, 1854
Jan. 16, 1932
"Weep not she is not
dead but sleepeth."

John Wesley Woody
July 18, 1851
March 16, 1918
"He was the sunshine of
our home."

HAMMONTREE

Mother
Mary J. Hammontree
July 2, 1849
Feb. 1, 1924

Father
Harvey A. Hammontree
Oct. 5, 1844
Dec. 23, 1916

CORPL.
Harvey A. Hammontree
Co. 1
5 Tenn. Inf.

MASON

B. A. Mason

S. O. Mason

KERR

F. L. Kerr
Oct. 11, 1868
Aug. 2, 1913
"Gone but not forgotten."

WHITE

Carles V. White
June 26, 1897
Oct. 12, 1918
Married
June 19, 1917
to Alice Cunningham

HARRIS

Johnnie E.
Daughter of
T. H. & C. H. Harris
Oct. 29, 1921
May 21, 1923

JONES

Polly Jones
1855--1920
"A tender Mother and a
true wife."

MONROE COUNTY

TOMBSTONE INSCRIPTIONS

WATKINS FARM CEMETERY

Copied by: Lawrence McConkey, Englewood, Tennessee.
Date: Jan. 6, 1939

This cemetery never has had a name, nor is it known when it
was established.   There are no dates on the field rock markers
to indciate when any of the persons buried here were born or
died.   It is thought that Mary Harris was the first person
buried in this cemetery.   She selected the place where she
wanted to be buried so probably the graveyard site was on the
Harris farm.

This cemetery is in the Notchey Creek Knobs about 6 miles South
of Madisonville on the farm of B. C. Watkins.   It is near the
Hauns old mill, now known as Watkins Mill, on the road leading
toward Tellico Plains.

There are approximately nine unmarked graves in this cemetery.

HARRIS

Mary Harris

Joseph Harris

Sarah Harris

Infant
Harris

NEWCOMBE

John Newcombe

Harriet Newcombe

PATTERSON

Infant
of
Mr. & Mrs. Robert Patterson

Infant
of
Mr. & Mrs. Robert Patterson

Infant
of
Mr. & Mrs. Robert Patterson

Copied by: Lawrence McConkey, Englewood, Tennessee.
Date:

The Webb Family Cemetery is the burial ground of the family
of Eligah (E. N.) Webb. His father is buried here but his
mother is buried at Prospect cemetery. His grandfather,
William I., and his grand mother are probably buried at
Hopewell Baptist Church Cemetery. Harrison (W. H.) Webb was
high Sheriff of the County. William Webb selected the location
for the Webb Cemetery on the Webb farm before his death and was
the first one buried here. Later his grandson, Harrison (W.H.)
owned the farm and deeded the burial plot for a graveyard. The
cemetery is about four miles East of Madisonville and can best
be reached by following the Ballplay road to the farm of
Harvey Belcher then turning right on to the road leading to
Anderson Belcher's. There are 22 inscriptions and 4 unmarked
graves.

MCCONKEY

Lora Webb
Wife of
D. W. McConkey
Nov. 29, 1896
Feb. 23, 197
Gone but not forgotten.

Infant
of
D. W. & Lora McConkey
Gone but not forgotten.

Infant
of
D. W. & Gertie McConkey
Our Darling

LAWSON

Infant
of
Mr. & Mrs. James Lawson
Our Darling.

WEBB

E. N. Webb
Mar. 7, 1837
Mar. 1, 1917

S. V. Webb
Sept. 10, 1861
Aug. 10, 1929

William Webb
Dec. 10, 1801
July 19, 1876
In God we trust.

(Member Jr. O.U.A.M.)
W. A. Webb
Dec. 25, 1895
Feb. 4, 1927

(Masonic member)
W. H. Webb
Sept. 20, 1869
Aug. 19, 1919
Gone but not forgotten.

(Note: W. H. Webb had been
High Sheriff of Monroe County.
LMcC.)

WEBB FAMILY CEMETERY

Gibbie Webb
May 18, 1905
Apr. 13, 1926
Asleep in Jesus.

Raymond Leon Webb
Died May 11, 1938
Aged 8 months 11 days.

Infant
of
Carl & Pearl Webb

Infant
of
Grant & Lillie Webb

DEWITT

H. L.
Infant of
C. H. & Etta Dewitt
Died July 30, 1927
Aged 11 months and
14 days.

Hattie Dewitt
Daughter of
Hattie & Arthur Dewitt
Died 1915
Aged about 10 years

Sallie
Daughter of
Arthur & Hattie Dewitt

Lela Dewitt
Died 1927
Aged about 19 years.

STAPP

Allie Webb
Wife of
Jess Stapp
Died Aug. -- 1933
Aged ---

Infant
of
Mr. & Mrs. Arie Stapp

Arie Stapp

C. B. Stapp
May 9, 1900
Oct. 23, 1932
Gone but not forgotten.

Infant
Stapp

WEBB FAMILY SKETCH

Three Webb brothers migrated to this Country from Ireland.
One settled in North Carolina and one in Upper East Tennessee.
Their names and exact location of settlement are unknown. The
other brother settled in Monroe County, Tennessee. His name
was William. He was the father of a son by the same name,
William. This son married and it is believed that his wife's
maiden name was Easter Matthews. William and Easter Webb were
the parents of: Thomas, William, Eligah, John, Elisha, Betty,
Millie, Huldia and Sallie. Eligah (E.N.) married Betty Duggan.
They were the parents of Doke, Ona, Allie, Hattie and Harrison.
Doke married Ella Hicks. Ona married Albert Castell. Allie
married Jess Stapp. Hattie married Arthur Dewitt. Harrison
married Arlee Dewitt. Elijah's first wife, Betty, died and he

WEBB FAMILY CEMETERY

WEBB FAMILY SKETCH

then married Samantha Ivens. (Their inscriptions on the
tombstone have initials E. N. & S. V. instead of names.) They
were the parents of: Dee, Etta, Navada, Grant, Daisy and Lara.
Dee married Gussie Tallent; Etta married Homer Dewitt; Navada
married Harvey Belcher; Grant married Lillie Tallent; Daisy
never married and Lora married Wesley McDonkey.

MONROE COUNTY

THOMAS WHITE FAMILY
TOMBSTONE INSCRIPTIONS

WHITE

Jane White
Oct. 5, 1795
June 26, 1869

Thomas White
June 26, 1799
June 7, 1876

(Masonic emblem)
E. Y. White
Mar. 1, 1830
July 5, 1900
"Gods ways are Just White."

Margaret White
June 1, 1844
May 23, 1923
"Gods ways are Just White."

CUNNINGHAM

John Cunningham
July 3, 1869
Aug. 30, 1931
"All is Well."

Annie Cunningham
Jan. 28, 1862
Nov. 5, 1890
"Blessed are the pure in
Heart for they shall see God."

Masonic emblem
James Cunningham
Mar. 21, 1866
July 8, 1912
"Blessed are the pure in
Heart for they shall see God."

(Note: The Cunninghams are
related to the Whites.)

MONROE COUNTY

TOMBSTONE INSCRIPTIONS.

WILSON-JOINES CEMETERY

Copied by: Lawrence McConkey, Englewood, Tennessee
Date: Nov. 1938

Buried in the Wilson-Joines Cemetery are members of the family
of Solomon Wilson, his descendants and their consorts; also
Isaac Wilson who was the son of John Wilson; and members of
the Reynolds family who were related to the Joines family and
not the Wilson. Jessee Wilson gave $500 in a trust fund, the
interest to be used on the up-keep of this cemetery. The location is 5 miles South of Madisonville, in front of the Chestua
Baptist Church.

There are 50 inscriptions and 2 unmarked graves.

TORBETT

William Herschel Torbett
July 15, 1936
Aged 6 mos.

STALCUP

Hattie
Daughter of
J. D. & Elizabeth Stalcup
Born July 31, 1892
Died Oct. 16, 1896
Those whom God love
die young.

REYNOLDS

Our Babyy
Infant
Daughter of
Ross B. Reynolds and wife
June 3, 1927
June 17, 1927

James T. Reynolds
Mar. 29, 1848
Nov. 3, 1917

Louise Dodson Reynolds
Aug. 28, 1849
Nov. 5, 1916
Gone but not forgotten.

ROGERS

James C. Rogers
Dec. 24, 1887
Jan. 1, 1916
Asleep in Jesus.

Hubert E. Rogers
Nov. 7, 1910
June 10, 1911

Heppie A. Wilson
Wife of
J. C. Rogers
Born Aug. 2, 1887
Died Dec. 7, 1918
At Rest.

WILSON

Solamon Wilson
Died Aug. 19, 1889
Aged 74 years.

Mary Wife of
Solomon Wilson
Died Aug. 17, 1873
Aged 62 years.

Elizabeth
Daughter of
Solomon & Mary Wilson
Born Oct. 4, 1837
Died Nov. 1, 1867

WILSON-JOINES CEMETERY

(Note: Elizabeth Wilson was the
first one buried here, and at
her request her grave is in
front of the Chestua Baptist
Church. LMcC.)

Laren
Son of
J. & H. Wilson
Born Dec. 1867
Died Nov. 1868
Aged 11 months.

Sollie
Son of
L. J. & H. M. Wilson
Born & Died
Oct. 1, 1885

Lawrence J. Wilson
Feb. 1849
Dec. 8, 1925
At Rest.

Matilda Denton
Wife of
L. J. Wilson
June 21, 1852
Nov. 20, 1889
At Rest
Father & Mother

Essie
Daughter of
J. W. & I. M. Wilson
Aug. 11, 1900
July 21, 1901

Wilson
Minervia J. Reynolds
Wife of
Jesse Wilson
Sept. 24, 1855
Sept. 17, 1921
Gone to rest.

Jesse Wilson
Born Nov. 5, 1850
Died --- ---------

Rebecca A. Wilson
Oct. 23, 1832
Apr. 18, 1917

Isaac G. Wilson
June 13, 1822
Mar. 22, 1889
Mother & Father

TOOMEY

Emma Joines
Wife of
O. A. Toomey
Nov. 1, 1873
Jan. 24, 1922
At Rest.

Ollie A. Toomey
Died July 5, 1933
Aged 62 years, 5 months
and 28 days.

Infant
of
O. A. & Emma Toomey
Of such is the Kingdom
of Heaven.

JOINES

G. F. Joines
Born Nov. 1, 1825
Died Feb. 11, 1882
(Masonic Member)
Father

Our Mother
H. C. Joines
Born Aug. 1, 1834
Departed this life
Mch. 19, 1894

Mary Allice
Daughter of
G. F. & H. C. Joines
Jan. 25, 1861
Nov. 11, 1886
Gone but not forgotten.

J. L. Joines
Born Oct. 4, 1853
Died May 10, 1907

Susie
Daughter of
John L & Mary A. Joines
Born July 11, 1888
Died July 28, 1888

WILSON-JOINES CEMETERY

Mother
Fannie Dyer
Wife of
J. L. Joines
Nov. 8, 1856
Nov. 4, 1922
Her spirit smiles from
that bright shore
and softly whispers
weep no more.

Alta May
Daughter of
J. L. & Fannie Joines
Jan. 9, 1895
Feb. 7, 1897
She was the sunshine
of our home.

Kattie
Daughter of
J. L. & Fannie Joines
May 21, 1892
Sept. 4, 1892

Carrie
Daughter of
J. L. & Fannie Joines
Sept. 10, 1896
Oct. 414, 1896
Of such is the
Kingdom of Heaven.

Bennie
Son of
J. L. & M. A. Joines
Jan. 16, 1879
Aug. 31, 1880
Our darling gone to
rest in Heaven.

Mary A.
Wife of
John L. Joines
Daughter of
H. C. & Elizabeth Reynolds
May 7, 1854
July 20, 1888

William N. Joines
Aug. 2, 1856
Apr. 28, 1929

His wife
Huretta C. McCaslin
Feb. 8, 1858
June 8, 1910

Our Darling
Emma Sue
Daughter of
Ott & Clara Joines
May 18, 1916
June 29, 1920
We miss you.

Hugh D. Joines
May 31, 1876
Dec. 18, 1932

His wife
Ella Joines
Jan. 21, 1882
July 22, 1937
I'll be looking for
you.

George Hugh
Son of
Mr. & Mrs. Clyde Joines
Nov. 30, 1935
Jan. 1, 1936
Budded on earth to
bloom in Heaven.

Hazel I.
Daughter of
J. W. & J. C. Joines
Apr. 7, 1907
May 12, 1907
Budded on earth to
bloom in Heaven

Nellie May Joines
Born Sept. 4, 1904
Died Sep. 11, 1904
Budded on earth to
bloom in Heaven.

Infant
Son of
Mr. & Mrs. H. D. Joines
March 16, 1916

WILSON-JOINES CEMETERY

Infant
Son of
Mr. & Mrs. H. D. Joines
June 9, 1921

C. W. Joines
Oct. 4, 1858
Dec. 21, 1892

M. E. Joines
Oct. 26, 1862
Aug. 3, 1991
Charles W. Joines
        and
Martha E. McDonald
were married
Oct. 19, 1886
They steered their
course to the same
quiet shore, not parted
long and now to part
no more.

Father
At Rest
H. C. Joines
May 1, 1877
Oct. 31, 1921
Gone but not forgotten.

Ralph
Son of
H. C. & Verra Joines
Mar. 10, 1906
Oct. 5, 1910

RAPER

Maude Joines
Wife of
C. D. Raper
Daughter of
J. L. & Fannie Joines

WEBB

Infant
of
Wm. & Inez Wilson Webb
        1927

FAMILY SKETCH

John Wilson of Washington Co., in or about the year 1838,
brought six of his sons Solomon, John, Elijah, Charles and
David Lawrence, to Monroe Co., and George to McMinn Co., and
bought them large farms. Solomon Wilson married Mary Glaze
before leaving Washington Co. Their children's names and who
they married are as follows: Hannah, married Gabriel (G.H.)
Joines; Eliza, married Robert Patty; Elizabeth never married;
Isaac, married --------, lived in the West; John, married -----;
Charles married, went West; George, married Nealy Taylor. She
died and he married Callie Cobble; Lawrence, married Matilda
Denton; Jessee, married Manervia Reynolds; Richard (Dick) married
Susie Reynolds. As above stated, Hannah Wilson married Gabriel
(G.H.) Joines. Their children's names and who they married are
as follows: Johnnie married Mary Reynolds. She died then he
married Fannie Dyer; Will married Huretta McCaslin; Charles married
Ellen McDonald; Hugh, married Ella Maxwell; Allice, never married;
Elizabeth, (Lizzie), married Jess D. Stalcup; Tezzie, married
Will Lee; Ida, married Robert Cochran; Emma, married Ollie A.
Toomey. Sherman's Army on its March through the South destroyed
a large amount of timber and also took or destroyed much personal
property of Solomon Wilson.

HENSON F., 18
RANSEY, 18

-A-

ABERNATHY
B.M., 46
BONNIE, 105
C.H., 46
FLOYD, 46
J.L., 105
M.A., 105
MYRA J., 46
POLLIE BARNET, 46
R.P., REV., 46
ADAMS
MAUD ILENE, 284
WASH, 262
ADKINS
EARNEST E., 156
ED., 156
JOHN, 154
M.L., 156
POLLIE, 154
AKINS
A.L., 225
B--- ----, 156
C., 225
CHARLIE, 156
CLERSA, 225
ED, 156(3)
FLOYD, 74
FRED, 172
H.N., 172
HENRY, 172(2)
INFANT, 156
INFANT DAUGHTER,
156
J--- B---, 156
J.H., 202
JOHNFANT, 156
L.C., 202
LIDA OLEY, 172
M.L., 156(2)
MARGARET L., 156
MARY NEAL, 73
MOLLY, 172
URMA, 82
VENIA, 172
VIRDA, 225
ALABAMA
DECATUR, 86
LOWNDESBORO, 159

ALEXANDER
DELIE S., 304
NELSON, 304

ALLEN
ALICE, 8
CHARLIE, 8
DOROTHY ANN, 258
INFANT SON, 39
J.C., 39
J.R., 8
ALLISON
---, 2
E.P., 1
ELIZABETH, 2
JESSEE, 2
LOWERY, 2
POLENIA, 2
SUSAN JANE, 2
W.D., 1(2), 2
W.P. REV., 1
W.P., REV., 2
WILLIAM D, 1
ALLMAN
FAY, 236
ALMON
JOE CLYDE, 236
AMMONS
GEORGE, 53
JANE, 53
ANDERSON
ELMER, 337
EMMA, 86
FRANCIS PAUL, 299
GEORGE, 337
IDA, 337
M., 299
MINNIE CAROLINE, 284
MOLLIE, 289
W.P., 299
WM., 123
ARDEN
FRANK, 205
FRED H., 48
G.W., 181(4)
INFANT DAUGHTER,
181
JOHN, 181
JULIA, 181
MAMIE, 181
MARGARET, 48
MOLLIE, 181
NANNIE, 205
NOAH J., 181
S.C., 181(3)
SAM, 48
SUSIE, 181
ARIZONA
SUMMERTON, 86
ARK
INFANT, 126
ARNOLD
BELLE LONG, 159
GEORGE, 159
GEORGE E., 241

JUNIOR RAY, 241
PAUL, 159
PAULINE, 159(2)
REV., 159
ARP
AUSTRIA, 49
BETTIE, 323
D.L., 49(2)
ESQ., 49(2)
LILLIE, 338
LONEY, 49
ROY, 309
SQUARE G., 49
ARRANTS
JACOB, 29
POLLY, 29
ASHE
LONESOME S., MRS.,
312
ASHER
RACHEL, 123
ATKINS
ALEX SANDERS, 240
ALICE, 204
ANDY, 200(2)
ANNIE, 200
CALLIE McCLELLAN,
239
CARL, 200
CAROLINE, 200
CORA, 200
DOLLIE WATSON, 200
ELIGAH, 200(2)
FANNIE, 241
HORACE, REV., 81
INFANT, 200(2)
INFANT DAUGHTER,
200
INFANT SON, 200
J.E., 200
J.M., 240(2)
J.N., 200(2), 201
J.W., 200
JAMES N., 240
JOE, 200
JOHN, 200, 239
JURETTA TALLENT, 200
LUDA, 200
LUDA ERVIN, 201
M.E., 200
M.J., 200
NANCY JANE, 77
R.B., 240
R.W., 200
ROBERT, 200
SARAH, 200
T.R., 200
THOMAS, 200
THOMAS R., 200
W.L., 240
WILLARD, 200

WILLIE, 200
WORTH, 201(2)
ATLEE
ELIZABETH, 158
AVANS
ELISABETH, 13
I.A., 4
INFANT SON, 4
J.P., 4, 5
S.E., 4
AXLEY
A.L., MRS., 325
BRUNER, 132
E.J., 85(2)
HENRY MAYER, 85
INFANT DAUGHTER, 85
JAMES, 282(2)
S.D., 85(2)

-B-

BACON
JAMES L., 136
JAMES L., MRS., 136
JAMES LYDALL, 137
NATHANIEL L., 136
NONA E., 136
ROSA H., 136
BAILEY
CHARLES M., 124(2)
GEORGE W., 124(2)
JAMES H., 123(2)
JAMES M., 124(2)
LILLIE, 238
LUCILE INMAN, 238
MINNIE E., 124(2)
MYRTLE Q., 124(2)
NANCY O., 124(2)
SARAH, 123
WALTER R., 124(2)
BAKER
G.W., 95
JAMES HARVEY, 95
JULIA, 95
LOUISE, 95
THOMAS, 273
BALL
BEATRICE, 203
BERNARD ISHAM, 202
C.W., 203
CORNELLIUS, 202
DOLLIE, 37
H., 202
HENRY, 202
I.E., 203
INFANT, 202(5)
ISAAC, 202(2)
ISHAM, 203
J.D., 202(3)
J.H., 37
JOHN E., 203

MOLLIE, 202
NANIE, 202(3)
BALLARD
    CALLIE S., 217
    M.R., 217
    W.L., 217
BARB
    J.C., REV., 247
BAREFIELD
    AMOS, 269
    COLONEL J., 269
    ETHELLEAN, 269
    J.B., 269
    J.S., 269
    LINA, 269
    M.L.J., 269
    THOMAS, 269
BARNARD
    J.H., 50
BARNEL
    EULA, 159
BARNETT
    J.M., 59
    J.R., 316
    OCIE, 160
    RACHEL, 148, 150
BARNNARD
    W.L., 306
BARR
    ADAM, 35
    ELIZABETH LOWRY, 35
    LOUVENIA, 35
BARRETT
    G.W., 307
    L.E., 307
    U.W., 307
BATES
    CLIF, 93
    CYNTHA, 94
    E.M., 94
    INFANT SON, 313
    MAMIE, 313
    O.S., 93
    ROBERT, 313
BEALS
    MARY, 13
BEAVERS
    ALICE, 312
    JOE, 312
BEIGHTOE
    H.E., 304
    H.L., 304
    INFANT SON, 304
BELCHER
    A.R., 173
    A.S., 8
    ALEX, 334
    ALEX., 200
    ANDERSON, 341
    BERNICE, 242
    BEUNA, 205

CHARLIE, 204
CLARASA E., 8
DANUL LAFAYETT, 8
H.A., 173
HARVEY, 341, 343
HORACE RAY, 334
J.A., 242
J.B., 204
J.H., 205(2)
LILLARD, 334
M., 205
M.C., 334(2)
M.J., 173
MOLIE ANGELINE, 8
MOLLIE, 205
NANCY, 204
TILDA, 334
TILDIA, 200
BELL
    DORTHY C., 305
    EMELINE, 305
    FRANK B., 160
    JOHN, 305(2)
    MARY JEAN, 160
    NANCY, 160
    NELLIE, 124
    WASH, 225
BENINE
    ELIZA, 38
    J.L., 38
    JOSEPH, 38
BENTON
    —, 159
BERRY
    JOSEPH W., 333
    MELTON, 73
    OPLINA, 73
    W.A., 333
BEST
    BETTIE, 294
    CARRIE JANE, 293
    CLARA, 294
    ELIZABETH, 294
    GEARLDINE, 293
    HENRY, 293
    INFANT, 293
    JAMES ERNEST, 293
    JOHN, 298
    JOHN C., 294
    JOHN, REV., 293
    KATHRINE, 294(2)
    MARGARET, 298
    MARTHA, 298
    MARTHA J., 293
    RENA, 296
    S.F., 293(3)
    SARAH, 293
    SINA, 294
    SITIA, 293
    W.L., 293(3)
    WILL, 293

WILLIAM, 294
BETIFISH
    S.F., 86
BIBEE
    ANNIE, 206
    DORTHEY E., 203
    PLEASIE, 203
    R.B., 203(2)
    R.E., 203
BILLINGSLEY
    B.F., 162
    JOHN F., 221
    MARGARET L.H., 162
    MARY E., 221
BINGHAM
    BILLIE S., 337
    HARRIET S., 337
    INFANT DAUGHTER,
        337
    M.E., 337(2)
    MARTHA, 317
    W.B., 337(2)
BIRCHFIELD
    HENRY, 252
    J.B., 304
    LOYD, 304
    WILLA REE, 304
BIVANS
    E.C., 42
    S.E., 42
BIVENS
    B.F., 153
    INFANT, 153
    INFANT SON, 153
    JOE, 153
    MARY ETTA, 283
    MILLIE, 153
    NANCY D., 153
    PINK, 153(2)
    SALLIE, 153(2)
BIVINS
    JAMES, 298
    MARGARET GILES, 298
BLACK
    A.L., 216
    A.M., 312
    ANNIE L., 216
    CHARLES, 103
    ESSIE, 103(2)
    G.W., 103
    INFANT DAUGHTER,
        216, 312
    J.M., 312
    JAMES M., 114
    LAURA ETHEL, 103
    MARY P., 114
    S.N., 103(2)
    W.E., 103
    W.T., 216
    WILLIAM T., 216

BLACKMAN
    CALLIE, 19
    ELECTA, 19(2)
    LOU EMMA, 19
    LUTHER M., 19(2)
    MARGARET, 19
    MOLLIE, 19
    NEWLAND, 19(2)
    WILLIAM D., 19
    WILLIAM D., J.P., 19
BLACKWELL
    A.M., 310
    MAYDELL, 310(2)
BLAIR
    ALBION, 160
    BEN C., 160
    BETTY CATHERINE, 160
    CARROLL K., 160
    CHARLES L., 71
    CHARLIE, 71
    ELIZABETH FRANCES
        LONG, 160
    FLORA, 160
    GILFORD, 115
    INFANT SON, 116
    J.T., 20(2), 21(2)
    JOE, 21
    JOHN, 20
    JOHN J., JUDGE, 20
    JOHN R., 116
    JOHN, JUDGE, 128
    JOSEPH, 114
    LAURA, 21
    LAURA E., 315
    LILLIE, 71
    MAHALA, 326(2), 328
    MARTHA W., 21
    MARY SNEED, 23
    MATTIE J., 116
    O.P., 116
    SARRAH, 115
    WILLIAM, 21
    WILLIAM B., 159, 160
    WILLIAM S., 328
    WM. S., 326(2), 328
BLANKENSHIP
    BERTHA A., 58
    I.E., 58(3)
    M.E., 58(3)
    MARGARET, 58
    NANCY E., 58
    T.E., 58
BLANTON
    ETHEL, 267
    J.B., 267
    N.J., 267
BLUFORD
    ANDERSON, MRS., 331
    JAMES, 331(2)
    SARAH C., 331
BOATMAN

AMOS, 211
ELLEN, 294
J.S., 294
THURMAN, 294
BOGART
JOHN T., 211
BOGGESS
—, 159
FRANK, 160
MARY LEE, 160
NANNIE SHUGART, 160

WILLIE, 160
BOLIX
W.E., MRS., 170
BOLTON
OSCAR, 122
BOOKOUT
DAVID, 210(2)
BORDEN
A.R., 327
ANNA REBA, 179
ARTHUR, 163
INFANT SON, 327
LUCY, 327
SAM, 325
BORIN
A., 258
E.J., 258
E.W., 258
EMMA, 258
J.A., 258
JOHN M., 258
MATTIE A., 258
NICK, 258
BORING
JACOB, 259
JOHN, 258
JOHN D., 259
MARY E., 259
MARY J., 259
SARAH A., 258
BOSWELL
ELIZABETH, 77
BOWERS
A.M., 96
E.M., 96
ELIZA, 286
J., 328
NELSON, 286
BOWMAN
—, 227
A.M., 227(2)
L.A., 227
BOYD
ERBY, 27
JESSEE, REV., 111
JINSEY, 27
JOSEPH, 87, 95(3),
112
JOSEPH C., MAJOR, 95

JOSEPH, C., MAJOR,
95
JOSEPH, COL., 87,
112(3)
MARGARET, 87, 95(2)
THOMAS M., 87, 95
BOYLSTON
C.M., 218
LINNIE BELLE, 218
T.A., 218
BRACKETT
F.P., 190
HORACE N., 190
JOHN W., 190
L.A., 153
N.D., 190
SARAH, 190
T.G., 190
BRADEN
—, 123
BRADLEY
ELIZABETH, 189
JAMES, 189(2)
JOHN A., 70
KENNETH, 103
LAFAYETTE, 189(2)
VINIE, 189
BRADSHAW
—, 113
J.R., 113
JOHN, REV., 113
BRAKEBILL
ETHEL L., 334
J.E., 253
MARTHA, 253
MILBURN C., 328
SARAH ISABELLE, 253
BRANNON
ANNIE, 332(2)
BETTIE, 108(3)
ELIHU, 108
F., 332
FRANCES, 108
G.A., 332
I.A., 332(2)
INFANT DAUGHTER,
332
JAMES, 108(5)
JOE REED, 332
LEE, MRS., 108
M.A., 332
MATTIE LEE, 332
OPAL, 108(2)
TINEY, 108
BRAY
CATHERINE, 238
CHARLES, 238
CHARLES F., 237
LOIS LEE, 237
WILLIE, 238
BREEDEN

A.B., 159
CARROLL C., 160
CARROLL, JR., 160
EDNA, 160
FRANK, 160
GEORGE, 160
HENRY, 168
JOHN, 9(2)
KATE, 160
KATHERINE, 160
MARY LOUISA LONG,

160
NANCY C., 9(2)
PAUL, 160
SAM, 160
BREWER
JOSEPH, 221(2)
KATHERINE WYETT,
221
M.R., 221
M.T., 221
MARY ALICE, 221
BRIDGE
LINDSEY, 148
SINK CREEK, 24
BRIENT
N.C. ANNA BELL, 262
BRIGHT
C.C., 179
E.M., 179
ESEYBEL, 153
GENEVA REE, 179
H.E., 179
HATTIE, 179
INEY MAY, 179
J.H., 179(3)
J.L., 179
JOHN, 148
JOSIE, 179
L.L., 179
MYRTIS, 179
NANCY A., 179
NETTIE, 153
W.C., 179
W.J., 179
W.L., 179(2)
WORTH, 179
BRITTON
BELLE, 54
CHARLIES C., 54
G.W., 54
JAMES, JR., 309
REED VERLIN, 309
BROOKS
D.C., 49
D.E., 190
DAVID, 33
DELENA E., 190
DORA, 48
EMMALINE, 299

FLOYD, 49
HIRAM, 299
INFANT, 190
J.A., 299
J.F., 190
J.J., 299
S.L., 49
WILLIAM, 299
BROOKSHEAR
A.W., 337
BIRDIE, 337
FINLEY ROSS, 337
MARY BELLE, 337
BROOKSHIRE
JOHN WESLEY, 337
NANCY, 337
BROOM
ZEBBIE FRANCIS, 211
BROTHERS
SWAINSON, 302
BROWDER
FANNIE, 85
MATILDA JANE, 221
BROWN
—, 158
BERLIN W., 306
BERLIN WESLEY,
SERGT., 306
HARRISON, 186
HENRY, 274
JAMES, 246, 274
JOE, 26
JOSEPH, 190
NARCISSAS, 306
PLEASANT, 66
SARAH, 190, 246
VESTA, 306
ZENES, 306
BROWNLOW
WM. G., 112
WM. G., REV, 112
WM. G., REV., 87
BRUNER
BILLY L., 6
MARGARET JOAN, 6

BRUNNER
T.W., 86
BRUSTER
ALICE, 53
W.J., 53
BRYANT
MARY, 319
BRYSON
A.L., 59(2)
BESSIE, 92
INFANT, 59(2)
J.H., 190
M.L., 59(2)
MARY —, 190
NERVEY E., 190

WILLIAM J., 59
BUCKNER
  AMANDA, 228
  CORDELIA, 228
  DELIA, 228
  GEO., 228
  HENRY, 228
  HORACE, 228
  INFANT, 244(2)
  JANE, 228
  RUBY, 244
BURCH
  AUGUSTA LOU IDA, 29

  ETTA, 29
  J.B., 29
BURCHFIELD
  CECIL M. AKINS, 82
  EDD, 186
  ELISABETH, 148
  EVALENER, 126
  GEORGIE, 304
  INFANT, 186
  J.M., 126
  J.R., 126
  LEVIND, 126
  ODIS N., 186
  ROBERT C., 186
  ROBERT, MRS., 134
  V.W., 82
  W.E., 304
BURGER
  ELSIE, 102
  INFANT, 102(2)
  J.H.L., 90, 102
  J.L., 102(3)
  JOHN, 102, 112
  JOHN, REV., 101
  JOHN, SR., REV., 87,
    101
  KATHLEEN, 102
  LUCIOUS C., 306
  MARTHA EMALINE, 101

  MARY, 101
  TABITHA, 102(3)
  W.N., 306
BURGESS
  SAMUEL LUTHER, 311

BURGIN
  JOHN, 335
BURK
  INFANT, 12
  JAMES, 12
  JANE, 12
  V.B., 12(2)
BURLESON
  JOSIE, 234
BURNETT
  F., 162

JJ., 213
JACK, 310
MARY, 310
S.F., 162
WILLIE, 310
BURNS
  LUCY A., 221
BURRELL
  JOHN, 29
BURRIS
  M.M., 292
BURTON
  ALICE M., 251
  DAVE M., 32
  DAVID, 251
  ELBERT W., 32
  HENRY N., 31
  HENRY P., 31
  INFANT DAUGHTER, 31

  J.M., 31(4), 32
  JACK, 32
  JAMES MADISON, 31(2)

  JANE, 31
  JOSEPH, 32(2)
  LUCY, 31
  M.J., 31
  M.M., 31
  MAGGIE, 31
  MARY JANE, 31
  MILDRED, 31
  NANCY, 31
  NANCY J., 31, 32
  NELLIE, 178
  R., 31
  ROBERT, 31(2)
  S., 31, 32
  SARAH, 31
  W.P., 31
  WILLIAM P., 31(2)
BUTLER
  A.D., 69
  ALICE, 69
  B.T., 69
  N.J., 69
  NELIE, 69
  WILLIE, 69
  WM., 69
BYERS
  —, 68
  C.L., 68
  HAYNES, 68(2)
  LEE, 68
  RUTHEY, 68
  WILLIAM DAVID, 68
BYOTT
  W.W., REV., 112
BYRUM
  —, 300
  JOEL, 220

JOHN J., 220
MARTHA, 220
MARY J., 220

-C-

CABLE
  JAMES, 302
  JAMES ARTHUR, 312
  NANCY, 194
CAGLE
  —, 10
  ALVIN WALTER, 10
  AMANDA ROGERS, 284

  AMY JANETTE, 10
  ARGIN, 10
  BLANCHE, 10
  BLANCHE ELISABETH,

    10
  BRUSCILLA, 291
  E., 10
  ELIJAH, 3, 10(3)
  IDA, 10
  JANE, 10
  MARTHA A., 10
  MARTIN, 10
  ROBERT, 10
  ROBERT N., 10, 12,
    13
  ROBT. N., 3, 9, 14
  SUSIE, 10
  W.H., 10
CAIN
  ANDREW H., 28
  C.A., 28
  E.K., 28
  ELIZABETH, 28
  ELVIRA K., 28
  GEORGE, 28
  HENRY, 28
  INFANT, 28(2)
  JACOB, 28
  JOHN, 28
  JOHN, MRS., 28
  MARTHA, 28
  S.P., 28(2)
  SUSAN A. ALLISON, 2
  WM. R., 2
CALIFORNIA
  LOS ANGELES, 160
  PORTERSVILLE, 86
  RICHMOND, 86
  SAN FRANCISCO, 163
CALLAM
  POLLEY, 227
  POLLY, 226
CAMPBELL
  COLEMAN, REV., 112
  J.S., 14

M., 14
M.R., 14
CANDLER
  JOHN C., 282, 284
CANE
  CORA BELL, 227
  E.K., 227
  ELIZABETH, 227
  JACOB, 227(2)
  JAMES, 227(2)
  MARY JANE, 227
  TEMPY, 227(2)
  W. CHARLES, 227
CANNON
  ADDIE RAY, 324
  CHAS., 214(2)
  J.B., 214
  L.C., 214
  SALLIE, 65
CANSLER
  MARY, 58
CANTREE
  S.I., 338
CANTRELL
  DAVID, 157
  H.D., 233
  JOE, 233
  M.M., 233
  M.M., MRS., 233
  MARY, 279
  SIMON, 25
CANUP
  J.T., 25(2)
  MARY E., 25(2)
  OLLIE, 25
CAPPINGER
  EDITH LUCIEA, 74
  GEO, 74
  MARY, 74
CARDEN
  AMOS R., 93
  ELBERT, 93
  ESAU, 111
  FAYETT, 267
  GRACIE, 93
  INFANT SON, 93
  J.B., 93
  J.M., 93
  J.R., 93
  JOE, 93
  JORDAN, 93
  L., 266
  MAGGIE, 93
  POLLY, 92
  SARAH, 267
  W.J., 92
CARDIN
  ALEX, 228
  ALEXANDER, 92
  AMERICA, 93
  CHARLES C., 228

19, 57, 62
OLD SWEETWATER, 66,

213
OLD SWEETWATER

BAPTIST, 213
PRESBYTERIAN, 275
PROSPECT BAPTIST,
230
PROSPECT
MADISONVILLE, 66
REEDS SPRINGS
BAPTIST, 235
ROCKY SPRINGS
BAPTIST, 230,
239(2)
RURAL VALE, 243
SHADY GROVE, 146
SHADY GROVE
BAPTIST,
258
SINK PRESBYTERIAN,

275
SOUTHERN
METHODIST,
162
ST. PAUL EVAN.
LUTHERAN, 247
ST. PAUL LUTHERAN,

254
SWEETWATER, 66
TELLICO BAPTIST, 166
TELLICO PLAINS
BAPTIST, 302
UNICOI BAPTIST, 318
UNION HALL
PRESBYTERIAN, 320
VONORE SOUTHERN

METHODIST, 326
CLARK
ALEEN, 86
ARTHUR, 86
BRYAN, 160
CLIFFORD, 86
CORNELIA THOMAS,
114
ERNEST, 86
ETHEL, 86
EUGENE, 86
HELEN, 86
J.D., 86(2)
J.F., 114
JAMES F., 114
MORRIS, 86
OSCAR M., 86(2)
OWEN, 86
RICHARD, 86

SADIE, 86
WALTER, 86
CLAYTON
FRANK, 234
MARGARET, 234
CLEMMER
BEN, 117
CLINTON M., 57
DOROTHY E., 117
FINIS H., 57
FLOID M., 58
G.S., 58
GRATUS DALE, 332
H.H., 57(2), 58
HANNAH, 58
HUGH, 57
I.E., 58
J.E., 332
JAMES E., 58
JAMES I., 254
JOHN, 57, 58
JOHN F., 58
JULIA A., 58
M.A., 58
M.M., 57(2), 58
MARY E., 58
P.P., 332
S.J., 58
WM., 58
CLEVELAND
A.M., 216
ALEY M., 215
ALIE, 213, 216
BENJ., COL., 222
D.H., 214(2), 215
E.A., 215(2)
ELI, 216, 222(2)
ELI NELSON, 215
ELI, REV., 213(3),
214
ELIZABETH, 216
ELIZABETH A., 214
H.H., 216
J.F., 215
JOHN SHEARMAN, 214

LOUIS J., 215
M.N., 214
MARTHA ANN, 215
POLLY, 214, 216(2)
PRESLEY, 216
R.R., 214
ROBERT R., 214
ROBERT, CAPT., 222
S.H., 215
WM., 216
CLICK
CATHERINE, 59
MARTHA E., 59
NANCY C., 59
W.M., 59

CLINE
A.B., 286
A.D., 286
CARRA, 184
CARRIE, 286
E.M., 270(3)
ELIZABETH, 270
ELIZABETH M., 269
HENRY, 270
J.E., 286
J.L., 329
J.S., 270(3)
JAMES A., 270
JAMES S., PROF., 269
LEE, 286
LENORA ARISTA, 269
REUBEN, 270
VIOLA, 286
VIRA, 286
WILLIE, 286
CLONINGER
CATHARINE, 253
J.W., 253
JACOB, 253
JOHN W., 253
MARGARET E., 253
CLOWERS
ELISHA T., 138(2)
JAMES, 58
MARTHA, 58
COBBLE
CALLIE, 348
COCHRAN
JANE, 62, 63
JOHN, 62, 63
MARTHA E., 64
R.L., 62, 64(2)
ROBERT, 348
COFFEY
JOHN G., 244
COLE
A.S., 242
COLEMAN
ESTELL E., 224, 225
FREDRICK MILLS, 241
J., MRS., 300
J.A., 174, 224, 225
J.C., 300
JESSE, 174
JESSIE ANDERSON, 225

JOHN B., 241
JOHN W., 174
L.A., 174
L.E., 224, 225
W.A., 241
WALTER, 300
COLLAKE
ANNIE, 11
C.V., 105
INFANT, 104(2)

J.C., 104(2)
M.M., 104(2)
COLLAQUE
CHARLES, 105
CRAWFORD, 112
HARVEY, 105
JOHN W., 105
JOSEPH S., 105
SALLIE, 105
SARAH JANE, 105
COLLEGE
CARSON, 146(2)
HIWASSEE, 31, 62,
138, 162, 163,
235
METHODIST, 146
MOSSY CREEK, 146
COLLINS
J.E., 314
J.H., 314(2)
COLORADO
COLORADO SPRINGS,

121
COLTHARP
ELSIE S., 37
JOHN, 35
COLTHORP
A.J., 41
A.L., 41(2)
ADA E., 41
ADDIE L., 42
ALVA M., 41
ARA M., 44
CAROLINE E., 41
CORNELIA, 41
ESTHER A. LEE, 41
G.H., 41(2), 42(3)
GEORGE HAMNER, 42

HENRY H., 41
HUGHIE H., 41
INFANT, 42
J.H., 41(2)
JANE C., 41
JOANAH B., 42
JOHN, 41(2)
M.A., 42(3)
M.J., 41
MAGGIE J., 41
MARTHA A., 42
NELLIE L., 42
O.H., 44
S.J., 41
SUSANNA, 41
W.D., 42
COMBS
M.E., 308
RUBY L., 308
T.C., 308
COMMUNITY

S.E., 207
VIOLA, 207
WALTER, 308
WILLIAM, 207
CROW
LENA E., 315
W.T., 315
CROWDER
— F., 80
A.D., 6(2), 7
A.O., 80(2), 231
AMANDA, 7
ARRIE, 6
ATLES O., 80
BERTHA, 7
C.A., 7
DANIEL B., 80
E., 187
EARL, 7
ELISEBETH, 300
ELLIE, 7
ETTA, 7
FREDDIE, 6
INFANT, 187
J., 187
J.A., 7
J.E., 231
J.R., 6(2), 7(2)
J.T., 231(2)
JOHN, 61
JOHN, MRS., 61
M.C., 7
M.D., 6(3)
M.L., 231
MARGARET, 320
N.C., 80(3)
NEAL C., 7(2)
RACHEL, 231
ROBERT A., 6
S., 232
SUSAN A., 6
TEMSY, 80
THOMAS, 7
W.C., 7
W.J., 6(3)
WILLIAM E., 6
CROWE
MARIE, 314
WILLIAM THOMAS, 314

CUNNINGHAM
A., 268
ADALINE, 268
ALICE, 339
ANNIE, 344
C.C., 245(2)
D., 268
D.B., REV., 54
DAVID, 268
EARL W., 268
JAMES, 344

JOHN, 245, 344
JOSEPH, 257(2)
M., 268
M.C., 268
MAHALA C., 268
MARY, 54
MARY RUSSELL, 245
PHOEBE, 257
ROBERT, 268
RUTHA, 268
CURD
RICHARD, 277
CURTIS
A.G., 313
BURT, 79(2)
E.J., 17
ELLA, 187(2)
EMMA E., 264(2)
F.C., 187
FABER R., 324
G.W., 16
GENIS, 187
GLIAN, 313
HARLESS, 264
INES, 187
ISAAC, 187
J.A., 313
J.H., 17
J.R., 264
JENNIE, 187
JOHN, 187
JOSEPH, 17
LIZZIE B., 187
LONNA V., 264
MAMIE, 16
MATTIE, 264
MINNIE, 16
NANNIE, 16
R.F., 187(2)
RILEY, 79(2)
T.J., 264(2)
THOMAS, 264
WILLIAM GARRETT, 187

WINCE, 187

-D-

DAILEY
C.W., 203
CARRIE MAE, 203
JOHN R., 17(2)
LENA MERELE, 203
SENIA, 17
DALE
M.E., 287(2)
VIRGIL A., 287
W.M., 287(3)
DANIEL
JAMES NEWTON, 94
LILLY GERTRUDE, 94

MARY, 94
DARNES
J.G., 26
MARY ANN, 26
DAUGHERTY
ALEX., 260, 261
ALEXANDER, 261
BETTIE, 260
BRAZEAL, 260
CARRIE, 261
ELIZA, 260
JOHN, 260(2)
KATE, 261
LINDA, 260
MARGRET, 260
NANCY J., 261
NANNIE, 260
RALPH, 260(2)
S.C., 261
SALLIE, 260
SPICIE G., 260
SPICY C., 261
SUSAN CORDELIA, 260

T.A., 261
W.A., 279
WILLIAM, 260
DAVENPORT
CLARENCE, 315
DAVIS
ANDREW, 284
BEN, 165
C.R., 251, 254
ETHEL, 57
HUGH, 121
J.C., 51
J.L., 319
JACOB N., 57
JENNIE, 51
JOHN, 167
JOSEPH C., 57
LAURA ELSIE, 57
LORENZO, 57(2)
LUTHER ERNEST, 57
MARGARETT D., 251
MARY JOSEPHINE, 57

MARY M., 57
N.J., 57
NELLIE LOUISE, 251
NORA ISABELLE, 251
O.R., 57
PETER, 91(2)
PETER, JR., 91(2)
PETER, PVT., 87
PLEAS, 121(3)
ROBERT R., 324
SARAH, 121(2)
SUSAN, 57
W.A., 11

W.E., 57
WALTER C., REV., 254
WILLIAM, 57, 121
WM. E., 57
WM. HENRY, 251
DAWSON
BETTY E., 330
HENRY F., 330
LAVENIA TIPTON, 330
MARY M., 330
WILLIAM H., 326(2),
330
DEAN
BOYD, 155
BRUCE, 155
DAVID, DR., 264
INFANT, 155
J.J., 155
L.Z., 155
VINSON, 155
WATTACE, 155
WAYNE, 155
DELASHMITT
ISAIAH, 249
DENNEDY
C.A., 185
DENTON
A., 21(3)
ALPHERD, 61
AMANDA, 21, 44
AMANDA C.L., 21
ANNIE, 33
CALVIN, 21
DAPCUS, 61
ELIZABETH, 21
FRANCIS A., 21
GEORGE, 13
JOHN, 232
JOSEPH, 44
MARY, 21
MATILDA, 348
PATTON L., 21
WILLIAM, 21
WM., 21(4)
DEVINE
CLIFFORD, 156
THOMAS L., 186
DEWITT
ARLEE, 342
ARTHUR, 342(3)
C.H., 342
ETTA, 342
H.L., 342
HATTIE, 342(3)
HOMER, 343
LELA, 342
SALLIE, 342
DIAL
—, 10
DILLS
ALLIE, 180

JAMES LEE, REV., 180
DISHROON
    HANNAH, 103
DITMORE
    H.M., 333
    VIVIE, 103
DIVINE
    A., 14
    E.V., 14
    J.L., 14
    JOSEPH, 13, 14
    JOSEPH M., 13
    M., 14
    MATILDA, 13
    R.R., 14
    THOMAS, 3, 13(2)
    W., 14
    W.H., 13
DOCKERY
    MARY, 138
DOCKREY
    NOAH, 171
    REBECCA J., 171
DONOHOO
    MATTIE A., 139, 140
DOTSON
    A.J., 48(3)
    A.N., 47
    ANDREW, 47
    ANNA, 47
    ARENIE, 47
    B.D., 47
    BOYD, 47
    CLIFFORD R., 48
    FLOYD, 47
    IKE, 182
    INFANT DAUGHTER,
182
    J.E., 182
    J.F., 47(2)
    JAMES A., 48
    JOHN, 48(2)
    JULIA ANN, 182
    LAURA, 47(2), 48
    LONEY, 48
    LUDIE, 182
    LUTHER, 48
    M., 47
    M.D., 47
    MARTHA, 48
    N.A., 48(2)
    TALAR, 47
    W.T., 182
DOYLE
    JACOB, 5, 6, 17
    JAKIE, 5
    M.S.C., 16
    SALLIE J., 6(2)
DUCKETT
    ADRA, 170
    ANDERSON, 170

ARIZONIA, 169
D.M., 169
ELIZABETH, 273
FANNIE, 169
IDA, 30
INFANT, 169
J.J., 169(2), 273
JESSIE, 169
JOHN, 169
L.A., 30
M.E., 169(2)
M.H., 170
ROBERT C., 169
SARAH, 169(2)
SINTHA J., 169
W.J., 169
DUGGAN
    BETTY, 342
    D.B., 229
    GEORGE, 229
    GRACE E., 109
    HENRY, 267
    HUGH, 83
    INFANT, 83(4)
    J.A., 207
    J.C., 83(4)
    M.R., 229
    MARGARET, 83
    MATILDA, 83
    S.L., 83
    SARAH, 83
    W.H.H., REV., 112
    W.H.L., 267
    W.H.L., MRS., 267
    WM., 83(4)
DULIN
    MARTHA, 168(2)
DUN
    ARCH, 188
    JANE, 188
DUNKIN
    A.C., 49
    INFANT, 49
    J.B., 49
    J.I., 49
    J I., 49
    J.W., 49
    JOHN L., 49
    MODENA, 49
    NOAH, 50
    OLLIE, 50
    TINIE, 49
DUNN
    ARCH, 188
    ELLA, 158
DURHAM
    —, 159(2)
DYE
    JANE, 298
    MANDA, 297
    WILLIAM, 298

WM., 298
DYER
    ARTHUR, 199
    CASPER, 199
    FANNIE, 347, 348
    GRADY, 199
    INFANT, 200
    JAMES A., 112
    MARGARET, 190
    MARVIN, 199

-E-

EAKIN
    DORA, 26
    J.A., 26
    LELLIE, 26
EATON
    BETTY, 28
    C.H., 243
    G.W., 28
    JOHN, 229
    JOSIE, 28
    NANCY, 229
    SAMUEL, 28
EDDINGTON
    A.A., 262
    M.J., 262
EDICK
    SAMUEL R., 281
EDINGTON
    ASENITH J., 277
    E.E., 277
    ELIZA JANE, 85(2)
    FANNIE, 85
    FANNY, 84
    JESSEE, 85
    MARY ANN, 85(2), 86
    P.C., 277
    SAMUEL, 84(3), 85(2)
    WALTER, 262
EDMONSON
    INFANT, 246
    REECE, 246
EDWARDS
    BESSIE, 237
    BULAH, 236
    EDNA R., 236
    ERVEN, 237
    FRANK, 237
    INFANT SON, 221
    JAMES C., 221
    JAMES EVERETT, 236
    ROBERT, 236, 237
    SAM, 236(2)
    SARAH J., 221, 222
    W.T., 221
EGBERT
    KING, 137
ELEXANDER
    FAY, 304

ELLIS
    AUGUSTUS WEISSERT,

34
    B.D., 91
    BENJ., 112
    BESSIE, 92
    HATTIE, 91
    HATTIE LOU, 91
    INFANT, 92
    JACK, 109
    JAMES, 92(2)
    JOHN, 91
    SALINA, 91
    STARLON, 91
EMORY
    BETTIE GARREN, 72
    T.A., 72
ENGLAND
    DEVONSHIRECOUNTY,

66
ERVIN
    A.S., 89
    ALBERT, 229
    ALEX, 88(2)
    ALICE, 89, 90
    ALICE CHESTER, 90
    B.E., 89
    BEATRICE JANE, 88
    BERTHA, 90
    CALVIN, 88, 89
    CARROLL, 90(2)
    CATHERINE, 89, 90
    DORA ELLEN, 90
    DORCAS, 90
    EARL, 89
    GEORGE, 88
    HENRY M., 89
    INFANT, 88
    J.M., 88, 89, 90
    J.W., 116
    JAMES, 88(2)
    JOSEPH, 89(2), 90
    LOW, 77
    M.A., 88
    M.J., 90(2)
    MARGARET, 88, 89
    MARTHA, 89, 90
    MARTHA AUSTIN, 88

    MARY, 90(2), 299(2)
    MATTIE RIDER, 90
    MINNIE, 89
    N.A., 89
    NANNIE, 88
    O.R., 78
    PATRICK, 89(3)
    R.H., 90(2)
    REBECCA, 88
    RISPA, 89(2)

ROBERT W., 88
RUBY LEE, 89
S.M., 90
SARAH JANE, 90
STEVE, 299(2)
SUSAN, 90
SUSAN A., 90
W.L., 89, 90
W.L., JR., 89
ERWIN
DEE, 299
ESTES
KERMIT B., 237
EUBANKS
HANNAH, 123
KATTIE, 123
EVANS
BILLY, 70
G.W., 70
J.H., 4
JASPER, 4
JENNIS UGENE, 4
LULA, 29
M.A., 4
MARION, 4
ROLLIE, 70
EVERHART
AMERICA, 109
FLORENCE, 109
ISAAC, 109
JESSIE B., 269
LILLIE V., 269
N.G., 269
R.M., 109

-F-

FAGG
HELEN, 338
J.W., 338(2)
N.M., 338
NELLIE, 338
FARLEY
NINA, 160
FARM
CHESTNUTT DAIRY, 157

KEFAUVER DAIRY, 65

STOKLEY BROTHERS,
79
FARMER
BENJAMIN FRED, 319
J.R., 324
VIOLA CURTIS, 324
FARNER
C.W., 173
GRADY, 173
I.D., 173
L.P., 173
W.I., 173

FARR
J.A., 178, 286,
287(3)
JAMES, 286
LOUIS, 287
LUCINDA, 286, 287(3)
MYRA E., 287
ROBERT, 287
FELTY
ELIZA, 188
FERGUSON
BARTLETT N., 280
MARGARET, 280(2)
W.H., 280(2)
FERRY
BACONS, 136, 151
NILES, 136, 144, 165
FIELDING
ROBERT, DR., 65
SARAH, 66
FIELDS
CYRUS, 79
PRUDIE, 79
FISHER
B.F., 171
MARTHA A., 171
FLETCHER
ALLIE VINCENT, 58
B.W., 334
J.C., 58
FLOYD
HOMER J., 73
JOHN, 73(2)
RICHARD, 268
SUE, 73(2)
FLOYED
JOSEPH, 268
FORKNER
BETTIE, 121(2)
CLARA N., 119
D.P., 119
E.I., 119
ELIZABETH, 122
EVA WILKERSON, 122

FRANKLIN, 122(2)
FRED, 122
FRED (FERD), 122
GRACE, 122(2)
INFANT, 120
J., 119, 120
JAMES, 121(2), 122
JESSIE, 122
JESTINA (JESTUANA),
121
JESTUANA, 119,
121(3), 122
JOE, 122
JOE (JOSEPH), 122
JOHN, 121(5), 122
JOSEPH, 121(2), 122

JOSEPH FRANK, 113,
119, 122
JOSIAH, 120
JULIA A., 120
LAWRENCE, 113,
119(3), 121(12),
122
LAWRENCE, SR., 113,
119
LELA, 122(2)
LIZZIE, 122
M., 120
M.A.W., 119
M.F., 119
NANCY, 122(2)
NANNIE, 121(2)
R., 119
SARAH, 121(2)
SCRUGGS, 122
STEVE, 121(2)
SUSIE, 121
T.A., 119
THOMAS, 113(2),
120(2), 121(9)
WILLIAM, 122(2)
FORRIESTER
B.A., 301(2)
JAMES, 301
W.M., 301(2)
FOWLER
ABIJAH, 84(4),
85(2), 86
ELIZA JANE, 86
MARY A., 84
MARY ANN, 85
MARY ANN EDINGTON,

86
MARY JANE, 85, 86(2)
SAMUEL A., 84, 85,
86
SARAH FRANCES, 85,
86
SARAH FRANCIS, 86
FRANK
ESTIE, 58
WILLIAM, 58
FRANKLIN
BENJ., 277
HENRY, MRS., 150
HENRY, REV., 150
FREDLE
DAVID, 17
JAMES, 17
FREEMAN
CHARLIE, 29
G.H., 29
H.C., 229
HOWARD C., 29
JOHN, 169
JOHN A., 172, 173

L.S., 229
MARY, 228
P., 229
R.S., 29
ROE, 297
SUSSIE, 29
FREEMON
BELL, 68
FRIDLEY
B.L., 120
BENJAMIN L., 117
ROAS A., 120
ROSEANNA, 117
WILLIAM H., 120
WM. H., 119
FRITTS
ADDIE BELLE, 74
H.J., 74
FRY
A.P., 70(2)
BEN, 70
M.A., 70
FRYE
BETTY, 321
CAROLINE, 321
E.L., 69(4)
EFFIE, 69
G.C., 69(4)
INFANT, 69(4), 83,
244
JOHN, 321
JOHN, MRS., 321
S.L., 83
SAMUEL, 321
SHERMAN, 83(3)

-G-

GADD
---, 168
GAINES
CORA, 102(2)
J.R., 102
R.J., 65
ROBERT COOKE, 65
SARAH, 65
SARAH J., 267
THOMAS H., 267
GALLAHER
A.H., 164
F.L., 164
INFANT DAUGHTER,
164
GAMBLE
D.A., 97, 104
ELIZABETH, 296
HENRY, 296
J.H., 296
JOSEPH, 296
SARRAH, 296
GANN

HENRY, 10
GARDNER
CORA, 246
NANCY E., 29
GARLAND
R.L., 274
GARREN
ELIZA, 72
ELIZABETH, 271
FREDIE, 271
H.G., 270
J.A., 271
J.W., 72
LEANDER, 206
LEE, MRS., 271
LIZZIE, 271
MARGARET, 72, 73
MURTLE, 271
GARRETT
BESSIE, 73
GASTON
J., 247
M., 247
PEGGY, 247
GAY
E.J., 276
ELIZABETH, 101
INFANT, 98, 101
MARY E., 98
MARY J., 101
WILEY J., 98
WILLIAM R., 276(2)
WILLIAM WALKER,

276(2)
WM. R., 276
GENTRY
ALLEN D., 130(4)
ALLES, 177
ALSIE ANN, 176
ARVALE, 177
CATHERINE E., 130
D.M., 176
E., 177
E.C., 176
E.H., 176, 177(3)
E.J., 176
E.M., 177(3)
EFFIE M., 176
ELL, 177
GEORGE, 177
INFANT, 156, 177
J., 177
J.A., 156
J.M., 177
JAMES, 130(2)
JOE ALLEN, 177
JOHN, 177
JONT L., 156
JOSEPH E., 177
LENEY, 156

M.M., 176
MARGARET, 148
MARTHA, 176
MARTHA MILTILDY, 176

MARY, 130, 145
MARYELLIE, 177
NANCY, 130
NEARVY, 177
NELLIE M., 177
PLEAS, 130
R.N., 176
ROBERT, 145
SARAH, 177
UNIS, 176
VIOLA, 176
W.A., 176
W.H., 177
W.J., 156
W.M., 176
W.N., 176
WILLIAM A., 177
GEORGIA
ATLANTA, 159(2), 160
GADDIS TOWN, 242
GERDING
EDWARD MONTEGRE,
175
INFANT, 335
GHORMLEY
A., MRS., 274
AMANDA E., 273
ELIZABETH, 273, 274,
278
J.H., 278
J.L., 278
JAMES, 273
JAMES L., 278
JAS., 274
LILLIE L., 277
LORENZO, 274
LOUIE, 300
MARY ANN, 274
NANCY K., 278
R.T., MAJ., 278
ROBERT T., 277
ROBERT T., III, 277
ROBERT T., MAJ., 275
W.A., 300
W.H., 274
GIBBY
FLORENCE, 241
G.T., 241
GEORGE, 241
J.T., 241
GIBSON
A.L., 204
BERNARD EARL, 204

EARL, 203
ELIGA, 203, 204

ELIGAH, 203
ELIGE, 203
FRANK, 204
G.W., 204
GEORGE, 204
J.W., 204
JIM, 203
JOHN, 204(3)
JOHN WESLEY, 204
LUCRESIE, 203
M., 203, 204
MARTHA M., 203
MARY, 199
TANE, 109
GILES
—, 166
ANNIE, 86
DELIA, 23
FRANK, 174
GERTIE, 174
GRACE, 166
HORACE, 166
INFANT, 23(2)
JOHN, 109(2)
M., 109
MAE, 109
MALICY J., 53
MARY, 109
MYRTUS, 86
SALLIE, 23
GILREATH
NANCY A., 242
GIVENS
ELIZA J., 8
HENCE, 294
JAMES, REV., 8
ZACHARIAH, 290, 294
GLAZE
MARY, 348
GOFORTH
JAMES, 54
LOUISA, 54
GOGGIN
THOMAS C., 66
GOLDEN
JESTINA, 121
JESTUANA, 121
GOODEN
BETTIE, 189
J.H., 189
GOODNER
JOHN, 158, 159(2)
GOODWIN
REBA, 47
GOURLEY
J.H., 148
JOHN H., 148
LEE, 148
SALLIE, 148
GOWAN
MYRTLE Q., 123

ROBERT, 124
GRAHAM
L.A., 92
GRASON
S.M., 184
GRAVES
ABRAHAM, 11(2)
ALFRED, 123
ALLEN, 319
ALPH, 11
B.C., 123
BENJAMIN, 123
BESSIE, 315
BETHIA C., 123
BETTIE, 11(2)
BETTY, 123
CATHERINE, 123
ELIZA, 123(2)
FREDIE, 266
G.W., 123
GRANVILLE, 123
GRANVILLE W., 123(2)
HARRISON, 123
J.L., 123
J.R., DR., 66
JAMES, 123
JOHN L., 123(2), 124
MARY, 11(2)
MARY KATHERINE, 266

MILLIE, 123
NANCY, 123
NANNIE, 110
PEGGIE, 11
POLLY, 123
RACHEL, 123(2)
S.H., 11(2)
S.S., 123
SAMUEL, 123
SAMULE, 316
SARAH, 123(2)
SARENNE S., 124
SOLOMON, 123(2)
VERTIE, 11
WEBSTER, 11
WILLIAM, 123
WINNIE, 11
GRAY
ADDIE, 180
BESSIE, 180(2)
CLARENCE, 314
ELIZABETH, 79
FANNIE, 184
H.B., 325
HENRY, 79
INFANT, 179, 180(4)
JOE, 180(2)
JOHN, 79
JOSEPH, 179
LAWSON, 179, 180
LUTHER, 180

MAGGIE, 179
MART, 179
MARY, 79
MARY JANE, 180
MARY NELL, 314
MODEANIA, 180
MODENA, 180
NANCIE C., 13
NELLIE REBA, 179
R.W., 314(2)
RAFE, 314
S., 183
S.B., 13
S.C., 180
SALLIE, 180(2)
SAM, 180(4)
SAMUEL, 180
SARAH, 79
W.M., 180
W.R., 180
W.W., 179
WARREN, 180
WILLIAM, 176, 180
WM., 179
ZADIE, 314(2)
GRAYSON
  ANNIE LAWSON, 324
  ETHEL C., 218
  JOHN, 339
  JOHN CALVIN, 218
  LENA M., 218
  LOUISA, 339
  SIDIE, 218
GREEHR
  ARLIE, 30
GREEN
  ARLIS, 30
  ELISHA H., 30
  ELIZABETH A., 30
  HARRELD, 308
  I.F., 243
  IDA F., 243
  INFANT, 309(2)
  JOHN, 236
  JOSEPH, 308
  LILLIAM FAIE, 241
  LOICE K., 243
  M.L., 308
  MARY J., 309
  N.T., 308, 309(2)
  PEARLEY E., 30
  POLLY, 138
  ROSCO, 226
  SARAH, 36
  THOMAS E., 30
  V.R., 243
  VESTER, 138
  WILLIAM, 241
GREGORY
  C. WALTER, 233
  C.L., 233

C.W., 233(2)
E.E., 233
EASTER E., 233
INFANTS, 233
JENNIE, 233
S.E., 233
S.W., 233
T.J., 45(2)
WILSON, 45
GRIFFIN
  J.T., 312
  MARY LEA, 312
GRIFFITH
  BRANTLY C., 125
  CALLIE, 125
  CHARLES, 126
  CHARLES E., 126
  CHARLES F., 125
  CORDIE, 125
  DETIE, 125, 126(4)
  E.E., 125
  E.L., 299
  ED DUNCAN, 126
  ELISHA E., 125(2)
  INFANT SON, 126
  J.L., 125
  JAMES, 317
  OLIVER Y., 126
  PAULINA LOUISE, 125
  R.L., 125, 126(2)
  RAHETT, 317
  REBECCA J., 125
  RICHARD L., 126(3)
  SALLIE J., 125
  SARAH S., 125
  WILLIAM, 125
GRIFFITHS
  LAURA JOSEPHINE, 330

GRIFFITT
  WM., 31
GRIGSBY
  MARANDA, 77
  THOMAS, MRS., 339
GRIMSHAW
  DR., 123
GROVES
  M.L., 226
  W.E., 226
GRUBB
  DERIAS, 175
  MARTHA C., 175
  SOPHIA A., 175
GUINN
  EMILY L., 133(2)
GUNNING
  HARRY, 86
GUNTER
  ANNIE, 310
  C.T., 310(2)
  C.W., 49

CLORENCE T., 238
D.L., 310
DOVIE LEE, 310
FRED, 310
GLADYS, 310
GLEN ALBERT, 310(2)
M.C., 49

-H-

HAGLER
  B.B., 22
  MARY JANE, 22
HALE
  S.P., 243, 245
  SARAH G., 243, 245
  WILLIAM, 104
HALEY
  MINERVIA, 121
HALL
  ALICE, 303(2)
  ALLEN, 86
  ARTIE LOU, 86, 330
  BARKSDALE, 86
  BEN, 86
  BESS, 128
  BETTIE, 86
  CHAS., 303(2)
  DORTHA, 86
  EDD, 159
  FRANCES, 86
  GEORGIA A., 303
  H.E., 303
  JAMES, 86
  JAMES C., 326,
    330(2)
  JAMES K., 303
  LESTER FAREE, 303
  LOTTIE, 86
  LOTTIE Q., 330
  LOU O., 329
  LULA MAE, 303
  MAGGIE, 86, 330
  MAGGIE HENLEY, 329

  N.B., 330
  NICK B., 86(2), 329
  P.H., 330
  RUTH, 128
  S.B., 303
  THOMAS, 86
  WM., 128(4)
HAMBEY
  LEURISE, 298
HAMBY
  BOOIS, 305
  CHARLES B., 305
  CORDELIA, 306
  DAVIE J., 83
  J.C., 83(2)
  K.E., 243

LILLY L., 83
LIZZIE, 83
M.A., 83
RICHARD, 305
WM., 83, 129
HAMILTON
  EDITH, 212
  H.T., 110
  IRA CLIFORD, 306
  J.B., 32(2)
  JANE, 169
  JOHN B., 32
  JOSIE, 212
  LIZZIE COLLAKE, 110
  LON., 212
  M.A., 306
  MARTHA E., 306
  MARY J., 32(2)
  MARY JANE, 32
  R.M., 306
  ROBERT H., 32
  THOMAS, 306
HAMMOND
  W.J., DR., 311
HAMMONTREE
  HARVEY A., 339(2)
  HIRAM, 192
  MARY J., 339
  PHOEBE, 192
  RUTH, 130
HAMPTON
  BETTIE, 324
  CALLIE, 227
  D.C., 29
  E.J., 97
  FRED, 29
  IDA, 28, 29
  INFANT, 97
  J.B., 226
  J.H., 97
  JOHN, 227
  LONIE, 316
  LOUISA, 97
  NANCY, 316
  PERKY, 123
  R.J., 28
  ROBERT, 29
  S.C., 226
  SUSIE, 28
  T.M., 97
  VIOLA, 226
  W.M., 316
HANKINS
  CORNELIOUS, 231
  E.E., 231
  E.E., CAPT, 231
  J.A., 231
  JOHN H., 230(2), 231
HARBIN
  S.A., 25(2)
  WILLIAM EDGAR, 25

HARDIN
FANNY M., 183
J.C.R., 165, 183(2)
JOHN B., 43
M.A., 43
M.F., 43
MARY E., 183
POLLY, 165, 183
POLLY L., 183
THOMAS J., 183
VICIE, 165
W.A., 165
W.W., 165(2)
WM. E., 183
HARLESS
INFANT, 115
THOMAS, 115(2)
HARPER
FRED M., 113
INFANT, 113
HARR
F.M., REV., 254
HARRILL
CORNELLIA, 46
EARL, 46
ELIZA STEPHEN, 46
ELLA E., 46
JAMES, 46(3)
JAMES R., 46
JOE V., 45
RICHARD, 46
HARRIS
ANNIE, 297
ARCHIE, 207
BEUNA, 297
BOYD, 186
C.H., 339
CARRIE, 173
CYNTHA, 174
DORTHIE M., 173
ELIGA, 193
ELIZABETH, 16
ETHEL CROFT, 78
EZEKIEL, 207
FANNA M., 193
FANNEY, 207
G.W., 243
GEORGE C., 269
H.H., 186
HENRY, 148, 193(2)
IDA M., 186
INFANT, 340
J.A., 297
J.C., REV., 112
J.F., 297
J.H., 303
J.M., 174
J.S., 46
JAMES, 16
JIMMIE H., 25
JOHN, 46

JOHN AKIN, 297
JOHN C.V., 269
JOHN F., 297
JOHN J., 268
JOHNNIE E., 339
JOSEPH, 340
L., 186
LAURA, 303
LEONA, 25
LIZZIE, 174
M.L., 159
MARTHA BLY, 186
MARY, 46, 340(2)
MARY JANE, 297
MARY R., 268
OSCAR, 186
S.P., 25
S.T., 193
SADIE, 25
SARAH, 133, 340
T.H., 339
W.C., 186
WILL, 173
WILLIAM C., 268
WILLIE, 46
WM., 25
HARRISON
ANNIE, 278
CHARITY A., 235
E.W., 24, 278(3)
EDWARD M., 235
G.W., 252(2)
INFANT, 278
JAMES, 235(2)
JANE, 217
LIZZIE J., 278
LOUISE J., 235
MARGARET, 216
MILARD, 99
NATHANIEL, 217
SARAH ANN, 307
HARTSELL
AMANDA, 60
C.R., 60
HARTSOOK
G.L., 253(2)
JAMES A., 253
N.G., 253
NANNIE G., 253
HARVEY
E.E., 333
G.S., 333
INFANT, 333
M.J., 333
N.L., 333
WILLIE IRINE, 333
HAUN
A., 39
A., REV., 39
A.W., 205(7), 206
ALICE, 202

C., 205(2)
CALLIE, 205(3), 206
CORDELIA ELIZABETH
  GUDGER, 39
EARL, 205
F.L., 205
INFANT, 205(5), 206
J.C., 205
J.L., 205
JAMES O., 39
LESLIE, 205
LUTHER, 205
MARY A., 206
NETTIE, 39
ORA, 205
RANKIN, 39
S.M., 206
SALLIE MILLER, 39
THOMAS E., 39
W.S., 39
HAWKE
GEAN, 76
IDA, 76
RALPH, 76
HAWKINS
—, 60
A.R., 239
ANDERSON, 97(2)
ANILEA, 332
BARBARA, 332
BETSEY A., 97
BETTIE, 75, 278(2)
BETTIE JANE, 79
E.C., 131(2)
EARL, 332
GOLDIA NORMA, 14

GREGG, 79(3)
INFANT SON, 75
J.M., 75, 278(2)
J.N., 131
J.R., 332(2)
JOHN, 60
JOHN H., 60
JOSHUA, 131
MATTIE, 332(2)
NANCY, 131
PARLEY, 332(2)
POLLY, 131
R.A., 332(2)
R.P., 14
RACHEL, 79(2)
REBECCA, 130
REED, 310
THOMAS PORTER, 278

VENIE M., 79
HAYNES
A.J., 104
M.M., 104

HEISKELL
DANIEL, 132, 133(5)
ELIZABETH, 133
MARY, 133
HELEMNS
JOHN A., 279
M.A., 279
HELEMS
JOHN, 26
MARGARET SHADDEN,
26
W.W., 26
HELMES
ANNIE, 297, 298(2)
HENRY, 297, 298(2)
LITHIE, 297, 298
LUTHER, 298
WALTER, 298(2)
HELMS
ELSIE MAE, 26
HENRY, 297(2)
S.J., 26
VIRGIL MUNSEY, 106
W.W., 26
HELTON
ELIZA, 123
MARY, 123(2)
NANCY JENNY, 123(2)
SOLOMON, 123(2)
THOMAS, 123(2)
HENDERSON
AMANDA, 134
AMANDA L., 134
BENJAMIN P., 276
C.L., 152
CARRIE, 135
DARCUS, 276
EDWARD, 152
FRANK C., 134
G.L., 135
GEORGE LAWRENCE,
135
GEORGIA A., 189
HATTIE A., 134
HERMAN, 135
HUGH K., 135(2)
INFANT DAUGHTER,
  135, 189
INFANT SON, 189(2)
JANE E. McG., 280
JOHN, 276(2)
JOHN E., 189
JOSEPH L., 134
LAWRENCE, 135
M.L., 189(5)
MARGARET R., 134
MARTHA E., 134
MARY, 152
MARY E., 134, 211
MARY F., 135

MARY J., 146
MATTIE E., 135
NANCY, 134(3)
NANNIE C., 134, 195
OLIVER C., 134
OTHER, 152
RACHEL ALLISON,
    276(2)
S.P., 135(3)
SADIE, 135
SALLIE M., 134
SAM'L L., 134
SAMUEL, 134(4)
SARAH, 189(6)
SARAH B., 135(2)
THOMAS A., 276
THOMAS ANDERSON,

    276(2)
WILLIAM, 134, 211
WM., 134(2)
HENLEY
A.H., SR., 136
A.M., 84(2)
ALLEN M., 84, 85(2),
    86
ANN, 137
ANN E., 136
ARTHUR H., 136
ARTHUR H., SR., 136,
    137
ARTHUR R., 85, 86
BETTIE, 84, 85, 86
CHARLES, 85, 86, 137
CHARLES FAIRFAX,

    136, 144
DAVID, COL., 137(2)
E.J., 85
ELIZABETH M., 137
FRANK, 85, 86
GEORGIA, 85(3),
    86(2)
GEORGIE, 85
INEZ, 85, 86(2)
J.R., 85
JAMES R., 85, 86
JOHN, 85, 86
JOSEPH, 85, 86
JOSIE, 85, 86(2)
KITTIE JONES, 136
LENA MOORE, 136
M.A., 84
MAGGIE, 85, 86(2)
MARY, 85, 86
MARY K., 137
MAUDE, 85, 86
NELL, 85, 86
SAMUEL, 85, 86
THOMAS OWEN, 85, 86

HENRY
---, 130
A.D., 192
ADDIE, 192
CALVIN, MRS., 284
EULA RAYMOND, 294

FLORA, 294
HUGH L., 294
INFANT, 192(2),
    284(2)
INFANT DAUGHTER,

    294(2)
IRA, 284(2)
JAMES, 192
L.T., 294
MARY, 130
PAUL, 192
S.C., 335
SARAH ANN, 294
SARRAH A., 294
SOPHRONIA, 233
W.C., 192
WM. T., 294
HENSLEE
F.H., 237(2)
HENSLEY
H.M.C., 72
JESSIE, 72(2)
JULIA MAE, 237
LELA FAY, 237
MARY E., 309
MARY J., 327
R.M., 72
R.M. (MATT), 72
THOMAS, 5
HERRON
INFANT SON, 52
JOHN, 52
MARY, 52
MARY J., 52
WILLIAM, 52
HI-S---
HAIRL, 18
HICKS
---, 168(2)
A.T., 162(2)
ABRAHAM, 3(2)
ALFORD, 3
B.H., 3
BERRY, 211(2)
C.A., 226
E., 192
ED, 192
ELBERT, 192
ELIZABETH V., 44
ELLA, 342
F., 162
G.W., 162
HERBERT R., 44

INFANT SON, 162
J.C., 162(2)
J.D., 4
JESSIE E., 162
JOHN, 187
JOHN A., 3
JOHN S., 44(2)
JULIA WATSON, 211
KATE, 117
L.V., 3
LILLIA, 226
LOISE, 3
LOUCINDA, 4
M.A., 4, 118
M.E., 4, 162
M.F., 162
MAGGIE, 192
MAGGIE R., 162
MARIAH, 211
MARK, 117
MARTHA, 162
MARY, 3
MARY ---, 211
MARY C., 252
MARY L.H., 44
N.J., 117
PAUL, 44
PHEBA, 192
R.K., MRS., 4
RITTIE, 3
ROE, 226
RUBY MAY, 304
S., 252(2)
STEPHEN F., 117
T.P., 4
VENA, 187
VESTIE, 4
WESLEY, 211
WILLIAM OSBIN, 3
WILLIE LEE, 304
HIGHTOWER
MARGARET, 273
MARGARET H., 273
T.H., 273
THOS., 273
HINES
INFANT, 74(2)
JOHN, 74
PEARL, 74
HITCH
A.J., 338
A.L., 139, 140
J.A., 338
JAMES A., 339
JOSIE M., 338
P.L., 139
ROY R., 139
HITSON
B.C., 301
JOE, 10
NELTER, 116

ROSIE LEE, 116
ZELTER, 116
HODGE
ADALINE, 182
ANDERSON, 182
EARNEST, 182
ELBERT W., 182
LOLIE DE LILIAN, 182
NELLIE B., 182
SELLIS P., 182
WILLIAM A., 182
HOGUE
NANCY E., 217
HOLCOMB
ARA, 108
BRIN, 108
CARRIE, 108
D.M., 108(2)
INFANT, 108(3)
PONEY, 108
SAMPS, 108
SAMPSON, 112
HOLDER
LEE ORIE, 274
HOLLOFORD
MARY ELIZABETH, 109

HOLLOWAY
GLENN, 63
J.H., 63(2)
J.W., 62, 63
JERRY, 63
L.U., 62
M., 63
M.E., 62
M.J., 63
PAUL, 62
R.E.L., 63
SAMUEL A., 63
SUSAN FARMER, 63
HOOPER
A.C., 108
JUANITA, 108
NARVEL, 108
HOPE
JACK M., 116
LUTHER CECIL, 116
LYDIA F., 116
SAMUEL, 116
SAMUEL E., 117
SAMUEL   EDWARD,
REV.,
    113, 116
SAMUEL, REV., 116
HORNER
MARY E., 42
PAT, 86
HOSPITAL
FOREE, 160
HOWARD
A.D., 178

ADELINE D., 178
ALLIENE, 140
B., 178(2)
D.B., 178(2)
EARNEST G., 139, 140
EARNEST R., 178
FANNIE L., 178
G.S., 139(2)
GEO. S., 139
GEORGE, 140
GEORGE S., 139, 140
HENRY J., 139, 140
I., 178
INA, 178
INFANT, 178(2)
IRENE, 140
J.B., 178(4)
J.H., 178
L.E., 178
L.M., 178
LUCY L., 178
M., 178
M.A., 139(2)
OSCAR, 178
P.L., 140
SALLIE, 178
SALLIE S., 140
THOMAS C., 140
THOMAS G., 139
W.B., 178
W.M.R., 178
WALTER, 178
HOYL
ELIZABETH, 141(2)
JOHN B., 141(3)
THOMAS, 141
HOYLE
ELIZABETH, 141
JOHN B., 141
HUES
RACHIEL, 270
HUFF
ALEZAN, 14
EMMA, 14
G.W., 14
GEORGE, 298(2)
INFANT, 14, 78
LUCILE, 14
W.H., 14
W.H., MRS., 14
HUGHES
EARNEST, 305
EDWARD P., 305
FANNIE, 236
ROBERT C., 236
WASHINGTON, 305
HUGHS
BETTIE, 305
JUDY, 305
HUMES
A., 338

N., 338
T.W., 338
HUMPHREY
MARGARET, 296
HUMPHREYS
ALFRED, 23
ALFRED, MRS., 23
WASHINGTON, 299
HUNNICUTT
E.L., 232
ETHEL, 232
H.G., 232
INFANT, 232
J.D., 232
JOSEPH B., 232(2)
L.D., 232
MARGARET, 232
P.H.M., 232
W., 232
HUNT
BARBARA, 182
BESSIE, 181
C., 271(2)
CALVIN, 181
DARTHULA K., 182
E.D., 181(3)
G.W., 319
GUSS, 275
INFANT, 181
LOUIS H., 319
M.L., 182
MATTIE, 306
OREN L., 271
ROY, 315
RUBIE, 181
SUSIE, 181
VINIE, 181(3)
VIRGIL, 181
W.A., 271
W.M., 181
WALTER, MRS., 315
HUNTER
ISAAC, 145
SUSAN, 145
HURST
CHARLES, 296
JOHN, 296
NANCY, 296
HUSKEY
INFANT, 78(2)
MARY, 78(2)
SAM, 78(2)
HUSTON
LOUELLA, 86
MARY, 56
HUTCHISON
H.G., 317(2)
HUTSON
P. & T., 143
PEYTON, 142(2),
143(2)

R.N., 306
TEMPERANCE, 142, 143
HYATT
C.W., 44
INFANT SON, 44
M.B., 44
HYDE
J.M., 310(2)
M.E., 310
NORA MYRTLE, 310

-I-

ILLINOIS
CHICAGO, 66, 86
INGRAM
EMMA JANE, 325
JIMMIE EDWARD, 282

MARYBELL, 245
SUSIE, 245
INSTITUTE
HOLLINS, 66
IRONS
A.J., 114
ALVIN, 208
F.M., 114
INFANT SON, 114
JULIA ANN, 114
MARTHA A., 207
MATTIE L., 207
RAYMOND R., 208
IRVIN
A.C., 84
ISBELL
G.C., 327
NICK, 86
ROSA, 327
ISBILL
ANNIE, 11(2)
ARTIE, 239
C.P., 11
CALLIE D., 231
COL. P., 10, 14
ELIZABETH, 239
ELIZABETH ANN, 11
EMERSON O., 11
EMERSON W., 11
ETTA SUE, 231
EULA, 231
G.W., 231(8)
I.A., 11(4)
IDA, 231(2)
IDA MAE, 240
INFANT, 231
ISAAC, 231
J.B., 239(2)
JOHN ROSS, 239
LEE, 327
M.J., 231(3)
MARY JANE, 11

MARY M., 11
OTA LOU, 231
RUFUS R., 11
SALLIE McCLELLAN,
239
WASH, 239
IVENS
ATHALONIA L., 15
CARELEE, 15
ELMER LEON, 15
H. CLAY, 15
JAMES M., 15
KENNETH KEITH, 15
LILLIAN, 14
LOUVENIA, 15
M.L., 15
MAMIE LOIS, 15
R.A., 14
ROBERT L., 15
SAMANTHA, 343
V.G., 14
W.S., 14
IVY
ELIZABETH, 186
JAMES B., 186

-J-

JACK
J.E., 72
JACOBS
J.S., 149
JAMES
C.M., REV., 87, 105
JARVIS
A.J., 43(2)
JOANNA, 43
R.B., 43
REBECCA B., 43
WM. S., 256(2)
JENKINS
A.J., 152, 153
ANDREW J., 153
ANNA MAE, 118
BLANCHE, 242
C.S., DR., 302,
311(2)
CARDELIA, 244
CORDELIA, 244
ESTIE, 152
GRACE, 242
HENRY, 153
INFANT, 153
INFANT SON, 311
J.C., 244(4)
JAMES, 192
LOIS, 238
LORA, 153
LOYD HUBERT, 152
MARY, 192
P.C., 118

SARAH J., 244
W.A., 244
JOHNSON
ADDIE, 310
ADDIE MAE, 49
ASHLEY, 86
B.S., 330
BEN, 81
BEN L., 216
C., 49
CATHERINE, 217
EARL, 330
ELISA ANN, 217
F.B., 324
FRANK LEE, 330
HARVEY, 219
INFANT, 217
J., 310
J.A., 49(2)
J.R., 153(2), 217(2)
JAMES R., 216
JOHN K., 216
KATIE C., 216
L.S., 310
LEWIS, 217
LOUIS, 217
M.E., 217(2)
MARGARET J., 330
MARY DEAN, 236
MOLLIE, 153(2)
NANCY CARRIE, 216
ONNIE A., 153
R.J., 289
R.J., MRS., 289
RESSA, 86
W.S., 217
WILLIAM E., 217
WM., 217
WM. L., 221
JOHNSTON
C., 175
CLARA, 122
CLARISSA, 175
FRANK, 86
FRANK LEE, 254
J.K., 175
J.N., 252
JOSIAH K., 175(2)
MARGARETT J., 252
NANCY ANN, 252
NANDY, 86
SUE E., 175
JOHNSTONE
C., 175
J.K., 175
JOINER
TILDEN, 124
JOINES
ALLICE, 348
ALTA MAY, 347
BENNIE, 347

C.W., 348
CARRIE, 347
CHARLES, 348
CHARLES W., 348
CLARA, 347
CLYDE, 347
D.H., 38
ELIZABETH (LIZZIE),
    348
ELLA, 347
EMMA, 346, 348
EMMA SUE, 347
FANNIE, 347(3), 348
G.F., 346(2)
GABRIEL (G.H.),
    348(2)
GEORGE HUGH, 347

H.C., 346(2), 348(2)
H.D., 347
HAZEL I., 347
HUGH, 348
HUGH D., 347
HURETTA C. McCASLIN,

    347
IDA, 348
INFANT SON, 347, 348
J.C., 347
J.L., 346, 347(5),
    348
J.W., 347
JOHN H., 38
JOHN L., 346, 347
JOHNNIE, 348
KATTIE, 347
M.A., 347
M.E., 348
MAGGIE, 38
MARY, 38
MARY A., 346, 347
MARY ALLICE, 346
MAUDE, 348
MOSES, 38(2)
NELLIE MAY, 347
OTT, 347
RALPH, 348
SUSAN, 38
SUSIE, 346
TEZZIE, 40, 348
VERRA, 348
WILL, 348
WILLIAN N., 347
JONES
A.B., 105(2)
A.J., 192
A.M., 215(2)
APHELIA, 137, 144
B.C.M., 192
BARRETT, 144
BENJAMIN FRED, 199

BERT, 240(3)
BETTY, 192
CHARLES C., 144(3)
CHARLES, JR., 144
CLARISSA H., 214
D.W., 311(3)
E.C., 214
E.S., 192
EMMA S., 214(2)
EPHRAIM G., 300
FLORENCE, 213
HATTIE, 231
INFANT, 192, 215,
    240(2)
J.D., 215(3)
J.R., 144
JESSEE F., 213, 214
JOHN, 144
JOSHUA, 137, 144
JOSHUA R., 144(2)
KITTIE, 137, 144(2)
L.C., 214
LENARD, 237
LENNIE, 311
LILLIE, 311
LODUSKY, 215
MANDY, 192
MARGARET McGHEE,
144
MARTHA C., 300
MARY, 231
MARY E., 105
MARY ISBILL, 231
MARY L., 215
MOULTRIE, 144
NANNIE A., 217
NELLIE, 214, 311(3)
NEPPIE BRADLEY, 70
NEWTON, 231(3)
O.J., 192
O.L., 144(2)
POLLY, 339
R.A., 217
RALPH, 240
SARAH, 144(2)
THOMAS, 144
THOMAS C., 144
WILLIAM, 144, 311
WILLIE, 318
JORDAN
INFANT, 312
J.T., 312
M.O., 312

-K-

KEENER
AMOS, 310
JON F., 167
MAUD, 310
RACHEL, 310

KEFAUVER
CHARLOTTE, 66
D.F., 65
ELIZABETH, 65
ESTES, 67(2)
J.P, REV., 65
J.P., REV., 65, 66,
    67
JACOB, 66
NANCY (VINEYARD), 66

P.E., 65
PAUL, 66
R.C., 65(2)
ROBERT COOKE, 66
ROBERT FIELDING, 65

VENIA, 66
KELSO
HARRIET J., 104
INFANT, 104
INFANT   DAUGHTER,
104
J.H., 104(4)
JOHN C., 104
KEZIAH A., 104(4)
KENNEDY
ARTIE, 184
C.A., 185(5), 282,
    283
CHELNELSEY, 185
CICERO A., JR., 185
E., 185
EUNICE L., 185
EUNICE LEE, 184
FLORA E., 185
INFANT, 185
INFANT SON, 185(2)
J.F., 185
J.M., 184
J.P., 185
JOE E., 283
MARY, 184, 185(5)
NEOMA I., 185
P.E., 185
R.L., 185
ULIS, 185
W.B., DR., 338
WILLIAM M., 185
KERR
F.L., 339
KETTRELL
WM. P., 32
KEY
WESLEY EDWARD, 204

KEYEES
M.E., 22
KEYES
JOHN, 22
VIOLA, 323

KILBY
  E.J., 228
  INFANT, 243
  J.M., 228
  J.S., 243(2)
  W.G., 269
KIMBLE
  INFANT, 242
  JOHN, 242
  NANNIE, 242
KIMBROUGH
  ADDIE, 135
  BRADLEY, 145(2)
  BRADLEY, SR, 145
  DUKE, 145(5), 146(4)
  DUKE, REV., 145(2)
  ELISHA, 145
  ELIZABETH, 146
  ISAAC, 145(2)
  ISAAC BARTON, 146(3)
  J.C., 147(2)
  JACOB, 147
  JOHN, 145(2)
  JOHN MOHLER, 146(2),
    147(2)
  M.A., 147(2)
  MARY, 145
  RAGON, 147
  ROBERT G., 145, 146
  SPENCER COKE, 147
  SPENCER H., 147
  WILLIAM, 145, 146(3)
  WILLIAM H., 147
KING
  BETTIE, 233
  C.B., 209
  CALLIE, 209
  CARL T., 209
  E.L., 307
  ELIZABETH HAWKINS,

    261
  H.L., 262
  IDA, 231
  J.H., REV., 262
  J.K., 209(3)
  JOHN C., 262
  LOUISA J., 265
  M.N., 307
  MARY, 262
  MARY E., 216
  MOLLIE RICE, 209
  N.C., 271
  NANCY JANE, 209
  REBECCA, 262
  S.M., 209(2)
  SARAH, 209(2)
  SARAH J., 262
  W.B., 209(2)
KINNICK
  NANCY, 123

KINSER
  F.J., 335
  J.H., 237
  N.I., 335
KINSLOW
  TEXIE, 16
KIRKLAND
  A.C., 50(4)
  A.D., 54
  ANDERSON G., 50
  C.M., 172
  C.W., 174
  CECIL, 73
  CLARA, 172(2)
  DELILAH, 50
  DELLA, 50
  INFANT, 50(2), 172
  INFANTS, 50
  J.A., 271
  J.C., 50(2)
  JAMES L., 50
  JAMES T., 186
  JAMES, JR, 51
  JOHN, 50(2)
  L.C., 174
  M.A., 186(2)
  MATTIE, 73
  N., 50(2)
  NANCY, 50
  NANCY A., 50
  NELLIE, 271
  NONIE, 186
  OTIS, 50
  SAMMIE W., 186
  SUSIE, 50(2)
  W.D., 186(2)
  W.H., 186(2)
  WILL, 186
KITTRELL
  COLUMBUS, 32
  N.J., 32
  NANCY, 32(2)
  W.P., 32
  WM. P., 31, 32
KNOBS
  NOTCHEY CREEK, 340

-L-

LACEWELL
  A.E., 38
LACKEY
  A.E., 285
LAKEY
  A.E., 288
  C.A., 51
  N.W., 288
  ORA, 288
  RACHEL A., 288
LANCASTER

  C.W., 86
LANCE
  —, 117
  BOB, 311
  INFANT, 117(4)
  JOHN W., 311
  LAURA, 311
  LOUEASE, 311
  SARAH, 117
LANCLEY
  CHARLIE J., 238
  FRANK M., 238
LAND
  BETSY ANN, 92
  DORA, 270
  E.J., 270(3)
  EFFIE LEE, 102
  ELIZABETH, 270
  ELIZABETH J., 270
  I.S., 270(3)
  ISAAC S., 270
  ISAAC S., SR., 270
  JESSIE, 102(2)
  MAGGIE, 270
  MANDY JANE, 102
  STELLER, 102
  THOMAS S., 270
  WILLIAM, 270
  WILLIAM E., 199
LANKFORD
  D.H., 278
  INFANT, 278
  M.L., 278
LAUDMILK
  ROBERT FRANKLIN, 237

LAUGHTER
  GEORGE, 13
  J.W., 156
  LOUISA, 13(2)
  SARAH, 156
  THOMAS H., 156
  WILLIAM H., 13
LAWSON
  INFANT, 341
  JAMES, 341
LAY
  W.B., 240
LAYMAN
  ALBERT C., 283
  SARAH A., 283
LAYNE
  CARL R., 323
  EARL, 323
  VINA RASAR, 323
LEDFORD
  B.A., 170(2)
  CALLIE, 232
  D.B., 170, 174
  D.O., 232
  ED., 232

ETHEL, 171
FLORENCE, 170
G.L., 170, 174
G.W., 232(2)
GEORGE, 170(2)
INFANT, 29
INFANT SON, 170
J.B., 170(3)
J.M., 232
J.T., 232
JANIE, 170
JASPER, 170
JOHN, 29, 232
M.A., 232
SARAH, 29
W.C., 170
LEE
  A.R., 204
  ALICE, 204
  AMANDA, 244
  ARTHUR A., 91(2)
  BELL, 309
  BOB, 263
  BUNA, 204
  C., 245
  C.N., 40
  CALLIE S., 39
  CALVIN, 245(2)
  CHARLIE, 204
  CLAUDE FRANKLIN, 282

  DELLA M., 40
  E.B., 91
  EDD, 264
  EDD, MRS., 264
  EDWARD, 244, 245,
    263
  ELIZA, 40
  EMMALINE, 263
  ESTHER A., 263
  ETHEL, 263
  G.C., 263
  G.W., 263
  H.E., 263
  HUBERT, 193
  HUBERT ROSS, 245
  I.C., 204(4)
  IDA, 263
  IDA SUE, 40
  INFANT, 263
  INFANT DAUGHTER,

    204(2)
  J.E., 40
  JAMES E., 39
  JAMES M., 245
  JAS. W., 204
  JOHN, 87, 88, 99,
    100, 102, 263(2)
  KATTIE, 40
  KITTIE LOU, 263

L., 204(2)
LESTER, 244
M., 245
MARGARET, 263
MARSHALL, 263
MARTHA, 40, 204
MARTHA ANN, 91
MARY, 245
MAUD, 91, 264
NEAL, 204(2)
OSCAR J., 40
P.N., 40(2)
RALPH DAVIS, 91
RALPH H., 40
RANDA, 91
RAS, 91
REX, 282(2)
ROBERT, 91(2)
ROBERT E., 263
ROBERT E., GEN., 137
ROBT., 263
ROXIE, 263
S.J., 40
SARAH, 263
SUE, 263
SUE ELLA BERNICE,
   263
SUSAN, 40
T.B., 40
T.J., 245
THOMAS J., 245
TROY BLANE, 204
VASSIE, 40
W.W., 309
WILL, 348
WILLIAM, 263
WILLIAM HOBART, 91

WILLIAM R., 40
WM., 263
WM. M., 87, 91(2)
ZILPHA, 40
LEFTWICH
   GEO. W., 66
LEGUIRE
   WM., MRS., 54
LEMING
   —, 152
   CORA, 323
   D.F., 323
   ETHELLONE, 186
   JOHN, 152
   MARY, 152
   ROE, 152
   SARAH E., 186
   W.D., 186
   W.G., 323
LEMONS
   BLANCHE DELENA, 115

   DEWEY, 115

ELIJAH, 115
LENOIR
   W.B., 132
LEONARD
   MATTY, 220
LEROY
   BEN, 76(3)
   ETHEL, 76
   INFANT, 76
LESLEY
   NANCY, 280
   THOMAS, 280(2)
LESLIE
   JAMES, 280
   LEE, 19
   SUE L., 273
   SUSAN L., 273
   THOMAS, 273(2)
LESTER
   C.L., 303
   HOWARD, 315
   O.E., 303
LETHCOE
   F.H., 308
   G.W., 308
   GEORGE R., 308
LETTERMAN
   EFFIE, 236
   FRANK, 236
   JESSEE K., 236
   ROSCOE, 236
   S.M., 218
   TENNIE C., 218
   W.J., 218
LEWIS
   FANNIE, 272
   N.B., 272
LILLARD
   DOUGLASS, 63
   J.B., 63(4), 220
   JOHN B., 62(2), 63
   JOSEPH BERRY, 216
   M.J., 220
   MARTHA E., 63
   MARY CAROLINE, 217

   N.A., 63(4)
   NANCY, 217
   NANCY A., 63
   NANCY E., 220
   PENELOPE S., 63
   WILLIAM, 217
   WILLIAM L., 62, 63
   WILLIAM W., 217
LIMTNER
   —, 229
LINDSEY
   A., 149
   ADLINE, 149
   ALABAMA, 148(2)
   ALEXANDER, 148(2)

C.H., 149
DAVID, 148(2), 149,
   150(2)
DAVID M., 148
DAVIED M., 149
E., 149(2)
ELISABETH, 149
ELIZABETH, 149
GERTIE, 149(2)
HARRIET, 148(2)
HARVEY, 148(2), 149
I., 148, 149(2)
INFANT, 149, 150
INFANT DAUGHTER,
149
ISAAC, 148(2),
   149(2)
ISAAC SAMUEL, 189
J.E., 149(2)
J.H., 149
JAMES, 149
JAMES I., 149
JOHN, 148(2)
JOHN H., 149
M.L., 149
MARTHA, 189
MARY, 148(2)
MARY JANE, 189
MELVINA, 150
PIERCE, 148(2)
RUSSELL, 191
S.E., 149
W.B., 189
WILLIAM, 148
WM., 148
LINGERFELT
   ELIJAH, 227
   MARY ANN, 228
LINN
   ELIZABETH A., 171
   WM. H., 171(2)
LOFTISS
   JACKSON, 259
   JACKSON, MRS., 259
   JOSEPH, 259
   JOSEPH, MRS., 259
LOGAN
   ELIZABETH, 63
LOMAX
   BESSIE, 86
   J.B., 324
   NANCY ISBILL, 324
LONDON
   ROB'T, 88(2)
   ROBERT, PVT., 87
   SARRAH E., 8
LONG
   ALBERT, DR., 158(3),
   159
   ALICE, 159
   ATLEE, 159

BASCOMBE, 159
BELLE, 159
BEN C., 160
BUD, 283
C., 157
CARROLL, 159, 160
CARROLL, DR., 159
CARROLL, REV.,
   158(3), 159, 160
CHARLES, 160
CLARA, 159
CLARENCE, DR., 160
DUDLEY, 159
E.A., DR., 158, 159
EDDIE, 159
EDITH, 159
ELIZABETH FRANCES,

   159(2)
EMMA, 159, 160
EUGENIA, 159
FANNY, 159
FRANCES, 159
FRITZ, 160
GEO. W., 320
GEO., MRS., 320
GEORGE, 160, 257
GEORGE R., 160
GEORGE RUFUS, 159(2)

HANNAH, 158
J. RUFUS, REV.,
   158(2), 159
J.A., DR., 157(3)
J.C., 160
JAMES B., 160
JAMES CARROLL,
   159(2), 160
JAMES W., 157
JAMES WRIGHT, 157,
   158(3), 159(2)
JEWELL, 160
JOHN A., DR.,
   158(2), 159(2)
JOHN ALBERT, 159(2),
   160
JOHN CARROLL, 160
KATE FOSTER, 160
KATHERINE, 160
LOUISA, 158(2)
LUCY A., 158(2)
M.J., 157(2)
MAGGIE REYNOLDS,
160
MAHALA, 159
MAHALA J., 157
MAHALA K., 157
MARY, 159(2)
MARY HARRIET,
   158(2), 159
MARY LEE, 160

329
GRACY MAE, 190
INFANT, 190
M.L., 165, 190
MARY L., 190
NANCY A., 329
T.D., 165, 190
THOMAS D., 165
W.T., 165
WILLIAM, 329
McDANIEL
BERTHA L., 45
BIRDY, 267
CALLIE, 305
CORA E., 45
G., 267(4)
J., 267
J.H., REV., 45(2)
JAMES, 267
JESSY, 267
JOHNIE R., 267
JOSIE MAY, 210
L.F., 210
M.V., 45(2)
MARTHA A., 45
MARY D., 267
N.M., 282
PETER, 305
R., 267(4)
RHODEN C., 45
ROSS, 305
TENNESSEE, 209
TENNIE, 45
THOMAS, 210
McDERMOTT
GEORGE P., 111
JANE E., 280
JOHNNIE, REV., 111
WM. P., 280(2)
WM. P.H., 280
McDONALD
ALIE N., 210
ELLEN, 348
MARTHA E., 348
McDURMOTT
W.R., 111
McGHA
MARREN, 114
R.M., 114(2)
W.R., 114
McGHEE
ALVA, 140
BARCLEY, 137(2), 144
BETSY, 137
ELIZABETH M., 137
JOHN, 20, 137(2)
JOHN B., 140
LAVENIA, 144(2)
MARGARET, 144(2)
MARY K. HENLEY, 144

ROBERT, 137
SARAH, 140
McGINTY
—, 123
McGUIRE
CY, 222
D.J., 216
JULIA ANN, 121
NICHOLAS, 216
SARAH, 222
McINTIRE (McINTOSH)

—, REV., 159
McINTOSH
ANDREW, 213
DAVID M., 213
MYRTLE, 213
McINTURFF
G.A., 181
NORMA L., 181
McJUNKIN
G.M., 319
McKEEHAN
G.W., 328
McKEEHEN
ANNIE, 185
CHARLIE, 328
JIMMIE, 185
M.C., 185
MARY, 328
MISSOURI ANN ISABEL,

328
N.J., 330
NANCY, 185
NELLIE A., 328
PETER, 185
REVEBELL, 328
W.M., 185(2)
McKELVY
HUSTON, 53(2)
JOHN, 53
SALLY, 53
WILLIAM J., 53
MacKENZIE
ALICE, 160
McKINNEY
SUSSIE, 168
McKINZIE
—, 159
McLEMORE
ARCHIBALD, 59
DONIE, 191
L.L., 191
MARGARET, 191
MARRY, 191
MARY JANE, 191
W.M., 191
WILLIAM IRA, 191
McLENDON
I.H., 254

RUTH, 19
McMAHAN
ASHLEY N., 155
D.E., 155
H.M., 155
HARVEY M., 155
JAMES ROBERT, 155
MARTHA, 155
MELLVINEY, 155
McMULLIN
JASON, 299
SARAH A., 299
McNABB
JAKE, 307
LUCINDA, 279(2)
McNUTT
JOHNNIE, 315
McPEEK
ALFRED, 38
C.H., 38(2)
E., 38
EDWIN S., 38
EPHRAIM, 38
FANNIE MAY, 38
L.L., 38(2)
McREYNOLDS
SAM D., 67
McSPADDEN
ARNOLD, 295, 296
FLETCHER, 295
H.L., 254
HANNIBAL, 166(6)
HARVEY L., 254
HENRY M., 295(5)
HOBART, 295
INFANT DAUGHTER, 295
INFANT SON, 254, 295
JAMES, 279
M.A., 295(3)
MARGARET A., 295
MARGARET L., 295, 296
MARTHA, 295
MARTHA J., 295
MARY A., 295
MELVEN, 295
MOLLIE, 295
NELLIE, 295
NICY, 166(3)
OLLIE, 295
S.K., 279
SALLIE L., 296
SAMUEL, 166
SARAH, 295
SARAH MAUDE, 295
T.T., 295
TEED, 166
TINE, 166
TOM, 324
VIOLA, 295

W.H., 295
MAGILL
JOSEPH, 164
S.H., 164
W.N., 164
MAHAN
JARIAH, 300
MANDA E., 299
R.S., 300
MALONE
JAMES, 210(2)
JOSIE, 201
LOLA MAY, 210
MOLLIE, 210
S.B., 210
SARAH JANE, 201
VINIE, 210
W.Z., 210
MALONEY
RACHEL, 124
MANIS
BETTY, 211
CALLIE, 211
CARRIE, 211
G.S., 45
GEO., 211
GEORGE R., 242
GEORGE R., MRS., 242
JEANETT, 101
JOSEPH A., 45
JOSEPHINE J.
FALCONER, 45
MYRTLE JOSEPHINE,

211
N.C., 45
ROBERT L., 211
STRODE, 211
VIRGIE E., 211
MAPLES
WILLIAM, 157
MARKIN
G.W., 52(2)
INFANT SON, 52
MARTHA L.M., 52
TINA, 52(3)
MARKINS
CHESTER, 52
MARR
GROVER C., 98, 99
JOHN F., 98, 99(2)
JOSEPH, 99, 112(2)
JOSEPH, CAPT., 87, 98, 99
MARSHALL
ALGIA, 329
CHALES WILFORD, 329

CHARLIE, 329
ELISHA R., 329
EMMA, 329

HARRIET, 329
ISAAC, 103
J.H., 329
JAMES, 329
JAS., 329
NANCY E., 329
R.G., 329(2)
RICHARD, 112
W., 329
WILLIAM, 103
WM., 329
MARTIN
CAROLINE, 218
INFANT, 52(2)
M.B., 52
S.J., 218
W.D., 52, 53
W.R., 52(2)
MASON
A.W., 126
ARCHIBALD, 321
B.A., 339
CHARLES, 321
EARNEST B., 312
FRANK M., 296
FRANKEY, 297
HENRY, 297
J.C., 296(2)
J.D., 312
JOHN, 54
JULIE, 312
LILLIE, 54
LOUISA, 202
LUTHER RAGON, 297

MARY, 321
MARY J., 321(2)
MARY SUE, 199
NANCY, 297
NANCY JANE, 297
NELLIE, 172
RASTUS, 296
RUFUS M., 126
S.C., 339
SAMUEL, 321
SAMUEL II., 321
SARAH E., 296
TOMMIE, 172
W.M., 172
WILLIAM, 297
MASSACHUSETTS
GEORGETOWN, 137

MASSENGILL
LENA, 118
MASSINGALE
JOHN OSCAR, 82
MATHIS
ALEY, 215
MATTHEWS
EASTER, 342

SARAH, 31
MAXWELL
ELLA, 348
MAYFIELD
G.F., 312(2)
H., 312(2)
H.G.F., 312
LEE OLIS, 312
MINNIE LOU, 312
WALTER, 312
MAYNARD
RACHEL E., 149
MEEK
SUE, 162
MELTON
C.E., 337
CALLIE, 337
LEONA, 337
MERCER
FOSTER, 99
MINNIE A., 99
WILLIAM JAMES, 99
MILL
HAUNS OLD, 340
LONGS, 141
WATKINS, 340
MILLER
ADAM, REV., 247
ALEX, 242
AMOS K., 235
ANNIE MAY, 242
ARLIE, 110
BOB, 110
C.H., 74
CHARLES WILLIAMS,

110
D.D., 188
E.S., 274
F.A., 110
GENEVRA V., 274
GROVER C., 110
HUBERT D., 188
J.E., 110
J.T., 188
JAS. W., 309
KINWOOD F., 235
L.E., DR., 111
L.J., 309
L.L., 274
LOUIS, DR., 112
LOUIS, REV., 87
LULA, 111
MARY HELEN, 235
MARY J., 110
OLLIE, 74
R.V., 309
RACHEL, 242
RICHARD W., 309
ROBERT M., 235
S.A., 274

STELL, 235
STELLA, 235
TEDDY, 235
VIRA, 111
W.C., 111
W.L., 111
WILLIAM HARDIN, 235

MILLIAGAN
JOHN HARRISON, 333

MILLIGAN
ADDIE, 333(2)
FERRING, 161
J.L., 333
JAMES L., 333
WILLIAM HOMER, 333

MILLS
A.H., 241
A.N., 152
AARON N., 151
AMBROSE, 151
ANNIE MAY, 151
AUTHOR J., 152
GEORGE LEE, 241
HENRY, 151, 152(3)
INFANT, 152(2)
J.R., 152(2)
L.A., 152
L.L., 151
LAURA, 151
LOLIE E., 152
LOUIS, 152(2)
M.L., 151
R., 151, 152
T.H., 151
WILLIAM T., 151
MILLSAPS
—, 148
ALF., 51
ALFRED, 54
ANDREW, 54
ANDY, 55(3), 56(2)
ANNA HAZEL, 55
ARIE, 152
AVERY, 56
BERTHA E., 56
C., 55, 288
C.L., 55(3), 56
C.M., 56
CALLA, 55
CALLIE, 55
CARL, 317
CARL CLINTON, 317
CARL HENRY, 55
CARTER, 55
CATHERN, 288
CHRISTEENA, 305
CLINT, 56
CLINTON, 307

EAS, 47
ELCIE, 288
ELIZ. E., 56
FANNIE, 188
FAY, 56
FLORIDA J., 56
I., 55
INFANT, 54, 56
J.A., 288
J.B., 54(3)
J.M., 56
JAMES, 56
JASON, 55
JESSE, 47, 55
JESSEE, 55(4), 56
JOE, 56
JOSE, 55
JULIA, 56
L.M., 56
LILLIE ANN, 274
LOUCINDA, 55(2), 56
M., 54
M.A., 54
M.I., 56
MARTHA E., 54
MARY, 55, 167
MARY A., 54
MARY F., 56
MOLLIE, 56
OLLIVER, 54
OVIE, 56
POLLY, 56
RANCE, 288
RAY, 56
REBA, 317
RILEY, 54
ROSE DOROTHY, 55

S.C.F.M., 56
SALLY, 55
SAM, MRS., 285
SAMANTHA, 288
SARAH, 55(2)
SARAH C.F., 55
SARAL L., 55
TENNIE, 55
TOM, 317
WM., 288
MILSAPS
THELMA, 274
W.A., 189
MINCEY
WILL, 62
MITCHELL
AUBREY ALFRED, 284

BURT, 77
CALLIE, 205
CATHERINE, 100, 310
ELMER G., 100
IRA, 205

J.E., 310
J.F., 40
J.G., 100
J.W., 205(2)
JAS. G., ESQUIRE,
   310
LEWIS A., 205
LIZZIE H., 205
M.J., 205
MALINDA, 205
MARY SUE, 205
MIZE
   J.S., 99
   JANE, 99
   JIMMIE, 99
MOLDER
   ELIZABETH, 146
MONTGOMERY
   GILLESPIE, 31
MOODY
   —, 86
   CARL, 252
   FLETCHER, 252
   JOHN, 252
   JOSEPHINE, 252
   L.B., 252
   M.T., 252
   MYRTLE, 252
MOORE
   ANN EVELYN, 137
   E.D., 73(2)
   INFANT, 73, 236
   M.E., 73
MOREE
   ERSKIN, 327
   M.M., 250
   NANNIE, 327
   RANSOM, 327
   SARAH, 327
MORELAND
   CHARLES O., 219
   MARY MALINDA, 220

   SAMUEL L., 220
   WILLIAM H., 220
MORGAN
   ANDREW, 43(2)
   CARL, 7
   CORA MAY, 94
   DENY, 8
   FRANCES, 7
   FRANCIES, 7
   HENRY, 7
   J.B., 43
   JAMES, 7
   JAMES R., 273
   JOHN JORDAN, 181
   LILLIAN, 8
   LITTLE TAYLOR, 94
   LOUISE, 73
   MARTHIE, 73

MARY J., 273
MARY JANE, 8
MATILDA, 94
O.A., 43
POLLIE, 168
POLLY, 7(2)
ROSS, 73
ROY LESTER, 138
TINIE PITTMAN, 43
WILLIAM, 7
Z.T., 94
MORRIS
   BERTHA, 49
   C.M., 49
   SALLIE LUCILE, 218
MORROW
   ARMSTRONG, 20(3), 21
   MARGARET, 20, 21
   MARTHA W., 20
MORTON
   NANCY, 80
MOSER
   —, 16
   A. LAFAYETTE, 248
   A.A., 254, 255
   A.M., 249
   ANNIE BELL, 331
   ANNIE L., 332
   AUSTIN, 331
   BELLE, 284
   C.L., 248
   C.V., 331(2)
   CARL, 331
   CARLETON, 60
   CHAS. IVAN, 138
   CROFT V., 331
   D.M., 248
   DENVER, 331
   DOKE, 16
   E., 247, 248
   ELIZA J., 248
   ELIZABETH BINGHAM,

      331
   ETHEL MAE, 149
   F.M., 248(2)
   FRANCIS, 247(3)
   G.L., 331(2)
   HAROLD HUGH, 249

   HENRY, 248, 254
   HENRY, JR., 323
   INFANT, 16, 247(2),
      248(2)
   INFANT DAUGHTER, 79,

      247, 331
   INFANT SON, 249, 255
   INFANTS, 331
   IVA LEE, 16
   IVAN, 249

J., 249
J.A., 247(2), 248
J.B., 139, 140(2),
   186
J.E., 148
J.F., 148
J.M., 249
J.O., 323
J.P., 16
JAMES C., 247
JESSE, 149
JOHN, 248(2)
JOHN FOX, 247
JOHN H., 248(2)
JOHN N., 248
JOSEPH, 16
JOSIE P., 148
JULIA A., 248
KATIE, 79
L., 332
L.S., 331
L.W., 331
LINDELL M., 331
LUCINDA, 16
LUTHER I., 148
M.A., 248(3)
MAGDOLINE, 248
MAGGIE, 252
MARTHA, 140, 186
MARY, 16(2)
MARY A., 248(3)
MARY C., 248
MARY E., 249
N., 248
NELLIE, 331
NEPPIE BELL, 331
NOAH, 247, 248(4)
NOVA, 323
OSCAR J., 139
P., 79(2), 248
P.F., 16(2)
PETE, 16
PETER, 79(3)
PHILIP, 247(2),
   248(4)
ROSS, 149
S., 249
SALLIE, 139
SALLIE S., 139
SILES, 60
V.M., 79(2)
VERA, 323
W.H., 254, 255
WANDA CHRISTINE, 138

WILLIAM C., 248
MOSES
   A., 9, 14
   ALTA MORROW, 199

   ANDERSON, 168(3)

ANDREW, 168(5)
ANDY, 9
ANEY, 9
ANNIE, 193
BIRDIE D., 9
CATHERINE, 321
CHARLES L., 9
CLESTER, 9
CONNIE, 9
DANIEL, 321
EDWARD, 168(2)
FRANCIS, 9
GEMILIA, 9
HENRY, 199, 316
INFANT, 9
J.B., 9
J.M., 9
JACK, 9
JAMES, 168(5)
JAMES R., 316
JESSEE, 9, 168(2)
JOE, 316
JOHN, 9, 168(2),
   321, 338
JOHNIE, 9
JOSEPH, 17, 61,
   168(2)
JOSHUA, 168(5)
JULEY AN, 9
MARGARET, 338
MARTHA, 168
MARY, 321
MOLLIE, 9
NANCY, 168(3)
O.G., 9
R.E., 9, 14
REN, 9
ROBERT, 9
S.C., 9
SAMUEL, 168(2), 199
SARA, 9
SARAH, 321
TOMMIE, 9
W.A., 338
MOSIER
   PHOEBE, 305
MOUNTAIN
   LAUREL, 168
   STAR, 28
   STARR, 226
MOUNTAINS
   UNICOI, 167
MUELLER
   CHARLES WILLIAMS,

      110
   EASTER, 110(2)
   ENOS C., 110
   LEWIS E., 110
   T.C., 110
   THEODORE CHARLES,

110
THEODORE CHARLES,

DR., 110
MULLENS
B.E., 233
ILAMAE, 233
J.H., 233
ZYMBLEE, 199
MULLINS
A.L., 191(2)
BEULAH, 232
CHARLIE, 60
CLARENCE, 233
DORCAS, 234
EDITH MARTIN, 283
GEORGE, 233
HARTSELL R., 283
INES EONA, 8
INFANT, 191
J.C., 232, 233
J.R., 191(2)
JAKE, 233
JOE H., 233(2)
JOSEPH WESLEY, 8
KITTIE, 191
LEWIS L., 191
MARGARET, 233
ROBERT, 191
WILLIAM P., 230, 233
MURPHY
—, 160
ROWENA M., 268
MURR
A.H., 60
ALFRED, 60
ANDY, 60
ANDY H., 60
INFANT, 69
JOE, 69
LILLIE, 69
MARGARET E., 60
MARTHA, 60(3)
ROY A., 38
RUBY RHEA, 38
MYERS
BERTHA, 54
JESSE, 262

-N-

NAILER
B.F., 99(2)
INFANT, 99
J.N. AGNES, 99
MARY L., 99
NANCE
J.P., 144
NELMONS
FLOYD, 307

NELSON
JAMES L., 286
M., 188
SARAH E., 286
SYDNEY G., 214
W.L., 187
NEW YORK
TARRYTOWN, 122
NEWCOMBE
HARRIET, 340
JOHN, 340
NEWKIRK
JOSEPH H., 272
NEWMAN
A.R., 258
CLEVE, 206(2)
ERVIN, 193
J.C., 193
J.W., 206
JESSIE SAMUEL, 308
JOHN F., 308(2)
JOHNNIE WILLIAMS,

258
L.C., 206
M.M., 206
MAHALA, 158
MARINDA, 206
SAM W., 193
SARAH C., 308
SARAH J., 308(2)
WINNIE MAE BILLE,
193
NEWTON
BESSIE, 159
CHAS., 159
DOC, 159
MARY LONG, 159
MAUDE, 159
WALTER, 159
NICHOLDS
JEFF (THOMAS J.),
122
JOSEPH, 122
MARY ANN, 194(2)
THOMAS J., 120
NICHOLS
BETTIE, 121
HAZEL, 53
ILLIE, 53
J.D., 80
WESS, 53
NILES
E.L., 274(2)
J.W., 336
JOHN D., 274
ORRA WESLEY, 336
PHILLYS H., 274
W.H., 274(2)
NORRIS
LOLA M., 97

LYTTON, 98
W.T., 97
NORTH CAROLINA

NEW RIVER, 123
NORWOOD
ANELANDEE, 246
F.A., 246
FLORENCE, 246
FRANK, 246
IDIA, 274
J.C., 246
JOHN, 246
KITTIE, 272
LEE VESTAL, 246
M.G., 246
SARAH, 246
NUNN
MAGGIE, 86

-O-

ODELL
DORTHA, 224
ELLA MAE, 224
JANE, 171, 224(4)
JOHN, 224(4)
LETHA, 224
LOUIS, 224
LUCILE, 224
OGS
—OMHI, 281
OKLAHOMA
ELK CITY, 148
OLIVER
CARNELL, 236
O'NEAL
A.M., 271, 272
ALICE MAY, 271
E.V., 271, 272
KATE, 272
ORR
C.O., 53
F., 162
G.A., 53
S., 162
SALLY, 122
W.A., 53
OSBORNE
JOSEPH R., 217
OURY
NANCY SANDERS, 158

OWNBY
ETHEL, 37

-P-

PAINTER
MARY E., 159
PARKS

ANNIE, 25
LAURA C., 222
PARSHALL
ANN E., 137
JOHN R., M.D., 136
JOHN ROSS, 137
PARSLEY
CAP, 122(2)
JOSEPH, 122
JOSEPH (JOE), 122
LAWRENCE, 122
LESTER, 122
NANCY, 122
RICHARD, 122
PASCHAL
GUSSIE B., 219
T.G., 219
PASSMORE
H.J., 45
J.C., 45
LAURA C. THOMAS, 45

PATTERSON
—, 166
CHARLIE, 195
CHAS., 195
EASTER, 195
GEORGE, 195
INFANT, 340(3)
LEE, 195
RACHEL, 195
ROBERT, 340(3)
SAM, 275
SUSAN, 195
VESTIE, 195
VIRGEL, 25
WILLIAM FRANK, 166
PATTY
ROBERT, 348
PAYNE
ANNIE, 16
C.C., 52
F.M., 25
FRED C., 81
GEORGE, 25
HETTIE ANN, 16
J.W., 16, 24, 25(2)
JENNIE, 16
JOHN HENDERSON, 24,

25(2)
JOHN HENDERSON

(JACK), 24
M.E., 25
SARAH SHADDEN, 25

URIAH, REV., 112
WM. W., 306
PEARCE
CARRIE OTTO, 216

MARY J., 58
PEARSON
 ART, 26
 INFANT SON, 26
 LOVIE, 26
 LULA M., 303
 MOLLIE, 303
 W.G., 109
 W.H., 303
 WILLIAM L., 303
PECK
 JACOB, 145
 JACOB F., 277
 JACOB FRANKLIN, 275,
  277
 JAMES M., 276
 JANE, 276
 JOSEPH, 276
 JOSEPH A., 276(2)
 MINERVA A., 276
 MINERVIA, 276
 MINERVIA A., 276
 NERVEY ALICE, 276
 SUSAN, 277
PEEL
 ELIZA, 1
 EVELINE, 2
 GEORGE, 1
 HENRY, 1
 JOHN, 1
 MARY, 1
 ROBERT, 1
PEELER
 INFANT, 100
 NANNIE, 100
 R.L., 92, 100
 S.E., 100
 W.D., 100
 W.H., 100
 W.W., 100
PEEPLES
 D.M., 241
PENNINGTON
 B.J., 311
 B.J., JR, 311
 CORDIE M., 44
 ELIZABETH, 219
 FLORENCE, 311
 HUBERT A., 44
 JOHN B., 44
 LUCINDA E., 219
 SARAH, 219
 W.J., 221
 WM., 219
PERKINS
 MIKE, 123
PERRINE
 ESSIE, 259
 JOHN H., 259
 LIZZIE, 259
 MARTHA E., 259

N.A., 259
W.H., 259
PETTETT
 CECIL C., 338
 MOLLIE, 338
 RUFE, 338
PETTIT
 EDITH ALINE, 338
 OSCAR, 338
PETTITT
 B.C., 210
 EARL, 210
 IDA, 210
PHILIPS
 BOYD, 39
 E.L., 39
 LIZIA BRADY, 39
PHILLIPS
 EUGENE, DR., 159
 MARTHA E., 253
 T.L., 253
PICKELSIMER
 MARGARETT, 103
PIKE
 TELLICO PLAINS, 195
 W.K., 243
PINKINGTON
 ---, 86
PITMAN
 JOHN N., 37
PITTMAN
 E.M., 37(2)
 ELIZABETH, 37
 H., 234
 JAMES F., 37
 M.A., 37
 MARGARET AMY, 37

 MARTHA SLEDGE, 221

 N., 37
 NARCISSA, 37(4)
 S.A., 37(5)
 S.B., 37
 S.E., 234
 SARAH, 37
 SMITH, 37
 TIP, 37(2)
 WALTER WORTH, 234

PITTY
 MAMMA PITTY, 69
PLANTATION
 HENLEY, 136
PLASTER
 CLARA, 173
 W.M., 173
 WILLIAM E., 173
PLEMMONS
 INFANT, 319
PORTER

A.J., 313
ELIZABETH A., 62
W.W., 62(2)
POWELL
 AMANDA McGAHA, 52

 CLAY, 52
POWERS
 INFANT, 170
 M.A., 170
 Z.B., 170
PRESLEY
 BILLIE W., 334
 GLENN B., 334
 JOSIE, 75(2)
 MANUEL, 75(3)
 NELLIE, 334
 R.M., 334
 WILLIAM, 75
PRESSWOOD
 E.F., 70
 E.W., 46
 EMMA, 76
 G., 70
 HERBERT, 76
 J.H., REV., 206
 JACK BRADLEY, 70
 JOSEPH, 70(2)
 LUCY J., 46
 MARGARET, 70
 VELMA L., 70
 WM., 76(2)
PRESWOOD
 AUGUSTINE, 226,
  227(2)
 MARTHY, 227
PRICE
 ANNIE, 86
 CHARLES, 86
 CHAS., 86
 DANELLA, 86
 EMMA, 86
 MARY, 86
 WESLEY, 86

 -Q-

QUEEN
 FREDA, 74
 JOHN, 74

 -R-

RABURN
 HENRY, 46
 MARY L., 46
RAGAN
 DANIEL, 214(2)
 ELIZABETH, 214
RAGON
 A.M., 214(2), 215(2)

ALBERT, 214
BETTIE C., 215
CLARISSA E., 214
DORA A., 215
J.E., 214, 215
JESSE J., 214
L.E., 215
L.J., 214, 215(2)
M.A., 214
MARY, 222
MARY E., 146, 147,
 215
W.H., 214(2), 215(2)
RAILROAD
 L & N, 160, 193, 326
RAINS
 AMANDA A., 292
 D.A., 293
 INFANT, 293
 J.E., 293
 J.M., 293
 JAMES A., 293
 JANE, 148
 L., 293
 LINA, 293
 MACK, 293
 MARY L., 293
 VERGIL, 293
RAMSEY
 J.D., 128
RANDOLPH
 JAMES, 145
 MARY, 145
RAPER
 --- WATSON, 199
 C.D., 348
 CAROLINE, 8, 199
 CORA, 100
 ELLA V., 100
 I.C., 13
 INFANT, 199
 J.H., 199(2)
 J.M., 199
 J.R., 199
 J.S., 13, 199
 JOHN, 199
 L.W., 13
 LENA, 199
 LISLIE, 100
 M.C., 241(2)
 M.E., 10
 M.H., 10
 M.L., 13
 MARY A., 199
 R.A., 100
 R.C., 13
 RILEY, 199(3)
 SARAH, 199
 VIOLA, 100
 W.J., 199
 WOM, 241

RATLEDGE
  BEN, 210(2)
  SALLIE, 210
RAUSIN
  M.H., 19
  MALLISSA, 31
RAY
  CHAS., 140
  FRANK A., 328
  G.W., 328
  GEO. W., 328
  GEORGE W., MRS., 322
  J.B., 328
  NELLIE J., 301
  S.A., 328
  SALLIE A., 328
  WILEY, 258
READMON
  ELVIRA J., 148
READMOND
  BART, 184
  G.W., 184
  JOHN H., 184
REAGAN
  B.P., 99
  BENJ. P., 99
REAGLE
  MARY A., 237
REAGON
  ATTIE, 91(2)
  BENJ. P., MAJOR, 87
  ELIZA, 99
  M.A., 99
REED
  J.M., 235(2)
  SUSON ADALIN, 126
REYNOLDS
  — KESTUTON, 158
  ALICE, 157
  ALICE McPEEK, 43
  ANNE, 157
  E.A., 43
  ELIZABETH, 157, 347
  EMMA, 159
  GEORGE R., 158
  GREEN, 158
  H.C., 347
  HANNAH, 158
  INFANT   DAUGHTER,
345
  ISHAM, 157, 158(3)
  JAMES T., 345
  JANE, 157
  JOHN, 158
  LOUISE DODSON, 345

  MAGGIE, 159
  MANERVIA, 348
  MARY, 348
  MINERVIA J., 346
  NANCY, 158(2)

ROSS B., 345
SALLIE, 222
SUSAN ELLEN, 43
SUSIE, 348
T.E., 43(2)
THOMAS E., 43
WILLIAM, 158(6)
ZILPHA, 158
RHEA
  JESSE, 280
  MARGARET, 280(2)
  WILLIAM R., 313
RICE
  AMANDA, 245
RICHARD
  A.B., 8
RICHARDS
  L.L., 8
RICHARDSON
  EMMA, 103(2)
  JAMES, 159
RICHESON
  ARCHIE, 101
  C.L., 101
  E.S., 101
  I.R., 101
  J.B., 110
  MARGARET, 101
  MARGARET S., 315
  MARTHA A., 101
  MARY ANN, 101
  WILLIAM, 101
  WM., 112
RIDEN
  GEORGE, 70
  MAMIE, 70
RIDER
  A.R., 96(8)
  ALEX R., 96
  E.J., 97
  IDA, 96
  INFANT, 96(5), 97
  J.L., 97
  J.S., 96
  LIDA J., 97
  LOUELLA, 96
  M.C., 97
  MALT, 97
  MARTHA, 97(3)
  MARY, 96(8)
  MARY L., 96
  ROBERT S., 97
  S.R., 97
  W.B., 97(2)
  WM., 97
RINES
  H.H., 236
  INFANT SON, 236
  J.H., 218
  MARTHA BELLE, 236

S.M., 236
SIDNEY, 218
RITCHIE
  ALEX., 266
  MARGARET, 266
  SYNTHIE, 266
  W.C., 266
RIVER
  LITTLE TENNESSEE,
    128, 167, 194,
    285(2)
  TELLICO, 20, 130(2),
    148(2), 166(2),
    168
  TENNESSEE, 136(2),
    139, 144
ROAD
  BALL PLAY, 20, 79,
    151, 290, 320,
    341
  BALLPLAY, 176
  BELLTOWN, 3
  BIG CREEK, 3, 24
  CITICO, 47, 139,
    144, 317
  IVY, 243
  LAKESIDE, 62
    MORGANTON   TO
ACORN
    GAP, 84
  MT. VERNON, 123
  NILES FERRY, 139,
    151
  OLD FEDERAL, 78
  POVO, 59, 130, 148,
    191
  ROCKVILLE, 119
  ROCKY SPRINGS, 239
  SINK, 275
  TELLICO PLAINS, 239
  TELLICO RIVER, 161
  VONORE, 151, 176
  VONORE   BALLPLAY,
165

VONORE-SWEETWATER,

    57
ROBERSON
  MARTHA ANN, 109
ROBERTS
  A.P., 154
  BOB, 174
  CARTER R., 98
  CATHERINE, 98
  DELENA EVALINE, 269

  EARNEST H., 154
  FRANCES, 225
  HARRIET, 170, 174
  HOWARD, 225

INFANT, 44
INFANT TWINS, 170
J.J., 98
JAMES, 110
JAMES R., 154
JOE, 225
JOSEPH L., 269
LISA, 44
M.A., 154
M.E., 44
MARY E. LEE, 44
NELLIE, 110(2)
P.M., 98
RODA AN, 98
TEDDIA, 110
W.J., 44(3)
W.M., 170, 174
WILLIAM, 109
ROBINSON
  ELISHA, 126
  FRANK, 116
  THOMAS, 113
ROBISON
  SARAH, 96
  W.B., 336
RODGERS
  DAVE, 331
  JAMES L., 331
  LAURA B., 331
  NELLIE ANN, 294
  NOLA ISABELL, 335
  SUSAN, 209
  T.J., 330
ROGERS
  A.A., 209
  ANDREW, 77
  CORA, 86
  GEO., 209
  GEORGE, 209
  HUBERT E., 345
  INFANT, 209
  J.C., 345
  J.M., 209
  J.W., 94
  JAMES C., 345
  JESS, 27
  JOSIE, 314
  LOUISA E., 209
  LUTHER, 267
  M.L., 94
  ORA, 267
  S. G. HOYT, 314
  THOMAS, 209
ROLEN
  DORA BELL, 115
ROLLINS
  HELEN, 144
ROMAN
  BERTHA E., 277
  ELISHA, 277
  F.A., 277

ALEX., 87
AMOS R., 272
DORA, 272
E.J., 87
FLORENCE, 88
G.C., 87, 272
GEORGE BROWN, 88

IDA, 87
INFANT, 87(7), 272
J.A., 272(4)
J.H., 87
J.O., 272
JANE, 88
JOSEPH, 88
LITTLE MAGGIE, 272
LOU, 87
LOUIS S., 183
LYDA, 272
MAGGIE, 88
MARGARET, 87
MARY, 272(3)
NINA DELORIS, 272
SPICIE, 272
THOMAS L., 87
URMA J., 88
W.M., 88
WILLIAM A., 280
WILLIAM H., 272
SHADDON
A.W., 280(2)
MARY LESLIE, 280
SHAFFER
W. —, 252
SHARP
DOCTOR, 139
ERMA GERALDINE, 209

H.H., 209
INFANT DAUGHTER, 6

INFANT SON, 6(2)
LENA, 209
M.J., 6(2)
PEARL, 6
R.P., 6(2)
ROBERT P., 6
SHAW
B., 171
B.B., 171
ETHEL, 309
F., 171
INFANT, 171
J., 171
JANE, 171
JASPER R., 34
LUTHOR, 309
MAGGIE, 34(2)
MARY NEAL, 309
NEALIE, 34
NELLIE, 171

REBECKAH, 171
SHEETS
FRANK, 298
HENRY, 64
INFANT DAUGHTER, 298
JACOB, 253(3)
JOHN AIKEN, 284
JOHN C., 253
MARTHA J., 298
MARY J., 64, 253
MARY JANE, 253
ROBERT T., 298
SINA, 299
T.F., 298
SHELDON
JAMES J., 133
MOLLIE E., 133
SHEPARD
DOLLIE, 313
EARNEST, 313
J.W., 313
SHIELDS
J.D., 251
JACOB, 250
JOSEPH, 250
LUCINDA J., 251
MARGARET, 250
SARAH A., 251
SHIRK
BRUCE BOOT, 180
IDA, 180(2)
JAMES W., 52(2)
JOHNNIE R., 180
M.L., 181
MARY, 52
MODEAN, 180
W.G., 180
W.J., 180(2)
SHRYOCK
HENRY S., 133(2)
SHUGART
E.A., REV., 159
JAMES, 159
LESLIE, 159
NANNIE, 159
WILL, 159
WILLIAM, 158, 159
SHULER
G.E., 53(2)
GEORGIA, 53
M.P., 53(2)
ROY, 53
SHULTS
SALLIE, 218
SHULTZ
R., 274
SINGLETON
ARTHUR, 182
S.E., 182
W.E., 182

SITZLAR
CLYDE, 107
FANNIE, 107(2)
MESCAL, 107
N.S., 107(3)
NEWTON S., 107
WILLIAM R., 107(2)
SIVELY
SARAH, 66
SKIDMORE
CHARLES, 154
RUFUS, 154
T.J., 154
TURNER, 154(2)
SKINNER
WILLIAM KENNETH, 236

SLEDGE
CHAS. F., 219
SLOAN
—, 158
APCH. M., 292
ARCH, 292
ARCHIBALD, 292
ARNOLD, 327
ARRIE, 291
BEN, 327(2)
BERTHA, 291
BOYCE, 290, 292
C.W., 291
CALLIE, 290
CARL, 290
CARROLL, 159, 292
CATHERINE S., 292
DAISY, 201
E. SAPHRONA, 291
E.L., 290(4)
EDNA MAE, 291
ELIZABETH, 292(2)
EMMA, 292
EMMA GHORMLEY, 291

ERSKINE LOWRY, 293

FLOYD, 290
FRANK, 291
FRED, 291
G.W., 292
G.W., MRS., 292
GEO. W., 300
GEORGE, 292
GEORGE W., 291
GILLIS, 291
HILDA MARY, 327
HUGH L., 282
INFANT, 290, 291
INFANT SON, 327
ISAAC, 291(2)
J.A., 290
J.C., 201(2)
J.C., JR., 201

J.E., 9
JAMES RILEY, 290
JAMES S., 292
JOHN A., 290
JOHN R., 290
JOSIE P., 291
K.A., 291
KADA, 327(2)
LEE, 327
LEE R., 327
LOUISE A., 282
LUCILE, 290
M.J.C., 291
MARRY C., 292
MARTHA L., 291
MARY, 327
MARY CAROLINE, 290

MASON, 292
MATTIE, 290
MOLLY, 159
NELLIE, 291
NEOMA, 292
NETTIE, 291
O.B., 290
OMA ELIZABETH MASON, 282
OSTON, 291
R.B., 292(2)
RAY, 291
REBA, 10
ROBERT, 291, 292(2)
ROBERT CARROLL, 290

RUTH ELLEN, 291
S., 291
S.L., 10, 290
SARAH A., 290, 292
SARAH L., 290
SARAH LONG, 159
SUSANAH, 292
T.B., 292
T.C., 292(2)
THEADORE, 159
THOMAS F., 282
W.R., 291, 292
WILLIAM, 291
WILLIAM H., 291
ZELMA, 290
SLUDE
NANCY, 108
SLUDER
NANCY, 108
SMALLIN
DAISY D., 259
DAISY DEAN, 259
E.J., 259
JEFF, 259
W.O., 259(2)
WILLIE D., 259

SMALLING
  DOSSIE, 182
SMILEY
  A.M., 188
  W.G., 188
  W.P., 188
SMITH
  A., 22
  A.L., 327
  ALICE HASELINE, 53
  ASENITH A., 262
  BETTY JO, 117
  C.D., 286
  CHARLEY, 170
  CHARLOTTA, 262
  CLYDE D., 43
  DAVID, 210, 211
  E.A., 43
  E.C., 227
  E.L., 43
  EDITH EDNIA, 227
  FRANK, 210
  FRANK, MRS., 210
  GEORGE, 129(2)
  GEORGE R., 286
  GEORGE, JR., 286
  GRACE, 244(2)
  GRACE RITCHIE, 244
  H.L., 170
  HENRY, 327
  HERMAN, 286
  HORACE, 244
  HUGH, 123
  I.A., 244
  INFANT, 244(2)
  IRENE, 286
  J.H., 281
  J.J., 262
  J.M., 106
  JAMES L., 262
  JOHN, 327
  JUDSON, 286(2)
  L.E., 281
  L.H., 227
  LEONA, 22
  LYLLIAN, 71
  M.A., 281
  M.J., 281
  MARTHA, 95
  MARY, 286(3)
  MARY E., 262
  MELVIN, REV., 87
  MINNIE, 170
  NANCY JANE, 262
  OLIE, 115
  P.M., 281
  PEARL, 244
  ROSTEN, 170
  SARAH, 129, 327
  T.H., 71
  TEXIE, 244

THOMAS M., 281
VIRGINIA, 86
W.H., 244(4)
WILLIAM HENRY, 262

WM. M., 22
WM. R., 262
SMYER
  E.E., REV., 252
SNEAD
  NANCY P., 175
  WM. E., 175
SNEED
  BELL, 210
SNIDER
  A.H., 331
  INFANT, 331
  J.A., 331
  JENNIE, 99
  LIZZIE, 99
  PAUL W., 325
  W.R., 99
  FLORENCE, 184
  FRED, 184
SORTON
  SAM, 58
SPARKS
  RUTH, 128
SPILLMAN
  G.A., 105(2), 112(2)
  GRIMES A., 87
  JOHN C., 105
  JOSEPH B., 105
  M.A., 105
  M.C., 105(2)
  N.J., 105(3)
SPRADLIN
  INFANT, 151(2)
  JANIE, 151
  P.L., 151(2)
SPRINGS
  BIG, 62
  CRAIGHEAD, 256
  HENSLEY, 275
  HOWARD, 113, 119
STAKELY
  A., DR., 42
  ABRAM, 42
  ELISABETH L., 42
  F.L., 42(3)
  JOE M., 42
  JOHN O., 42
  LUCY LEE, 42
  MOSTON H., 42
  N.C., 42
STALCUP
  ELIZABETH, 345
  HATTIE, 345
  J.D., 345
  JESS D., 348
  MARGARET, 211

STALEY
  DAVID, 66
STAMEY
  ALICE, 317
  CHARLES D., 320
STANDEFER
  ---, 159
STANDIFER
  CLYDE, 160
  HARRY, 160
  HERMAN, 160
  JOE, 160
  MAE, 160
  MATTIE LONG, 160
  WILL, 160
STANDRIDGE
  NANCY, 93
STAPP
  AMANDA, 294
  ARIE, 342(2)
  C.B., 342
  INFANT, 342(2)
  JESS, 342(2)
  SALLIE, 300
  WM., 294, 295
STARRITT
  HELEN   MARGARITE,
333
  J.M., 333
  JOSEPH, 326(2)
  LILLY, 333
  MARY, 333
  MONROE, 326(2)
  TYE, 333
STEAMSHIP
  CORTEZ, 163
STEED
  JOHN, 300, 301
  SARAH JANE, 300
STEEL
  JAMES F., 327
STEELE
  ELBERTA, 86
  MARGARETTE A., 327

STEPHEN
  ABSOLUM, 44
  AMANDA, 44
  JA-, 44
  RUFUS, 44(2)
  VISE E., 44
STEPHENS
  ANDERSON, 335
  BEN H., JR., 34
  BETHIA C., 123
  C.B., 123
  CALLIE STONE, 115
  CHARLES W., 278
  EDNA, 335
  ETTA FRANCES, 34
  FLORENCE, 117

GEORGE, 256
GORDON H., 206
H.C., 278
H.L., 12(2)
HENRY CLAY, 278
INFANT, 316
INFANT SON, 335
J.H., 206
J.L., 117
J.T., 206
JAMES, 12
JORDAN, 251
L.A., 206
MARY, 232
R.E., 316
RACHEL, 204
ROBERT, 206
ROBERT HARRISON,

34(2)
S.H., 117
S.I., 206
SALLIE L., 278
SAMP A., 114
SUSAN, 78
SUSIE, 77
T.J., 26
VIRGIE LEE, 12
STEPHENSON
  ELIZABETH P., 1
STEPP
  ELIZABETH P., 221
  WILLIAM, SGT., 221
STEWART
  INFANT DAUGHTER, 26

MILTON, 25, 26
OLLIE, 26
SINTHA, 109
STILES
  A.S., 106
  CHANLER K., 106
  CHIPPY, 106
  CORA LEE, 106
  EASTER A., 106
  ELIZA, 105, 106
  ELLA, 90
  H.E., 106
  INFANT, 90, 106(2)
  J. PASCHAL, 106
  J.L., 106
  J.P., 106
  JACK L., 106
  JOHN, 106
  KITTIE, 106
  L.A., 46
  LILLIE, 106
  MARY, 46
  NELLIE DORRIS, 106
  R.A., 106
  SARAH J., 106

W.H., 106
W.P., 90
WILLIAM M., 106
WM. M., 105
STILLWELL
J.M., 273
STILWELL
J.M., 273
REBECA S., 273
STIZLAR
NEWTON S., 87
WM. M., 87
STOCKDALE
FRANCES, 38
STONE
CLARK W., 114(2)
FRED, 160
JAMES H., 115
SARAH D., 114
STRATTON
A.J., 287
ARMINDA, 287
H.A., 336
JOHN R., 298
KAIR, 287
L.O., 298
M.C., 287
M.D., 336
M.V., 336
MANDA, 287
NANCY, 298
NELSE, 298
NELSON, 298
R.R., 287(3)
RICHARD R., 287(2)
ROSCOE, 287
STEVE, 298
SUSAN, 287(4)
W.A., 336
STRICKLAN
AMANDA, 60
G.W., 60
JAMES E., 60
MANDA H., 335
MARY J., 335
N.A., 60
STRICKLAND
J.F., 301
JAMES ROBERT, 301
STUART
DELILAH, 152
JANE, 94
MAY, 94
STYLES
FRAZIER, 24
SUMMEY
EVIE, 178
FANNEY MEANS, 177
FANNIE, 177
HORIES D., 177
JAMES M., 177

PETE, 177(3)
ROSCO, 177
SALLIE, 177
TEX, 177(2)
WALTER, 177
SUMMIT
DANIEL, 250(2)
H.A., 250
HETTY ANN, 250
JONATHAN, 250
JOSEPH, 250(2)
PHILIP, 250
SARAH, 250
SUMMITT
CALLIE, 250
DARIUS E., 250
DAVID L., 249
DENVER W., 249
E., 249(2)
ELLA F., 250
ISABELLA, 252
J., 249(2)
J.S., 249
J.W., 249
JACOB E., 249
JOHN S., 249
JOSEPH, 249
JOSEPH C., 254
L., 249(2)
LULA MAE, 249
M.C., 249(2), 250(2)
M.E., 249
M.L., 249(2), 250(4)
MARTIN LUTHER, 250

MARY T., 249
MINNIE E., 254
NANCY JANE, 250
PETER, 250
R.C., 250(2)
ROBERT D., 250
SARAH, 249
SUSIE, 254
W.L., 249
SUTTON
G.H., 4
J.L., 315
J.O., 4
JESSE H., 4
JOHN, 4
MARTHA ALSA, 211
W.H., 4
SWABE
CHARLOTTE B., 322
H.E., 322
R.M., 322
SWAINSON
CHARLES, 68, 312
CHARLES S., 302, 312
MARY, 312
MARY GLADYS, 312

SWANEY
ALBERT M., 330
SYLVESTER
—, 71
ALLEN, 72
ANNIE, 71
BERTHA, 71
BITHA ANN, 71
BOB S., 316
D.W., 72
E., 72
E.C., 71
EFFIE, 71, 72
ELCIE SUE, 71
ELIZABETH, 72
GIRTIE, 71
HATTIE, 71
INFANT, 72
INFANT DAUGHTER, 72

INFANT SON, 72
JOHN, 72
JOHN R., 71, 73
L.S., 316
LUCIE, 71
MYRTLE, 71
NANIE S., 316
R.T., 72
ROBERT, 72
ROYE, 71
S.S., 316
SAM, 319
T.A., 71
TEXIE, 319
VERGIE, 71
W.T., 71, 72

-T-

TALLENT
A.B., 307
A.R., 320
BESSIE, 307
BETSY, 17
BUD, 202
BULA ELIZABETH, 51

C.H., 172
CARRIE, 201
CARRIE VIOLA, 201
CATE, 202
DIXIE ILA, 202
E.C., 296
EASTER, 240
ELIZA J., 201
ELIZABETH, 202
FANNEY, 201
FLORIDA, 323
GEO., 202
GUSSIE, 343
HENRY, 154

HOMMER, 307
HUGH, SHERIFF, 282
I.M., 307(2)
INFANT DAUGHTER, 296
ISEY, 154
J.C., 201
J.H., 202
JACKIE, 320
JAMES, 201, 202
JANE, 296(2)
JANE WILLIAMS, 173
JASPER C., 201
JENNIE, 282, 283
JEP H., 323
JEPP, 17(3)
JOHN, 201(2)
JOHN OLIVER, 154
JOSIE, 148, 240
JULIA ANN, 154
JURITTA A., 320
KATIE, 296
LILLIE, 343
LIZZIE, 307
M., 202
M.D.L., 296(2)
MALINDA C., 201
MARTHA J., 209
MYRTLE, 201
NANCY JANE, 201(2)
OPHA MARIE, 296
RACHEL, 307
RANKIN, 282, 283
S.H., 296
S.L., 307
SALLIE A. MANIS
WILSON, 41
SAM H., 296
SAMEY, 153
SAMIE, 320
SAVILLA, 202
T.R., 201(2)
THOS., 17
VADDIE, 320
VESTA, 201
W. MORRIS, 17
W.P., 307
WORTHEY, 154
TATE
ADA E., 261
DAISY, 261
G.W., 98(2)
GEO. W., 98
GEORGE W., 98
INFANT SON, 98(2)
ISAAC, 261
JENNIE, 98(2)
JOHN A., 261(3)
M.W., 98
MAGGIE, 271
MARY J. SMALLIN, 261

BERTHA, 184
C., 184
JOHN, 184
LULA, 184
MAGGIE MAYS, 184
MARY, 184
S.E., 184
TREW
  JOHN, SR., 219
TRUE
  CHARLES M., 307
  JUNIOR, 225
  MINNIE, 225
TUCKER
  BURLIN, 173
  KATE, 173
  OSCAR, 173
TUCKERS
  J.B., 178
TURK
  C.L., 104
  CAROLINE, 104
  V.W., 104
TURNER
  LIZZIE, 288
  T.F., 288
TYLER
  ANNIE M., 337
  J.C., 183
  JOHN, 337
  MARION J., 324
  MARTHA ANN POPLIN,

    324
  MARY, 337
  NORA GLAN, 183
  SAM, 183
  SAMANTHA, 183
  W.J., 324

    -U-

UNDERWOOD
  ARKEL, 336
  CARLIN, 261
  D.M., 336
  ED, 336
  ED., 336
  ELIC, 336
  GEORGE HOWARD, 336

  HENRY M., 336
  INFANT SON, 336
  JOHN, 173
  LOUISA, 336
  M.L., 336
  MARTHA, 336(2)
  MARY, 336
  S.L., 336
UPTON
  BETTIE, 326, 335

BOYD, 282, 284
C.A., 219
DR., 14
HENNIE, 219
ISAAC, 326(2), 335
J.F., 219
MAGGIE, 219
SAMUEL, 219

    -V-

VALLEY
  SWEETWATER, 213, 222

VANCE
  ANNIE, 48
  FLOID, 156
  MARTELLIS, 48
  MARTELLUS, 48(2)
  MARY, 48
VAUGHN
  —, 148
  INFANT, 95(2)
  J.C., 95(4)
  J.C., MRS., 95
  MARY ANISE, 260
  N.S., 95(2)
  ROY, 237
  WILLIE H., 95
  WM., 260
VEAL
  C.J., 172
  CLEMMA, 155
  CYNTHA, 172
  INFANT, 155
  INFANT SON, 155
  J.H., 172(2)
  JAMES, 172
  JOHN, 155
  JOHN B., 172
  LEE, 172
  MEDY, 155
  PEYTON, 155
  S.E., 155
  WILLIAM H., 172
VINCENT
  G.W., 250
  JOSIE, 116
VIRGINIA
  BRISTOL, 159, 160
  MARION, 159
  ROANOKE, 66(2)
  WYTHEVILLE, 158
VISAGE
  P.J., 98

    -W-

WADE
  M.C., 182
WALKER

CORA LEE, 311
ELIZABETH J., 215
G.W., 109
JOHN H., 311
JOSEPH, 215(3)
ROY EMERSON, 225
SARAH E., 109
TEXIE, 168
TROY, 225
WALL
  VIRGIL F., 302, 313
WALLACE
  MARY, 309
WARD
  ADDIE H., 135
  ISAAC A., 235
  ISAAC, MRS., 317
  SAM, 59
WASHINGTON
  D.C., 66
WATKINS
  B.C., 340
  HENRY, 209
  HENRY C., 209
WATSON
  A.J., 43
  ADLINE, 198
  ALBERT HOYET, 198
  ALICE RAPER, 198
  ARCHIE, 197
  AUSTIN C., 197
  B., 196
  B.C., 198
  B.W., 198
  BEDDIE, 197
  BERDIE, 196, 197,
    210, 240
  BETTIE, 207
  BETTIE JANE, 197
  C.C., 156
  C.J., 173
  CALLIE, 241
  CHARLOTTE, 196
  CHAS. E., 197
  CRICKET, 198
  DANIEL, 43
  DANIEL, MRS., 43
  DAVID, 197
  E.L., 198
  EFFIE, 197
  ELBERT, 240
  ELIHU, 197
  ELSIE, 198
  ETHLEEN, 197
  EVA E., 304
  FANNIE, 196
  FLOSSIE MAE, 196
  FRANCES, 197(2)
  GEORGE, 198
  GILFORD C., 304
  GORDON, 240

HARTSELL, 197
HENRY, 198, 274
HOLSTON, 196
I.H., 198
INFANT, 173, 197,
  198, 240
INFANT SON, 274
J., 197
J.A., 187, 274
J.B., 197
J.H., 43
J.N., 196(2)
J.S., 198
J.W., 240
JAMES, 196, 197(2)
JAMES E., REV., 198
JANIE, 196
JOE, 196
JOHN, 43(2), 77,
  198(2), 200(2)
JOHNIE, 196
JOSIE, 197, 198
KENNETH, 17
LAURA, 274
LETHIA, 198
LOCHIE, 196
LOIS, 17
LOTTIE NEWMAN, 197

M.E., 187
MACK, 240
MADILENE, 240
MAGGIE, 187
MARGARET, 77
MARIAN, 240
MARION, 197, 198
MARTHA, 198
MARTHA A., 43, 199
MARY, 198(2), 200(2)
MARY A., 196, 198
MARY ANN, 196
MATTIE, 198
MOLLIE, 198
NANCY JANE, 77, 207
NELLIE, 198
OSIE, 173
PHEBE, 196
PHEBIE, 196
R.B., 196
R.D., 240
RACHEL, 198
REBECCA, 195, 196
REBECKEY, 196
RHODA, 77
ROBERT, 196(2)
RUFUS, 197(3)
S.F., 274
S.M., 198
SAM, 196
SARAH, 43
SARAH A., 197

SARAH GENEVA, 240

SUSANNAH, 67
TAYLOR, 198
TENNESSEE, 197
THOMAS, 196
TITIA, 196
TOM, 197
URIAH, 197(2)
VERNA SUE, 196
W.H., 196, 198(2)
WALTER, 304
WILLIAM, 195(3),
  196(2), 198(2),
  241
WILLIE, 193, 240
WILLIE MERLE, 198
WATTS
  MARGARET, 308
WAYMAN
  C.W., 187(3)
  HOWARD, 336
  JULA ANN, 22
  M.L., 187
  MARY NELL, 187
  N.F., 187
  REAGAN SILES, 187
  SUSAN, 187
  WALTER OTTO, 187
  WILLIAM THOMAS, 313

WEAR
  DONNIE, 260
  F.B., 329
  HOMER, 259
  JAMES P., 299
  JEAN LEA, 329
  JESSE, 281
  LELIA MAY, 259
  R.J., 329
  SALENA, 299(2)
  W.J., 299(2)
  WILLIAM J., 299
  WILLIAM S., 275, 281
WEBB
  ALICE, 342
  ALLIE, 342(2)
  ASTHER, 234
  B., 234
  BERTHA, 233
  BETTY, 342(2)
  CARL, 342
  DAISY, 343(2)
  DEE, 343(2)
  DOKE, 342(2)
  E.N., 341, 343
  EASTER, 234, 342
  ELIGAH, 234(2), 342
  ELIGAH (E.N.), 341,
    342
  ELIJAH, 342

ELISHA, 342
ETTA, 343(2)
GIBBIE, 342
GRANT, 342, 343(2)
HARRISON, 342(2)
HARRISON (W.H.),
  341(2)
HATTIE, 342(2)
HULDIA, 342
INEZ WILSON, 348
INFANT, 342(2), 348
ISABELLA, 234(2)
JAMES, 234(2)
JAMES HOWARD, 234

JAMES M., 12
JAMES ROCHE, 12
JASPER, 12
JENETTIE, 10
JOHN, 342
LARA, 343
LARKIN, 12(4)
LILLIE, 342
LORA, 341, 343
LU—, 234
LUCINDA DIVINE, 12
M.A., 234
M.R., 234
M.S., 234
MARY J., 231
MILLIE, 342
NAVADA, 343(2)
NELSE, 300
ONA, 342(2)
PEARL, 342
RAYMOND LEON, 342

REBECCA, 12(2)
RHODA, 12
S., 12, 300
S.V., 341, 343
SALLIE, 342
T.N., 300(2)
THOMAS, 342
W.A., 341
W.C., 234
W.H., 341(2)
WILLIAM, 234,
  341(2), 342(4)
WILLIAM I., 341
WILLIE, 300
WM., 348
WEBSTER
  ADA, 116
  ALICE LOUISE, 116
  H.L., 116
WEISS
  ENA, 69
  MOLLIE, 69
  WALTER, 69
  WM., 68, 69

WM., MRS., 76
WELDIN
  ANN, 279
  HARVEY M., 275, 279
WELLS
  GEORGE, 39
  JAMES, 39
  M.D., 185
  SIS, 39
  W.W., 185
  WILLIAM, JR., 185
WEST
  INFANT DAUGHTER,
155
  JOE, 51
  LEWIS, 155
  MARY, 155
WEST VIRGINIA
  BECKLEY, 160
WHEELER
  ELIZABETH, 146
  LEMIRA A., 146
  THOMAS, 146
WHIRE
  NERVIE, 191
WHITAKER
  JOHN J., 145
  MARTHA H., 145
WHITE
  — KESTUTON, 158
  A., 321
  A.I., 131
  A.L., 192
  ALLEN N., 191
  AROEL, 314
  B.F., 282
  B.F., SR., 282, 283
  B.L., 183
  BERTHA, 182
  BETSYAN, 130
  BULAH MOSER, 324
  CARLES V., 339
  CECIL, 15
  DAVID, 15
  DEWEY, 15
  E.A., 314
  E.L., 314
  E.M., 302, 314
  E.Y., 344
  ESTHER, 191
  EVE, 191
  HOWARD, 94
  HUGH CLENTON, 191

  I.S., 297(2)
  I.W., 297
  INFANT, 183
  INFANT TWIN SON, 15
  IVA, 314
  J—, 260
  J.C., 183

J.E., 321(2)
J.H., 183
J.N., 191
J.W., 15
JAMES, 15, 314, 321
JAMES B., 16, 130,
  131
JAMES C., 324
JAMES HARBERT, 94
JANE, 344
JOE, 183(2)
JOHN, 283, 297
JOHN A., 284(2)
JOSEPH, 321
KITTY, 15
L.E., 314
M.L., 182(2)
M.M., 15
MAGGIE, 297
MARGARET, 130, 344
MARTHA, 183(2)
MARTHA LINDSEY, 283

MARY, 192, 260, 321
RACHEL, 183, 307
RANDA, 183
ROXEY MAE, 15
RUTHEY E., 203
SERENA, 321
T.E., 182(2)
THOMAS, 344
THOMAS H., 182
TRACY, 314
VERNON DOYLE, 314

W.B., 130
WALTER, 183
WILLIAM GATH, 191
WM., 183
WORTH, 297
WYATT, 314
WHITESIDE
  J.H., REV., 51
WICKINSON
  JOHN, 123
WIDNER
  MICHAEL, 226, 227
  SARAH, 226(2), 227
WIGGINS
  ANNIE F., 338
  G.W., 338
  GEORGE W., 337
  JOSEPH, REV., 112
  MAGGIE, 338(2)
  NANCY, 338
  O.H., 338
WILBURN
  E.F., 234
  E.J., 192(3)
  ELBERT F., 234
  GEORGE, 234

HOUSTON, 102(2)
HOUSTON, PVT., 87
INFANT, 192
M.J., 192
P.A., 192(3), 233,
234
WILFORD
J. HUGH, 115
WILKINSON
BENJAMIN, 123(2)
HOMER, 123(2)
HOUSTON, 123(2)
JOHN, 123
NEOMA, 123(2)
RACHEL, 123
SALLIE, 123(2)
WILLIAMS
ADA PEARL, 328
ALEXANDER, 129
ALLEN, 29
ANDREW J., 283
ANNIE, 265
ANNIE MAY, 154
ARTTY, 51
B., 215
B.W., 265
BARBARA, 215, 264
BENN F., 51
BETTY, 129
BIRTHA, 288
BRICE, 326
BRYSON, 59
C.J., 51(2)
C.L., 154
E.L., 154
EDWARD, 288
EDWARD MARTIN, 265

ELIZABETH, 264,
265(2), 274
ETTA, 264
EUGENE, 288, 328
F.P., 29, 228
FINIA, 288(3)
G.W., 265(4)
GEORGE, 265(2)
GEORGE W., 264
GEORGIA M., 265
H., 189
H.P., 264(5)
INFANT, 228, 264
INFANT DAUGHTER, 51,

265
INFANT SON, 154, 265
IRENE, 154
J., 264
J.A., 265(3)
J.E., 154
J.N., 304
JAMES, 258, 264, 265

JAMES F., 265
JAMES H., 215
JAMES H.E.Z., 265
JANE, 228
JAS., 274
JESSE, 154
L.B., 59
L.D., 29(2), 228
L.H., 288(3)
LADY KATE, 265
LAURA, 51, 154
LEE, 264
LORA, 51
M., 265
M.F., 51
M.H., 51
M.J., 29, 265(3)
MALOWINEY, 288
MARCUS, 323
MARGARET F., 264
MARY J., 265
MELISSA C., 265
MELTON, 51
MELTON F., 51
MILLIE, 264
N.A., 154
N.J., 264(2)
NANCY JANE, 264
NANIE PIRL, 265
NANNIE, 265(2)
NELSE R., 129
NETTIE, 265
O.H., 51
OMA, 288
ORALEE, 304
OSCAR, 29
P.A., 154
POLLIE AN, 154
ROBERT, 329
RUTH LEE, 328
RUTH S. CLICK, 329
S.Y.B., 215(3)
SAM, 265
SAMUEL, 265(3)
SAMUEL R., 265
THENE, 51(2)
V., 265
VADA LEA, 323
W.B., 51(2), 154,
328
W.H., REV., 304
W.O., 51(3)
W.P., 154(2)
W.W., 264
WILLIAM, 169
WILLIAMSON
INFANT, 271
R.F., 271
W.H., 271
W.W., 271
WELLA NELL, 316

WILLIAX
---, 151
J.D., 49
JANEY, 49
JOHNEY JACKSON, 49

LOU ELLA, 151
WILLSON
E.F., 220(2)
EARL HENRY, 220
EUGENE, 220
JIM, 72
MARY LOUISE, 220
W.P., 220(2)
WILSON
BENJAMIN, 35
BETTIE, 202(4)
CHARLES, 35, 348(2)
DAVID LAWRENCE, 348

DIANAH, 96
E., 95
ELIJAH, 348
ELIZA, 348
ELIZABETH, 345, 346,
348
E L I Z A B E T H
(BROYLES),
35
ELLA, 41
ESSIE, 346
F.M., 95
FRANCIS M., 96
GEORGE, 348(2)
GEORGE LEE, 95
H., 346
HAIRSE, 202
HANNAH, 348(2)
HEPPIE A., 345
I.M., 346
I.N., 202(5)
IDA, 95
INFANT, 40(2), 41,
96
INFANT SON, 95
INIS, 202
ISAAC, 345, 348
ISAAC G., 346
J., 346
J.M., 72
J.T., 96(3)
J.W., 346
JESSE, 346(2)
JESSEE, 345, 348
JOHN, 345, 348(3)
JOHN B., 35(2), 40
JOHN CLINTON, 136
L.J., 346(2)
LAREN, 346
LAWRENCE, 348
LAWRENCE J., 346

LEE, 41
LOUVENIA BARR, 41

LUCINDA, 40(2)
M.M., 346
MARY, 345(2)
MARY A., 96
MARY ALICE, 95
MATILDA DENTON, 346

MILLY, 72
REBECCA A., 346
RICHARD (DICK), 348
S.J., 96
SAM, 305
SAM, MRS., 305
SOLLIE, 346
SOLOMON, 27, 345(4),
348(3)
T., 95
THOMAS, 40(2)
WILLIAM L., 41
WM. L., 41
WIMBERLEY
HAM, 201
WIMBERLY
HAM, 211
WINN
R.R., 100
ROBERT R., 100
ROBERT R., LT., 87
WINTERS
LILLIAN, 283
WISE
ELLIE B., 2
WOLDRIDGE
ELAM, 147(3)
HOYT, DR., 147(2)
MANERVA, 147
STELLA, 147
WOLF
SAM, REV., 34
WOOD
EFFIE, 234
G.W., 234
NORA, 232
RETTA, 234
WOODS
DIXIE MAY, 101
FRANCES VIOLA, 101
HUGH KING, 101
LIZZIE CLEMENTINE,

101
ROBERT CLIDE, 101
WOODY
JOHN WESLEY, 339
MARTHA J., 339
WORTHY
WM., 138
WRIGHT

www.ingramcontent.com/pod-product-compliance
Lightning Source LLC
Chambersburg PA
CBHW080243030426
42334CB00023BA/2683